CLARENDON LAW SEF

CLARENDON LAW SERIES

Policies and Perceptions of Insurance Law in the Twenty-First Century

MALCOLM CLARKE

OXFORD
UNIVERSITY PRESS

This book has been printed digitally and produced in a standard specification
in order to ensure its continuing availability

OXFORD
UNIVERSITY PRESS

Great Clarendon Street, Oxford OX2 6DP
Oxford University Press is a department of the University of Oxford.
It furthers the University's objective of excellence in research, scholarship,
and education by publishing worldwide in
Oxford New York
Auckland Cape Town Dar es Salaam Hong Kong Karachi
Kuala Lumpur Madrid Melbourne Mexico City Nairobi
New Delhi Shanghai Taipei Toronto
With offices in
Argentina Austria Brazil Chile Czech Republic France Greece
Guatemala Hungary Italy Japan South Korea Poland Portugal
Singapore Switzerland Thailand Turkey Ukraine Vietnam

Oxford is a registered trade mark of Oxford University Press
in the UK and in certain other countries
Published in the United States
by Oxford University Press Inc., New York

ISBN 978-0-19-922764-8

Preface

In 1994 I had the good fortune to be invited to contribute a book to the Clarendon series published by Oxford University Press, which was published in 1997 under the title *Policies and Perceptions of Insurance*. The present book, which is not in the Clarendon series, is less a second edition of that book than a successor. It purports not only to update but also to amplify the themes of the 1997 book. It is intended to be a critical introduction to the English law of insurance contracts and seeks to present the rules in their socio-economic context. It also seeks to set the rules of insurance contract law in the wider setting of contract law at large, in an endeavour to demystify them and make them more intelligible to lawyers with a general legal background. At the same time I hope to provide a springboard for further study by those thus inclined. Selective reference is made to the corresponding rules of law in other countries—not only common law countries but also major jurisdictions in western Europe. The law is stated as I believe it to be on 1 April 2007.

Malcolm Clarke

Cambridge
April 2007

Summary Contents

Contents

Bibliographical and Other Abbreviations

ABI	The Association of British Insurers
Abraham	K. S. Abraham, *Distributing Risk: Insurance, Legal Theory, and Public Policy* (New Haven, 1986)
APIL	Association of Personal Injury Lawyers
ATE	after the event
AUTH	*Authorization Manual* of the FSA
Basedow and Fock	J. Basedow and T. Fock (eds), *Europäisches Versicherungsvertragsrecht* (Tübingen, 2002) vol. 1
Bernstein	P. L. Bernstein, *Against the Gods, The Remarkable Story of Risk* (New York, 1996)
Birds and Hird	J. Birds and N. J. Hird, *Bird's Modern Insurance Law*, 6th edn (London, 2004)
Butterworths	M. P. Furmston (ed.), *Butterworths' Law of Contract*, 2nd edn (London, 2003)
Cane	P. Cane, *Atiyah's Accidents, Compensation and the Law*, 6th edn (London, 1999)
CAR	construction all risks
CFA	conditional fee agreement
Clarke	M. A. Clarke, *The Law of Insurance Contracts*, 4th edn (London, 2002)
CMC	claims management company
COB	Conduct of Business, requirements drawn up by the FSA for most firms with business investment customers, including certain insurers (http://www.fsa.gov.uk/vhb/html/cob/toc.html)
CUE	Claims and Underwriting Exchange
DSU	delay in start-up
ELC	English Law Commission
Farnsworth	E. Allan Farnsworth, *Farnsworth on Contracts* (Boston, 1990)
FOS	Financial Ombudsman Service
FSA	Financial Services Authority (http://www.fsa.gov.uk/)
FSMA	Financial Services and Markets Act 2000

GAIC	Genetics and Insurance Committee
GISC	General Insurance Standards Council
ICOB	Conduct of Business, requirements drawn up by the FSA for firms with insurance business customers (http://www.fsa.gov.uk/vhb/html/icob/ICOBtoc.html)
IFA	independent financial adviser
IOB	Insurance Ombudsman Bureau
K & R	kidnap and ransom
LEI	legal expenses insurance
Markesinis and Deakin	S. Deakin, A. Johnston, and B. Markesinis, *Markesinis and Deakin's Tort Law*, 5th edn (Oxford, 2003)
MIA	Marine Insurance Act 1906
OFT	Office of Fair Trading
PM	*Post Magazine*
RAO	Financial Services and Markets Act 2000 (Regulated Activities) Order 2001
Risk	*Risk is a Construct*: *Perceptions of Risk Perception,* (Bayerische Rückversicherung AG, Regensburg, 1993)
Treitel	G. H. Treitel, *The Law of Contract*, 11th edn (London, 2003)
VVG	Versicherungsvertragsgesetz

Table of Cases

Table of Legislation

1

Policyholders

Risk

To actuaries, risk is the 'probability that a particular adverse event occurs during a stated period of time or results from a particular challenge', where 'an adverse event is an occurrence producing harm'. This was the conclusion of a report of the Royal Society'[1] about a broad spectrum of human activity, be it insured or not. Nonetheless, to insurers, probability matters greatly in order to rate the risk and calculate premium.[2]

To insurers, risk is the chance of loss of the kind insured. Loss means both loss in the literal sense of deprivation (e.g., robbery) and financial loss—the impact of events (e.g., storm damage) on the economic well-being of policyholders. Insurers are concerned not only with whether the loss will occur (e.g., fire), but also, in cases in which loss is expected to occur, with when it will occur (e.g., death) or how much of it will occur (e.g., the damage to London taxis in the course of the period insured).

To insurance policyholders, as conceived by the insurance economist, the 'concept of risk comprises two components—a detriment aspect and an uncertainty aspect'.[3] As regards the detriment, by taking insurance, the element in the detriment, although no longer a risk but a certainty, is reduced to the level of the premium; and the inconvenience element is curtailed to the time it takes to find insurance and, if the risk strikes, to obtain indemnity. As for the uncertainty and whether the risk will strike, that is not reduced objectively. Subjectively, however, just as some people say that as long as they take an umbrella it never rains, some people feel that insurance serves as a 'charm' which wards off the danger. Uncertainty is reduced objectively, however, as to the extent of the detriment, notably the cost. Moreover, when insurers offer advice on or incentives to risk avoidance, the likelihood of the occurrence and thus, if policyholders respond appropriately, the amount of uncertainty are reduced further.[4]

To ordinary policyholders, who may well not be models of behaviour or rationality, something is risky if loss is relatively likely to happen, or, although it is not likely to happen, if the effect will be disastrous if it does. An instance of the first is an injury playing rugby; an instance of the second is an accident at a nearby nuclear reactor. Policyholders are less concerned with the precise probability than with whether the risk seems probable or bad enough to justify paying (premium) to soften its effects; that depends on their view of things, i.e., what psychologists call risk aversion.

[1] Royal Society, *Risk Assessment* (London, 1983).
[2] See Chapter 2, p. 48 ff.
[3] P. M. Wiedermann, 'Taboo, Sin, Risk: Changes in the Social Perception of Hazard', *BayerischerR* 44.   [4] See Chapter 2, pp. 53–4.

Risk Aversion

In the words of *The Economist*,[5] risk aversion is the feature of human nature that explains why, 'when given a choice between, say, losing 1 dollar and a 10 per cent chance of losing 10 dollars, most people would prefer a certain outcome (losing 1 dollar) to a risky one (losing 10 dollars or nothing)'. 'Prospect theory' tells us that people making decisions in uncertain conditions weigh prospective losses twice as heavily as prospective gains. If people know that there is a 1 per cent chance of total loss of their £100,000 house, they may be willing to pay more than £1,000 for insurance, and one of the main reasons is that they are willing to pay to offload anxiety. Such people are 'risk averse'. The Association of British Insurers (ABI), the organization that speaks for the insurance industry, projects insurance as something that enables people who are insured to organize their household budgets, or plan their business activities, with greater certainty. Indeed, although the usual period of commercial risks cover is one year, some insurers have offered businesses a fixed premium for two or more years, because research indicated that stable insurance-planning could be used as a selling point in the UK, as it has been in other countries such as Germany. This raises the question: What is it that makes a risk so unacceptable that people decide to do something about it and, in particular, to buy insurance cover?

Stress Aversion and the Purchase of Peace of Mind

Risk aversion grows from stress aversion. One of the causes of stress in human beings—in the motor car, the work place, or anywhere else—is a sense of not being in control of their situation, or of themselves. For many of those who avoid flying, the reason is not only fear of an air crash but also fear of losing control of themselves, as a result of stress.[6] Research also shows that, in a given risk situation on the roads, the anxiety levels among passengers are higher than among drivers.[7] Drivers feel in control; passengers do not. At the same time, drivers frustrated by traffic congestion, about which they can do nothing, suffer what a psychologist has called 'rumination road rage', and become more dangerous to themselves and to others.[8]

One of the ways in which people seek to regain control of their lives, to reduce stress and to move towards some kind of peace of mind, is by taking out insurance. That is why some insurers send their sales staff on courses to learn about the 'emotional needs' of the customer. That is also why some insurers advertise life insurance for 'life-long peace of mind' and travel cover 'to give you peace of mind when

---

[5] 3 December 1994.

[6] E. I. Foreman, 'Fear of Flying' in R. Bor (ed.), *Passenger Behaviour* (Aldershot 2003) 45–59.

[7] H. D. Somen, 'Experience of Risk in Road Traffic Situations' in *Risk is a Construct: Perceptions of Risk Perception* (hereafter '*Risk*') (Bayerische Rückversicherung AG, Regensburg, 1993) 119–53, 136.

[8] *Guardian*, 18 December 2002.

travelling'. A major bank has offered 'a free home insurance review to ensure peace of mind'. Insurers also point to peace of mind when underlining that the cheapest insurance is not always the best insurance. Advertising of this kind has an enduring appeal, and even the courts have recognized this—in other countries.[9]

Associated with the wish for peace and certainty is a desire for security. Sociologists tell us that on a descending scale of priorities, just after people's basic needs for food, clothing, and shelter, comes the need for security.[10] Insurers know this too, and security is another prominent feature of the image that insurers project of their products to the insured.[11]

Indeed, some have gone further. Recently a life insurer has offered term life insurance with counselling for the bereaved survivor; and a pet insurer has even offered bereavement counselling to pet owners. A motor insurer has offered counselling to policyholders who have been the victims of 'road rage'. An important feature of insurance contracts is that a significant part of what policyholders are paying for is peace of mind.

Litigation

Aversion to Litigation

Associated with the desire for peace and security in the past has been a general aversion to 'aggravation', and thus to litigation. For some the 'day in court' is a day out. For others, people in business, it is also a 'day out' but in a different sense: a waste of time. For most, it is an alien and unnerving experience, but one that, more recently, many have been willing to brave.

In the 1980s a leading commentator could contend that the court process got people to settle rather than to pursue their claims to judgment.[12] A seriously injured racing cyclist was quoted as saying that the pain and anguish of a prolonged court case was at least as bad as the pain and anguish of his injuries. Tort litigation in those days was described as a 'compulsory long-distance obstacle race', in which the amount of the prize 'must remain uncertain until the last moment because the umpire has discretion to fix it individually for each finisher. None of the runners is told the distance he must cover to complete the course; nor the time it is likely to take.'[13]

Certain sectors of business, such as the international commodity markets, are notorious for litigation; but on the whole, businessmen today still want to keep

---

[9] E.g., Canada: *Fowler v Maritime Life Ass. Co.* (2002) 217 DLR (4th) 473 at [44]. See Chapter 6, p. 247.
[10] B. Strumpet and P. Michael, 'The Security Requirements of Private Households', *BayerischerR* II 3–33.   [11] See Chapter 2, p. 46 ff.
[12] H. Genn, *Hard Bargaining* (Oxford, 1987) 111.
[13] D. Harris *et al.*, *Compensation and Support for Illness and Injury* (Oxford, 1984) 132–3.

out of court. The reasons are escalating cost and the weeks of executive time that may be involved, not least in attending the court. What they want is 'to be allowed to go on running a business instead of sitting for days in court, while the competition make hay in their absence'.[14] At an oversubscribed conference held in Cambridge in April 2003 on 'Dispute Resolution', the main session was titled 'Monsters: Discussion of the monstrous length, complexity and cost of current proceedings'. The session was planned and chaired by an experienced arbitrator and former Law Lord, Lord Mustill. The discussion was off the record and the dissatisfaction with the current court process only too apparent. At the end of the same year a London survey among FTSE companies, including some well-known names, found a perception that litigation lawyers were letting their clients down.[15] One dispute in five of those that got as far as their lawyers went on to trial and that, thought the executives in the survey, was far too many. Settlement soon or sooner was the call—in business.

Conditional Fee Agreements

Until recently, the man in the street tended to litigate less in England than, for example, in Germany and the United States.[16] Such people did not buy legal expenses insurance, which sold well in other countries, but preferred insurance which gave them the clear prospect of indemnity without having to sue their neighbours. However, the man, woman, or even child, in the street is now being reminded, sometimes months later, that he or she fell in the street and suffered hurt—reminded by touts not of tickets but of the promise of compensation because someone with insurance is to blame. As one claims management company (CMC) said in an advertisement, 'where there's blame there's a claim'. Insurers have expressed alarm at the arrival of 'US-style scan vans' at or near industrial sites in the UK where there might have been asbestos, offering free scans to locals for a lung shadow;[17] or cold calling to ask people whether they have worked in the mining industry, with a class action in mind.[18] Insurers also point to newspaper reports of 'claims farmers', touting for business in hospital accident departments; and of doctors giving patients appointment cards for the next visit and with the contact details of CMCs marked on the back. An unofficial survey of doctors in late 2004 shows that the vast majority of doctors were against proposals that doctors could charge for such referrals.

Behind the advertisements, the more or less unspoken implication is that insurers have lots of money and settle claims rather than spend the cost of a full investigation

[14] Staughton LJ, 'Good Faith and Fairness in Commercial Contract Law' (1994) 7 JCL, 193–6, 194.
[15] *Financial Times*, 4 November 2003.
[16] Generally, see S. Deakin, A. Johnston, and B. Markesinis, *Markesinis and Deakin's Tort Law*, (5th edn) (hereafter *'Markesinis and Deakin'*) (Oxford, 2003) ch. 1.1.
[17] See below, p. 10.
[18] *Post Magazine* (hereafter *'PM'*), 13 March 2004.

in the hope of paying nothing at all. Indeed, it has been alleged that some lawyers have been 'unfairly raising expectations of instant relief without liability to the payment of any costs by the claimant'.[19] So in their new role as outraged victim, injured people make a claim against the wrongdoers and their insurers.

To claim, people have to overcome their former fears of court proceedings and, especially, cost. On these points the change in attitude to litigation seems to lie less in any change in the man or woman in the street than in the advent of conditional fee agreements (CFAs), whereby claimants and their lawyers agree that the latter get paid only if the claim succeeds. With CFAs came matched insurance. Claimants who win are allowed to recover the success fee payable to their lawyer, as well as the ATE (after the event) LEI (legal expenses insurance) premium they are wise to contract against any outstanding costs, win or lose, from the other side. With CFAs and ATE insurance providing the vehicle, the driving force behind a proliferation of claims, it has been argued, lies in the emergence of a 'compensation culture'. As a prominent social commentator put it, the 'concept of Act of God died along with God himself'.[20] In 2006 an official report concluded that the introduction of CFAs had adversely affected the reputation of legal service providers and advocated the regulation of CMCs.[20a] Such regulation is contained in the Compensation Act 2006.[20b]

A Compensation Culture?

A 'compensation culture', or 'blame and gain culture', is the feeling in society that, if ill befalls people, somebody else must pay. The slings and arrows of outrageous fortune no longer come from fate and are no longer to be borne with stoicism, especially in relatively wealthy communities.[21] Widely reported, for example, was the action in the USA against a fast food retailer in respect of the ill health suffered by a customer from obesity. Less widely reported was the action in Scotland by an alcoholic against the whisky manufacturer whose wares he had enjoyed for many years. Both actions are likely to fail, but what is remarkable is that they were commenced.

Associated with the alleged compensation culture is the more sophisticated form of consumerism now found in our society, spurred by organizations set up to support consumers or groups more or less openly hostile to 'big business'. The story has been told[22] of marketing liability insurance during the glasnost years in Eastern Europe, when transport companies began buying relatively small amounts of insurance to cover their liability exposures. In the face of alarm at the apparent inadequacy of

    [19] R. Dadak, 'Time for action on CFA abuse', (2004) 194 NLJ 1466–8, 1468. The comment concerns threats to the media, and thus to freedom of expression, posed by media facing large costs defending dubious libel claims run on CFAs by claimants with neither money nor ATE insurance to cover liability for costs. See *King v Daily Telegraph Group Ltd* [2004] EWCA Civ 613, [2004] EMLR 23.
    [20] Polly Toynbee, *Guardian*, 20 February 2004, p 21.
    [20a] House of Commons, Constitutional Affairs Committee, Report on 'Compensation Culture', 14 February 2006, p. 35 ff.   [20b] See section 4. The Act is not yet in force.
    [21] See H. A. Cousy, 'Tort Liability and Liability Insurance: A Difficult Relationship', *Tort and Insurance Law Yearbook* (2001) 18–55, 26 and references cited.
    [22] S. Ignarski, *Wavyline*, 9 November, 2003.

cover, an old hand in the local insurance industry replied that 'first they must learn how to claim, and this will take many years'. Indeed, knowing how to make a liability claim against a business supplier backed by a practised industrial liability insurer and the best commercial lawyers money can buy requires a great deal of skill, education, experience, and strategic sense. It is the by-product of mature economies and prosperous societies, such as those now found in Western Europe.

Some deny the existence of a compensation culture, or belittle its impact. Insurers do neither. In 2004, several conferences were organized by leading insurers, with titles such as 'Confronting the Compensation Culture'. Even so, the evidence is that only one-third of potential claimants do claim; and of those who do not, nearly one-third had little or no idea where to find the legal service to help them to claim. This emerged from an extensive survey by the Claims Standards Federation in 2004, which indicated that many people do not see compensation as a sufficiently important objective to submit themselves to the litigation process; and some of them were even quoted as saying that they hated the idea of 'turning into a nation of US-like ambulance-chasers'. Others who did claim were keen to give a reason other than cash, as if 'money' were a dirty word. At the same time, a leading insurer has published its own survey suggesting that people believe that *other* people are more likely to claim than they are.[23] Whether or not it is accurate to speak of a compensation culture, it is clear that insurers are paying out more money to meet claims. So there is something of the kind out there, but what is it?

The Claims Crisis: Cloud or Mirage?

What appears to have increased is not so much the number of claimants as the amount of compensation awarded to those who make certain kinds of claim.[24] Certainly the total bill paid by society is large. In a report published in December 2002, for example, the Institute of Actuaries estimated that the annual cost of compensation claims had reached £10 billion.[25] Of that £10 billion, £7 billion was paid under insurance claims and 40 per cent of that went in legal fees.

The report was described as 'alarmist' by the President of the Association of Personal Injury Lawyers (APIL). 'Compensation culture', he said, was a misleading description of current society; the number of claims had stabilized since 2000; although amounts awarded in clinical injury cases had considerably increased, the number of claims had gone down; and 'it is the insurance industry which lies behind this latest attack on the tort system' because it needed to 'justify a rise in insurance premiums'. This, he alleged, was really 'a result of long-term underpricing of both

---

[23] Specifically, that 'society is more stressed; less community spirited; less prepared to save for personal wants; less prepared to take responsibility; and that every one is out for themselves': Supplement to *PM*, 13 May 2004.

[24] David Howarth, *The Times* (Law Section), 1 June 2004, pointing to a 1999 decision on lump sum compensation.

[25] Reported in *The Economist*, 21 December 2002, which also reported the case of a soldier paid £387,000 by the Army because it had failed to treat his warts properly.

motor and employers' liability policies leading to massive year on year underwriting losses'.[26] This, of course, has been denied by insurers, who point the finger of blame at the CMCs, as regards personal injury litigation, for 'claims cost inflation'. That, they argue, is due to lawyers and their 'success fees', and so on.[27] Also insurers point to the Ogden Tables, prepared by actuaries, accountants, and lawyers, which measure life expectancy and enable courts to project the compensation required for a victim; and to the 'Judicial Studies Board Guidelines for General Damages'. Both are due for upward revision in the near future.

The President of the APIL also drew attention to part of the Institute's report, apparently overlooked when the report was highlighted in the newspapers, that the UK had the lowest 'tort cost expressed as a percentage of GDP' in the industrialized world.[28] Indeed, in the latter part of 2003, the Compensation Recovery Unit, part of the Department of Work and Pensions, published a report that between 2000/2001 and 2002/2003 the number of employers' liability cases had fallen by 16 per cent and the number of disease claims by 26 per cent. Nonetheless, the President of the APIL was able publish his riposte in a journal devoted to personal injury law and litigation; and whereas a journal of that kind has flourished for some years, attempts to market a journal of insurance law in the UK in that period have failed.

In contrast, the APIL[29] was quick to indorse a Government-backed report,[30] published in May 2004, which found that although the public perception of easily available compensation was still alive,[30a] in reality the compensation culture was an 'urban myth' because the number of accident claims was falling; and that one reason was that the judicial system was efficient in weeding out spurious claims.[31]

The Response of the Courts

In the report published in May 2004 (see above), some of the main recommendations included better publicity of the Financial Ombudsman Service (FOS),[32] more mediation, and, if claims must go to court, channelling more claims into the small claims track to court. CMCs were regulated by statute.[32a] In February 2005 the government announced its intention to regulate CMCs. Moreover, if claims subsequently continue to rise, there are clear signs that in future judges will take a stand against spurious claims.

---

[26] D. Marshall, 'Compensation Culture' [2003] JPIL 79–82, 79, 80. However, there was said to be an appreciable rise in the number and quantum of claims brought against retailers, particularly in the food and drinks sector, which is the largest manufacturing sector in the UK: D. Fanning, Supplement to *PM*, 25 September 2003.
[27] This element was recognized in that it was felt necessary to agree a fixed amount in late 2004: *Liability, Risk and Insurance*, No. 170, October 2004.
[28] P. Marshall, op. cit. above, n. 26, 81.   [29] *Financial Times*, leading article, 28 May 2004.
[30] 'Better Routes to Redress', published by the Better Regulation Task Force: http://www.brtf.gov.uk/taskforce/reports/entry%20pages/Litigcompensation.htm.
[30a] Likewise in 2006: House of Commons, Constitutional Affairs Committee, Report on 'Compensation Culture', 14 February 2006, p. 35 ff.   [31] *Financial Times*, 31 May 2004.
[32] See Chapter 6, p. 239 ff.   [32a] See the Compensation Act 2006, s. 4.

In *Tomlinson*,[33] Lord Hoffmann, with whom other members of the House of Lords agreed, said that 'the majority of the Court of Appeal appear to have proceeded on the basis that if there was a foreseeable risk of serious injury, the [defendant occupier] was under a duty to do what was necessary to prevent it. But this in my opinion is an oversimplification.' The question of what care can be expected of an occupier (or anyone else) depends upon assessing 'not only the likelihood that someone may be injured and the seriousness of the injury which may occur, but also the social value of the activity which gives rise to the risk and the cost of preventative measures. These factors have to be balanced against each other.'[34] On balance their Lordships found against the claim and, in particular, Lord Hoffmann said that an important point

is the fact that it is not, and should never be, the policy of the law to require the protection of the foolhardy or reckless few to deprive, or interfere with, the enjoyment by the remainder of society of the liberties and amenities to which they are rightly entitled. . . In truth, the arguments for the claimant have involved an attack upon the liberties of the citizen which should not be countenanced. They attack the liberty of the individual to engage in dangerous, but otherwise harmless, pastimes at his own risk and the liberty of citizens as a whole fully to enjoy the variety and quality of the landscape of this country. The pursuit of an unrestrained culture of blame and compensation has many evil consequences and one is certainly the interference with the liberty of the citizen.[35]

Further, in *Bhamjee*,[36] the Court of Appeal was concerned with what Lord Phillips MR described as the 'very serious contemporary problems created by the activities of litigants like Mr Bhamjee who are bombarding them with applications which have no merit at all'. He continued:

Many of these litigants have no fees disincentive because they automatically qualify for fees exemption. The problem created by these hopeless applications is not only a serious financial one . . . [it] is also that the court is having to divert the skilled attention that ought to be paid to cases of real merit which warrant early hearings to cases which have no merit at all. A further problem is created by the fact that these litigants are often without the means to pay any costs orders made against them, and the parties in whose favour such costs orders are made are disinclined to throw good money after bad by making them bankrupt, particularly as the vexatious conduct may spill over into the bankruptcy proceedings themselves.[37]

This appears, however, to be the first occasion on which a court has had to consider whether the totally unmeritorious waste of the resources of a court (whether in terms of staff, lawyer or judge time or in the expense involved in procuring necessary transcripts at public expense for a litigant without means) is itself sufficient to justify the granting of some form of injunctive relief.[38]

Lord Phillips MR concluded with a summary of the various steps that the court could take, including civil restraint orders.[39]

---

[33] *Tomlinson (FC) v Congleton BC* [2004] 1 AC 46, in which the House, reversing the decision of the Court of Appeal, decided against a claim based on occupier's liability.   [34] Ibid., [34].
[35] Ibid., [81].   [36] *Bhamjee v Forsdick* [2004] 1 WLR 88 (CA) at [3].
[37] Ibid.   [38] Ibid., [10].   [39] Ibid., [53].

Statements such as these have been seen as amounting, if not to a red light, to an orange light to the gravy train. Practitioners believe that these decisions may well mark a radical shake-up of the courts' approach, and that CMCs will have to reconsider their practices.

Clouds on the Horizon

Insurers' fears are also directed to certain categories of claim which are anything but the work of CMCs. These are brought by the victims of asbestosis. Associated with these is a large cloud on the western horizon in the form of the possible advent from the USA of the practice of 'bundling' of asbestosis claims,[40] that is, group actions that mix malignant cases with non-malignant cases, thus increasing the size of claims' settlement overall. A report published there in 2002 estimated that about 65 per cent of the compensation thus far had gone to claimants with non-malignant conditions. This refers to claims by people ('the worried well') with scars on the lining of their lungs (pleural plaques) caused by asbestos, but who have no symptoms, are not ill, and may never be ill on that account. This has been called compensation for the fear of getting disease.[41] Lawsuits in the USA have been described as a 'malignant enterprise' based on 'no illness recognized by medical science',[42] but they continue to come. A study reported in January 2004[43] that more than 100,000 new asbestos claims were filed in 2003, the most in a single year. This record number of claims is added to the 700,000 claims that already have been filed, as asbestos litigation: 'a combination of Pac-Man and the Energizer Bunny' continues to extend its reach to gobble up new pools of assets.[44]

In the UK, insurers now have reason to fear. Deaths from asbestosis are not likely to peak before 2015–2020 and, according to one oncologist, virtually everyone in the UK over 30 years of age has been exposed to asbestos in some degree.[45] It has been estimated that one in every hundred men born in the 1940s will die of malignant pleural mesothelioma, which is almost exclusively the result of exposure to asbestos. The cloud arrived.

Premiums

Clearly, insurers do not believe that the 'blame and gain' culture is a myth, nor are they using it as cover themselves for other kinds of loss. In the television series 'Coronation Street', once described as a 'bastion of social realism', one of the characters fell and banged his head, and a claim was started as part of the story. This provoked real-life concern among insurers, lest some of the 12 million

[40] *Liability*, issue No. 162, February 2004.   [41] *Economist*, 6 November 2004.
[42] Ignarski loc cit.   [43] *Insurance News*, January 2004.   [44] L. Brickman, ibid.
[45] D. Fanning, *PM*, 30 October 2003.

viewers think about following suit. In a prominent public statement that year, the President of the Chartered Institute of Loss Adjusters pointed out that,[46] myth or not, insurance premiums were rising steeply in response. Indeed they are, with stultifying effects on the rest of society.

Between 2002 and 2003, for example, one outdoor centre in the hills found that its third party and equipment premium rose from £1,400 to £15,000. In 2004, another found that its annual liability premium had risen from £1,050 to £8,600. The effect of such rises has been not only to drive out careless operators, but also to inhibit competent and useful enterprises. In October 2003, for example, the British Caving Association had to shut down its operations, albeit temporarily, because it could not afford to pay the premium. The number of 'outward bound' adventure courses for companies seeking to promote 'corporate bonding' is now but a trickle—in easy terrain. In 2004, golfers were being advised not to set foot on a golf course without £2 million of liability cover. In September of that year, according to the *Daily Mirror*, thousands of window cleaners threw in the shammy (sic) due to spiralling insurance costs, a message as sadly probable as its spelling. Hospitals, however, have little choice. In 1990, the cost of claims to the National Health Service was £53 million, whereas in 2004 the amount of claims pending stood at £5 billion.

Evidently there is crisis of insurance cost—for those who want to be in a position to pay for their sins: another consequence has been that some people have stopped buying insurance altogether but continued the activity nonetheless. At least one in twenty motorists were driving without insurance in 2004. The amount paid out by the Motor Insurance Bureau, which is there to fill the gap and compensate the victims of uninsured or unidentified drivers,[47] rose from £11 million in 1988 to £225 million in 2000 and is still rising. Will the insurance industry be able to rise with it—to the occasion?

Insurers: Spreading Risk

In *The Merchant of Venice*, Shakespeare's Antonio had few anxieties about commercial risk because, he says:

> My ventures are not in one bottom trusted,
> Nor to one place; nor is my whole estate
> Upon the fortune of this present year.

If Antonio were an exporter of eggs today, he might well have to put all of them in one container on a single ship. He might not be able to spread the eggs between different ships, but he could nonetheless spread and share the risk of loss or breakage.

---

[46] *PM*, 15 July 2004.
[47] See M. A. Clarke, *The Law of Insurance Contracts*, 4th edn (hereafter 'Clarke') (London, 2002) ch. 5–9E.

The risk that the ship will sink is spread by insurance among all those who insure risks of that kind with the same insurer, who may well pass on some of that risk to other insurers, reinsurers. The availability of insurance encourages new ventures and new adventurers. One of the main purposes of insurance is to achieve a rational and reasonable spread of risk, and to help people to do things which, otherwise, they would hesitate to do—not only litigation (above), but also mineral exploration and medical research. If Antonio turns out to be a bad businessman who chooses badly maintained ships, his premium will rise to reflect the 'moral hazard' he presents. If risk is spread efficiently, not only the risk presented by Antonio but also the risk of random loss (from swordfish and typhoons) is spread among all in the group (the pool of policyholders). So is the random element provided by inaccuracies in the underwriting, such as the classification of the risk group: lines between good and less good risk groups are not always perfectly drawn, but, on the whole, these errors are sufficiently evenly spread for the insurance to be sold at what is perceived to be a reasonable price and for a reasonable return.

The efficiency of the spread depends also on the data available to those who spread the risk. Insurers must rely on information from other experts—who may strive for objectivity but not always achieve it. Studies speak of 'affiliation bias'; for example, toxicologists working for industry see chemicals as more benign than do their counterparts in academia and government. Still, relatively speaking, and with one reservation concerning their fear of fraud,[48] the approach of insurers to risk is apparently objective and rational.

People: Assessing Risk

Homo Oeconomicus

The model policyholder is a close relative of *homo oeconomicus,* a species said to be 'rational maximizers of their satisfactions'.[49] These people are supposed to be concerned mainly with the maximization of personal material self-interest, which their creator proudly called 'utility'. They make wise decisions in the light of personal goals. At worst, they can be tricked into collectively irrational behaviour by systematic errors in the social rules of the game. So as long as insurance products are fairly presented to them, they will make wise choices and all will be well. This is the 'assumption of rationality'.[50]

This model of mankind was dismissed as long ago as 1938 by John Maynard Keynes as 'disastrously mistaken'. Rather, he saw mankind as prone to 'deeper and blinder passions'.[51] More recently, the prototypical behaviour of *homo oeconomicus*

---

[48] See Chapter 6, p. 201.
[49] R. A. Posner, *The Problems of Jurisprudence* (Cambridge, Mass., 1990) 353.
[50] Cousy, op. cit. above, n. 21, 39.
[51] J. M. Keynes, *My Early Beliefs* (London, 1949) 20.

was denounced as leading to outcomes that 'are at odds with most people's sense of justice'.[52] Be that as it may, *homo oeconomicus* was an invention of economists and no more a figure of 'real life' than the model policyholder.[53] Nor is a more sophisticated descendant of the species, the person of qualified economic 'rationality'. The latter is characterized by self-interest in a broader sense that includes non-material factors, such as a desire for more leisure, and consistency. Having decided what they want, these people then work out correctly how to get only as much of it as they want. This model too is accepted even by many economists as unrealistic.

The well-known exponent of law and economics, Richard Posner, once observed that the

basic assumption of economics—that people are rational maximizers—seems not only counterintuitive . . . but also seriously incomplete. People have difficulty in dealing with low-probability events, which are important in many areas of behavior studied by economists; and much human behavior appears to be impulsive, emotional, superstitious—in a word irrational.[54]

Indeed, in 1911, when Germany was the UK's largest trading partner and most German merchant ships were insured at Lloyd's, a book, *The Great Illusion*, was published, written by a journalist called Norman Angel. Angel predicted that there would never be a European war because it did not make economic sense.

Economists have also conceded that predictability of behaviour is also limited by *bounded* rationality: although, in their view, people still pursue self-interest rationally, they are constrained by lack of information and the cost of getting it.[55] So, if the human condition is thoroughly understood and the insurance market perfectly transparent, all will be well. Apparently some economists think that this is because there has been yet another development of the species in recent times based on 'quasi-rational economics'. This looks to experimental psychology and cognitive sciences, and has led, for example, to the setting up of 'risk appraisal initiatives' on an inter-disciplinary basis. But the figure of bounded rationality is still a model which ignores other factors that influence actual decisions, including both fashion and fear, as well as those referred to by Posner. G.K. Chesterton has been quoted as saying that the 'real trouble with this world of ours is not that it is an unreasonable world, nor even that it is a reasonable one. The commonest kind of trouble is that it is nearly reasonable but not quite.'[56]

---

[52] Gordley, 47 Am J Jur 1, 15 (2002).

[53] H.-W. Sinn and A. J. Weichenrieder, 'Biological Selection of Risk Preferences', *Risk* 67–83, 68 ff.; see also Tyler and Dawes in B. A. Mellers and J. Baron (eds), *Psychological Perspectives on Justice* (Cambridge, 1993), ch. 5; R. Baldwin, in the introduction to R. Baldwin (ed.), *Law and Uncertainty, Risks and Legal Process* (London, 1997) 1–18, 5 ff., and, in particular, A. Ogus, ibid., 139–53.

[54] Op. cit. above, n. 50, 365.

[55] See, e.g., R. B. Korobin and T. S. Ulen, 'Law and Behavioral Science: Removing the Rationality Assumption from Law and Economics', 88 Cal L Rev 1051–1144, 1075 (2000).

[56] P. L. Bernstein, *Against the Gods, The Remarkable Story of Risk* (hereafter 'Bernstein') (New York, 1996) 331.

Perhaps neither G.K. Chesterton nor Judge Posner had met Sir Phillip Brocklehurst. He was the insurers' and the economists' nightmare, but, evidently, Lord Denning found him rather endearing. Although Sir Phillip had 'had a conventional upbringing at Eton and Trinity Hall', he was, said Lord Denning,[57] 'the most unconventional of men' because he took the 'line that the insurance company never paid him anything, so why should he go on paying them?' Most people are not quite like Sir Philip; but many people, who have had a less conventional upbringing than Sir Phillip, share his view of the world and of insurance, in that they sometimes take a less than objective perception of risk. Their perception of risk, however, is not for that reason alone inferior to that of the expert in a free society. It is simply different. For those people whose concerns do lead to insurance, one of the goals is peace of mind, and whether their fears are rational or not, they are real to them and cannot be ignored. After all, in the 1990s a few people bought insurance against being abducted by aliens. Although Posner concluded that as 'a universal social norm' wealth maximization is unsatisfactory,[58] he also insisted that economics is not a 'false science' but has a part to play in explaining human behaviour in the insurance market. Perhaps so, but the problem is to measure that part.

Knowledge of Risk

Self-evidently, people's fears, and hence the kind of insurance they may seek to buy, depend on their perception of risk; this is sometimes called 'risk cognition'.[59] Their perception of risk depends, first, on their knowledge of risk. People may be unaware of the very existence of risk. In the seventeenth century, for example, people smoked (pipes) in the belief that smoking was good for their health. In the late nineteenth century, Marie Curie worked unprotected with radium. In the mid-twentieth century, asbestos was hailed as the wonder material. In the internetted world of today people are better informed, but rarely enough. They may be aware of the risk but not of its extent. For example, in spite of ministerial statements to the contrary, many people believe that the State provides a sufficient safety net for long-term illness and disablement, and an adequate pension for their retirement. As it is, therefore, many more people take life insurance than any form of disability insurance, even though, for all but the oldest or terminally ill, the likelihood of illness or injury is appreciably greater than the likelihood of death. The average person in business has a one in three chance of contracting a critical illness before reaching retirement age, but only one person in four is even aware that insurance against critical illness is available.

---

[57] *Re Brocklehurst* [1978] 1 All ER 767, 769–70 (CA).   [58] Op. cit. above, n 50, 366 ff.
[59] Somen, op. cit. above, n. 7, 120.

Experience of Risk: Media Impact

Perception of risk also depends on people's experience of risk, directly or indirectly. One factor that plays a part in risk assessment 'is the gearing of judgments towards the cognitive "prominence" or "availability" of events. The lay person regards an event as being more probable, the easier it is to recall or imagine similar events.'[60] Psychologists speak of the 'availability heuristic', which is the human tendency to assess the frequency of an event by how quickly instances of the event come to mind; and of the 'simulation heuristic', which is the tendency to assess frequency by how quickly an image of it comes to mind.[61] The quicker it comes, the more likely it is thought to occur. The person who has experienced an event of loss directly knows, of course, that it does not happen to other people only, and is more likely to register the event when it happens to others, thus reinforcing the process. To register events, of course, people must be aware of them; and this depends on how and where they are reported.

Headlines

Experience of risk may be acquired indirectly, that is to say, secondhand from others, whether from the man in the pub, from the morning newspapers, or from the evening television. After the Great Fire of London in 1666, fire insurance spread too. Personal accident insurance surged on a sense of the destructive power of railway trains in the 1800s. With industrialization came special cover, such as boiler insurance. Burglary insurance was largely born of the fears of houseowners in London, fuelled by the newspapers, of a successful burglar from Yorkshire called Charles Peace.

In the seventeenth century an attempt to market ransom insurance for travellers was unsuccessful. More recently, the number of kidnaps rose from 784 in 1995 to 1,367 in 1997. Today we do not know the exact number, but it is clear that the demand for kidnap and ransom (K & R) cover is growing—from companies, such as oil and gas, mining, communications, construction, and engineering companies, which send staff to work overseas for relatively long periods. Indeed, in some countries, for example France in 2004, it is illegal for insurers to refuse it. K & R rates, however, have been largely unaffected since 2001, although events in Iraq makes this unlikely to continue.

Although sometimes costly, there has also been a bigger demand for cover against terrorist activity since the attack on the World Trade Center in New York in 2001.[62]

---

[60] H. Jungermann and P. Slovic, 'Characteristics of Individual Risk Perception' in *Risk*, 85–102, 87; R. Kemp, 'Risk Perception: The Assessment of Risks by Experts and by Lay People—A Rational Comparison?' in *Risk*, 103–18, 107.

[61] S. T. Fiske and S. E. Taylor, *Social Cognition*, 2nd edn (New York, 1991) 384 ff.

[62] However, even in the USA, there had not been a 'stampede for coverage' according to a survey by the Council of Insurance Agents and Brokers published in March 2003. Nearly 50 per cent of member brokers who provided information said that fewer that one in five of their largest clients had purchased terrorism cover.

A poll of over 2,000 people on the electoral roll in England was conducted in September 2004. It found, on the one hand, that although there had been no terrorist outrage in England in the previous nine months, 68 per cent said that they were worried about terrorism and 29 per cent that they were 'very worried' about it. On the other hand, one man in two and one woman in three will suffer some kind of heart disease in their lifetime, and about 100,000 people die of heart disease every year, however, only 17 per cent said that were very worried about that.

Well researched and established is the fact that the media tend to select alarmist reports or opinions, which distort people's perception of those risks; but the reports are useful nonetheless. Emotions aroused by media reports 'act as controls on cognition, alerting people to important goals'.[63] In other words, emotions are the 'springs of action', which spur people to avoid risk, *inter alia* by seeking insurance, and on which the media play. Scare stories sell newspapers. The effect of the media on the popular perception of risk has been the subject of considerable study in the recent past.[64] This shows, for example, that the public perception of the risk of death is less in line with the hard statistics than with the amount of media coverage.

A striking current example of this kind is fear of crime, fuelled by the media, which is out of all proportion to its reality according to government statistics. So people tend to stay at home even though, according to a study approved by the Royal Statistical Society at its annual conference in 1999, people are more likely to die as the result of an accident at home than being killed elsewhere. Most householders regard burglary cover as a priority. In contrast, newspapers rarely run stories about heart attacks on holiday unless the victim is a celebrity. Only one-third of those who follow the current middle-class (householder) trend to take weekend holiday breaks, even as far as New York, have travel insurance, even though an air ambulance back from the Costa Brava costs upwards of £12,000 and heart surgery in the USA could cost £35,000 or more.

National media tend to focus on large-scale accidents, such as air crashes, rather than more frequent but small-scale accidents, such as befall motorists, whereas in the local media the latter feature more frequently. Thus it is a commonly held myth that aircraft emergencies are non-survivable, whereas, having examined air accidents worldwide, the European Transport Safety Council estimated in 1996 that 90 per cent of such accidents are 'survivable or technically survivable'.[65] In 2004 not a single person died in an accident involving a western airline.

Within the scope of any one medium, people, politicians among them, tend to take their cue from the headlines. Obviously headlines catch the eye and are read, even if the eye goes no further. Moreover, the very location of the information

[63] Fiske and Taylor, op. cit. above, n. 62, 433.
[64] See S. Dunwoody and H. P. Peters, 'The Mass Media and Risk Perception', *Risk*, 293–317 and references cited. Also G. Loewenstein and J. Mather, 'Dynamic Processes in Risk Perception', 3 *J Risk & Uncertainty* 155–75, 158 and 172 (1990).
[65] E. Galea, 'Passenger Behaviour in Emergency Situations' in op. cit. Bor, above n. 6, 128–82, 129. The definition of 'survivable' is that nobody was killed in the accident, and the definition of 'technically survivable' is that at least one person survived.

implies its importance. The consequences may be a distorted perception of risk and a misallocation of resources. For example, *The Economist*[66] has pointed out that the money spent on fire-proof doors at King's Cross Railway Station after a fire there in 1987, would have saved more lives if spent on smoke detectors elsewhere; and that speed restrictions on the rail network after the Hatfield rail crash in 2000 drove so many people on to the roads that more deaths were caused than saved. Whereas on average at least ten people die on the roads every day, of the 217 people who died in 2002 on British railways, 198 were trespassers and only nineteen were passengers.[67] In the five years up to 2007 and the Cumbria crash, ten rail passengers were killed but 15,000 people were killed on the roads.

The Economist has also written of the 'near-hysterical reaction' to certain 'relatively minor incidents', such as derailments on the London Underground, which, it said, had 'more to do with politics than with safety' on a network that recorded just one passenger death for every 300,000,000 passenger journeys.[68] It reported the view of the director of the passenger-transport executive for an area in the north east of England, that the cost of making what is already the safest form of transport even safer is crippling the rail industry and will result in higher fares and a smaller network. As in 2002, decanting 'frustrated passengers on to the roads, where the accident rate per mile travelled is more than ten times that of rail, may appease politicians but it is certainly no way to improve safety'.[69] Politicians ride the safety wagon and pronounce that 'even a million to one risk of death is unacceptable', and people nod their heads—unaware, perhaps, that risk analysts in the USA have pointed out that a list of 'million to one' death risks includes eating forty tablespoonfuls of peanut butter. To little avail. Security, it has been argued, is open to a powerful form of political exploitation,[70] not least the temptation to exaggerate risk in order to increase the apparent importance of the politician who promises to do something about it. Arguably people in relatively wealthy communities elect leaders who can be trusted to keep them safe[71]—safe from whatever they perceive as the greatest threat.

The Quality of Reporting

If insurers could manipulate the media, they could manipulate the market for insurance; there is no evidence that they do. Individually, however, journalists are not immune to influence, and this affects what they write. Some are specialized, but in many cases it has been shown that journalists are less educated in scientific subjects than their average readers, and that they are often unable to judge the soundness of their scientific sources. Moreover, they 'need' a story and, for reasons of speed and economy, there is now less investigative and searching reporting than before and more reliance on 'sources' such as the company press release.[72]

---

[66] 13 September 2003.   [67] *Financial Times*, 2 May 2003.
[68] Leading article, 13 September 2003.   [69] Ibid. See also *The Economist*, 25 October 2003.
[70] See, e.g., L. Zedner, 'The concept of security: an agenda for comparative analysis', (2003) 23 LS 153–76, 155 and references cited.   [71] Andrew Rawnsley, *The Observer*, 7 November 2004.
[72] Dunwoody and Peters, op. cit. above, n. 65, 301 ff. Marr, 'My Trade' (London, 2004), 253–4, 276.

So some simply select the most striking source, which may well reflect opinions of the eccentric. Others, journalists seeking a selection of views, may consider that they have complied with a standard of 'truthful' reporting if they present a range of views without any real assessment of their relative merits; equal space is given to the ideas, whether respected by others in the field or not.

Freedom from Distraction

People's perception of risk may also be affected by the pull of other worries, some real, others not. On the one hand, people who know that they have terminal cancer may neglect to renew their house insurance—but not their life insurance. On the other hand, people who walk the streets in fear of being hit by muggers should be more concerned about the chance of being struck by a car. Those who walk the jungles of Malaysia looking down in fear of snakes should be looking up for falling coconuts. In many areas of England, those who worry about radioactive waste are more likely to be damaged by natural radiation in the soil; and a study in New Zealand once showed that those who had the highest aversion to the dangers of technology were more ready than most to assume the risk of smoking. In these examples, the dominant anxiety is that which subjectively arouses the most fear. In other instances, the dominant anxiety may simply be that which is associated with what happens next. Smokers may promise themselves that they will give up smoking if they get the job they so desperately need. Not surprisingly, people worry most about the risks that seem to them most directly to threaten their well-being at the time.

The Context of Society: Time and Place

As a general predictor of risk aversion, the personality of the policyholder is not always helpful, because individuals who take high risks of certain kinds often avoid other risks at all costs. Cultural and social factors are thought to be more significant.[73] In more affluent and leisured societies people are more willing to put money against the odds, whether a low chance of winning or a low chance of losing:

We gamble because we are willing to accept the large probability of a small loss in the hope that the small probability of scoring a large gain will work in our favor; for most people, in any case, gambling is more an entertainment than a risk. We buy insurance because we cannot afford to take the risk of losing our home to fire—or our life before our time.[74]

In poorer societies people are less likely to contract insurance; and when they gamble, it is more likely to be out of desperation than for fun.

---

[73] A. Wildavsky, 'The Comparative Study of Risk Perception: A Beginning', *BayerischerR* 179–220, 188–90.   [74] Bernstein, 203.

In England, the cult of the self-reliant consumer, encouraged by governments into the 1990s, led *inter alia* to more purchasing of insurance, such as health insurance. But the sense of risk and the focus of fears often differ from country to country. A widespread factor is wealth. In Europe, as people became richer after 1945, fewer went to church but more bought insurance. Worldwide, most of the premium for life insurance comes from a cluster of wealthy countries, including Japan, Switzerland, and the United States. In some countries in the Far East, however, life insurance has been relatively slow to develop, because people saw taking out life insurance less as a wise precaution against premature demise than as a foolish temptation to fate. In 2004, whereas 77 per cent of residents of Hong Kong had life insurance, the corresponding figure in urban China was just 18 per cent,[75] albeit rising. This seems to be a case of culture overcoming the wealth factor which is found in North America and Europe. Again, in the United Kingdom the number of households without contents insurance in Northern Ireland is about three times higher than in East Anglia. The more people have got, the more they are afraid of losing it, and the more they are willing to pay to protect it. That includes their pets. A growth line born of recent affluence in the 1990s is pet insurance. Owners have been insuring not the life of the beast but its body—to pay the rising cost of veterinary fees—and not only for dogs and cats but also more exotic companions, such as crocodiles and scorpions. By 2007 the cost of comprehensive cover for a large dog was not much less than that for a small car.

These examples seem to show that there is a 'difference between societies dominated by wants and those dominated by worry, between societies who cannot pay enough for safety and those who can. The biggest worry of all, for those in the second category, is that they are slipping back into the first.'[76] Moreover, people in the second category have more leisure to worry. They have more 'information' to feed their anxiety; but living in the security-fenced social isolation that wealth has enabled, they are less well placed to keep it in perspective. Their perception of insecurity has increased.

A particular anxiety for people in the more 'advanced' countries, who have become more aware of their world, lies in the potential hazards over which they, as individuals, have no control. Examples are pollution, climate change, the spread of nuclear or chemical weapons, and, more recently, the associated threat from terrorists who, to a greater degree than those who hi-jacked passenger aircraft in the 1970s, are willing to 'go down with the ship' or aircraft. That kind of anxiety is not eased by the knowledge that they cannot live in society without trusting the skill, knowledge, and care of others, whether of other people with whom they must share the roads, or of governments. All this fosters a general sense of insecurity, exacerbated because sections of the public now feel that in times past, trust in their experts and in public institutions (especially, in the United Kingdom, those

---

[75] Lex Column, *Financial Times*, 26 August 2004.
[76] Martin Woollacott, *Guardian* 24 February 1996. See also R. B. Bovbjerg, 'Liability and Liability Insurance: Chicken and Egg', 72 Tex L Rev 1655–79, 1669 (1994).

concerned with food and agriculture) has been misplaced. Once again we see a sense of helplessness (lack of control) that leads to stress and to attempts to avert risk.

Compulsory Insurance

Whereas most people worry too much about travel by air, they worry too little about travel by road which, on any statistical basis, is more hazardous. 'Shortfalls in the cognition of danger and playing down of the probability and consequences of accidents go hand in hand with the conviction of being in complete control.'[77] It is one of the attractive features of motoring that drivers are led to believe, not least by advertisements for cars, that they are in control of a marvel of technology, that they are masters of the situation, monarchs of the road and even the glen, as they see the latest model gliding through beautiful landscapes. Moreover, because 'driving is an activity which everyone, or almost everyone, practises successfully, it is generally felt to be an easy task, an everyday activity at which everyone is almost perfect and whose risks are therefore underestimated. Accordingly, a failure in this apparently easy task is particularly wounding to self-esteem'[78] and defence mechanisms are triggered which, for example, deny mistakes and thus deny risk.

At the same time, drivers are more conscious of the threat posed by others but tend to underestimate the dangers they pose themselves, not only in respect of how they drive but also in respect of what they drive. An old example is that of vehicles with bull bars or sharp ornaments. Marketing studies say that in them people feel safer, although accident surveys indicate that certain types are more likely to turn over. A more recent illustration in the UK is the 'Four by Four', known to its detractors as the 'Chelsea tractor', which ploughs a furrow of danger and fear in narrow city streets and leafy country lanes alike.

A survey conducted for the British School of Motoring in 1995, like similar surveys in other parts of Europe,[79] indicated that over 75 per cent of drivers considered themselves to be above-average drivers. An empirical survey in Washington DC[80] found that the 'averagely good' driver (one uninvolved in a traffic incident in the previous four years) made roughly nine driving errors during every five minutes of driving. There is surely little reason to believe that the 'averagely good' driver in congested England does any better.

Motoring is one of several spheres of human activity for which Parliament has been convinced that the experts are right and the people are wrong: that most people underestimate and underprovide for risk, and that the cumulative actual loss and damage to the community is unacceptably great. So this is one of the situations for which Parliament has made insurance compulsory. Another

---

[77] H. D. Somen, 'Experience of Risk in Traffic Situations', *Risk*, 119–53, 136. See also Jungermann and Slovic, op. cit. above, n. 61, 92 ff.; Kemp, op. cit. above, n. 61, 107; B. Corby, 'On Risk and Uncertainty in Modern Society', *Geneva Papers on Risk and Insurance* 19 (No. 72, July 1994) 235–43, 241.   [78] Somen, op. cit. above, n. 7, 137.

[79] Somen, ibid., 134.   [80] Quoted in *Markesinis and Deakin*, 38.

instance is the liability of employers to their employees. Insurance for that was first required in England in 1969, whereas insurance against liability incurred on the roads was first required in England by the Road Traffic Act 1930 but had been foreshadowed by legislation in other countries, such as Sweden (1906), although it was not found until 1939 in Germany and 1958 in France.[81] Such is its importance today that it has been the subject of several EC Directives designed to ensure and to harmonize compulsory motor insurance in Europe.

Less well known is that by an international convention agreed in 1999, which came into force in the UK and other countries in 2004 and which increases appreciably the liability of airlines to passengers, governments are obliged to require airlines registered with them to maintain adequate insurance covering their liability.[82] This is a first for compulsory cover of this kind. Indeed, there is no clear pattern of public policy as regards where insurance is compulsory and where it is not. Whereas insurance is compulsory for drivers of motor vehicles, for drivers of motor boats or jet skis, for example, even near crowded beaches, it is not. What is clear is a trend in society in the direction of compulsory insurance.

The Demand for Insurance

The lines of insurance available depend on demand and, thus, largely on people's perceptions of the risk that they need to cover. In the eighteenth century, there was an 'assurance of female chastity', a very personal line, for which, it seems, there is insufficient demand today. A line that prospered mightily in the last 100 years or more is life insurance. Life insurance has origins both commercial and non-commercial. Life insurance in England may have begun not as a matter of family provision but because creditors realized that their chance of repayment depended largely on the labour, and thus the longevity, of the debtor.[83] Today life insurance is seen not only as a means of family provision, but also as a means of investment.[84] In England past, life insurance, together with fire and marine insurance, was the first on offer. Most of the other established classes of cover offered by insurance companies were introduced between 1840 and 1900.

More recent developments include contractors' all-risks insurance. As building and engineering projects have grown larger, so has awareness of the need to cover work under construction, work in which much time and money has been invested. Customized insurance cover of great complexity is arranged for new airports, railway stations, tunnels under the sea, and so on.

Another recent development of a more personal kind concerns people whose continued prosperity depends on all or part of the anatomy—their own, or that of those in their employment. What is true of the whole may also be true of the parts.

---

[81] For the historical development, see A. Tunc, *International Encyclopedia of Comparative Law*, vol. IX, Part 1, paras 90 ff. [82] Montreal Convention 1999, Article 50.

[83] See *Hebdon v West* (1863) 3 B & S 579.

[84] See *Feasey v Sun Life Assurance Corp. of Canada* [2003] Lloyd's Rep IR 637 (CA).

The famous film stars Marlene Dietrich and Betty Grable insured their legs for what would now be £8 million; a British film actress of the 1950s insured her bosom, albeit it for a lesser sum. And a high priest of *haute cuisine* once sought to insure his sense of taste, but was unable to do so because the insurer could not see how a claim could be proven and assessed. In late 2003, however, it was reported that a supermarket chain had insured the taste buds of its senior wine buyer for £10 million.

Large sums like that are relatively new. A century ago the sum allowed by law was no more than a month's salary.[85] When the racing driver Ayrton Senna was killed in 1994, Lloyd's paid his sponsors over $17 million. When Sir Richard Branson set out on a long journey by hot air balloon in 2002, his company insured him for £50 million at a premium of £850,000. This kind of cover, the legality of which is dubious but which would be questioned only by the liquidator of an insolvent insurance company, is sometimes called 'keyman' insurance.[86] Almost anything and anyone can be insured, if insurers can assess and quantify the risk, but is there any limit?

A Mori survey in the autumn of 2004 found that only three people in ten had the faintest idea of what we mean by 'insurance'. So, what is it? In the insurance marketplace visited in the next few pages, a variety of insurance products are on sale. A generic definition of insurance is conspicuous by its absence. The long title of an article in a law journal[87] published recently was this: 'Life Assurance: Effective Inheritance Tax Planning—Isn't Insurance Supposed to be Simple?' Perhaps it should be, but the short answer is that it is not. Even the best lawyers in the field have been unable to agree.[88] Some readers of detective stories go straight to the last chapter to discover 'who did it': thoughtful readers about insurance, who may be asking 'what it is', should do likewise and turn to Chapter 9, but be warned that, unlike the writer of detective stories, the author cannot offer a clear answer that ties up the loose ends. That is one reason why the question has not been addressed here in Chapter 1. What we can do is describe the main features of insurance. So, like the manual that comes with audio equipment, the technical specifications of insurance are set out at the end.

The Insurance Marketplace

Traditional Products

If people demand insurance, the next question is whether they can get it—which is really not one question but two. Is it available at all, or at a price people can afford; and, if so, is it available to the person who wants it? The answer to the second question depends on whether the person in question has what the law

85 *Simcock v Scottish Imperial Ins. Co.* (1902) 10 SLT 286, 288.
86 See below, p. 27 ff.
87 *Private Client Business*, September 2004.
88 See *Fuji Finance Inc. v Aetna Life Ins. Co. Ltd* [1997] Ch 173 (CA).

regards as an insurable interest in the subject-matter of the insurance proposed.[89] The answer to the first question depends on whether the risk is one that insurers can rate, or, if it is expensive, the cover is one that insurers can sell.

For cover to be offered at all, the risk must be one which can be assessed and to some degree controlled by human action. Partly this is a question of technological advance, such as the invention of the lightning conductor in about 1750. Partly it is a question of the existence of information, such as the development of probability theory and data to which it can be applied.[90] Partly it is a question of whether insurers think there is enough information. Some insurers are more cautious than others. Demand for cover that is not offered by market insurers, because they are unwilling to take on that kind of risk, has led to mutual self-protection in 'clubs' of those who want the cover concerned.[91]

Generally, however, the appearance of insurance companies marked the point in time when the need was sufficiently widespread for cover to be offered to people who wanted it by others with money to invest, and who then formed companies for profit for this purpose. Today, potential buyers find that most insurance is offered by companies; and that these companies market standard insurance 'products' by reference to the peril against which cover is offered, or to the subject-matter of the insurance, the person, or property at risk.

Personal lines, they will find, include not only life and accident insurance but also, for instance, health and long-term care insurance. Accident insurance began with the railways as personal accident insurance, but has since acquired a different meaning. Although people think first of personal accident insurance and of what befalls the human body, the insurer thinks first of property and loss or destruction of that. For insurers the primary meaning of accident insurance embraces all commercial insurance, including motor and liability insurance, except marine, aviation, fire, and life. From accident insurance in this sense, the premium income (in the United Kingdom) is greater than all the rest together except life insurance, which, since the 1990s, has outstripped the rest.

Property insurance, buyers will find, is separated into insurance on tangible property, including specific items of money, and insurance on intangible wealth, known as pecuniary-loss insurance. Insurance of tangible property is divided according to the kind of property (livestock, cargo, house, etc.) and also according to the peril (fire, theft, burglary etc.). Pecuniary-loss insurance includes cover against the insolvency of debtors, loss sustained by guarantors under their contracts of guarantee, and consequential loss, which is also called business interruption cover.

Cocktails of different kinds of cover may be offered in one package for the convenience of customers. Just as audio equipment is sold both as separate units and as integrated 'systems' of units, fire cover, for example, can be bought on its

---

[89] See p. 26 ff.   [90] See Chapter 2, p. 48 ff.
[91] See Chapter 2, p. 39 ff.

own or as part of a package, such as 'householder's comprehensive' cover. This may be divided into sections covering not only fire and theft, but also the liability of the householder for things that go wrong (e.g., falling slates), with an 'all-risks' extension (e.g., for protection against theft) on valuables when taken out of the house and some cover for legal expenses (e.g., for proceeding against noisy neighbours).

If none of the standard products meets the perceived needs of purchasers, they can ask their broker to seek customized cover in the market or, perhaps, at Lloyd's. At Lloyd's, some insurers are celebrated for covering non-standard risks, whether the movement of satellites in space, of paintings by Raphael to London for exhibition, or, on one occasion, of an elephant from England to Israel to be mated. An older case was that of the person who voyaged from Dover across to France in a bathtub—on condition that he did not remove the plug. Customized cover can be obtained, but at a cost.

Meeting Current Needs

The insurance market has responded to the needs of the time in many ways, mostly by development of existing products. Sometimes, however, the scale of the need has been a challenge too far. For example, since September 2001, the exposure of the organizers of certain high-profile sporting events has been regarded as so great that the existing sports insurance market has been unable to carry it. The organizers have had to go to the capital markets and much of the risk has been securitized. The problems are seen as terrorist attacks, or threats leading to restriction or cancellation. The cost of such insurance to the Athens Olympic Committee in 2004 was estimated to be £42 million. For London in 2012 it is likely to be much more. In 2002, Selfridges, a high-profile store in London, found that its premium for property damage and business interruption (loss of profit) cover rose by no less than 375 per cent for that kind of reason.[92] In the USA the perception is that, as the Government provided financial assistance after the terrorist attack in September 2001, it will find it difficult to refuse assistance in the event of further attacks,[93] not only because it has done so in the past but also because of the way that such attacks are perceived: 'A natural disaster will trigger a weaker reaction than an enemy assault; hurricanes do not hit Florida *because* it is part of the United States, whereas terrorists struck New York and Washington precisely because of what they signified about our nation.'[94] Competitors in other countries, such as major airlines, see this rather differently.

A more down-to-earth dilemma is that of farmers, who may not be able to get cover against crop disease. That was both the plight and the blight of a farmer in England in late 2003, who lost his entire potato crop (worth £50,000) to a disease

[92] *Insurance Day*, 19 November 2002.
[93] See S. Levmore and K. D. Logue, 'Insuring Against Terrorism—and Crime', 102 Mich L Rev 268–327, 278 ff. (2003).   [94] Ibid., 279.

that came in with the potato seeds that he had bought from Holland. Farmers in Holland have their own problems. Although there is a sophisticated and relatively large insurance sector (10 per cent of GDP) in Holland, market cover for natural disasters such as floods, as well as earthquakes and landslides, is not available for certain areas. In that case there may be some kind of indemnity fund paid for and run by the government concerned.[95] The same is true in parts of Belgium, where the Government has tried for years to persuade people of the merits of compulsory private insurance against such risks, and legislation was finally introduced in 2003.[96] In the 1990s in the United Kingdom (and most other European countries), cover for flood damage was a standard feature of private house policies, but that can no longer be said. The perceived probability of volatile weather and rising sea levels attendant on global warming has led insurers to revise their policies. It remains be seen whether and when farmers in East Anglia will have the same problem as some of their competitors across the North Sea; and to what extent government support will go further than improving sea defences.

The Choice of Insurer

At the point of choice, like purchasers of any other product, purchasers of insurance may be torn between price and reliability, that is, security. Some will go for the lowest premium; others for the insurer with the reputation for support and prompt payment.

The choice may depend on whether they have to live with consequences of the decision. A longer view may well be taken by policyholders such as householders buying fire insurance than, for example, by exporters of goods who sell an occasional buyer a package including insurance on the goods; such sellers are obliged only to provide commercially acceptable insurance and, if there is a claim and if insurers are slow to pay, it is the buyers rather than the sellers who suffer, and there are no insurance repercussions unless a buyer is a regular customer with clout. In between, perhaps, are buyers of private motor insurance, who wear risk lightly and buy insurance only because they must. Convinced that 'it won't happen to them', they often seek the cheapest insurance they can find.

The choice may also depend on the past experience of the purchaser. Some recent surveys suggest that, although price is still a factor, among buyers of commercial lines, security, integrity, and continuity are now more important. The speed with which Lloyd's paid on the Californian earthquake of 1906, when other insurers were dragging their feet through the dust and the small print, did much for the prosperity of Lloyd's in subsequent years. Likewise, a controversial ruling of

---

[95] See C. Van Schoubroeck, 'Legislation and Practice Concerning Natural Disasters and Insurance in a Number of European Countries', *Geneva Papers on Risk and Insurance*, 22 (No. 83, April 1997) 238–67.

[96] Law of 21 May 2003: C. Van Schoubroeck, 'The Quest for Private Insurance for Damage Caused by Natural Disasters' [2003] JBL 558–71, 570.

the court in late 1993 that, under a compensation scheme, the insurance industry at large must pay claims against a failed insurer not only to policyholders in the United Kingdom but also to policyholders abroad,[97] although painful in the short term, probably benefited the image and thus the longer-term prosperity of the English insurance industry. Moreover, there is some evidence that Lloyd's is currently reaping the rewards of relatively rapid payment of claims arising out of the terrorist attacks in New York in September 2001. Lloyd's promptly paid a large sum, about £5 billion prior to recovery from reinsurers, after the attack on 11 September 2001; and resumed offer of cover against terrorism within 48 hours.[98]

If the choice is difficult and insurance buyers are uncertain about what to buy and how, they may well seek advice; but from whom? Traditionally they went to brokers, who see their role as specialist retailers of insurance.[99] But many potential purchasers are confused about that too. A short walk down the High Street will reveal a variety of insurance intermediaries: not only insurance advisers and insurance consultants, as well as banks and building societies offering advice about insurance. Moreover, having heard that something called ABTA is responsible for travel agents, buyers of insurance may want to know who or what is responsible for controlling the sale of insurance. In the 1990s they would have found an array of acronyms, ranging from FIMBRA and LAUTRO to SIB, IBRC, and PIA. No longer: the Government has set up the Financial Services Authority (FSA), which does not sell insurance but is responsible for the way it is sold. The *Insurance: Conduct of Business Sourcebook* contains rules that came into force on 14 January 2005. An important part of the FSA is the Financial Ombudsman Service (FOS), which deals with complaints from the public about insurance cover.[100]

Insurable Interest

If a person has decided on the particular kind of insurance to buy, the next question is whether the law allows that person to have it at all. The law states that buyers of insurance must have an insurable interest in the subject-matter concerned: they must stand in the 'right kind of relationship' to the person or property that they want to insure. They must be acceptable as an insurance risk-taker not only to the particular insurer, but also to society at large. Society must be satisfied that their purpose in seeking insurance is a proper purpose and, indeed, takes the matter so seriously that an insurance contract made in the absence of insurable interest is void in law. The exact requirements of insurable

---

[97] *Scher v Policyholders Protection Board (No 1 and No 2)* [1994] 2 AC 57. The matter is now regulated by the Financial Services Compensation Scheme set up under Pt XV of the FSMA 2000.
[98] Special Report on Lloyd's of London, *The Economist*, 18 September 2004, p. 90.
[99] See Chapter 3, p.69 ff.   [100] See Chapter 6, p. 239 ff.

interest vary according to whether the insurance is indemnity insurance or non-indemnity insurance, which is also called contingency insurance.

Indemnity insurance pays compensation up to the amount of actual measurable loss. An obvious example is the amount recoverable under property insurance against fire. Contingency insurance pays a pre-determined sum on the occurrence of a specified event, and the *amount* payable does not necessarily turn on the nature or importance of the event or any assessment of money lost thereby. The main example is life insurance payable on death: the amount does not usually depend on how the insured dies, or how much the insured was 'worth' to family and friends, but on how much premium was paid for the cover. Some kinds of insurance, such as personal accident (PA) insurance, have both features. A market value cannot be put on a leg, so what the skier gets for breaking one is an arbitrary amount determined partly by the amount of the premium. That part of the cover is contingency insurance. However, PA insurance also covers medical expenses—the actual cost of treatment. That is indemnity insurance.

The distinction between indemnity insurance and non-indemnity insurance leads to important differences in the law. For indemnity insurance, policyholders are required to have an insurable interest at the time of the actual loss, that is, the time at which the amount of the indemnity is measurable. Thus people can insure property, such as the house they have agreed to buy, some time before they actually own it, against its loss by fire. For contingency insurance, however, measurement is neither necessary nor, usually, possible at any time. The rule is that policyholders are required to have an insurable interest at the time they contract the insurance, which is when it can best be seen whether the insurance is really a wager, or whether, in the example of life insurance, society might want to ask whether it is likely that the insured will be tempted to take the life insured. Moreover, when life insurance is a vehicle for investment, calculations have to be made at the time of contract based on as few variables as possible; so that is when the life insured must be identified and, incidentally, when the insurable interest must exist.

Insurable Interest in Life

Ties of Affection

The classic case of contingency insurance is life insurance.[101] In theory the traditional rules survives: people are allowed to insure only the lives of those whom, as the law sees it, they will not be tempted to kill. English law's view of human nature is dismal. The list of insurable lives is short: spouses. The law's view of human nature is also uninformed, unconvincing, and—if it were ever otherwise—out of date. It is uninformed because many, if not most, murders are committed inside the family. It is unconvincing because it can scarcely be said, for example, that at 3 am, in a state of postnatal depression, a mother is less likely to

---

[101] Clarke, 3–1 ff. and 4–4A.

kill her crying child than her husband; or that she will telephone for life insurance on the child first. It is out of date *inter alia* because it takes no account of stable and loving relationships outside marriage.

A more positive view of human nature has been taken in the United States. In many, if not most, states, life insurance is allowed not only by spouse on spouse, but also by one sibling on another and by children (legitimate or not) on parents. Moreover, some state courts have allowed insurance between engaged persons, 'partners', and 'significant others', although others have not. In Texas, for example, the court disallowed insurance between unmarried couples because, said the court, it 'is a matter of common knowledge that the practice of such relations often results in a fertile field for the breeding of violence which too frequently ends in the wanton destruction of human life'.[102] Clearly, some states of the Union are more conservative than others. Perhaps the only real lesson to be drawn from these differences is that general assumptions about human behaviour based on formal relationships are unsafe. Indeed, English law today looks less to the ties of love in a relationship than to the purse strings.

Dependence

The restriction relating to natural affection, on which the traditional rules about insurable interest are based, is neither natural nor normative. So, an alternative basis for the requirement of interest in England was found in financial dependence. This explains the early decision that the life of a debtor far outside the family circle could be insured by his creditor: if a creditor's best chance of repayment lay in the continued life and labour of the debtor, society had no reason to worry about the life of the debtor.[103] Inside the family circle, however, insurable interest based on financial dependence was recognized more slowly. In 1830 the argument, that a father had an interest in the life of his son because the death of the son might mean that the father would not be maintained in old age, was rejected. The court said that, as the parish was bound to maintain him, it was a matter of indifference to the father whether he were maintained by the parish or by the son.[104] This was probably no more true then than now. Children are still seen as a source of security in old age, not least by those who would rather starve than take 'handouts' from the State and by those who are being told that there is a pension gap and that they must provide for old age in large part themselves.

The argument for an insurable interest fared no better when it came from children claiming to have an interest in the life of their parents. Was it because judges feared the thin end of a wedge, whereby a range of poor relations might insure the life of a prosperous relative on whose generosity they depended? The reason given at the time was that children had no right to maintenance,[105] albeit

[102] *Biggs v Washington National Life Ins. Co.*, 275 SW 2d 566, 569 (Tex, 1955).
[103] *Hebdon v West* (1863) 3 B & S 579.   [104] *Halford v Kymer* (1830) 10 B & C 724.
[105] *Bazeley v Forder* (1868) LR 3 QB 559, 565.

with the corollary that the argument succeeded in a few cases when children did have a right to maintenance. A similar reason was given for rejecting the argument that the potential burden of funeral expenses gave children an insurable interest in their parents: children were not obliged to pay for the funeral—in law.[106] Eventually, however, the law relented on this and allowed limited cover for this kind of expense under the Industrial Assurance and Friendly Societies Act 1948.[107] When financial dependence inside the family was finally recognized in 1909, it was not to extend the range of insurable interests but as an alternative basis to natural affection for allowing insurance between spouses.[108] The idea was that, when one alone was earning, there might nonetheless be mutual financial dependence because, as one judge put it, the cock bird can feather the nest only because he does not have to sit on it all day. That left English insurance law looking censorious but clear; yet, if the law is clear, insurance practice is not.

In practice, although the law says that there is no insurable interest in the life of a cohabiting 'partner', some insurers do offer cover and we know that the FOS is likely to enforce it.[109] Further, although, by analogy with the established case of debtors (above), firms can insure the lives of key employees, the law says that the amount must be limited to the pecuniary value of the employee's unexpired period of employment. The limit matters little to those who have contracted golden handshakes, but for the lives of those who have not, in practice the limit is widely ignored.[110] This is the kind of muddle that occurs when a rule does not appears to have a rationale that meets the needs of commerce or commands respect. Can a rationale be found for the rule?

The Problem of Finding a Rational Basis

Affection is clearly some kind of guarantee against murder; but what is not clear at all is when affection can be presumed. Marriage is not always a bond of affection; like charity, murder begins at home. But murder at home is mostly hot-blooded murder, whereas the requirement of interest only makes any sense at all if people think before they kill. Nor, of course, is marriage the only bond of affection. Indeed, it is strange that, on the one hand, tort law states that a third party owes a duty of care to co-habiting partners A and B because, if the third party kills one in front of the other, the other will be so upset that nervous illness is a reasonably foreseeable result.[111] Yet, on the other hand, the same partners are not allowed to insure each other's lives, because the law presumes they might be tempted to kill each other. So much depends on the particular relationship that categories of relationships are a poor guide.

---

[106] *Harse v Pearl Life Assurance Co.* [1904] 1 KB 558 (CA).   [107] Section 2.
[108] *Griffiths v Fleming* [1909] 1 KB 805 (CA).
[109] This was made clear by its predecessor, the Insurance Ombudsman Bureau, in its Annual Report 1989, paras 2.31 ff.   [110] See above, p. 21.
[111] See *Markesinis and Deakin*, 106.

Financial dependence, as we have seen, is also given as a rationale for the interest rule. However, readers of Agatha Christie's *Murder on the Nile* will recall that it was financial dependence within a family, and abuse of power, which bred resentment among the dependants, leading to murder. Still, the idea of dependence does reflect what is often the purpose of those who take out life insurance: to indemnify the survivors against the financial consequences of the death of the life insured—consequences which may be difficult to measure or predict, and upsetting to have to prove, but real nonetheless.

Were it regarded as the sole and sufficient rationale of the rule requiring insurable interest, however, financial dependence would go too far. If a bomb blasts a tourist to death in London's Oxford St, that is bad not only for the tourist but also for the revenue of hotels and shops in the neighbourhood. Likewise, if the monarch dies today, that is bad for business throughout the realm tomorrow. But, just as hotels and shops are not allowed to insure the lives of visitors, neither they nor the loyal citizen can insure the life of the sovereign—as such. In the realm of reality, what business needs and what it gets is not insurance on the life of the tourist or the life of the sovereign but insurance of the 'bottom line' of the business—against loss to the business caused by the event in which the death occurs.

For example, although promoters cannot insure the life or health of star performers booked to appear at a concert, profits can be insured against the loss resulting from stars' non-appearance.[112] The death of the actor Oliver Reed while filming in 1999 was reported to have been covered by the producers against consequent loss. Moreover, a firm that signs up a star athlete to endorse its health-related products can insure against, for example, the banning of that athlete from competition for having taken unlawful substances: the death of an image. Similarly, a star footballer is an asset insured by his club—usually for the amount of the player's potential value in the transfer market. Even lost expenditure on a wedding can be insured against non-appearance of the bride or bridegroom who is indisposed on the appointed day—as long as it is not a case of 'cold feet'!

For many businesses the most valuable assets are its people—not only the stars of stage and boardroom, but also researchers and others lower down the corporate hierarchy. Such people are regularly insured for their value to the company, usually an estimate of the loss of revenue to the company should they die or be rendered unfit to work. To meet such needs insurance practice has either stretched the law of life insurance, in the case of keyman insurance, or outflanked it altogether, by calling it consequential loss (or business interruption) insurance. And, indeed, why not? In each case the amount recoverable is based on a bona fide estimate, or on actual proof of what the employer has lost.[113] By thus respecting the principle of indemnity, underlying concerns of public policy are respected too.

---

[112] See *Quinta Communications v Warrington* [2000] Lloyd's Rep IR 81 (CA).

[113] Cf 'delay in start-up' (DSU) insurance, e.g., for a construction project, which is available but where the assessment of loss may be more conjectural, as in most cases the work will be associated with a new venture with no track record of past turnover.

It does little for the image of the law that the law says one thing and that remains apparently the law only because those who practice in the field have been ingenious in outflanking it. An alternative rule to one based on affection or dependence is found in certain other jurisdictions,[114] where there is the same social concern. The rule there is that insurance on the life of a third party is valid with the written consent of the life insured. Of course, consent is no guarantee against murder unless the consent is independent and informed. Consent might be obtained by the influence of charm or sophistication over innocence or age; however, such instances do not seem to be frequent enough to cause concern. It is a rule that appears to work elsewhere and, unlike current English law, it is a rule that in practice is what it appears to be.

Insurable Interest in Property

The paradigm of indemnity insurance is property insurance. People have an insurable interest in property if, first, they have an 'economic interest' in the property. This is simply a 'factual expectation' of loss, that is, that if there is physical damage to (or loss of) the property insured, that will cause the policyholder financial loss.[115] A factual expectation should have been enough for the law of England, as it is today in most other countries, to allay any anxiety about why the property was being insured; but it is not. In England, secondly, people are also required to stand in 'a legal or equitable relation' to the property they insure. The 'legal or equitable relation' is an interest recognized by the law of property. This requirement seems to have arisen because, in a society which valued and protected property rights, there was a feeling that a solid factual expectation of loss, about which society could be sure, would be found only among those with that kind of relationship to the property. Like many another dubious rules of law, it arose out of a controversial case.

In *Macaura*,[116] the claimant insured the timber on his estate, and then sold it to a company of which he was the main shareholder and the main creditor. Soon after that, the timber was destroyed by fire. Although, for all practical purposes, he was the company and the person who stood to lose by the fire, his insurance claim failed. The reasons given were that the insurance was in his name and not that of the company; and that neither his role as shareholder nor his role as creditor gave him a legal relationship of any kind, such as ownership or possession, with the timber. After the sale that relationship with the timber was that of the company and the company alone. The House of Lords affirmed on those grounds the decision of the Court of Appeal in Northern Ireland, and indirectly that of the arbitrator who had first considered the case there. However, it has been suggested

---

[114] E.g., France (Code d'assurance, Art. 132–2), Germany (Gesetz über den Versicherungsvertrag (VVG), Art. 159), New York State (Ins. Law, § 146(3)), Switzerland (Loi fédérale sur le Contrat d'Assurances (LCA), Art. 74). [115] *Lucena v Craufurd* (1806) 2 Bos & Pul (NR) 269 (HL).
[116] *Macaura v Northern Assurance* [1925] AC 619. See further, Clarke, 4–3.

in the USA that the British courts were motivated to take a hard line because the case 'involved charges of fraud that, though not proved, proof usually being difficult', 'influenced the court to reach a theory of insurable interest that is nothing short of pernicious'.[117]

Be that as it may, the effect of the decision has been that an insurable interest in property is enjoyed by people such as owners, trustees, personal representatives, mortgagors, mortgagees, lessors, lessees, and bailees; but that many people with a significant economic interest in property are left out. They include beneficiaries named in a will, as well as people who put money, time, and effort into a business, whether as investor, employee, or sub-contractor: these people cannot insure the factory or equipment on which the work or the venture depends. Also left out are people who have agreed to buy goods but have yet to acquire possession or ownership, in particular the distance buyer of goods in transit, even though the very future of the buyer's business may depend on their safe arrival. With two exceptions (discussed in the next section) such a buyer cannot insure the goods against the perils of the sea or the intervention of thieves.

These limitations help to explain why the requirement of 'legal or equitable relation', which had been imported as part of the common law from England, was later dropped in Australia,[118] Canada,[119] and the United States.[120] In these countries the law is now satisfied with the requirement of factual expectation of loss, the economic interest, alone. Indeed, the logic of the step taken by the law in these countries suggests a further step, a step away from a rule that requires expectation of loss at the time of contract, to one which drops that too and, like the law of France[121] and Germany,[122] for example, is content simply with proof of actual loss at the time of claim. In the case of property, the law does not need a rule of insurable interest; all it needs is what it has already got: a rule against voluntary destruction[123] and a principle of indemnity.[124] This was the view of the Australian Law Reform Commission back in 1982[125] and, although it was not implemented by the legislature there, it still seems to be sound advice.

As often happens when English law is too constricting, it has been stretched by the pressure of commerce. Such a strict requirement no longer meets the needs of the day and the rule has been stretched by the realities and requirements of practice. The law states a rule, which most people do not expect in the first place, and then confuses them further with special cases. The most important special cases are those of buyers and bailees.

[117] R. E. Keeton, *Insurance Law—Basic Text* (St Paul, Minn., 1971) 117.
[118] Insurance Contracts Act 1984, Pt III.
[119] *Constitution Ins. Co. v Kosmopoulos* [1987] 1 SCR 2.
[120] *Hayes v Milford Mutual Fire Ins. Co.*, 48 NE 754 (Sup Ct, Mass, 1898).
[121] Code d'assurances (c.ass.), Art. 121–1.   [122] VVG 1908, Art. 55.
[123] See Chapter 7, p. 255 ff.
[124] See Chapter 6, pp. 219–20.
[125] The Law Reform Commission, Report No. 20, *Insurance Contracts*, para 117.

Buyers

People who have contracted to buy land acquire at the time of contract an equitable interest in the property, and thus an insurable interest in the property. Not so buyers of goods. Generally buyers of goods, who have yet to acquire possession or ownership of the goods they have contracted to buy, cannot insure them in transit. However, exception is made when the goods are at the buyer's risk—which is usually from the time of shipment.[126] Until shipment, the buyer stands in no legal or equitable relation to the goods. After shipment the buyer's position is no different, except that, as a matter of contract with the seller, the goods are at the buyer's risk because the buyer must pay for the goods if they are lost or damaged. However, the obligation to pay is less a legal relation with the goods than clear confirmation of factual expectation of loss—payment to the seller come what may—and that is the explanation of the extension. Once risk has passed, it is clear beyond doubt that damage to the goods will damage the buyer financially. A fortiori, the same can be said of buyers who have actually paid a seller. So, the second exception concerns buyers who have paid all or part of the price. Payment, said the courts of the nineteenth century, gave buyers an 'equitable lien' on the goods and thus an equitable relationship to them.[127] But the lien is window-dressing. Again, the real explanation is that the payment is evidence enough that damage to the goods will damage the buyer; that is what matters. Any social concern that there might be the evil of wagering in such a case can be laid firmly to rest.

Bailees

People have a legal relation to any goods in their possession—not only their own goods, but also goods of others in their possession for which, therefore, they may be liable as bailee if the goods are lost or damaged. This is easy to understand in the case of bailees in business, such as repair shops and warehouses, but the rule has been extended to private houses. A householder may insure not only his wife's jewellery but also his son's bicycle, even though the jewellery is in his wife's handbag and the bicycle is at his son's college and neither son nor bicycle spend much time at home; once a year is enough. The explanation, like that for other bailees, is that the father's insurable interest lies in liability to members of the family, if their property is stolen because, for example, the father did not mend the lock on the back door. This explanation does not bear close examination, but it is not meant to: everyone agrees that it is sensible to allow the insurance. Indeed, the good commercial sense of the device is such that it explains a number of other extensions of that same idea.

The first concerns the warehouse, where the rule has been stretched further by what is called (confusingly, as it is not a trust at all) a commercial trust. Not only is

---

[126] *Inglis v Stock* (1885) 10 App Cas 263.
[127] *Ebsworth v Alliance Marine Ins. Co.* (1873) LR 8 CP 596.

a warehouse allowed to insure the goods of its customer, but, in the event of loss or damage, it may recover the full value of the goods from the insurer, even though the actual loss has been suffered not by the warehouse but by the customer. If, however, the warehouse does claim and recover the insurance money, it cannot keep it: the customer can compel the warehouse to account for the money over and above the insured loss, if any, suffered by the warehouse itself.[128]

Builders

The second extension concerns a more diffuse group of bailees in commerce. On a construction site, especially large ones like that currently at the King's Cross and St Pancras railway stations in London, there can be no doubt about the convenience for all concerned of allowing one person, usually the head contractor, to take out a single policy covering the whole of the risk and for the benefit of all those working on site. Otherwise each sub-contractor would have to take out a separate policy. This would mean, at the very least, extra paperwork; at worst, in the event of an accident, there would be multiple overlapping claims and cross-claims or, possibly, no cover at all. One solution to the problem might be for the head contractor to contract insurance as agent for all the sub-contractors concerned, but there are difficulties here about the well-worn agency device. One is that the law does not allow agents to contract for unknown principals: the head contractor cannot insure sub-contractors that have yet to be appointed. Another is that the cost of separate liability insurance might be too much for the small sub-contractor, who would then be tempted to under-insure. So, in situations like this, the courts have held that the position of a contractor in relation to contract works is sufficiently similar to that of a bailee in relation to goods bailed that a co-contractor, usually in practice the head contractor, is entitled to insure the entire contract works, and in the event of a loss to recover the full value of the loss on behalf of the losers.[129]

The cover makes evident commercial sense. Not only does it avoid multiplicity of paperwork and claims, but, as the judge pointed out in one case,[130] contractors want their insurance policy to be available to sub-contractors because it is

cheaper to give sub-contractors some benefits under their policy rather than for every party to have to enter into entirely separate policies, the cost of which would be reflected in the sub-contract prices, and . . . by controlling insurance protection [the contractor] could satisfy itself that if a claim did arise there would be no gaps in the cover available.

Moreover, this kind of cover, often called construction all risks (CAR) insurance, has another feature which promotes harmony and thus productivity on site.

---

[128] The leading modern case is *Tomlinson v Hepburn* [1966] AC 451. Alternatively, the policy may now be worded in such a way as to support a direct action by the goods owner under the Contracts (Rights of Third Parties) Act, 1999, s. 1.

[129] See *Petrofina (UK) Ltd v Magnaload Ltd* [1983] 2 Lloyd's Rep 91, 96–7.

[130] *National Oilwell v Davy* [1993] 2 Lloyd's Rep 582, 600, *per* Colman J.

Normally, any insurer who has indemnified a policyholder against damage to property is subrogated to any rights the policyholder might have, for example in tort, against a third party responsible for the damage. Not so under CAR cover. Although their interests are diverse, the various contractors and sub-contractors covered by a CAR policy are treated as co-assured and, as such, are immune to such claims. Although the legal basis of this is debatable,[131] the outcome is not: if contractor A drives into contractor B, the insurer which has indemnified B cannot bring a claim in negligence against A any more than if A and B were employed by the same firm.[132]

CAR cover of this kind has been held, on the one hand, to be confined to the site and not to extend, for example, to the work of sub-contractors working elsewhere on even large components to be installed on the main site.[133] Thus, *prima facie*, an Airbus wing made in Wales is not covered by the Airbus company at Toulouse before it arrives there for assembly with the other parts of an aircraft, unless the company has a separate transit policy for it, although it would be easy to justify insurance by the device of risk transfer or pricing.[134]

CAR cover has been expanded, on the other hand, in point of time in the form of 'delay in start-up' (DSU) insurance—for delay in commencing a construction project. Sensible enough from a commercial point of view, conceptually DSU cover is striking because it is essentially pecuniary—it may have not only an element of liability cover for breach of contract but, in particular, a large measure of business interruption (loss of profits) cover. Usually CAR insurance is associated with property (buildings, machines) to which the insured has a legal or equitable relation, but in this case there may be none. Usually, however, for practical reasons, DSU cover is 'bolted on' to CAR cover on the actual work, and that connection provides incidentally a tenuous (prospective) link to property to which the insured has or will have the requisite legal and equitable relation.[135]

Such extensions of liability cover have implications for any collaborative activity on a large scale, where there is a potential for damage to property and liability between collaborators. Factories, hospitals, and even colleges come to mind. As Lord Diplock has explained the original rule as one based on commercial practice,[136] however, we cannot predict a similar extension for these places unless it can be said that, on account of manifest convenience, the basis lies more in the element of convenience than in the element of commerce. Once again the law has been stretched to achieve a sensible result, but once again its extent is uncertain.

---

[131] See *Cooperative Retail Services Ltd v Taylor Young* [2002] UKHL 17, [2002] 1 WLR 1419 (HL).
[132] *Simpson v Thompson* (1877) 3 App Cas 279; Clarke, 31–5D.
[133] See *National Oilwell v Davy*, op. cit. above, n. 131.   [134] See above, p. 33.
[135] *Macaura*, op. cit. above, n. 117.
[136] *The Albazero* [1977] AC 774, 846.

Insurable Interest: Why?

The gambling known as business looks with austere disfavor upon the business known as gambling.[137]

One reason given in the past for the requirement of insurable interest is that it stops people using insurance for gambling. If I insure my own cargo worth £100,000 against total loss on a voyage to New York for a premium of £100, that is valid insurance. If, however, the cargo is not mine but that of someone else, the so-called insurance is a wager of a thousand to one on whether the cargo will get there and, as such, it is void. Why?

Gambling

Two hundred years ago the judges saw wagers less as a social or moral evil than as a nuisance. In *Gilbert v Sykes*,[138] P had paid D 100 guineas in return for D's promise to pay P a guinea a day for as long as Napoleon Bonaparte should live—a dinner table bet that Napoleon would be assassinated. The court refused to enforce D's promise simply on account of the 'inconvenience of countenancing wagers in Courts of Justice'. Wagers occupy the time of the court and divert 'their attention from causes of real interest and concern'.[139] Elements of this factor are still found today in the economists' notion of 'diminishing marginal utility': time and money, whether that of the insured or the insurer, should not be diverted to matters that serve no useful social or economic purpose.[140] Be that as it may, the use of insurance for wagering is surely a thing of the past. As the Supreme Court of Canada said in *Kosmopoulos*,[141] today there are 'many more convenient devices available to the serious wagerer'.

Temptation and Moral Hazard

A reason more commonly given for the requirement of insurable interest is that people with such an insurable interest are less likely to succumb to any temptation to bring about the loss insured against. A person with a large overdraft but little love for a neighbour might be tempted to insure the neighbour's warehouse against fire and then burn it; and also perhaps insure his life and burn it while his neighbour is there. The assumption is that, when it comes to their own life or their own warehouse, people are not subject to the same temptation; and that, as regards

---

[137] Ambrose Bierce (1842–1914), *The Devil's Dictionary*.
[138] *Gilbert v Sykes* (1812) 13 East 150.   [139] Ibid., 162, *per* Bayley J.
[140] B. Harnett and J. V. Thornton, 'Insurable Interest in Property: A Socio-Economic Revaluation of a Legal Concept', 48 Col LR 1162, 1179 (1948).
[141] *Constitution Ins. Co. v Kosmopoulos* [1987] 1 SCR 2, 22, *per* Wilson J.

property, sentiment or the inconvenience of being deprived of it will ensure that any such temptation is resisted.[142] This is not convincing without qualification.

On the one hand, the very fact that property is insured gives rise to 'moral hazard', that is, in the language of economics, 'the resulting tendency of an insured to underallocate to loss prevention after purchasing insurance'.[143] Or, in the language of Shakespeare and one of his witches, 'security is mortals' chiefest enemy'.[144] On the other hand, the impact of moral hazard can be overrated, if we ignore the countervailing factors of sentiment and inconvenience, and the fact that insurance money is not always paid promptly to restore the situation. One of the main criticisms of insurers in modern Britain is how long they take to respond.[145] For example, in late 2003 a leading insurer confessed at a conference that its offices took between 500 and 1,200 days to settle claims under £2,500.[146] In any event, people are only likely to set fire to their property when they are desperate. That is not good for the property or for other people who, indirectly or indirectly, may depend on it. However, it is when an arsonist is desperate that skilled investigators are likely to sense the desperation and a fraudulent insurance claim is unlikely to succeed anyway.

Removing both the Temptation and the Rule of Law

People have sometimes taken their own life in an attempt to pay debts and salvage honour; and, especially in times of recession, people have sometimes tried to reduce a large overdraft at their bank with a large fire at their warehouse: what has been described in the insurance industry as 'ash for cash'. An interest in, and thus an 'involvement' with, persons or property insured, whether as strict as that required by English law or not, does not appear to make it much less likely that insurance will be abused. What does appear, it is submitted, is that people should be allowed to insure whatever persons or property they wish, if they can find an insurer to provide the cover.

In many, if not most, cases of people succumbing to temptation, insurers can resist payment on other grounds. Although the law does not require people to prove their interest, either when contracting insurance or when making a claim, in practice they will find it difficult to insure property of any value and in which they have no interest at all other than crime without falling foul of the rules about misrepresentation or non-disclosure.[147] If they do insure it and then burn it, they will find it impossible to obtain the insurance money without committing fraud.

---

[142] See also S. A. Rea Jnr, 'The Economics of Insurance Law', 13 *Int Rev of Law & Economics* 145–62, 146 ff. (1993).

[143] K. S. Abraham, *Distributing Risk: Insurance, Legal Theory, and Public Policy* (hereafter 'Abraham') (New Haven, 1986) 14, See also Rea Jnr, op. cit. above, n. 143.

[144] Hecate, *Macbeth*, Act III, Scene 5.

[145] See Chapter 6, p. 244 ff.

[146] *PM*, 30 October 2003.   [147] See Chapter 4, p. 95 ff.

Of course, fraud is sometimes successful. However, although insurers may be reluctant to defend a claim on the ground of fraud,[148] crooked claimants may well find that the insurer concerned is very slow to pay and, if the insurer does pay, that even then their enjoyment of the insurance money is spoiled by the unwelcome attention of the police.

In these circumstances, it is submitted that the requirement of insurable interest, whether as strict as that required by English law or not, does not appear to serve its purpose; and that, in principle, people should be allowed to insure other people or their property. Why not trust citizen A to appreciate that there are better and safer ways of making money than insuring B one day and killing B the next? If A, for reasons which A knows best, values B's life enough to pay premiums, why not let A do so? Why not trust people? Why not trust the police, who will be the first to look at A if B dies suddenly, and society at large to see that B is safe from A?

If that is true, the question remains whether insurers, as an important part of that society, might owe any kind of duty of prevention *ab initio*, duty not only to their stakeholders but also to society at large. Their claims department can usually be relied on to smell rats and root them out. The same cannot be said of the sales department, which has little incentive to undertake more than a routine invest-igation of standard risks such as life policies, even policies taken on the life of a third person. In England, however, it has been suggested,[149] and in the USA it has been decided in some states, that if the seller of a gun was aware that the buyer intended to use it to shoot someone, the seller may be liable to the victim in tort. In the USA it has also been stated that a person has a duty 'to use reasonable care not to create a situation which may prove a stimulus for murder'; this statement was made not about a seller of guns but about a seller of insurance.[150] There is also precedent there to suggest that, if the seller of insurance to the spouse of the life insured is aware that the buyer has already got a gun for this purpose, the insurer may be liable to the victim in tort.[151] This is not to suggest that such an insurer would be liable in England. It does raise, however, and not for the last time, the difficult question of the extent to which insurers can be expected to investigate a risk proposed, to which we return in Chapter 4.

---

[148] See Chapter 6, p. 215 ff.
[149] *Paterson Zochonis Ltd v Merfarken Packaging Ltd* [1986] 3 All ER 522, 540, *per* Goff LJ (CA).
[150] *Ramey v Carolina Life Ins. Co.*, 135 SE 2d 362, 367 (SC, 1964).
[151] See Kingree and Tanner, 29 Tort & Ins LJ 761 (1994).

2

Insurers

The Emergence of Insurers

In Chapter 1 we saw that people buy insurance, in part at least, to find some degree of peace of mind concerning the risks insured. Insurers are aware of this and, to sell their insurance, have projected a certain image of themselves and of their products. Advertising that stresses the unpleasantness of risks has been censured by the advertising authority. Anyway, insurers have found that, if the presentation is too disturbing, people respond negatively, by pushing the issue aside, rather than positively, by seeking insurance. That is one reason why, for example, insurance against illness is sold as health insurance, and insurance against death as life insurance; it is the positive features of the product that are stressed. The image of insurance and insurers is the main subject of this chapter.

A Brief History

The earliest insurers were mutuals.[1] Their correct title today is 'protection and indemnity associations', informally known as P&I clubs. People in need of what we now call insurance got together in 'clubs' of such people in need for mutual protection and indemnity.[2] Today they are still there, but reinsure each other in the so-called International Group Pool, which is itself reinsured at Lloyd's and by insurance companies across the globe. The early mutuals were followed by companies which offered insurance on a commercial basis, companies set up to provide insurance for others and to make a profit for those who invested in the companies. In parallel, certain kinds of insurance, originally marine but later other lines too, were arranged at Lloyd's.

As the market grew, intermediaries came into the market to bring people together. Indeed, insurers have done much of their personal lines of business through intermediaries, usually brokers,[3] and in the past chose to have little direct contact with policyholders, until the mould was broken by the arrival of 'direct' insurers. These are insurers who market their products directly to the client by mail or by telephone. The older way of doing business left it to the broker to identify need and to design products; the new pattern found some insurers ill-equipped to take the initiative which the new marketplace required.

First, some insurers lacked the staff with the inter-personal skills necessary for dealing with customers in the flesh. Some simply did not listen to the customer; they were unable to appreciate the particular concerns of the customer and to tailor cover accordingly. Further, the older practice left the industry with a remote and monolithic image, which failed to attract the best graduates of the best business schools or, indeed, graduates of any kind at all. Those who did enter the industry were more likely to be promoted for loyalty than for talent. The 'successes' of this system reinforced the process by showing little enthusiasm for education, within the firm or in the world outside; and in turn they tended naturally to promote those they could trust and understand, cloning their own kind: the graduates of the university of life—company life.

Lloyd's

The insurance market at Lloyd's began in Mr Lloyd's coffee house centuries ago. The recent history of Lloyd's begins with recovery from its near collapse in the last twenty years. The Lloyd's litigation in the 1990s established, said an industry journal at the time, 'what we always knew—that some underwriters at Lloyd's during that period', the late 1980s and early 1990s, 'were simply not up to the job'.[4]

---

[1] See below, 'Mutuality', at p. 44 ff.   [2] See Chapter 1, p. 22 ff.
[3] See Chapter 3.
[4] *PM*, 13 October 1994, 19. See, e.g., *Henderson v Merit Syndicates Ltd* [1994] 2 Lloyd's Rep 193.

A particular strand of folly then was the assumption by some underwriters that the price of cover could be fixed without researching the risk. In those days people saw 'what happens when brokers of less than top draw quality are tempted to present bad risks to underwriters who are known to fly by the seat of their pants, particularly after lunch on Fridays'.[5] A senior industry executive was quoted as saying, 'those who insist on using a crystal ball often end up eating ground glass'.[6]

Today, insurance personnel both inside and outside Lloyd's are more likely to have been trained, *inter alia*, in the use of statistical data and drawn from graduate recruitment programmes. In underwriting, as in sport, apparently effortless reliance on natural ability rather than hard work, training, and research is a thing of the past. Underwriting is less a branch of white magic than a scrupulous science. Even so, some underwriters at Lloyd's still pride themselves that for an honest proposer they can put a price on anything and do it in about three minutes, as the broker waits. Nonetheless, today speed is less important than the sureness of touch that comes with experience and knowledge. In late 2003, the Chairman of Lloyd's could report that in 2003 it had filed the best results in its history of over 300 years.

The changes in the structure and operation of Lloyd's have also been considerable and now give some grounds for confidence in the future of the Lloyd's market. By 2005, 625 Names provided £1,445 million of Lloyd's capital, whereas 705 corporate members provided £12,277 million. Nonetheless, it seems that the new and revitalized image of Lloyd's has yet to reach a wide public. A survey of public perceptions of Lloyd's, part of a 'brand definition project' conducted in the first quarter of 2004 among Lloyd's 'stakeholders', concluded that, in so far as any consensus emerged, the image of Lloyd's was still of 'an old fashioned institution that insures anything and always pays up'![7] In the same year, *The Economist* described it as unique, a 'voluntary, mutual capitalist society' that is 'behaving more like a company' with a powerful brand, to which people come to cover 'big risks, complicated risks and weird risks'.[8]

Although by 2004 the capacity of Lloyd's to underwrite risk had expanded to an all-time high of just under £15 billion (and £16.1 billion in early 2007) from £10 billion in 1996, however, recently most new 'investment' money has gone to Bermuda where taxation is lower and regulation lighter. Moreover, its traditional marine business continued to show a long-term relative decline. In 1994, some 25 per cent of total Lloyd's income was derived from marine insurance, a quarter of which related to hull insurance. In 2004 these numbers were estimated at 17 and 4 per cent respectively,[9] simply because it had become difficult to make an underwriting surplus from this line of business. As for the future, a new determination

---

[5] M. Mendelowitz, 'Reinsurance Dispute Resolution—Recent Trends and Recent Cases' (1993) 83 BILA J 23–33, 27.   [6] *Insurance Day*, 18 November 2002.

[7] *PM*, 8 July 2004.

[8] Special Report on Lloyd's of London, *The Economist*, 18 September 2004, p. 89.

[9] The seven biggest hull markets in 2003 in $ millions were London (517), Japan (377), France (361), Norway (337), USA (299), Italy (266), and Spain (167): S. Ignarski, *Bow Wave*, 5 January 2004.

by shipbuilding insurers to charge much higher rates to the booming shipyards of the world has been noted; but with so much of the world's tonnage heading to the East, Lloyd's has established platforms for new business in both India and China.

Niche Insurers

In the 1990s it was predicted that general multi-line insurers would suffer in competition with specialist insurers who have identified and focused on a particular part of the insurance market. In recent times there have been signs that that prediction is coming true; it is the 'niche' underwriters that appear to prosper most.[10] Successful niches include space and satellite cover. On the edge of cyberspace is cybercover, which offers protection *inter alia* against hacking (but not yet indemnity against the impact of viruses). Down on Earth we find 'non-standard' motor cover for actors, publicans, and drivers with convictions. Other examples are kidnap and ransom (K & R) cover,[11] and cover against the possibility of unexpectedly finding pollution on sites acquired.[12]

Niche marketing is distinguished, in theory at least, from 'cherry picking'. That is when, for example, insurers rate risk with such precision (for example, by post code) that insurance (for example, against theft), is much costlier in one street than in the next. In extreme cases streets are 'red lined' and cannot get cover at all. In public the insurance industry condemns this practice as bad for its image, and dangerous for its future; the fear is of newspaper outrage such that pressure may build on the Government to intervene and compel insurers to offer the cover.[13] Indeed, it might seem odd that insurers should be so risk adverse; and no less odd that 'high net worth insurance' (covering the property of the rich) is regarded by the industry as a respectable niche, whereas refusing cover to the downtown poor is not. Be that as it may, the response of some other parts of the industry to some of the newer needs of society has also been impressive. Among them are transport insurance and innovation of various kinds brought in by mutual insurers, discussed below.

Meeting or Making the Need

Publicity

Insurers first appeared on the scene in response to the perception that people needed insurance. It remains the role of insurers to meet that need by spreading risk, with the aid of the law of large numbers and within the framework of the law

---

[10] See, e.g., *PM*, 13 November 2003, 23.   [11] See Chapter 1, p. 21 ff.
[12] *PM*, 13 November 2003, 23–4.
[13] See Chapter 7, p. 248 ff.

of the land. In some theatres of need they have played a reward winning role on a world stage, for example, their response to the sinking of the *Titanic* in 1912.

Simply covering ships like that, ships in the public eye, is an exercise in self-promotion. When the *Titanic* sank, the vessel was insured for £1 million. When the *Queen Mary* set sail in 1936, she was insured for £4.8 million, albeit with £1.8 million of that underwritten by the Government. When the *QM2* first set out for Fort Lauderdale in January 2004, the hull and machinery alone were insured for $500 million. Most insurance cover, however, is more mundane; it is a product which has to be marketed like any other product. Between 1992 and 1994, the amount spent by insurers in the UK on advertising in all parts of the media more than doubled, from £70 million to £163 million. In 1999, for example, a life company started a three-year television campaign costing £30 million over three years. The trend has continued since.

Trains and Boats and Planes

In spite of the adverse publicity surrounding deaths on railways in recent years, there has been no significant increase in the cost of personal accident cover for those travelling by rail in the UK. This is partly because the dangers have been exaggerated by certain sections of the media, but partly too because insurers have been covering this kind of risk for a long time. The same is true of ships, although the cost of cover for all that may happen to, on, and in large cruise ships has been the subject of extended debate. Above all, it has been true of passenger aircraft.

In 1969, some observers doubted whether the insurance industry had the capacity to cover the loss that might arise out of the crash of the then new Boeing 747 aircraft, the largest civil aircraft to take to the sky with passengers. By the 1990s, passenger miles had increased by a factor of four, the number of western passenger jets in service was over 10,000, and it was estimated that a serious crash of a 747 would cost insurers of the hull alone $15 million. Even so, in the late 1990s the cost of an airline's insurance for such an aircraft was only about 0.8 per cent of the operating costs of the aircraft. Fluctuations and losses of this magnitude can be covered only by spreading loss—over the years and over the market, through many insurers and many layers of reinsurance—but it could be done.

In January 2001, for a well-run, medium-sized western airline operating modern passenger aircraft of all sizes, the insurance cost was scarcely more than 1.5 per cent of operating costs. For a small airline of that kind, about twice that. The position since terrorists flew aircraft into the World Trade Center in September 2001 is still not entirely clear. Initially the market overreacted to the event, and rates are still unsettled. Analysts have been seeking to apply to aviation insurance the lessons of catastrophic modelling, which were applied by the insurance industry after the hurricanes of the early 1990s to life insurance and reinsurance.[14] A survey in 2004 quoted the then chairman of the Lloyd's Aviation Association as announcing a reduction in losses, with the result that losses were barely more than 60 per cent of premium received; and the survey found that aviation was one of the few sectors where the cost of liability cover was coming down.[15]

A tentative estimate today is that the insurance cost to airlines has doubled since 2001; but at 3 to 5 per cent of operating costs it is still a sustainable cost, in spite of a stricter passenger and cargo liability regime in the Montreal Convention 1999, which came into force in the UK on 28 June 2004. In a broadsheet newspaper analysis of the operating costs of a 'no frills' air carrier in the UK, the insurance ingredient was too trifling to make the pie chart. In addition, Lloyd's has offered tour operators insurance against 'air rage'—it can be costly to divert an aircraft to off-load a loaded passenger; but business interruption (loss of profits) insurance has been increasingly hard to get; and liability cover for air traffic control and other airport service providers had become considerably more expensive.[16] Of all the upward pressures on the cost of running western airlines, liability insurance does not appear to be among the most significant.

Mutuality

Another success story can be told of the mutuals, also known as P&I clubs. Traces of clubs can be found from Roman times and, later, in the protection offered by guilds. In 1782, sugar refiners, who were regarded as a bad risk by the market, formed the Phoenix Fire Office to cover their own fire risks. Today, at one end of the financial spectrum shipowners still 'club' together to take large liability risks. At the other end, we find mutual benefit societies, such as local burial clubs, which arose out of the custom of passing around the 'hat' on the death of a fellow workman to collect something for his funeral and his family; indeed, the earliest English life insurer was a mutual.

The recent history of mutuality shows that that part of the insurance industry has done more than simply react to the needs perceived by potential policyholders. Today the mutuals together insure the owners (and many of the charterers) of some 98 per cent of the world's ocean-going ships for their liabilities towards third parties—their traditional business. In the 1960s, the cover on offer was extended from that to the cost of strikes and cover to protect charterers against liabilities they may have for damage to the ships which they charter. In 1968, in response to the trend towards combined and intermodal carriage, the through transport mutual,

---

[14] Stuart Collins, *Insurance Day*, 14 August 2003. Farmer can buy crop insurance against bad weather. Moreover, *The Economist* (9 December 2004) reported a plan to offer a kind of 'drought insurance' by means of derivatives.

[15] *PM*, 4 March 2004. 2004 was the safest year ever: *Guardian*, 11 January 2005.

[16] *Insurance Day*, 18 November 2002, which also reported that the aviation sector was making good profits.

now known as the TT Club, was formed. This now insures some 70 per cent of the world's ocean-going containers, as well as associated facilities and those who operate in intermodal cargo transport worldwide.

In the 1980s, certain club managers reckoned, correctly as it turned out, that the traditional maritime market was more likely to retract than expand, and the search was on for new fields. A mutual was founded to cover the liabilities of ship agents and shipbrokers and, later, ship managers and other professionals engaged in maritime work. Other mutuals were formed to cover the professional liability of in-house architects and surveyors of housing associations, UK patent and trade mark agents, insurance brokers at Lloyd's, UK barristers, and, as regards a crucial upper layer of liability cover, UK solicitors in England and Wales. In 1990, a mutual was formed to cover against latent defects in the retained housing stock of UK housing associations.

From the beginning the clubs have been in the forefront of innovation, undertaking novel risks that others were too conventional to recognize or too cautious to rate.[17] A recent instance is the development of insurance products (*Takaful*), in particular property cover, for the estimated 350,000 Muslim households in the UK. Takaful is broadly similar to mutual cover, in that it involves participants sharing risk on a co-operative basis in pools in a way which is acceptable to Islamic law. Payment of a conventional insurance premium, non-returnable if no loss occurs, would be seen as a form of gambling (*Maysir*). Also prohibited is the earning of interest (*Riba*), so it is particularly difficult to market attractive life products.

A mutual of particular current interest is Pool Re, which was set up in response to the IRA bombing of the Baltic Exchange in 1992 in the City of London. Pool Re is a mutual, backed by the Treasury in case Pool Re's reserves are overstretched, set up under the Reinsurance (Acts of Terrorism) Act 1993. It is an excess insurer to cover upper levels of loss (only) caused by terrorism, which is there defined as the

acts of persons acting on behalf of, or in connection with, any organisation which carries out activities directed towards the overthrowing or influencing, by force or violence, of Her Majesty's government in the United Kingdom or any other government *de jure* or *de facto*.

Originally confined to damage caused by fire and explosion, cover was extended in 2002 to 'all risks' of contamination arising from chemical, biological, and radioactive causes, thus including 'dirty bombs'. However, it excludes not only war risks but also hacking and virus damage. Moreover, the requirement of connection with an organization is narrower than the definition used by other reinsurers and rules out the exploits of individuals acting alone. The requirement of affecting government rules out attacks by religious fanatics or animal rights protesters, for example, and there is no plan to extend it in that direction.[18]

---

[17] See above, p. 44.
[18] For discussion of the relative roles of insurers and government, see S. Levmore and K. D. Logue, 'Insuring against Terrorism—and Crime', 102 Mich L Rev 268–327 (2003).

Whether mutuals have a long-term future, however, is less clear. The sceptical view is that 'it is the qualities of mutuals themselves that make a further flourishing of the model unlikely in the 21st century. They are after all the product of a kind of thinking called self-help' and their operation called 'international functionalism', which is now less fashionable and less necessary.[19] Moreover, the mutual 'is a peculiarly unmodern way to own wealth. The mutual organisation is hard to sell, take over or merge with others . . . Mutuals can lock up capital very effectively.'[20]

Inspiring Confidence

When a serious smallpox epidemic hit London in 1901, a leading and celebrated underwriter at Lloyd's was Cuthbert Heath. He was 'quick to realize that, at a time of great anxiety, people needed some kind of talisman; and the talisman might be insurance'.[21] So he offered them insurance against their catching the disease, provided that they got vaccinated. While making a lot of money, Heath also promoted risk management and prevention,[22] as well as offering the possibility of some degree of peace of mind. That is a need that remains. To satisfy the desire of people today for peace of mind, insurers must offer cover in which the buyers have confidence. They must convince them that, if loss occurs, money will be paid—and paid reasonably quickly. To overcome the lingering *frisson* caused by the public perception of past scandals in the financial services industry about pensions, one of the main objectives of advertising by insurers has been to create an image of financial security, enduring trustworthiness, and fair dealing.

An Image of Trustworthiness

'When it comes to life', ran an advertisement in the United States, 'there are two things you can always count on. A mother's love and your State Farm agent.' In England the prose is more restrained, but the message is the same. This is an important aspect of the image that insurers wish to project, and of the relationship with their customers, the policyholders, that they would like to promote.[23] They have a long way to go. Surveys of public opinion indicate that, when it comes to the public perception of trustworthiness, general insurers, and financial services generally, come some way behind banks, building societies, and supermarkets. That is one reason why so much standard insurance is now sold through retailers with a good public image.

---

[19] S. Ignarski, *Bow Wave*, 7 October 2002.   [20] Ibid.
[21] A. Brown, *Cuthbert Heath* (London, 1980) 90.
[22] See below, p. 53.
[23] See Chapter 9, p. 341 ff.

Typically, an insurance company teams up with a particular retailer. In what the industry calls the 'affinity market', people can buy, in certain well-known stores and supermarkets, life, motor, household, travel, and even pet insurance. Even football clubs, such as Southampton Football Club, may sell a wide range of insurance products to their supporters. Given that insurers see exposure as a major factor in the extent of risk, there is surely some attraction in the idea floated in the USA, but as yet not in England, that motor insurance should be widely sold at petrol stations.[24]

An Image of Security

Security is associated with endurance and continuity—and thus with a known and, by implication, established name. To acquire this image, some insurers advertise simply to increase name awareness. As with washing-powder and whisky, people buying blind are more likely to choose a brand name that they have heard of. One of the major UK insurers ran the same short advertisement for over fifteen years, partly because repetition, while risking boredom, suggests consistency and stability. For similar reasons, life insurers more than other insurers have been slow to change their names, because research indicates that people want an 'old' name, a company with pedigree, which they can rely upon to be there in the future as in the past. Ecclesiastical, for example, with 'over 100 years of experience in property insurance', offers 'insurance you can believe in'.

The image of security is also built on associations with solidity—sometimes quite literally. One company advertised on television with pictures of the Great Wall of China and the claim that 'no-one protects more'. A Swiss insurer advertised in the UK with the image of a St Bernard dog, not only because it is seen as Swiss but also because it is a breed associated with rescue and reliability. Was there irony in the mind of the advertiser who chose the name 'Churchill'—and the picture of a bulldog—to market in England the insurance products of a German insurance company?

Sponsorship, which is often cheaper than advertising, is chosen with equal care. Some insurers have associated themselves with classical arts, and thus with enduring values, and others with community involvement, especially organizations concerned with caring for those in need. A number of insurers have chosen to sponsor sport. Most insurers today have some reservations about the image of association football. Cricket is another matter. For many people cricket still has connotations of fair play and honesty; and it is followed by many people of the kind that insurers want to attract.

Much remains to be done to give insurers the appearance that would promote their self-image. However, there is surely something to be said for the view of one public relations (PR) consultant that, although there is a PR problem, the

---

[24] *The Economist*, 25 October 2003.

solution is not to be found through PR, for PR should be used as a means of communication, not as a sticking plaster; and that images or reputations are built mainly on good products, service, and handling of complaints. The image of the industry will improve only when the volume of complaints goes down. If the desired image is to be created, the implied promise kept, reassurance and peace of mind provided, insurance and the law that underpins it must meet the expectations induced by the image: certainty of cover and reasonable speed of settlement. This book seeks to assess the law of England against these standards.

Risk Prediction

To market insurance successfully, insurers need to know the extent of the risk proposed, in order to decide whether to take the risk at all and, if so, what premium to charge and what conditions to impose. Broadly viewed, the risk contains two major elements. The first is risk on the ground, the obvious question of how likely it is that the insured event will occur. The second is harder to tie down. Most of what the insurer promises is to pay money in the event of loss; and for insurers a risky feature of promising money at some time in the future is inflation. For liability insurance, for example, the premiums collected this year must be enough to pay claims which may arise next year and which may not be quantified for some years to come, and in the light of prices and wages then. This depends not only on economic factors and the 'state of the art' in ways to mitigate loss, but also, especially in the case of liability insurance, on the state of the law, both liability law and rules of indemnity.

Risk on the Ground

Above all perhaps, insurers need to know about the peril to be insured. They must try to predict events, and to look forward insurers look back. 'I have but one lamp by which my feet are guided, and that is the lamp of experience. I know no way of judging of the future, but by the past.' The lesson thus expressed in 1775 by an American lawyer, Patrick Henry, was well understood by insurers then and now. This is the actuarial aspect of risk. Insurers must have enough data from the past to predict the future and, in particular, to have some idea about the largest possible single loss, the average size of the loss in question, and how frequently losses are likely to occur. Insurers prefer risks with a high frequency on a low scale.[25] They prefer, for example, to cover damage to taxis rather than damage to space vehicles.

[25] A. J. Vermaat, 'Uninsurability: A Growing Problem', *Geneva Papers*, No. 77 (1995), 446–53, 447; M. G. Faure, 'The Limits to Insurability from a Law and Economics Perspective', ibid., 454–62, 458.

The importance of data is illustrated by the history of life insurance. Lives were insurable only after Edmund Halley, the Astronomer Royal, had drawn up mortality tables and these had been published by the Royal Society in 1693. Insurance covering the consequences of disease was possible as regards many diseases (and then on a limited scale) only with the information resulting from the Infectious Diseases (Notification) Act of 1889. Indeed, until the middle of the twentieth century, many believed that the march of progress was such that uncertainty was a transient imperfection which, in time, would be eliminated by science and technology, thus rendering even insurance, or at least much of it, unnecessary.[26] As recently as the 1980s, current wisdom was that any risk could be insured at a price. However, although the global village today is overseen by a universe of computers, uncertainty is still there and, if anything, its impact has been underestimated. The mortality tables can still be rocked by a major war or a flu pandemic. Today it is safer and more accurate to say that any risk can be insured, if there is enough accumulated experience of, and data on, that risk; and that both experience and data are increasing. One example is that of large passenger aircraft.[27] Another example is that of people who are HIV positive. At one time they found it all but impossible to get life or health insurance; that is no longer true.

Nonetheless, the scale of some risks has changed almost out of recognition. Before 1988, no single natural disaster cost the insurance industry more than $1 billion, but by 1994 there had been fourteen of them, and there have been more since. Early estimates of insured losses caused by Hurricane Charley in Florida in August 2004, according to the United States' Insurance Information Institute, stand at $7 billion.[28] Not since Texas in 1886 had so many hurricanes struck a single American state in one season. The four hurricanes of 2004 together, according to Swiss Re in October 2004, will cost the insurance industry between $20 and $25 billion. The frequency of weather causing severe damage has tripled since the 1960s and, according to Munich Re, which is the world's largest reinsurer, insured losses have risen ten times in the same period.[29] The immediate effect is a quarterly loss for reinsurers, but over the relevant financial years their business remains 'highly profitable'.[30] There is no room for complacency but they can cope.

The Great Tooley Street Fire in warehouses along the Thames in June 1861 was a 'red card' for the less professional players in the field of insurance in London. Some observers believe that recent problems, such as long tail liability claims,[31] are having a similar effect. As soon as one tail (or tentacle) is cut off, another one appears. However, for the truly efficient insurers, disasters such as Hurricane

---

[26] O. Giarini, 'Insurability and the Economic Relevance of Insurance: A Historical Economic Perspective', *Geneva Papers*, No. 20 (1995), 419–22; Bernstein, Chapter 6.

[27] See above, p. 43.

[28] *The Economist*, 21 August 2004, p. 70.   [29] *The Economist*, 2 October 2004, p. 86.

[30] *The Rerreport*, 12 November 2004.

[31] See 'Issues in Law and Economics', *Geneva Papers*, No. 87 (1998).

Charley, while denting the balance sheet for the year, leave in their wake a climate in which the surviving insurers can hike premiums and in the medium term increase the profitability of insurance. That attracts capital to the industry and insurers are better placed to face the next disaster. So it was with the tsunami in December 2004, although the cost to London looks like being no more than £100 million.

Après Moi la Déluge: Clouds on the Horizon

Among the latest clouds on the horizon of the claims departments are 'sick building syndrome', the impact of nanotechnology, and the effect of mass air travel on the spread of seriously infectious diseases. In particular, fears are being expressed about liability cover for silicosis, a disease caused by the carcinogenic properties of silica.[32] There are also plenty of old clouds that have not blown away but grow in size. One was confirmed by a test case in 2004 awarding substantial damages to a teacher who suffered a breakdown as the result of class room stress.[33] Further impetus to this concern came in August 2004, when a Health and Safety Executive report expressed 'official' concern at the levels of stress in jobs such as teachers and health workers.[34] If insurers respond to threats like this by refusing cover or raising premiums, they fear that they may fall foul of the Disability Discrimination Act 1995.

Asbestosis

Perhaps the most enduring concern of insurers in recent times has been asbestosis. The use of asbestos in the UK peaked in the reconstruction period after 1945. It was the greatest source of work-related death and occupational disease in the UK in the twentieth century. It has not gone away, far from it. In 2004, the Health and Safety Executive estimated that a minimum of 3,500 people were dying every year in the UK from asbestosis, mesothelioma, and other asbestos-related cancers; and that mortality of this kind is likely to rise for at least ten, and possibly twenty, years. It has been estimated by the Institute of Actuaries that over the next thirty years it will cost the Government up to £4 billion, companies up to £6 billion, and insurers up £10 billion.[35]

The particular insurer most at risk at one time was Lloyd's Equitas, on account of insurance written by Lloyd's in the United States in the past.[36] Asbestos-related claims against a leading American motor manufacturer at December 2003

---

[32] *In House Lawyer*, No. 124, October 2004.
[33] *Barber v Somerset CC* [2004] UKHL 13, [2004] 1 WLR 1089.
[34] *Financial Times*, 10 August 2004.   [35] *The Times*, 2 November 2004.
[36] See, e.g., *Financial Times*, 9 November 2004. In late 2006 it was taken over by a large American investor and its future seems secure.

were one-third up on the figure at the end of 2002.[37] In 2004, the insurance world at large was reckoned to be under-reserved in respect of outstanding asbestos-related claims by anything from $11 billion to $36 billion.

Climate Change

Another concern, which for the insurance industry is not new at all, is climate change. In times past, uncertain weather might have been written off as an intervention of Fate, or even as an act of God. Today, on the one hand, the actions of Man have made weather more predictable and its effects therefore more insurable.[38] The latest computer models of the climate do not enable forecasters to predict the weather on a certain day more than ten days ahead, but the data are sufficient to enable firms in the City of London to lay off the risk by developing a weather derivatives market. On the other hand, the weather itself has become more volatile—more precocious in pattern and more severe in impact. For example, over just three days in November 2002, eighteen states in the United States reported 91 tornadoes, 182 hailstorms, and 351 ordinary windstorms.[39]

For some time insurers have been underwriting on the assumption that significant climate change, with associated extremes of weather, will occur. Indeed, in December 2003 the underwriting manager of one of the UK's largest insurance companies was reported as saying that climate change 'is the biggest issue facing the property insurance market and makes the risk of accidental damage and theft pale into insignificance'.[40] According to a report by the ABI in June 2004, 'A Changing Climate for Insurance', claims for storm and flood damage are set to treble in amount by 2050, such claims having doubled already in the period 1998–2003, compared with the five years before that; and that the cost of subsidence claims will have doubled in the same period. 2004 saw exceptional flooding not only in the well-reported cases of Cornwall and Bangladesh, but also in Brazil, Hungary, India, Iran, Japan, Kenya, Mexico, Nepal, Nicaragua, Pakistan, Peru, Romania, South Africa, and Zambia.

The ABI has proclaimed the insurance industry to be 'messengers of change', but offered something of a silver lining both for the world at large and for the insurance industry. Fewer people will die of cold in winter and there will be considerable market potential for the insurance of new energy technologies. Evidently, the risks associated with wind and wave power are considerable in every sense. By 2004, an all risks policy on the construction of off-shore wind farms was already available. Although it included business interruption cover, there was an exception for lack of wind!

[37] *Financial Times*, 25 March 2004, p. 31.
[38] E.g., in 2001 the Benfield Greig Hazard Research Centre at University College, London had developed a model of the English weather sufficiently reliable to predict the Spring temperatures through the UK correct to within 0.1°C. [39] *Insurance Day*, 18 November 2002.
[40] *PM*, 18 December 2003, p. 13.

Risk at Law

When insurance claims come to court in England, legal expenses amount to a large part of the overall cost. The decisions of the courts most welcome to insurers are those that settle points of law sufficiently to discourage further excursions to court. An insurance journal's 'best decision of 1993' award went to the decision of the House of Lords in a pollution case,[41] not so much because it decided against liability but because it settled doubts raised by the lower courts. The journal did not name a 'best decision' for 2003, but the accolade for that year might well have gone to the decision of the House that settled doubts in favour of liability, but a very limited liability, for the escape of potentially dangerous things stored or accumulated on private land.[42]

The accolade for best decision of 2005 or 2006, if there is one, may well go to that which settles the question, on which the lower courts have been contradictory, of liability for repetitive strain injury (RSI). Alternatively, it might go to the decision which settles liability for clearing up pollution and, in particular, any change in English law which might have the effect of making current insurance policies pay for 'historic pollution'. Whether regarding impending changes in the law or in the weather, uncertainty in any form is the bane of insurers.[43]

A nomination, if there were one, for worst decision of 2003 might go to that of the House of Lords in *Fairchild*.[44] *Fairchild* decided that a liability case could be established merely by showing that, on the balance of probabilities, the risk of asbestos-related disease had been materially increased by the defendant at the work place at a certain time; and that a claimant no longer had to show that but for that exposure, the liability would not have been incurred. The case was decided in 2002, but it took a while for it to surface in the consciousness of the insurance industry that what was true of exposure to asbestos at work could also impact any disease where various factors have increased the risk. Among the examples in the ongoing debate are those of lung cancer in a claimant who smoked various brands of cigarette, or obesity and associated illness in a claimant who had eaten a variety of fatty foods.[45] For the moment there have been conflicting decisions in the Court of Appeal on the more limited argument that *Fairchild* should impact all cases of alleged medical negligence, at least to the extent that a claimant could recover damages for loss of a chance of recovery.[46] Liability insurers are not happy.

The worst decision of 2004 may turn out to be the associated decision in *Maguire*,[47] that a firm is liable to the wife of a worker who contracts a disease by washing her husband's clothes. By a majority of the Court of Appeal, the decision

---

[41] *Cambridge Water Co. v Eastern Counties Leather Plc* [1994] AC 264.

[42] *Transco Plc v Stockport Metropolitan Borough Council* [2004] 2 AC 1.

[43] Abraham, 46 ff.

[44] *Fairchild v Glenhaven Funeral Services* [2003] 1 AC 32. But cf *Gregg v Scott* [2005] 2 WLR 268 (HL).

[45] *PM*, 5 February 2004, p. 1. See Chapter 1, p. 7 ff.

[46] See Amirthalingam [2003] CLJ 253.

[47] *Maguire v Harland & Wolff plc* [2004] EWHC 577; [2005] EWCA Civ 1.

was reversed in 2005, however, not because the firm did not owe her a duty of care but on the facts of the case as they were in 1965. If there were to be a nomination for the worst statute in 2004, it might be the Courts Act. The change in the law is as clear as can be expected; however, it will have the effect of making personal injury insurers pay periodic payments to victims, amounting in the end to a much larger sum than they bargained for when rating the risks years back. Uncertainty there will be not in the law itself but about the reserves required to pay claims; and this has been predicted to accelerate the dwindling market capacity for this important kind of cover.[48]

In 2006 the *Fairchild* saga continued. First, in *Barker* v *Corus*[48a] the House of Lords held that each employer was liable only for the amount of damage caused, the amount to be settled by apportionment between the employers. However, then the Compensation Act 2006, s. 3(2) effectively reversed the decision by making each employer jointly and severally liable for all the damage.

The Courts Act will benefit policyholders who need to claim. Uncertainty in the law, however, hurts policyholders when insurers raise premiums on the basis of 'worst scenario' in law, or withdraw cover altogether. Moreover, if the law is unclear and litigation in prospect, policyholders have the dim prospect of drawn-out litigation. Alternatively, if their chances in court are good, insurers may press for a settlement out of court to avoid a judicial precedent that goes against them at what might be a higher amount. Generally, however, what concerns insurers most about the law is not so much what it is but whether they know what it is.

Closing the Door: Risk Control and Risk Management

Risk control and risk management are possible both before and after the insured event. Prevention seeks to reduce the number of insured losses that occur. Cure and loss limitation reduce the extent of loss that did occur.

Measures of Prevention

Health insurers may offer medical advice by e-mail. Providers of legal expenses insurance (LEI) may offer legal advice on the phone. Services like this can be expensive for insurers, but the return is that a significant measure of loss prevention can be achieved. A simple and well-established measure, which costs insurers nothing, is to insist on anti-theft devices, such as locks on windows or immobilizers for motor bikes.

Motor insurers have found that 30 per cent of road deaths annually are work related, so some offer discounts to fleet buyers of insurance who give extra training to their drivers or monitor the number of hours spent at the wheel; or to employers who check the safety of employee-owned vehicles used for work. Encouraged by their insurers, some fleet operators have installed black boxes to monitor the location and speed of their vehicles. Moreover, given that exposure is

---

[48] *PM*, 22 April 2004.   [48a] [2006] 2 AC 572.

a major factor in the extent of risk, one insurer in England is experimenting with telematics. This is 'pay as you drive' insurance, whereby premium is payable according to the reading in a 'black box' installed in the vehicle. On the horizon is the image of a vehicle insured by mileage, tracked by satellite.[49]

In addition to locks and the like, a less obvious measure against theft and vandalism is that Ecclesiastical and others set up 'Churchwatch' in 1999 to monitor the safety and security of religious buildings. Many of their policies are still written for five years at a time. After five years of the scheme there was no significant rise in premiums, mainly because the incidence of theft was down by nearly 20 per cent, although assault on clergy, another risk covered, had increased by 25 per cent. Clergy today do not pursue their calling for a quiet life, or expect God or the Church to guarantee it.

English insurers have made a prolonged study of employers' liability risks generated by engineering, but they could do more. One American insurer, in the area of large industrial and commercial property risks, employs no actuaries but 1,400 engineers instead. The role of the engineers is to test things to destruction. The strategy of the company is less to calculate losses than to prevent them altogether. Clearly that is a costly measure aimed at a particular but well-capitalized section of the market. However, as we have seen,[50] many markets are driven by price, and potential policyholders go for the cover that is cheap today rather than that which is subsidizing research for improvements tomorrow. Insurers who spend little or nothing on loss prevention may be able to undercut insurers who do so spend. Moreover, the policyholders' perception of risk is subjective,[51] and, even when insurers do undertake or promote research, the research may not be directed to the most urgent concerns of society and is more likely to be aimed at the short-term hazard that concerns its policyholders than the long-term hazard which eventually poses a greater threat. In this situation there may come a point when insurers say that the responsibility for research to promote loss prevention and safety lies not with insurers but with Government; that is, for the Government to keep the North Sea out of London and to ensure an infrastructure that keeps sewage in.

Sharing Information: Collective Action

Undoubtedly, certain kinds of information generated by research are valuable in a competitive marketplace. It may, for example, enable insurers to identify and target a new niche in the market. Naturally, insurers are slow to share information of this kind with other insurers.[52] Insurers have their own priorities; market opportunities and conditions are high on the list. Nonetheless, in some areas insurers have been convinced of the value of collective action, which is usually carried out through or by the ABI.

[49] *Financial Times*, 12 March 2003.   [50] Chapter 1, p. 25 ff.
[51] Chapter 1, p. 12 ff.
[52] An important exception is the Transport Research Laboratory at Thatcham, which is financed by and for insurers.

Prominent in the work of the ABI is crime prevention. A notable venture is the Arson Prevention Bureau, which was set up by the Home Office and the ABI in 1991 and which has organized working groups such as the Fraudulent Arson Working Group. Arson currently costs insurers an average of £1 million per day and the trend is upwards. Associated with the Group is the Bureau's Schools Working Group, because about 70 per cent of all fires in schools are started deliberately. Out of the work of groups such as these comes advice to the insurance industry, which in turn advises policyholders directly, or indirectly by the message that comes from the terms of the insurance contract requiring fire-resistant panels and the like.

Loss Limitation and Cure

Prevention is better than either cure or mitigation, but these measures are by no means disregarded by the insurance industry. On the contrary, as one market analyst put it, an insurer should be a crisis alleviator rather than the final straw; or, we might say, a stitch in time is better than a finger in the dyke. . .

Among travel insurers, some use assistance companies, which may be their own subsidiaries, to organize repatriation by air ambulance or by liaison with airlines. One assistance company has thirty doctors at its control centre. Other measures to mitigate loss include property damage dealt with by telephone helplines and, for example, having bespoke plumbers on call. Stolen property may be recovered by the use of tracking devices. Specialist consultancies have sprung up. One, for example, assists in the salvage of documents not only after fires and floods but also following insect infestation such as book lice, which involves deep-freezing documents at $-20°C$ for two weeks.

A new development is cooperation between insurers and others concerned in what insurers find to be the more troublesome areas of insurance claims. One such is rehabilitation designed to reduce the extent of disability and the monetary cost of personal injury cases. A Code of Best Practice on Rehabilitation was drafted in 2000, with the support not only of the ABI and the International Underwriting Association of London but also of the Association of Personal Injury Lawyers and the Forum of Insurance Lawyers. Speedy agreement on what is best for the victim is also best for insurers as well as victims. To get a victim back to work as soon as possible, assuming that it is possible at all, is not only better psychologically for the victim but also tests whether a return to work is sustainable—as long as the victim understands that cooperation will not prejudice his or her insurance claim.

Such moves require the generation of an atmosphere of trust rather than the stand off and mutual suspicion that have been more typical in the past. After four years of operating the Code, a large majority of UK insurers involved thought it had been worthwhile, less because it saved money than because it promoted good relations with claimants. Even so, evidence about such schemes in other EU countries, where they have been in operation longer, indicates that that they do indeed save money.

On a wider front, in July 2004 a 'subsidence forum' of certain insurers and certain banks—and soon, they hoped, some intermediaries—was set up to agree best practice and share expertise in handling subsidence claims. On a yet wider front, in the same month, a Faculty of Claims was set up as a joint venture between the Chartered Institute of Insurers and the Chartered Institute of Loss Adjusters, for all in claims activities within the financial services and associated industries to promote good practice in claims.

3

Insurance Intermediaries[1]

[1] Generally, see Clarke, chs 7–9. C. Henley, *Law of Insurance Broking*, 2nd edn (London, 2004).

Agents and Independents

Until recently insurance intermediaries were of two kinds, tied agents and independent agents. Of the latter, those who registered as such were called insurance brokers. Today what counts is not the name or the label but what a person does, the activity undertaken. If the activity is a 'regulated activity', that person must comply with the appropriate regulations. In this book, however, unless the context otherwise requires, those whose are mainly occupied in selling insurance on behalf of insurers are referred to as agents; those who are mainly occupied with the role of intermediary between buyers and sellers of insurance, including those called insurance brokers in the past, are referred to as independents.

Before the status of broker was abolished, the director general of the British Insurance and Investment Brokers' Association once said that buying insurance 'is a little like buying bread'. Tied agents 'may sell you a loaf at a very attractive price, but it will be a standard, white, sliced pack', whereas a broker 'will sell you white bread, brown bread, granary bread, wholemeal bread and even the more exotic croissants and ciabatta, all at the best possible prices'.[2] The role of the broker is now that of the independent. Today's customers often do choose their bread with care, but are they really so discerning when it comes to insurance? Ten years ago a broker was quoted as saying that research among customers had shown that 'they don't understand insurance at all' and that brokers have to treat 'insurance as a commodity, just like selling beans or dog food', to be sold with supermarket tactics like own branding and money-off vouchers to sell it cheaper.[3] There is little reason to think that insurance customers are different today, or that they will change once the impact of the new line-up is felt.

Independent agents are indeed a kind of shop selling insurance; in the past, independents, notably insurance brokers, were the standard retail outlet for insurance. Like shopkeepers, independents have an interest in selling the products which they have in stock at the time. However, although computer links between some independents and insurers have brought the 'just in time' practice of supermarkets to the stocking of insurance, the similarity does not go much beyond the shop window. It is easier to 'stock' a large range of insurance than a large range of bread, as information no longer takes up shelf-space and does not dry up. Further, whereas most people can tell the difference between the bakery and the bread-shop, it has been sometimes difficult for buyers of insurance to tell the difference between agents and insurers. On the one hand, 'direct' insurers bypass retailers of insurance and sell directly to the public. On the other hand, in the past some independents were not averse to letting the buying public think that they were insurers. This was a serious source of confusion castigated by the courts to

[2] *PM*, 10 March 1994.   [3] *PM*, 23 February 1995.

little avail,[4] but now attenuated in so far as new rules, discussed below, require them to disclose their status.[5]

The ignorance of the public about the status of those selling insurance has been matched by the ignorance of some independents about the state of the law. In the general law independents are fiduciaries with a duty of disclosure.[6] Whether or not they are obliged to disclose their exact role, it is arguable that, if they were to use the description 'direct', that would be an actionable misrepresentation. Clearly, that would be a statement of fact about their business. Customers are drawn to 'direct' insurers to cut cost. What cost? Customers are likely to answer that it is the commission which intermediaries charge for their services. The reply might be that, in context, 'direct' does not mean without commission but simply 'cheap'. The *Financial Times* has even doubted whether it is cheap, but, be that as it may, the truth surely is that the appeal is to the belief of customers that costs are being reduced by cutting out the commission. If the independent is indeed getting commission, is this not misleading customers? Anyone who sells 'direct' insurance without disclosing their true role as agent or independent is surely misrepresenting their position.

Supposing potential customers who are better informed than most and have perceived that they need independent advice about what to buy, where should they go? They will find that there are independents large and small, local, national, and international. The large international adviser may put together complex schemes for new risks, selling these schemes not only to those seeking cover but also to insurers. What most ordinary customers need is the local 'high street' independent, 'independent' in the sense of this book but perhaps not of other independents. The situation is far from static.

Any outline of the current profile of independents may well be ephemeral. In 1994, a leading firm of solicitors organized a conference entitled 'The Next Decade for Brokers—Death of the Salesman?' Many, if not most, have survived the decade, but not without change. They have been stripped of the title 'broker', in so far as it is no longer possible to register as a broker; the profession of insurance broker no longer exists. George Bernard Shaw once famously described all professions as conspiracies against the laiety, so perhaps that is just as well. Since 1994, many former brokers have grouped together as networks in one way or another to defend their position in a hostile business environment, a circle of wagons against predators. As with the dinosaur, death it will be for those who remain as independents, if they stand on past achievement and do not evolve with the changing commercial climate, by adding greater value and professionalism to their service. To a large extent this is what is occurring. The species has not died but mutated. Indeed, reports of the death of the High Street broker may well have been exaggerated: in late 2006 it was argued that the species was making a comeback.[6a] Moreover, under the Financial Services Authority (FSA) regulations that

---

[4] *Roberts v Plaistred* [1989] 2 Lloyd's Rep 341, 345 (CA).   [5] See COB 5.1; below, n. 9.
[6] Below, p. 66 ff.   [6a] *Post Magazine*, 26 October 2006, Broking Supplement.

came into force in January 2004, these people are defined and judged not by what they call themselves, but by what they do and how they do it.

Regulation

Authorization in the United Kingdom

Section 19(1) of the Financial Services and Markets Act (FSMA) 2000 provides that no person may 'carry on a regulated activity in the United Kingdom, or purport to do so', unless they are '(a) an authorised person; or (b) an exempt person'. Section 327 excludes 'professions' from authorization if insurance services are incidental, for example, as in the case of solicitors. Section 327 says that in such cases the 'designated professional body' must make rules for them, but that these must be approved by the FSA.

Since 1 December 2001, the consequences for sellers of *unauthorized* insurance have been found in section 22 of the FSMA, which provides for imprisonment and/or a fine. The consequences for those who buy insurance from unlicensed operators are to be found, first, in FSMA, section 20. This provides that, if 'an authorised person carries on a regulated activity in the United Kingdom, or purports to do so, otherwise than in accordance with that person's permission to do so', that is a 'contravention' which, in certain 'prescribed cases', is 'actionable at the suit of a person who suffers loss as a result of the contravention', notably buyers of insurance, subject to certain defences; but the FSMA does not 'make any transaction void or unenforceable'. The Act also provides, in section 26, that an agreement 'in the course of carrying on a regulated activity' made by a person not authorized to do so, 'is unenforceable against the other party'; and the other party is entitled to recover (a) any money paid by them under the agreement, and (b) compensation for any loss sustained by them as result of having parted with the money.[7]

Further, under section 150(1) of the FSMA, a contravention of a rule for the conduct of business by a person *authorized* to carry on 'regulated activity', 'is actionable at the suit of a private person who suffers loss as a result of the contravention, subject to the defences and other incidents applying to actions for breach of statutory duty', unless otherwise specified.

Codes of Conduct

Until January 2005, the General Insurance Standards Council (GISC), an independent voluntary organization encouraged, but not set up, by government, regulated the sales and service standards of its members; membership was open to all who sold or gave advice about insurance. The intention was that GISC rules would replace the ABI codes which applied hitherto; however, until January 2005, the ABI codes still existed. At that point in time both were withdrawn. Regular

---

[7] See further Henley, op. cit. above, n. 1, ch. 5-003.

doubts had been expressed in the past about whether codes such as those of the ABI were 'working',[8] that is, being respected in practice. This was always hard to establish, but it was one reason among several why, in December 2001, the Government announced that in future the regulation of such matters was to be within the remit of the FSA, and thus subject to compulsion. From January 2005, the FSA rules have been those that matter. Broadly speaking, there are two sets of rules, those for investment insurance (COB), that is mainly life insurance, and those for general insurance, with which this book is mainly concerned, the Insurance Conduct of Business (ICOB) rules.[9] The latter rules affect all general insurance except large risks and reinsurance,[10] whether on the general market or at Lloyd's.[11]

The Insurance Mediation Directive

The Insurance Mediation Directive (IMD)[12] was implemented in the UK by regulation.[13] Under the Directive, agents are those who carry on 'insurance mediation'. For our purposes the impact of the Directive was mainly twofold. First, implementation compelled the UK Government to extend regulation to general insurance. Secondly, Article 3 of the Directive made the FSA responsible for the competence of individuals inside firms carrying on insurance mediation, both investment insurance and general insurance. To this end the FSA has published the *Fit and Proper Test for Approved Persons Sourcebook* (APER),[14] as well as making arrangements to ensure compliance with the financial requirements of the Directive.[15] Compliance with the Directive allows firms to sell insurance throughout the EU.

Rules and Principles: ICOB[16]

Scope

The ICOB seek to protect buyers of general insurance products, but in this respect draw a distinction between retail customers and commercial customers. Retail customers are natural persons acting for purposes outside their trade, business, or profession. Commercial customers are any customers other than

---

[8] E.g., P. Hart, 'The Insurance Ombudsman and payment protection insurance' (1997) 5 *J Financial Regulation & Compliance* 139–45.

[9] Respectively, http://fsahandbook.info/FSA/handbook.jsp?doc=/handbook/COB, http://fsahandbook.info/FSA/handbook.jsp?doc=/handbook/ICOB.

[10] See RAO, Art. 3(1) and Art. 12. Also exempted are certain insurance products associated with the public finance initiative.   [11] See ICOB 12.1.1R.

[12] 2002/92/EC.

[13] See the Financial Services and Markets Act 2000 (Regulated Activities) (Amendment) (No. 2) Order 2003 (SI 2003/1476). See also the Insurance Mediation Directive (Miscellaneous Amendments) Regulations 2003 (SI 2003/1473).

[14] http://www.fsa.gov.uk/pubs/hb-releases/rel27/rel27fit.pdf.

[15] See further Henley, op. cit. above, n. 1, ch. 15-033 ff.

[16] See The FSA Handbook: http://fsahandbook.info/FSA/handbook.jsp. Also J. Y. Lovells (ed.), *Practitioner's Guide to FSA Regulation of Insurance* (London, 2004). For a general introduction to the requirements relevant to insurance intermediaries, see the FSA's *Guide to the FSA Handbook for Small Mortgage and Insurance Intermediaries*: www.fsa.gov.uk/mgi/guide.html.

retail customers, and are also referred to as 'market counterparties'. The premise of the distinction is that commercial customers need less protection; however, exception is made for small businesses, for which there is some extra protection in respect of product disclosure and advice.[17]

The ICOB apply to any person carrying on a 'regulated activity'. Such persons may be insurers as well as insurance intermediaries. The FSMA, section 22(1), headed 'Classes of activity and categories of investment', provides that an activity

is a regulated activity for the purposes of this Act if it is an activity of a specified kind which is carried on by way of business and—

(a) relates to an investment of a specified kind; or
(b) in the case of an activity of a kind which is also specified for the purposes of this paragraph, is carried on in relation to property of any kind.

The notion of regulated activity is elaborated by the Financial Services and Markets Act 2000 (Regulated Activities) Order (RAO) 2001,[18] as amended.[19] Article 21 of the RAO[20] includes buying or selling rights under contracts of insurance as agent. Article 25 of the RAO[21] includes making arrangements for other persons to buy contracts of insurance. Article 39A of the RAO[22] includes 'assisting in the administration and performance of a contract of insurance', subject to activities excepted by Article 39B, such as expert appraisal, or loss adjusting or claims management on behalf of an insurer, if such activities are carried on in the course of a profession or business. Also excepted by Article 54 is advice given in newspapers, or periodicals, or other media, as long as the principal purpose of the advice is not advising on investments as there specified.

Core Principles

The Principles for Business, published separately from COB and ICOB, express the spirit of the more detailed rules found in both, although firms have been fined by the FSA for breach of the Principles *per se*. The FSA *Handbook* describes the Principles as 'the fundamental obligations of all firms under the regulatory system'.[23]

Principle 1 states that firms must conduct their business 'with integrity', and Principle 6 states that they 'must pay due regard to the interests' of their customers and 'treat them fairly'. In this connection Principle 8 provides that firms 'must manage conflicts of interest fairly', both between the firm 'and its customers and between a customer and another client'. Principle 5 requires firms to 'observe proper standards of market conduct'. When the terms of business are

---

[17] See Prin. 1.2.   [18] SI 2001/2635.
[19] SI 2003/1476. See also the definition of insurance mediation activities in the FSA *Handbook* Glossary.   [20] SI 2001/2635, as amended by Art. 4 of SI 2003/1476.
[21] SI 2001/2635, as amended by Art. 5 of SI 2003/1476.
[22] SI 2001/2635, as inserted by Art. 7 of SI 2003/1476.
[23] For the Handbook see http://fsahandbook.info/FSA/handbook.jsp; and for the 'core' Principles, i.e. the Principles for Business, see http://fsahandbook.info/FSA/handbook.jsp? doc=/ handbook/PRIN/2/1.

agreed, the record must, if relevant, contain a statement directing complaints to the Financial Ombudsman Service (FOS).

Principle 2 states that firms must conduct their business 'with due skill, care and diligence'. More specifically, Principle 9 provides that a firm 'must take reasonable care to ensure the suitability of its advice and discretionary decisions for any customer who is entitled to rely upon its judgment'. Principle 7 requires firms to pay due regard to the information needs of their clients, and communicate information to them in a way which is clear, fair, and not misleading.

Principle 3 (management and control) and Principle 4 (financial prudence) focus mainly on matters within firms. Matters within impact relations without, of course, and there is a reminder of this in Principle 10, which requires firms to 'arrange adequate protection for clients' when they are responsible to them. Moreover, Principle 11 requires firms to 'deal with its regulators in an open and co-operative way', and to 'disclose to the FSA appropriately anything relating to the firm of which the FSA would reasonably expect notice'. Thus, it has been suggested,[24] independents becoming aware that they had mishandled claims must notify the FSA. Failure to do so would itself be a serious regulatory breach.

Information Duties

Information initially required concerns the relationship of firm and customer. Firms are required (ICOB 4.2.2R) to disclose certain information of this kind to customers in a 'durable medium', at any time before conclusion of an insurance contract, unless, for example, customers require immediate cover or the contract is made on the telephone, when oral disclosure will suffice. The information is listed[25] and includes such matters as the firm's statutory status, the kind of advice it is willing to offer, whether it will seek terms from more than one insurer, and the firm's complaints procedure, including mention of the FOS.

Unless it is a distance contract, firms must supply retail customers with a summary of any policy proposed,[26] a statement of the premium payable, and certain other information[27] required by the EU Directive: ICOB 5.3.1R. In particular, firms must draw customers' attention orally to the summary and the section of the summary on 'significant and unusual exclusions or limitations'.[27a] On conclusion of the contract, firms must supply customers in a 'durable medium' with *inter alia* a 'policy document', and with information about the 'claims handling process'[28] and, where relevant, cancellation rights:[29] ICOB 5.3.4R. Comparable rules are provided for distance contracts[30] and group policies.[31] Firms are obliged to send

[24] Henley, op. cit. above, n. 1, ch. 15-031. [25] See ICOB 4.2.8R.
[26] For detail see ICOB 5.5.1R.
[27] See ICOB 5.3.20G and, in particular, the Table set out in 5.5.16R.
[27a] See also *Fisk v Brian Cahill* [2007] EWCA Civ 152, [2007] All ER (D) 374.
[28] Contact details and information to be required of a claimant: ICOB 5.3.9R. For detail, see ICOB, s. 7.
[29] E.g., how and when rights can be exercised: ICOB 5.3.12R. See also 5.3.16R and ICOB, s. 6.
[30] See ICOB 5.3.6R and 5.3.8R.
[31] See ICOB 5.3.29R.

renewal notices, where relevant, and certain information is required at the time: ICOB 5.3.18R. Comparable but less demanding rules are established for commercial customers: ICOB 5.4.

Contracting Insurance

Further to Principle 2, requiring 'due skill, care and diligence', and Principle 9, requiring 'care to ensure the suitability' of advice and decisions, firms are required (ICOB 4.3.1R) to take reasonable steps to ensure that, if they make any personal recommendation to customers to buy insurance, the recommendation is suitable for the customers' demands and needs at the time. To do this firms are required (ICOB 4.3.2R) to seek such information about customers' circumstances and objectives as might reasonably be expected to be relevant in enabling firms to identify customers' requirements, having regard to any relevant details about customers that are readily available and accessible to firms. An example given is that of information in respect of other contracts of insurance on which the firm has provided the particular customer with advice or information in the past.[32]

Firms are also required (ICOB 4.3.2R) to explain to customers their duty to disclose material information both before the insurance contract commences and throughout the duration of the contract, and the consequences of any failure to do so. This includes, of course, an explanation of what might be material, and the ICOB give the examples of existing medical conditions in relation to private medical insurance and, in relation to motor insurance, any modifications carried out to the vehicle.

Where firms have arranged for retail customers[33] to enter into an insurance contract (including at renewal), immediately before conclusion of the contract firms are required (ICOB 4.4.1R) to provide certain information to customers in a durable medium unless, for example, customers require immediate cover or the contract is made on the telephone, when oral disclosure will suffice. The information is listed and where, for example, a personal recommendation has been made, it must include an explanation of the reasons for the recommendation. The rule goes into considerable detail. For example, firms are instructed (ICOB 4.4.6G) to use simple and plain English and, when technical terms need to be incorporated, they should be explained if customers are unlikely to understand their meaning. Copies of certain statements must be kept for three years.

Integrity: Commission

Principle 1, requiring 'integrity' in business, and Principle 8, stating that 'conflicts of interest' must be managed 'fairly', lead *inter alia* to ICOB 4.6.1R. This rule

[32] Note that there is a special rule for the situation where firms are aware that customers' existing insurance cover is likely significantly to affect the suitability of any personal recommendation of cover: ICOB 4.3.5R.
[33] The information duty to commercial customers is more limited: ICOB 4.4.2R.

requires firms to disclose commission; however, controversially, the duty applies to commercial customers but not to retail customers, and only to commercial customers which ask about it. The commission is stated to be the commission received by firms in cash terms, or, to the extent it cannot be indicated in cash terms, the basis for the calculation of the commission. The guidance note published with the rule (ICOB 4.6.7G) advises that it includes

all forms of remuneration from any arrangements he may have for remuneration . . . including arrangements for sharing profits, for payments relating to the volume of sales, and for payments from premium finance companies in connection with arranging finance.[34]

As regards all clients, but commercial customers in particular, it should be noted that the guidance note (ICOB 4.6.2G) states clearly that 'ICOB 4.6.1R does not replace the general law on the fiduciary obligations of an agent'. In relation to contracts of insurance, the note continues:

. . . the essence of these obligations is generally a duty on the agent to account to his principal. However, in certain circumstances, the duty is one only of disclosure. Where a customer employs an insurance intermediary by way of business and does not remunerate him, and where it is usual for the insurance intermediary to be remunerated by way of commission paid by the insurer out of premium payable by the customer, then if the customer asks what the insurance intermediary's remuneration is, the insurance intermediary must tell him.[35]

Thus intermediaries must still respond to commercial customers in a similar way because that is required by the general law. Indeed, arguably, the law goes further than stated in the guidance note.

The Nature of Independents' Duties to Customers

Lawyers have commonly assumed that independents' duties are based concurrently in both contract and tort,[36] stiffened by an added element of equity. From equity independents get duties to their clients, duties called 'fiduciary' duties. From the contract with clients independents incur the obligation to do whatever it is that they have promised to do. That is a question of interpretation in each case, but it should be noted that for some years now larger firms have been undertaking not only the traditional functions of insurance mediation but also risk management.[37] As for the fulfilment of their promises, generally it will be

---

[34] See also the example given in ICOB 4.6.8G.

[35] The note goes on to point out that 'ICOB 4.6.1R is additional to this requirement in that it applies whether or not the insurance intermediary is an agent of the commercial customer'.

[36] *Caparo v Dickman* [1990] 2 AC 605, 619, applied to insurance brokers in *Punjab National Bank v De Boinville* [1992] 3 All ER 104, 117 (CA); see also the *Superhulls Cover case* [1990] 2 Lloyd's Rep 431, 456 ff.

[37] H. Thomas, 'The Insurance Broker—Intermediary of Advisor?' (1995) 87 BILA Journal 5–8.

inferred that independents undertake not to perform promises at all costs but to use best endeavours, reasonable care, and skill to that end.[38] From tort independents have a duty of care, and with it an obligation of reasonable care and skill similar to that implied in their contract. These duties are reinforced by the regulatory framework, such as Principle 2, which provides that firms must conduct their business 'with due skill, care and diligence'.[39]

As between contract and tort, in most cases the extent of independents' duties to clients is the same. When parties have regulated their relationship by contract, courts today are reluctant to impose duties in tort which extend in any way those imposed by the parties' own contract. Independents are undertaking to do things for particular clients and the natural legal framework for this relationship is contract;[40] that is how the courts see the situation, and that is how it is presented here. When it comes to clients' remedies against independents, however, it is still possible that clients will fare better in tort than in contract.[41]

Payment: Fee or Commission

A curious feature of the contract between independents and their clients is that, in the past, independents were generally paid not fees by clients but commission by insurers. In the general law, the answer to 'who pays the piper?' is one of the main tests of agency: the piper is the agent of the one who pays. This remains so in the law of other countries, not only in general but also for independent insurance intermediaries in the United States.[42] On account partly of the problems debated here, in recent times many independents in the UK have switched to a more transparent relationship whereby they are remunerated like any other profession, namely, by professional fees payable by clients. However, a large number still operate as before on commission from insurers. One reason is fear that clients would not appreciate the real value and cost of the service provided by independents and find the fees excessive; and that, in a market driven by price, the insurance buying public will be driven to direct insurers and that independents will be forced out of business. Be that as it may, the system of payment by commission poses problems of law.

The Problem of Consideration

Contracts between independents and their clients, under which independents are remunerated by getting commission from insurers, should surprise students of

---

[38] *Eagle Star v National Westminster Finance* (1985) 58 ALR 165, 174 (PC); *Youell v Bland Welch (No. 2)* [1990] 2 Lloyd's Rep 431, 458; aff'd [1992] 2 Lloyd's Rep 127 (CA).

[39] See above, pp. 62–3.

[40] *The Zephyr* [1985] 2 Lloyd's Rep 529, 538 (CA).

[41] See below, pp. 80–1.

[42] E.g., *Kioutas v Life Ins. Co. of Virginia*, 35 F Supp 2d 616 (ND Ill., 1998).

contract law. Students may well wonder whether independents get anything from their clients which can amount to consideration in law; and if not, whether their agreement can be enforced as a contract at all. This is not an easy question to answer.

One possibility is that, if and when client C pays premium to insurer B, C rewards independent A indirectly because the premium that C pays insurer B reflects the insurer's transaction costs, including commission payable to independent A. Clearly, that answer proves too little in cases in which independent A works for client C but no insurance results, unless it can be said that C provides A with a business opportunity—the chance of getting commission from B.[43] Equally clearly, the answer proves too much if it means that, beyond the world of insurance, anyone who contracts for any kind of service with B has a contract too with anyone else, including, for example, the employee whom B uses to carry out the service. Nonetheless, courts are currently more astute to find consideration than once they were. When it is clear that all parties to a transaction intended binding legal relations, courts today are not attracted by any contention that the relations were technically unenforceable for want of consideration.[44]

The Problem of Consent

Being paid by commission from insurers is perfectly consistent with the fiduciary role of agents, including independents, under the general law, if it is received with the consent of clients.[45] The corollary is that independents are not allowed to keep *secret* payments from insurers, that is, payments of which clients are unaware. Indeed, the general law of agency sees these as bribes.[46] The same is true of any other material benefit conferred on independents in order to induce them to act in favour of a particular insurer in transactions that independents undertake on behalf of a client. Although it might have been assumed that clients knew that independents got commission from insurers, the practice in the past was not to disclose the amount; this cannot be sustained. It is irrelevant that nobody concerned has a corrupt or an improper motive. To make and retain commission or any other benefit lawfully, the consent of clients must be given in full knowledge of the actual or potential conflict and of its implications.

The general law to this effect has now been reinforced by the rules (ICOB)[47] and Principles[48] promulgated by the FSA, which have been in force since January 2005. Principle 1 requires of independents 'integrity'; Principle 8 states that firms

[43] *Chaplin v Hicks* [1911] 2 KB 786 (CA). Analysis of this kind, it is submitted, also lies behind the courts' assumption that the contract was enforceable in *The Good Luck* [1992] 1 AC 233.
[44] See, e.g., *Williams v Roffey Bros. & Nicholls (Contractors Ltd)* [1991] 1 QB 1 (CA).
[45] *Phipps v Boardman* [1967] 2 AC 46.
[46] *Maheson v Malaysia Government Officers' Co-operative Housing Sy Ltd* [1979] AC 374 (PC).
[47] See n. 9.
[48] See n. 23.

'must manage conflicts of interest fairly'; and ICOB 4.6 sets out in some detail requirements of commission disclosure. The fully informed consent that suffices to vindicate independents under the general law is probably enough for ICOB too.

However, for retail customers the FSA has not required full disclosure, taking the view that it was enough that the price of general insurance products was sufficiently transparent for retail customers to make an informed choice. This position has been questioned, both as a matter of policy and as a matter of existing law—both before and since the Spitzer investigation (discussed below).

Conflicts of Interest: Spitzer

Large firms of intermediaries, still referred to internationally as brokers, have a role that goes well beyond that of the traditional independent or middleman. On the clients' side they have become corporate advisers, and for insurers they have become important distribution channels. In October 2004, three firms accounted for nearly two-thirds of brokerage revenue worldwide, when, following an investigation that had commenced at the end of the previous April, charges were brought against MM, the largest of the three. MM then described itself in its promotional literature as 'not simply an insurance agent' but a 'trusted business partner', and stated that its 'guiding principle is to consider our client's best interests in all placements'. Among others involved in the affair was AIG, the world's largest insurer. The charges were brought by New York's Attorney-General, Eliot Spitzer, described by *The Economist* at the time as being 'like the little boy announcing that the emperor has no clothes', because once again 'he has exposed practices as dishonest or even illegal that have long been accepted'.[49]

Charges against MM related to 'price-rigging'[50] and taking 'contingent commissions'.[51] Price-rigging refers to the production of false quotes so that brokers' clients would believe that the process of obtaining cover had been competitive. Contingent commissions are extra payments from insurers for sending more business their way. Clearly, there is a potential conflict of interest in these practices. The conflict is exacerbated if, as in some instances, the amount of the contingent commission is based on the insurer's profits. Brokers might be tempted not to push clients' claims against that insurer too hard lest the profits and the brokers suffer. Another practice being investigated by Spitzer was 'tying', whereby brokers bringing business to primary insurers also insist on reinsurance to go with it. Evidently the reinsurance may or may not be in the best interest of the clients in question.

At MM in 2003, contingent commissions accounted for 12 per cent of revenues and 48 per cent of profits. Even though the charges had yet to be substantiated, the immediate effect on MM was that its share price on the New York

---

[49] *The Economist*, 23 October 2004.   [50] Also called 'bid-rigging'.
[51] Also referred to as 'contingent payments' or 'incentive commissions'.

stock exchange plunged, and its market value halved. Moreover, the chief executive was replaced and the new chief executive announced 3,000 job cuts. Two months later a New York broker described the business situation of MM as 'trying to patch a hole in a ship taking on water, while selling tickets to the next cruise, in the hurricane season'.[52] Clearly the Spitzer investigation would not stop with MM, and the share price of other quoted insurance brokers also dropped, as did that of insurers. Among them was Munich Re, the largest reinsurer in the world, which was mentioned in the Spitzer investigation but not accused of any irregularity. Repercussions were felt worldwide.

In Europe the self-regulated French insurance industry professed itself to be shocked by the Spitzer allegations. Not so the industry in London. The practices of the London branch of MM became the subject of an investigation by a leading law firm which cleared it of price-rigging, and although it found 'examples of brokers being encouraged to use or not to use a particular underwriter', there was no evidence of clients suffering as a result.[53] The first reaction in London, however, both in the insurance press and in the financial papers, was to wonder about the effect on share prices rather than whether the allegations were true. As to truth, it was denied that 'price-rigging' occurs there, but it soon emerged that various players on the London scene were 'reviewing their practices'. The riposte that 'everyone else is doing it' is to no avail. At common law reference is often made to the accepted standards and practices of a profession,[54] but they have never been decisive.[55] A London independent was quoted as saying of contingent commissions that 'Spitzer has kicked the whole practice into touch';[56] and another leading figure in the UK brokerage industry was quoted as saying that the 'industry will never be the same again'.[57]

The Quality of Advice

Objectivity: Due Skill, Care, and Diligence

Recent history has not inspired public confidence. A number of people were advised to take endowment insurance, once described as 'the bread and butter of intermediaries and life offices', as a mortgage repayment vehicle, although for some time some analysts had been doubting, rightly as it turned out, whether this was indeed 'best advice'. Then there was the pension misselling scandal that surfaced in the 1990s. Doubts were reinforced by the shadows of suspicion cast

---

[52] *PM*, 2 December 2004.   [53] *PM* 'Legal Report', 9 December 2004.
[54] This was one of the issues in *O'Brien v Hughes-Gibb & Co. Ltd* [1995] LRLR 90, concerning the risks normally covered for racehorses.
[55] *Bolitho v City and Hackney Health Authority* [1998] AC 232.
[56] 'Commercial Broking', supplement to *PM*, 18 November 2004.
[57] *Financial Times*, 29 October 2004.

by allegations of conflict of interest that culminated in the Spitzer investigation in 2004 (above). Moreover, contingent commissions paid by insurers were not the sole concern. Another remains today. Not only do independents act for more than one client, they may also act for insurers in transactions where they are acting for clients. The best known and least objectionable instance of this is when they issue a temporary cover note to a client for motor insurance. Indeed independents' authority may well go beyond this and empower them to conclude the main contract within certain limits and to settle small claims—all on behalf of the insurer. In the general law, dual agency is lawful only with the fully informed consent of the client.[58] The clients of independents were rarely fully informed.

In these circumstances little confidence was inspired by the codes: the ABI Code, the Insurance Brokers' Code, and, latterly, the GISC rules. Not many clients have been aware of them. If they were and enquired, they would have discovered allegations that they were not observed in practice and that, anyway, they were not enforceable in law. The general law neither was nor is entirely toothless. Like any other agents, independents owe the legal duties of fiduciaries.[59] These include a duty to act bona fide, that is, in what they believe to be the interests of their principals, the clients. They also have a duty not to place themselves in a position in which duties to clients may conflict with duties to others. In case of breach, civil remedies are available, but to get them means a trip to court.

The Brokers' Code[60] contained not only principles of conduct, but also illustrations. The very first illustration required brokers to give clients 'best advice'. In essence this requirement has been reiterated and fleshed out by the rules of conduct (ICOB)[61] and Principles[62] promulgated by the FSA, and in force since January 2005. In particular, Principle 2 requires of independents 'due skill, care and diligence', and Principle 9 states that they 'must take reasonable care to ensure the suitability' of their advice to clients. This is also the rule of common law.[63] However, whereas high standards might be expected of the London branch of a multi-national firm, as Brooke LJ once pointed out, when the question is 'the standard of care reasonably to be required of a solicitor in a small country town who is instructed by a legally aided client to pursue what appears to be a comparatively small claim', it is 'of critical importance for the courts not to apply a too rigorous standard'.[64] This is no less true of insurance brokers or, as we now call them, independents. Unlike the codes, however, the ICOB has sharp teeth, in as much as the FSA may impose penalties on those who infringe its rules.

---

[58] *Anglo-African Merchants v Bayley* [1970] 1 QB 311.

[59] *Cook v Deeks* [1916] 1 AC 554 (PC).

[60] Insurance Brokers Registration Council (Code of Conduct) Approval Order 1994 (SI 1994/2569). Repealed.   [61] See above, n. 9.

[62] See above, n. 23.

[63] *Nederlandse Re v Bacon & Woodrow* [1997] LRLR 678, 744.

[64] *Belamoan v Holden & Co.* 1999 WL 477470 (CA).

Subjectivity: Suitability of Advice

Except as regards 'execution only' transactions, COB 5.3.5R requires independents to take reasonable care to ensure the suitability of their advice and discretionary decisions when recommending certain products. Further, firms are required by COB 5.2.5R to obtain sufficient information about their customers, that is, personal and financial information relevant to the services firms agree to provide. 'Execution only' transactions are those where firms make it clear that, while they undertake to carry out specific instructions from customers, they do not undertake to give advice relating to the merits of the transaction. Suitability varies according to the customer and the transaction, however detailed guidance on these matters is set out in COB 5.3. Note that COB 5.4.3R requires firms to take reasonable steps to ensure that private customers understand the nature of the risks inherent in certain transactions which customers are minded to enter, and lists the transactions, mostly investments such as securitized derivatives, in some detail.

The Content of Advice

Rating Insurers

Usually the main thrust of an independent's advice concerns the insurance that might meet the needs of the client and, perhaps, related matters of risk management. The policy must meet the needs of the client (above). For some quite standard risks there may be a bewildering choice of products on offer. The policy suggested by independents must be at a favourable rate, not necessarily the lowest rate. It must be with an insurer that will pay reasonably promptly, not one which has acquired any sort of reputation for resisting claims which other insurers would not; and, importantly, it must be with an insurer that is solvent. In the past this has not been easy for independents to assess.

To monitor the published accounts of insurers is burdensome, and thus expensive; it may also be futile, as even recent history has shown. In the 1990s, an authoritative survey indicated that only 31 per cent of brokers actually carried out any solvency assessment of insurers at all. Even today there have been reports of independents recommending cheap offshore insurers without warning clients of the associated risk. That would have been a specified breach of paragraph 4.1 of the Insurance Brokers Code of Conduct (now abrogated). Independents who make such recommendations are taking a risk themselves—that of liability birds that return home to roost.

Today, a check can be done relatively cheaply by reference to a credit rating agency. Beyond that, what more should independents do? Now that more stringent solvency requirements have been imposed on UK insurers, and now that the

FSA is monitoring compliance much more closely than did the Department of Trade and Industry before, arguably, independents are entitled to be less suspicious and less active in their own investigation. It might be enough just to refer to a credit rating agency and to check that the insurer in prospect has been licensed to carry on insurance activity in the UK; and to go further only in the case of long tailed cover.[65] In the past, before the existence of the FSA, it was only in quite extreme cases that a broker was liable in negligence when the recommended insurer turned out to be insolvent.[66]

Policy Terms

Independents must draw clients' attention to potentially onerous terms.[66a] Moreover, if clients ask independents about the meaning of the policy proposed, any advice that independents give must be competent professional advice. This is an important service to clients because, in the words of a management consultant brought in to look at the insurance industry, the 'customer must rely on an experienced and trained wizard to guide him through the maze of arcane language and apparently complex products', needlessly created by the industry, and the independent is the guide. That was in 1994 but, in spite of campaigns for plain English[67] and genuine attempts to make products more transparent, guidance is still needed. Some doubt has been expressed in the past, both in the industry and in Parliament, about the professional competence of agents to explain the products that they sell. That is one reason why some insurers have sought to devise simpler policies—they serve not only to facilitate quick sales, but also to make policies easier for others, agents or independents, to explain when they are sold. However, optimum clarity and transparency have yet to be achieved.

That is true not only when insurance is first purchased, but also when it is renewed. Policy terms are often adjusted on renewal; that is the insurer's opportunity to reconsider the risk.[68] Mostly insurers notify policyholders not with a new copy of the policy, still less a new copy with the changes highlighted, but simply with notes of amendments; many people find this kind of presentation hard to understand without professional advice. In a world of word processors and vastly improved printing facilities, this parsimonious practice is hard to justify.

Contracting Insurance

If clients accept the advice of their independent about what insurance they need, they are likely to instruct the independent concerned to arrange it, that is, to contract the insurance with the recommended insurer. As clients' agents for this

---

[65] See Henley, op. cit above, n. 1, chs 2-007 and 2-010.
[66] E.g., *Osman v J. Ralph Moss Ltd* [1970] 1 Lloyd's Rep 313 (CA).
[66a] *Fisk v Brian Cahill* [2007] EWCA Civ 152, [2007] All ER (D) 374.
[67] See Chapter 5, p. 147 ff.   [68] See Chapter 5, p. 161 ff.

purpose, independents' authority extends to all acts which are necessarily or ordinarily incidental to the execution of the instructions. Incidental authority extends to agreeing with the insurer the terms of the insurance. If clients do not hear from their independent to the contrary, they are entitled to assume that all is well and that the cover has been obtained, or will be obtained in due time.[69] If independents are uncertain about the scope of their instructions, for example about whether a term insisted on by the insurer is acceptable to the client, they must go back to the client for further instructions.[70] But if that is not viable, and if the independent interprets the instructions reasonably and in good faith, the client is bound by the contract of insurance that the independent makes. Analogy with rules for other kinds of agent (company directors, mercantile agents abroad) suggests that the reference to good faith allows for honest subjectivity in the independent's interpretation. However, those rules are based partly on decisions in old cases in times of poor communication. Today, if there is the slightest reasonable doubt about the instructions, and if there is time and opportunity to do so, independents must seek clarification from their client.

Disclosure

The incidental authority of independents, when contracting insurance for clients, extends to giving the insurer the information needed by the insurer to assess and to rate the risk proposed, that is, the material facts.[71] If an independent fails to disclose material facts, the insurer in question is entitled to rescind the contract and refuse to pay claims. If the insurer does so, that independent will be liable to pay the client the amount of insurance money which would have been payable by the insurer, if the independent had made proper disclosure and the insurance had not been vitiated. Obviously, independents are obliged to disclose only those facts which they know about the risk, or which they should have known. Sometimes independents are required to make enquiries. Less obvious, however, is what enquiries the independent should have made and what the independent should have found out: the law draws a difficult line between statements and omissions.

In one case[72] a broker prepared an application for motor insurance, which the client signed and which stated untruly that the vehicle was normally kept in a garage. The court held that the broker was entitled to assume that, before signing the form, the client had read it; and that the client assumed responsibility for the accuracy of what had been written. Clients do not, however, take responsibility for what has not been written, for what has been omitted. The completeness of the contents of the application form is the responsibility of the independent.

---

[69] *United Mills Agencies Ltd v Harvey, Bray & Co.* [1951] 2 Lloyd's Rep 631, 643.
[70] *Youell v Bland Welch & Co. Ltd* [1990] 2 Lloyd's Rep 431; *Harvester Trucking Co. Ltd v Davis* [1991] 2 Lloyd's Rep 638.   [71] See Chapter 4, p. 101 ff.
[72] *O'Connor v Kirby* [1971] 1 Lloyd's Rep 454 (CA).

So, in another motor case,[73] when the independent broker did not ask about, and the client did not disclose, the driving record of one of the named drivers, the insurer rescinded the contract and the broker was held liable to the client. Independents must enquire about any material facts which they have reason to suspect are a feature of the risk proposed. On the one hand, the second case shows that the independent mandated to obtain motor cover should enquire about the record of named drivers, as it is not unlikely that one of them will have had an accident in the past. On the other hand, an English court is likely to agree with a court in New South Wales that independents do not have to enquire whether people working for a company proposing fire cover have a criminal record[74]— unless there are grounds for suspicion. Indeed, 'illiterate, senile people and other such persons in similar categories' as clients may well call for independents to take 'unusual precautions' when application forms are filled in,[75] because the potential pitfalls for those seeking to please the 'prudent insurer' are many,[76] and it is the job of independents to guide them through. Even if an independent fails to do this, with the result that the insurer avoids the contract and the client is left uninsured, as we have seen,[77] the independent will be liable to the client but, of course, only if the independent's failure was the cause of the client's uninsured loss.[78]

Renewal

The authority of independents to contract insurance does not automatically extend to renewing that insurance. Nor are independents obliged to send a renewal notice or reminder. Of course, clients' instructions may include renewal, for example, an instruction 'to keep my Cambridge property covered'.[78a] Moreover, if an independent has renewed a policy or sent reminders in the past, it is arguable that an obligation has been assumed to renew the policy again, or at least to warn the client that it is about to expire. In general, in the current language of both tort and contract, it must be possible to say that a particular independent has 'assumed that responsibility'.[79]

Claims

When independents contract insurance for clients, it does not usually follow from that alone that, if need be, they are also mandated to pursue claims under the policy, but authority is readily inferred from subsequent conduct. For example,

---

[73] *Warren v Sutton* [1976] 2 Lloyd's Rep 276 (CA).

[74] *Panhaven Pty Ltd v Bain Dawes Northern Pty Ltd* [1982] 2 NSWLR 57 (CA).

[75] *Gunns v Par Insurance Brokers* [1997] 1 Lloyd's Rep 173, 177.

[76] See Chapter 4, p. 103 ff.　　　　[77] *Warren v Sutton,* op. cit. above, n. 73.

[78] See, e.g., *Darville v Notcutt & Co. Ltd,* 18 March 1991 (CA), unreported but discussed by Henley, op cit. above, n. 1, ch. 11-012.

[78a] Concerning post-placement duties, see *HIH v JLT* [2006] EWCA 485 (Comm), [2006] 1 CLC 499.

[79] See *Henderson v Merrett Syndicates Ltd* [1995] 2 AC 145.

generally an independent cannot enter a claim without information about the loss, so in such a case, authority to pursue the claim can be inferred, especially if, as is likely, the information was obtained from the client. On receiving clients' notification that they wish to make a claim, independents are required to 'respond promptly' (COB 8A.4.1R) and in the manner there detailed; and generally to 'act with due care, skill and diligence' (COB 8A.3.3R) in that regard. Claims sometimes pose problems for independents.

If a claim is disputed, the independent's interest is to handle the differences between claimant and insurer while retaining the goodwill of both. The insurer may distrust the claimant but trust the independent, and the independent may well be aware of this. If the independent has unsubstantiated doubts about the honesty of the claim, however, the independent's duty in law is not unlike that of a barrister: to press the client's case to the best of his or her ability, in spite of the doubts, although independents will be aware that the displeasure of the insurer may be incurred thereby.

If the independent expresses doubts about a claim to the insurer concerned, however, the independent will likely lose the client, but it is not likely that a court would hold the independent liable to the client for breach of contract. The *prima facie* breach of a duty in 'pulling the plug' on claim and client [80] is qualified in such circumstances.[81] As regards the possibility of liability in tort for defamation, communications in good faith to the insurer in such a case attract the defence of qualified privilege.[82] As regards claims for breach of confidence, the independent can raise the defence of public interest,[83] because the courts have 'always refused to uphold the right to confidence when to do so would be to cover up wrong-doing'.[84] As a matter of business judgement, independents might be inclined in this situation to 'pull their punches', but the law does not require this.

When claiming for clients, independents owe no duty to insurers except, of course, a duty not to be fraudulent and, possibly, a duty not to make careless misstatements actionable in tort.[85] On the one hand, the reliance placed in practice by some insurers on some independents may be used to argue that independents owe a duty to insurers actionable in tort. On the other hand, if their profession is really threatened with partial extinction, as some people have asserted, perhaps a court would hold that a tort duty would not be 'fair and reasonable': another liability might be the last straw that breaks the overly burdened back of the profession and, therefore, against the interest of a public that needs the services of independents. If an independent suspects that a claim is fraudulent, perhaps the best course is to pull out of the ring altogether and allow the insurer to draw whatever conclusion seems appropriate; the independent may

[80] *Southern Foundries (1926) Ltd v Shirlaw* [1940] AC 701.
[81] *Holman v Johnson* (1775) 1 Cowp 341, 343.   [82] *Watt v Longsdon* [1930] 1 KB 130.
[83] *Initial Services Ltd v Putterill* [1968] 1 QB 396 (CA).
[84] *A-G v Guardian Newspapers* [1990] 1 AC 109, 268.
[85] *The Zephyr* [1985] 2 Lloyd's Rep 525, 538 (CA).

lose the client, but at the same time the independent is likely to retain the confidence and goodwill of the insurer, as well as his or her integrity.

The Liability of Independents

Contract and Tort

Independents who advise clients without exercising the requisite care and skill and who cause loss, are liable to clients both in tort, usually but not invariably the tort of 'negligent misstatement', and in contract, for breach of an implied term.[86] Liability in tort is of particular importance when the liability in issue is not to clients, who have a contract with their independent, but to third persons, who have no such contract and must therefore base any claim against an independent in tort.

For any claim in the tort of negligence, claimants must establish that the defendant owed them a duty of care, broke that duty, and that, as a result, the claimant suffered loss of a reasonably foreseeable type. In general, no duty at all is owed by anybody when, as here, loss is purely economic. A major exception, however, concerns 'negligent misstatements', such as negligent advice by independents. Bad advice breaks no bones but does lead to bad cover, which may damage a client's business if the client loses the insurance money that would have been payable if the independent's duty had not been broken and the cover had been as good as it was supposed to be. This exception applies primarily to the liability of independents to their clients, largely overlapping with the contractual liability of independents to clients, but has been extended to third persons intended to be beneficiaries of the insurance.

Third Party Beneficiaries

The extension was the effect of the decision of the House of Lords in *White v Jones*,[87] a decision affecting solicitors but applicable to all 'professionals'. The professional for the purpose of the tort is not just a person who belongs to a recognized profession but any 'informed persons': persons, including independents, so placed that others might reasonably rely upon their judgement or skill, or upon their ability to make careful inquiry, and who undertake to give information or advice.[88]

The House of Lords ruled in *White v Jones* that professional D is liable in tort to P, someone who D's client, C, wanted to benefit from D's professional services to C, under the following conditions.[89] First, as is required of any duty of care, the loss

---

[86] Implied at common law, e.g., the *Superhulls Cover case* [1990] 2 Lloyd's Rep 431, 458, as well as under s. 13 of the Supply of Goods and Services Act 1982. See further *Henderson v Merrett Syndicates Ltd*, op. cit. above, n. 79, 184 ff.   [87] [1995] 2 AC 207.

[88] In a professional indemnity policy, 'professional' is often defined; see M. Simpson (ed.), *Professional Negligence and Liability* (London, 2000) ch. 5.83 ff.

[89] Derived from the famous case of *Hedley Byrne & Co. Ltd v Heller & Partners Ltd* [1964] AC 465.

or damage suffered by P must be reasonably foreseeable by D. Secondly, there must be proximity between P and D. Thirdly, liability must not be unfair or unreasonable on D. The key to the crucial second requirement, proximity, is an assumption of responsibility by D. Since *White v Jones* the key works differently according to whether D has undertaken to give advice, which is mainly the case of independents, or to take action.

In the case of advice, there is proximity when:

(1) the advice is required for a purpose, whether particularly specified or generally described, which is made known, either actually or inferentially, to the adviser at the time when the advice is given; (2) the adviser knows, either actually or inferentially, that his advice will be communicated to the advisee, either specifically or as a member of an ascertainable class, in order that it should be used by the advisee for that purpose; (3) it is known, either actually or inferentially, that the advice so communicated is likely to be acted on by the advisee for that purpose without independent inquiry.[90]

In the case of action undertaken by independents on behalf of clients, the impact of *White v Jones* is unclear. At least two different positions can be taken about the *ratio* of the case. First, there is the narrower common law position, the 'transactional' position whereby, in most instances, the rules for action undertaken are the same as those (above) for advice. Secondly, there is the 'Chancery' position of Lord Browne-Wilkinson, that professionals are quasi-fiduciaries: they owe a duty whenever they have assumed responsibility for a task knowing that P's economic welfare is dependent upon their carefully carrying out their task.[91] In this respect independents have been likened[92] to surveyors.[93] This is a wider rule than the first. 'Hell and Chancery', said Thomas Fuller, 'are always open.' Some fear that the Chancery approach might lead, if not to damnation, then to open season on liability on a scale that would beggar not only belief but also many firms of professionals. That has yet to happen, but it was the Chancery approach that was most in evidence when *White v Jones* was applied to the scandal of pension misselling in *Gorham*.[94] There it was held that an insurer was liable for bad advice not only to one of its policyholders but also to his wife, the claimant, who was clearly intended to be the beneficiary of his policy.

Lastly, whichever approach is taken, liability is not regarded as fair and reasonable, and a duty will not be owed to anyone other than client C, if it results in conflict between D's duties to client C and D's duty to third person P. Nor would it be reasonable if the result is that D has to pay twice for the same loss. In *Verderame*,[95] for example, claims in tort were brought against a broker not only by C, the corporate client, but also by P1 and P2, the sole directors and shareholders of C. The court held that broker D owed a duty, but to C alone. The overall effect is

---

[90] *Caparo Industries plc v Dickman* [1990] 2 AC 605, 638. See also *Customs and Excise Commissioners v Barclays Bank plc* [2006] UKHL 28, [2006] 3 WLR 1.
[91] [1995] 2 AC 207, 274.   [92] E.g., by Henley, op. cit. above, n. 1, ch. 11-001.
[93] *Smith v Eric S. Bush* [1990] 1 AC 831, applied in *Merrett v Babb* [2001] QB 1174 (CA).
[94] *Gorham v British Telecommunications Plc* [2000] 1 WLR 2129 (CA).
[95] *Verderame v Commercial Union Assurance Co. plc* [1992] BCLC 793 (CA).

that D will not be liable very often to persons other than client C. For some time the clearest case was *Punjab*,[96] in which P was a substantial creditor of client C and, as independent D well knew, P was not only to be an assignee of the policy but actively participated in giving instructions for the insurance. In this case, it was against the very possibility that a remedy against C would be worthless that P required insurance and assignment. However, *Punjab* has been followed in cases in which the involvement, and thus the rights, of claimant P were less obvious.[97]

Remedies

If independents are in breach of a fiduciary duty—if, for example, there has been an unacceptable conflict of interest in respect of a contract of insurance, which the independent has made on the client's behalf—the client is entitled to rescind the contract of insurance.

If independents fail to do what they have promised to do—either fail altogether, or fail to do it fully, properly, or carefully—clients may seek compensation from independents: a claim lies for damages for breach of contract. If the essence of the client's complaint is that the independent has acted (or advised) with insufficient care or skill, that is a breach of contract actionable as such. Also, however, it is negligence actionable in tort.[98]

As for the damages, if the claim is based on breach of contract and the loss was of a type that should have been reasonably contemplated by the independent at the time of contracting with the clients,[99] the clients can recover as damages the amount of their actual loss as a consequence of the breach of contract. If the claim is based in tort and the loss was of a type that should have been reasonably foreseen by the independent at the time of the act or omission which institutes the tort,[100] clients can recover as damages the amount of their actual loss as a consequence of the tort.

As regards the measure of recoverable damages for breach of contract, clients are to be put in the position they would have been in, if the independent's mandate had been performed.[101] For tort, clients are to be put in the position they would have been in, if the tort had not been committed.[102] Thus, in a case of failure to procure cover, clients can recover the amount of insurance money which they would have recovered from the insurer, if the independent's breach had not occurred and the cover had been obtained, whether the cause of action is contract[103] or tort.[104] This is the position whether the cover required is available

---

[96] *Punjab National Bank v De Boinville* [1992] 3 All ER 104 (CA).
[97] *Aiken v Stewart Wrightson Members Agency Ltd* [1995] 2 Lloyd's Rep 618, and *European Int. Re v Curzon* [2003] Lloyd's Rep IR 454.   [98] See above, p. 70; also FSMA 3150(1), above p. 60.
[99] *The Heron II, Koufos v C. Czarnikow Ltd* [1969] 1 AC 350.
[100] *The Wagon Mound, Overseas Tankship (UK) v Mort Dock & Engineering Co.* [1961] AC 388.
[101] *Robinson v Harman* (1848) 1 Ex 850; *Ruxley Electronics & Construction Ltd v Forsyth* [1996] 1 AC 344.   [102] *The Albazero* [1977] AC 774, 841.
[103] *Dunbar v Painters* [1985] 2 Lloyd's Rep 616, 620; aff'd [1986] 2 Lloyd's Rep 38 (CA).
[104] *Osman v Moss* [1970] 1 Lloyd's Rep 313 (CA): seen mainly as an action in negligence.

in the insurance market or not—on the assumption that, when cover cannot be obtained in the market and clients are told this, they will not pursue the activity for which cover was unobtainable. In one case,[105] however, the client recovered consequential loss in the form of the amount of a fine imposed by the court on the client who drove his car in the mistaken belief that the broker had got him motor cover. This is in line with the law of compensation but out of line with public policy, which generally rules out indemnity for criminal penalties.

Causation: Must Clients Check Their Policy?

Trite law tells us that clients' loss is recoverable, whether in contract or in tort, only if it was caused by an independent's breach of duty. In at least two situations, independents may argue that clients' loss was the result not of the independent's breach, but of some act or omission on the part of the client concerned.

First, let us suppose a client who was so determined to drive a new car that the client would have taken it out on the road anyway, whether covered by insurance or not; it cannot be said that, but for the independent's failure to obtain cover in time, the client would not have suffered loss such as liability to a pedestrian. If the injury to a pedestrian would have been caused anyway, it is caused not by the independent but by the client and the client's determination to drive at all costs.

Secondly, let us suppose a car used for motor sport but a policy that does not cover that; the independent might argue that, if the client had read the policy, the client would have realized that the sport was not covered and withdrawn from competition; and that, therefore, the cause of the accident that occurred during a race and associated liability to a spectator is not the independent's failure to get wider cover but the client's failure to read the policy, which failure is, in words well known to lawyers, a break in the chain of causation.

This argument assumes that clients can be expected to read their policy and check their cover. Between policyholders and their insurer, policyholders must indeed read and check their policy, not as soon as it arrives but before too long (perhaps with the help of an adviser) and, as regards the insurer, they cannot later plead ignorance of its contents.[106] Between policyholders and independents, however, the law is less clear, because it is central to the normal mandate of independents that independents undertake to obtain cover that meets the requirements of the client. In one case it was held that the client who failed to appreciate a flaw in the cover was negligent.[107] However, the case was one of reinsurance with trained parties on each side. Moreover, the client's negligence did not excuse the independent entirely: the client recovered from the independent,

---

[105] *Osman v Moss*, op. cit. above, n. 104.

[106] *Rust v Abbey Life Assurance Co Ltd* [1979] 2 Lloyd's Rep 334, 340 (CA). IOB, Annual Report 1990, para. 2.1.

[107] *Youell v Bland Welch (No. 2)* [1990] 2 Lloyd's Rep 431, 461; aff'd [1992] 2 Lloyd's Rep 127 (CA).

but some allowance was made for the client's negligence in the amount awarded to the client. Generally, however, clients can assume that the cover obtained complies with their instructions, unless the discrepancy is notified, or the non-compliance is obvious or concerns an aspect, such as a schedule of specified items, which clients know better than the independent.[108] Generally, therefore, the argument, that the cause of loss was the client's failure to read the policy, is likely to fail.

Loose Ends: Limitation

Although the duties of independents are unlikely to be any greater in tort than in contract, the remedies of clients are not quite the same. Conceptually, this is unsatisfactory; and practically speaking, it is potentially confusing. First, the discussion above assumes, as is most likely, that claims in tort against independents are based on the tort of negligence. If, however, the tort were the tort of deceit, different rules would apply: claimants recover all direct consequential loss, that is, all loss unless the chain of causation was broken.[109] Secondly, the rules of time limitation are different.

When the claim is for breach of contract, the limitation period is that of section 5 of the Limitation Act 1980, six years from the date on which the cause of action accrued. If the claim is in tort, the period is one or other of the two specified by section 14A of the Limitation Act 1980. The first, like that of section 5 for claims based in contract, is 'six years from the date on which the cause of action accrued'. The second, however, is 'three years from the starting date'. Here lies the difference between contract and tort: sometimes the second (tort) period, although of only three years, will end later than the first (contract and tort) period of six years.

The six-year period starts when the cause of action 'accrues': when the claimant client suffers loss as a result of the independent's breach of duty. In one case,[110] for example, action was brought in both contract and in tort against brokers in respect of insurance that did not pay because of misrepresentation and non-disclosure by the brokers who placed it. The claimants, the clients, argued that their action was in time, as the cause of action did not accrue until the insurance had actually been avoided by the insurer. The brokers, however, argued successfully that the action was time barred, because the cause of action accrued earlier, when the insurance, which was potentially voidable by the insurer, had been contracted. This was when the client suffered loss: financial loss, because the flawed contract of insurance afforded them lesser contractual rights and was less valuable than that which the brokers should have procured.

---

[108] *Dickson & Co. v Devitt* (1916) 86 LJKB 315; see Clarke, ch. 9-5C.

[109] *Smith New Court Securities Ltd v Citibank NA* [1997] AC 254.

[110] *Islander Trucking Ltd v Hogg, Robinson & Gardner Mountain (Marine) Ltd* [1990] 1 All ER 826; see also the *Iron Trade* case, below n. 111.

The three-year period for tort alone starts when claimant clients have 'both the knowledge required for bringing an action for damages in respect of the relevant damage and a right to bring such an action': section 14A(5). Knowledge means knowledge of 'facts about the damage as would lead a reasonable person who had suffered such damage to consider it sufficiently serious to justify his instituting proceedings for damages against a defendant who did not dispute liability and was able to satisfy a judgment': section 14A(6). In one case,[111] for example, the 'damage' was that reinsurance contracts were voidable, so the question for the court became 'when did the plaintiffs have sufficient knowledge of the facts concerning the voidability of the contract as would lead a reasonable person to consider it sufficiently serious to justify the taking of proceedings?'. This is knowledge not only that there has been a wrong, but also knowledge of who to sue.

Problems

Performance

Although the legal duties of independents are reasonably clear, in practice they are not easily fulfilled. The average independent is under pressure. Independents must meet the legal standards of care and skill and, if they do not, they are more likely to be sued than in the past or, indeed, than their contemporaries in other countries in Europe. This is partly the reward for past success: in England the market is more innovative and independents are more involved in other people's deals. It is also a consequence of rules of English law that make it relatively easy for insurers to refuse to pay on technical grounds, if so minded.[112] When that happens, outraged policyholders sometimes turn against the independent concerned:

... the inevitable corollary of insurers' right [*sic*] to avoid liability on technical or unmeritorious grounds is that brokers are expected to advise, warn and protect their insureds against just such a possibility. The risk returns to the market through the medium of brokers' liability.[113]

Profitability

In addition to the pressure of possible litigation, independents have been under market pressure which has led to falling returns. To meet this pressure one possibility is to sell more insurance and to cut costs. Another, a quite different strategic response, is to add value by offering more service.

---

[111] *Glaister v Greenwood* [2001] Lloyd's Rep PN 412; and *Haward v Fowcetts* [2006] UKHL 9, [2006] 1 WLR 682.   [112] See Chapter 6, p. 215 ff.
[113] J. Mance, 'Insurance Brokers' Negligence' (1993) 82 BILA Journal 32–53, 40.

Faster and fuller response on the part of independents has been made possible by various computer programs, including those which allow independents to compare insurance products quickly. An associated selling tactic is innovation, one suggestion being '24/7 web business': on-line marketing of personal lines of insurance to a public that has become increasingly 'at home' when buying a range of things from groceries to Christmas gifts. However, on the one hand, it is a public that has become increasingly demanding not only of products but also of websites. It is a public that is easily switched off. On the other hand, a public at home on the web may prefer to find its own way through the maze, and that has become increasingly possible.[114]

Simple products that independents might have sold are being sold by others. For example, in 2004 a major motor manufacturer, which had been selling insurance with its vehicles, decided to bite the bullet, seek FSA registration, and sell the insurance itself. Again, the sale of travel insurance remains a problem, but for the moment someone else's problem. It is more than ten years since an insurer was quoted as saying that 'in the real world', holidaymakers who buy travel insurance have no interest whatsoever in the cover provided but are far more concerned with their holiday, that we 'do not live in a perfect world' and that full discussion of the cover would make the cost of such insurance 'prohibitive'.[115] It seems that this world is still imperfect but that travel agents have not withdrawn. On the contrary, in 2003 the Association of British Travel Agents announced a new training programme for the staff selling insurance. However, one industry observation was that it might not be a case of teaching an old dog new tricks but it will take a bit more than a training programme to make this leopard change its spots.[116] This business may fall to independents in the end but, it seems, not yet.

On the service side, the natural area must be more complex products and more complex risks. A senior executive of the leading German insurer, Allianz, argued some years back that the effect of insurers marketing their products in other EU States will be that it will be harder for buyers of insurance to understand the products, so independent advice will be needed as never before.[117] That is still true, but one wonders whether buyers are aware of their need for advice and, if they are, whether they will not simply retreat to the home supplier rather than arm themselves with advice from independents and venture out. Moreover, at the other end of the spectrum of complexity, in late 2004 risk managers who buy insurance for large companies published the results of a survey indicating that in future they would prefer to deal directly with insurers rather than buy cover through independents, as most of them had done in the past. These are the very people who might be expected to appreciate the real value of the service that independents have to offer. For independents times are hard and times are still changing, however, not necessarily for the worse.[117a]

---

[114] E.g., http://www.insurancexpert.co.uk/.

[115] See O. Hameed, 'The ABI Code of Practice for the Selling of General Insurance' (1993) 3 Ins. L & P 37–41, 39.   [116] *PM*, 20 November 2003.

[117] H. Schulte-Noelle, 'Challenges for Insurers in the Nineties', *Geneva Papers on Risk and Insurance*, No. 72 (1994), 287–303, 294.

[117a] *Post Magazine*, 26 October 2006, Broking Supplement.

4

Contracting

Contract Formation

The rules of law governing the formation of contracts of insurance are the same as those which govern the formation of most other kinds of contract: the ritual matching of offer and acceptance. This is true of most kinds of insurance contract, including those contracted at Lloyd's; however, in the Lloyd's market the ritual takes a form rather different from that described here.[1]

In a simple case the person seeking cover (the 'applicant') considers the insurance described in some form of advertisement or brochure (invitations to treat). Then, with reference to the brochure or advertisement, the applicant responds with a written application—aka a proposal for insurance (offer)—to the insurer, who accepts it or rejects it. If, however, the insurer does not reject it outright but responds with policy terms, terms which differ from those expressed or implicit in the applicant's original offer, the insurer's response is a counter-offer, for the applicant to accept or reject. If the applicant rejects the insurer's counter-offer and comes back with a further proposition, he makes a further counter-offer, which the insurer may accept or reject, and so on. Note that rules issued by the FSA allow policyholders to withdraw from contracts to buy certain kinds of insurance, notably pure protection and life insurance, within periods that vary between fourteen and thirty days.[2]

If at any stage in this interchange the response of one party, let us say the applicant, is a prolonged silence, that is generally inconclusive; but, exceptionally, a long silence in the particular context has been held to be acceptance of the terms in question.[3] That is the traditional way of negotiating insurance, and in the past it has been commonly pursued through the medium of a broker or other intermediary.[4] However, a further possibility, increasingly common today for standard risks such as motor insurance and house contents insurance, is that of 'direct' insurance. This is usually contracted by the proposer in person directly with the insurer by telephone and confirmation later in writing.

In each case the various communications are effective in law only on receipt.[5] The exception is the communication of acceptance by post (or by any other authorized non-instantaneous mode of communication), which is effective when the communication is sent. This exception does not apply to telefax, but it may well apply to electronic mail as this is not an instantaneous mode of communication. By the late 1990s it became possible to contract insurance on an 'insurance exchange' on the Internet; this process is also outside the scope

[1] Generally, see Clarke, 11-1 ff. For contracting at Lloyd's see id., 11-3.
[2] COB 6.7.7R: see above Chapter 3, p. 61.
[3] *Rust v Abbey Life Assurance Co. Ltd* [1979] 2 Lloyd's Rep 334 (CA), approved [1996] 2 Lloyd's Rep 225, 230 (HL).   [4] See Chapter 3, Insurance Intermediaries.
[5] Concerning the meaning of receipt; see below, pp. 102–3.

of the exception. With well over 30 million regular users of the Internet in the UK, insurers see the Internet as an important marketplace. Moreover, there are now 'aggregator sites' which display a 'panel' of insurance products on offer from different insurers.[6] However, it seems that that is where potential customers survey the products available, and many people prefer to seek a human being, whether across a desk or on the phone, when it comes to actually buying the insurance they have surveyed.

The basic legal rules, in their application to the formation of insurance contracts, work well. The insurer and applicant know where they stand, as long as the chosen mode of communication leaves them with a record of what has (or has not) been agreed. The greatest uncertainty, however, arises out of the rules special to insurance concerning disclosure.[7] The effect and the effectiveness of the basic rules for the formation of insurance contracts rest on three assumptions which must be addressed in turn: that insurers are not bound unless they clearly indicate their intention;[8] that all the essential terms of the contract have been agreed;[9] and that the apparent agreement is unconditional.[10] First, however, we turn to the appearance of the agreement: its form.

Documentation

No particular contract form, not even an insurance policy, is required by law, except as regards marine insurance, for which statute requires a policy.[11] That reflects the maritime tradition. Recently, however, the FSA has required certain documents to be sent to the insured for the protection of the insured.[12] In practice most insureds are provided with a policy document of some kind when the insurance is first contracted. Moreover, insurers are making serious and welcome efforts to make their documents intelligible to ordinary people. Whether this can ever be entirely successful is debatable.[13] In New York, § 3102(c)(2) of the Insurance Law[14] requires *inter alia* that:

(A) For an insurance policy containing ten thousand words or less of text, the entire form shall be analyzed. For an insurance policy containing more than ten thousand words, the readability of two hundred word samples per page may be analyzed instead of the entire form. The samples shall be separated by at least twenty printed lines.

(B) The number of words and sentences in the text shall be counted and the total number of words divided by the total number of sentences. The figure obtained shall be multipled by a factor of 1.015.

---

[6] *PM*, 13 November 2003.   [7] See below, p. 98 ff.   [8] See below, p. 86.
[9] See below, p. 90.   [10] See below, p. 91.
[11] Marine Insurance Act (MIA) 1906, s. 22.   [12] See below, p. 131.
[13] See Chapter 5, p. 147 ff.   [14] http://public.leginfo.state.ny.us/menugetf.cgi.

(C) The total number of syllables shall be counted and divided by the total number of words. The figure obtained shall be multiplied by a factor of 84.6.

(D) The sum of the figures computed under subparagraphs (B) and (C) hereof subtracted from 206.835 equals the Flesch reading ease score for the insurance policy.

This is just a small part of § 3102 headed 'Requirements for the use of readable and understandable insurance policies'. English law is unlikely to go as far as that.

One effort that is made by very few insurers is to reissue a policy document to gather up, compress, and consolidate the litter of amendments made on annual renewals since the cover was first contracted and the first policy issued. The lawyer who has tried to read a statute subject to piecemeal amendments must surely have sympathy with puzzled policyholders, trying to make sense of the paperchase left by their insurers. In a world of word processors, reissue of the policy as amended should be easy. One objection, of course, is cost. However, in the current Banking Code of 2005 (clause 6.6), banks promise that if they 'have made a major change or a lot of minor changes in any one year, we will give you a copy of the new terms and conditions or a summary of the changes'. It is not clear why insurers cannot and should not do the same, preferably an integrated copy. Be that as it may, the FOS decides against insurers which have not made new terms sufficiently clear on renewal.[15]

Expectations of Cover

The brochure or other advertising material put out by insurers, like that of other suppliers of goods or services, is not intended as an offer which can become a contract simply by acceptance on the part of the recipient. Just as other kinds of supplier may not want to supply all and sundry, insurers too wish to consider the kind of person that they insure. In theory, at least, insurers are not obliged to quote (make an offer) in response to any and every applicant. Until the nineteenth century, for example, it was quite impossible to get life insurance for 'unhealthy lives', that is, people with gout, asthma, and so on. Today, for example, drivers with drinking convictions find it very difficult to get affordable motor insurance. One newspaper, in its campaign against insurance 'discrimination', gleefully highlighted the case of an insurance company which employed a certain actor in a television advertisement for its insurance, and then refused him motor cover. Insurers want policyholders but the right to pick and choose is a feature of the perfectly free marketplace, and that is what insurers want too. This is a controversial point to which we return.[16]

A feature of a free market is the possibility of negotiating terms of contract. Clearly, however, for most standard insurance risks negotiation is neither viable nor wanted—by either side: standard terms reduce transaction costs and thus

---

15 See *Ombudsman News*, December 2002.
16 See below, p. 88; also Chapter 5, p. 175 ff; and Chapter 7, p. 298.

premiums. The market, it is said, is still free because, although applicants may not be able to change the terms offered by insurer A, they can still turn elsewhere for different terms from insurer B or insurer C. But many, if not most, do not think that that is much of a choice on account of the time and trouble involved. True, they may cut cost by using the comparative tables published by consumers' organizations, but it still takes time and diligence, and then the 'best buy' cover may not be sold on every high street.

In California, home insurers have been required by law to offer earthquake cover; and Maryland once had a statute forbidding insurers from raising motor premiums for drivers over sixty-five on account of their age. In England, however, the rating practice of insurers, whereby some people or professions find it harder to get insurance than others, has been condemned as 'discrimination' by newspapers and pressure groups—but not so far by Parliament, unlike age: discrimination on grounds of age has now been regulated.[16a]

For example, the suggestion that lower household insurance premiums should be offered to non-smokers was attacked by a representative of the Tobacco Advisory Council as a discriminatory marketing gimmick. This objection got rather less sympathy than that of the Spinal Injuries Association, which complained of discrimination when disabled drivers were charged more for, or refused, motor insurance. The complaint was that some insurers do not understand the risks associated with disabilities and have thus been too 'careful' about taking on these risks. The practice has now been outlawed in principle by the Disability Discrimination Act 1995. The Act makes it unlawful to refuse to provide, or deliberately not to provide, any service, but special regulations allow insurers to treat the disabled less favourably than others.[17] A current issue being debated across Europe is whether gender underwriting, which usually favours men for health insurance but women for motor insurance, should be banned as unfairly discriminatory.[18]

One or two insurers use non-smoking together with home ownership and marriage to identify better motor risks. This has been called 'lifestyle underwriting', whereby insurers identify good risks on sociological or psychological criteria. An obvious instance is the belief that people who are careful with their cars are careful with other things, so the person's motor history is relevant to household cover and vice versa. Another insurer draws conclusions from the applicant's job, and loads premiums for people such as financial advisers, accountants, and doctors, because these professions are associated with stress. At the other end of the stress scale are not only retired people but also those who work on the land. Some insurers see such people as a market opportunity and are quick to offer them cover, pointing out that they are a special group, a pool in

[16a] See The Employment Equality (Age) Regs. 2006 (2006 No. 1031), Regs. 3 and 34, as well as Schedule 2.

[17] The Disability Discrimination (Services and Premises) Regulation 1996 (SI 1996/11). Insurers must be able to justify less favourable treatment on the basis of actuarial or other statistical information, or other information on which it is reasonable to rely, such as medical reports.

[18] See below Chapter 7, p. 243 ff.

which good risks are not compelled to carry bad ones. In the same way, one motor insurer targeted owners of expensive cars, who were aged over twenty-five and who had at least four years' no claims discount, emphasizing that the cover was exclusive in every sense. However, the corollary is that bad risks carry bad risks. This means, *inter alia*, that property and motor insurance is expensive in high-risk areas, which tend also to be where relatively poor people live, and this has been attacked as 'income-regressive'.[19] Moreover, sometimes these areas are where there is a high concentration of 'ethnic' groups and, once again, the cry is 'discrimination'. To a degree, therefore, rating becomes a political question which demands sensitivity of an industry that does not want government interference. The industry will insist that cover is available, but, like The Ritz, for some citizens it may be barred by cost.

The idea of insurance as a kind of public calling, and that the insurer has a responsibility (and even perhaps a duty) to provide cover,[20] is one for which English law and English insurers are not yet ready. It is one thing to expect some insurer or other (or all of them collectively) to provide some kind of cover; it is another to say that a particular insurer must accept a particular risk. So, any realistic appraisal of English law must start from the double baseline of traditional contract law that there is no legal duty to negotiate a contract in good faith, or indeed at all. But neither is there a complete vacuum. The market context is one in which there is a public expectation of cover; and in which the simple operation of the rules of classical contract law in a notionally free market may no longer be enough.

Expectations of Speed and Courtesy

If it cannot be maintained that a particular insurer is bound to accept a particular application, can any insurer simply ignore an application? In so far as English law says that it is an offer to contract subject to classical contract law, the answer must be affirmative. However, in some countries the position is less classical and, for consumers of insurance, less crude.

State law in the United States, for example, enforces an implied collateral promise to take prompt action on an application for an acceptable risk. If an insurer fails to accept or reject an application with reasonable promptness, and the applicant is thus led reasonably to believe that the application is acceptable, the insurer is considered to have accepted it.[21] More striking still is the rule in Belgium:

If, within 30 days of receipt of the proposal, the insurer does not notify the prospective policy-holder of an offer of insurance, or that insurance is subject to certain inquiries, or a

---

[19] See further Abraham, 76.   [20] See Chapter 7, p. 298.
[21] The seminal article is: F. Kessler, 'Contracts of Adhesion—Some Thoughts about Freedom of Contract' 43 Col LR 629, 639 (1943). See further Clarke, 11-2A3.

refusal of insurance, he undertakes to conclude the contract, in default of which damages shall be payable.[22]

In England the basic rule, which applies in most cases, is that consent to cover a risk cannot be inferred from silence alone. Two situations at least, however, invite argument against application of the basic rule.

One argument for a contract is that, if a particular applicant is prejudiced by the insurer's lack of response, the insurer may be estopped from denying that there is cover. If, indeed, the insurer is estopped from denying the formation of the proposed contract of insurance, there is some precedent in the general law of contract for the proposition that the insurer is bound by it.[23] The balance of opinion is against basing a cause of action in contract on (promissory) estoppel;[24] however, it has been forcefully argued[25] that an extension to found an action in cases, such as promises made during contract negotiations, would be a significant but nonetheless justifiable incremental development of the law. The obvious objection to an estoppel argument in the insurance situation here is that, generally, estoppel requires a positive representation and cannot be based on silence on the part of the insurer. Occasionally, however, a 'duty to speak' has been inferred from contexts other than insurance, with the corollary that silence speaks.[26] In a similar way, for example, if insurers indicate in any way that they will contact an applicant in case the application is unacceptable and they do not, a contract may be inferred from the insurers' silence;[27] and when, as is not unlikely, there is some dispute about what was said or done during negotiations, the FOS is likely to give the applicant the benefit of doubt—even though in law it is for an applicant to prove the existence of the contract.[28]

A second, but related, argument might be built on key features of an established practice of insurance contracting: what has been called in another context the 'clear, orderly and familiar procedure' and the 'prescribed common form'. The other context is that of the tender in the *Blackpool* case.[29] The argument by analogy is that an insurance company is obliged to give proper consideration and due response to an application for insurance on the company's form. Essential links in the analogy are an invitation to participate in a 'familiar procedure', that participation is in the business interests of all concerned, and that the prescribed common form is designed to suit the insurer. In the *Blackpool* case, the person who invited tenders but did not follow the procedure and consider an eligible tender, had broken the 'rules' and was liable. If the insurer leaves such an application unanswered, here too, it might be argued, the 'rules' have been broken and, if

---

[22] Art. 4 of the Insurance Act 1992. A similar rule is found in Finland for standard risks: section II of the Insurance Act 1994; and in other countries in Europe: see Basedow and Fock, 21 ff.

[23] See *The Henrik Sif* [1982] 1 Lloyd's Rep 456.   [24] R. Bradgate, *Butterworths*, 2.124.

[25] Ibid., 2.134.   [26] *The Stolt Loyalty* [1993] 2 Lloyd's Rep 281.

[27] See *Re Selectmove Ltd* [1995] 1 WLR 474 (CA).

[28] E.g., IOB Bulletin 2 (1994) case 94/21929.

[29] *Blackpool & Fylde Aero Club v Blackpool BC* [1990] 1 WLR 1195 (CA).

the applicant suffers as a result, the insurer should be liable—if not under an insurance contract implicitly agreed, then under a contract collateral to it which has been broken.

A court determined to distinguish the *Blackpool* case could do so without difficulty. For example, the defendant there chose to deal with a limited number of people; and the orderly procedure made sense only if the defendant could be kept to it. One might almost say that the decision was based on essential business efficacy.[30] However, in *Blackpool*, Bingham LJ[31] rejected one of the arguments against liability because it would lead to 'an unacceptable discrepancy between the law of contract and the confident assumptions of commercial parties'.[32] The Court of Appeal in that case wanted to protect ordinary commercial expectations of businessmen tendering for work. Why not also the expectations of the person tendering an application for insurance? According to Brownsword, the decision shows that 'the courts are sometimes ready to manipulate orthodox doctrine so that reasonable expectations are protected'[33] and that 'reliance in and around the formation of contract will be protected where it is reasonable'.[34]

Terms Offered

Like any other contractual offer, the application must be unambiguous and complete. Ambiguity depends on interpretation in context.[35] For completeness, the application must contain (expressly or by implication) all the essential terms for an insurance contract of that kind.

One essential term concerns premium. So, when an advertisement 'guarantees' life insurance to anyone over fifty who applies, that is not an offer that can be simply accepted by fifty-one-year-old applicant Joe. Nor is Joe's application an offer, because neither the advertisement nor Joe's response contains a key term: the amount of premium. In law, what is being 'guaranteed' is not insurance but a subsequent offer of insurance at a premium, determined after the insurer has seen Joe's details, for Joe to accept or not.

Generally, essential terms are of two kinds. First, some terms are particular to the contract in question and to no other; these must be agreed because that particular contract cannot do without them. In the example of fire insurance, these are the identity of the parties to the contract (Joe and the insurer), the kind of risk (fire), the subject-matter at risk (Joe's house), and the amount of insurance (an estimate of the value of the house, or of the cost of reconstruction).

Secondly, other terms are no less essential but are of a more general kind so that, if they have not been expressly agreed by the parties, they can be implied. For example, it is commonly inferred that fire insurance lasts for one year; that the

---

[30] In this sense Bradgate, op.cit. above, n. 24, at 2.8.
[31] With whom Stocker LJ and Farquharson agreed.   [32] Op.Cit. above, n. 29, at 1201.
[33] R. Brownsword, *Butterworths*, 1.11.   [34] Ibid., 1.75.
[35] See Chapter 5, p. 139 ff.

amount of premium can be implied, as long as the risk is a standard risk and there is an ascertainable market rate; and that notice of any claim must be within a reasonable time.

In addition, terms may be implied which are not essential but are general not to the industry but to that insurer; for example, the particular insurer's standard terms for fire insurance might include a term about a right of access to the house after a fire. Indeed, there is a presumption that when a person applies for a standard kind of insurance to a company offering that kind of insurance, the applicant does so on the implied basis of the insurer's standard terms for that kind of insurance.[36] Like any other standard form terms, however, to be part of the contract they must be available for Joe to read on request.

In most European countries insurers must provide a copy if the contract is to bind an applicant at all.[37] Indeed, some commentators there take the view that this is required in all EC countries for health insurance by the Third Directive on Non-Life Insurance.[38] In England, however, the traditional rule is that people are taken to know that insurers have standard terms and it is for applicants to enquire about them, if they want to know what they say. The picture in current practice is rather different. For some time past ABI codes of practice have exhorted insurers to draw to the attention of buyers of insurance the inevitable restrictions and exclusions that the policy on offer contains. The FOS insists on this,[39] and the practice has *obiter* support from the courts.[40] Moreover, if the relevant contract term is onerous and unusual, it is inoperative unless specifically drawn to the attention of the other party under general contract law.[41] In practice, however, complaints that have come before the Insurance Ombudsman, and later the FOS, suggest that this does not often happen.

Unconditional Acceptance

Like any other acceptance of a contractual offer, the acceptance, whether by insurer or applicant, must be unequivocal and unconditional. However, some acceptances, notably acceptance by life insurers, are often conditional.

A common example is an agreement for cover 'subject to payment of premium'. In that case either there is no contract and no cover at all, or there is a contract but no cover until premium has been paid. The correct analysis depends on the correct construction of the agreement.[42] Again, even if premium has been paid for life insurance, the agreement between insurer and applicant may be, for

[36] *General Accident Ins. Corp. v Cronk* (1901) 17 TLR 233.
[37] Basedow and Fock, 19, p. 31.   [38] 92/49/EEC, OJL 228; Basedow and Fock, 18 ff.
[39] E.g., for the widely misunderstood limits on cover of curtailment of travel: *Ombudsman News*, July 2003, p. 5; see also *Ombudsman News*, April 2004, p. 36. So does the FSA; see p. 63 ff.
[40] *Nsbuga v Commercial Union Assurance Co. plc* [1998] 2 Lloyd's Rep 682, 685.
[41] *Interfoto Picture Library Ltd v Stilleto Visual Programmes Ltd* [1989] QB 433 (CA); *O'Brien v MGN* [2001] EWCA Civ 1279.
[42] *Canning v Farquahar* (1886) 16 QBD 727 (CA). See Clarke, 11-2E.

example, 'subject to satisfactory medical report'. The effect of this too depends on construction, but in this instance, courts are most reluctant to construe against any cover at all. Unless told otherwise, most people who pay premium expect immediate, although perhaps temporary, cover, and in this situation are unlikely to withdraw the proposal during the period of investigation or look for alternative cover; meanwhile the insurer has the use of the premium money. So, acceptance of premium is strong evidence of contract and that some kind of cover has begun for, otherwise, the applicant, who might reasonably expect to get something for the money paid, is getting little or nothing.

English law could do worse than look west to Canada and the USA, where, unless insurers have made it very clear indeed that their applicants get no cover for their money yet, the courts are likely to find in favour of what they call 'temporary' or 'interim insurance'.[43] In such cases, said the Supreme Court of California, 'it would be unconscionable to allow the insurer, who had required payment from the applicant of the first premium, to escape the obligation of coverage which the applicant could reasonably assume and expect that the insurer was thereby undertaking'.[44] Subsequently, the Supreme Court of Canada drew the same kind of conclusion,[45] adopting the view of the Supreme Court of New Jersey that 'the very acceptance of the premium in advance tends naturally towards the understanding of immediate coverage though it be temporary and terminable'.[46]

In England, the matter is left to the interpretation of the courts, but the courts are likely to see such a case as one of conditional cover, although the exact analysis might vary. One possibility is a preliminary or interim contract at the time of agreement, under which the insurer promises immediate but temporary cover pending, for example, a medical report and, if the report is satisfactory, to enter the main contract later. This is also the analysis of motor insurance and the familiar cover note, when some aspect of cover remains to be sorted out. Another possibility is a main contract from the beginning, subject, however, to cancellation by the insurer later, if the medical report is not satisfactory. Further, note that, whatever the contract says, the FSA has given applicants a right to cancel life insurance within a statutory cooling-off period. A rule of this kind, formerly in a statute (now repealed), is contained in the FSA's *Conduct of Business Sourcebook*.[47]

Renewal and Variation

When the period of cover ends, policyholders may well wish to renew it. People often forget when their cover ends, and this has led to the practice whereby insurers send reminders in the form of renewal notices. These are offers of

---

[43] See, e.g., *Smith v Westland Life*, 539 P 2d 433 (Cal, 1975).   [44] Ibid., at 439.
[45] *Zurich Life Ins. Co. of Canada v Davies* 130 DLR (3d) 748, 750 (1981).
[46] *Allen v Metropolitan Life Ins. Co.*, 208 A. 2d 638, 642 (1965).
[47] Chapter 7. See COB 6.7: above, p. 61.

insurance for the next period (commonly one year), which policyholders can accept, usually by sending the premium required, or reject. In some countries, such as Switzerland,[48] insurers are obliged to send a reminder when premium is due, but this was not English law: insurers were not obliged either to send a notice, or, generally speaking, to renew the insurance at all, even when the consequences for a policyholder are dire, until new rules came into force in 2005.[49]

As regards renewal, a special case is that of life insurance. When policyholders pay second and subsequent premiums, the contract is not renewed but continued: provided that the policyholder pays premiums, the contract continues until the life insured 'drops' or a stated period of years has passed. Policyholders have a right to pay premium and to continue the cover, with the corollary that their insurer cannot refuse it because, for example, since the last renewal the policyholder has contracted a fatal disease. If policyholders fails to pay premium on time, however, the insurance lapses.[50]

In spite of what has just been said, both for life and other kinds of cover a special case *might* also arise out of the common practice of reminders. A policyholder could argue that the past practice of the insurer in sending renewal notices amounts to a waiver of the policyholder's duty to pay until the usual notice is sent; and that the past practice has lulled the policyholder into a sense of complacency about payment in time of which the insurer should not be allowed to take advantage. In law the argument might well be framed as one based on estoppel: insurer, you are estopped from pleading that my cover has ceased because you led, or at least allowed, me to believe otherwise. Indeed, if, as more than one court has held, insurers can be estopped from pointing out that the insurance has ended automatically on account of a policyholder's breach of warranty,[51] why not also when it has ended when cover has expired 'naturally'? The problem about this argument is that English courts are reluctant to infer estoppel from negative conduct,[52] except in the case of a commercial relationship closer and more cosy than that of insurer and insured.

An American court, however, observing a similar common practice among insurers there to send reminders with a view to retaining and furthering their business, upon which the general public had come to depend, once held that insurers had waived their right to require their insured to assume the burden of keeping track of dates on which premium was due.[53] The decision was a Pyrrhic victory for the public, as insurers responded with clauses to defeat it. The insured's case will be won in England only if the relationship between insurer and insured can be rid of the market image and seen as fiduciary, or at least one in

[48] VVG, Art. 20.1.   [49] See Chapter 5, pp. 63–4.
[50] For possible exceptions, see below, Chapter 6, p. 244 ff.
[51] See, e.g., *Kirkaldy & Sons v Walker* [1999] Lloyd's Rep IR 410, 422, *per* Longmore J; *Agapitos v Agnew (No. 2)* [2003] Lloyd's Rep IR 54 at [70], *per* Moore-Bick J. This is the courts' current view of what was formerly referred to in this context as 'waiver'.
[52] *The Scaptrade* [1983] 1 Lloyd's Rep 146 (CA), aff'd [1983] 2 AC 694.
[53] *Pester v American Family Mutual Ins. Co.*, 186 NW 2d 711, 713 (Neb., 1971).

which the insurer, like some brokers, has undertaken to see to the insurance needs of the insured in a more general way.

Alternatively to estoppel, it might be argued that insurers should send reminders as part of a duty of information based on general obligations of good faith and fair dealing. That too is the kind of argument that might succeed in the USA or some countries in Europe; however, the 'good faith' of English insurance law is little more than a duty of disclosure, which originally arose precisely because the parties, although facing each other across a cosy cup of coffee at Lloyd's coffee house, were in certain respects far apart. Failure to notify policyholders that cover is about to come to an end may be inconsiderate or discourteous, but the English courts have been unlikely to censure insurers by insisting that policyholders are still covered in cases such as this. Be that as it may, insurers are now obliged to send renewal notices.[53a]

Flawed Consent

In 1732, Thomas Fuller described trade and commerce as 'cheating all round by consent'. Be that as it may have been then, a contract between A and B today is vitiated if one of them 'cheats' to such an extent that the consent of either, let us say B, is fatally flawed. The consent of B is flawed if B is fundamentally mistaken about the subject-matter (operative mistake), whether A is mistaken or not. The consent of B is also flawed if B is induced to contract on the basis of wrong information (misrepresentation) or of insufficient information (non-disclosure) supplied by A. This is the law whether A is the policyholder or the insurer, but the typical case is when A is a policyholder who obtains cover from insurer B in that way.

The consequences of mistake and misrepresentation are explored further below.

Mistake

Operative fundamental mistake is rare. Unless the mistake has been induced by A, it is hard to convince a court that B's consent was so flawed by mistake that the contract is void.[54] There was once a case[55] in which A obtained life insurance by getting friend C to submit C's body for the required medical in place of his own which, in the event, proved to be on its last legs. Cases like that do not come up very often.

[53a] See pp. 63–4.
[54] Generally see *Great Peace Shipping Ltd v Tsaavliris Salvage Int. Ltd* [2002] EWCA Civ 1407; [2003] QB 679.   [55] *Obartuch v Security Mutual Life Ins. Co.*, 114 F 2d 873 (7 Cir, 1940).

A specific consequence of the strictness of the law about mistakes is that policyholders cannot get out of insurance contracts because of an uninduced mistake about the terms of the policy. Normally insurers are entitled to assume that policyholders read their policy and, if they did not understand it, sought advice. In the case of a genuine mistake about the policy as a record of the terms agreed, a policyholder may be able to obtain rectification of the policy so that it says what it should have said.[56] Otherwise, the policyholder may have a remedy against an intermediary, if there was one, for giving the wrong advice or getting the wrong policy: intermediaries are not entitled to assume that their customers read the policy to check that the intermediary has carried out their instructions.[57]

Misrepresentation

Much more common than consent flawed by operative mistake is consent flawed by misrepresentation. Usually the misrepresentation is that of applicants for insurance; but it should not be forgotten that insurers, especially those inviting people to contract insurance by way of investment, sometimes overstate the desirability of what they have to offer. Moreover, any person who publishes a false or misleading advertisement commits an offence under section 46 of the Consumer Credit Act 1974. Prosecutions are rare. More to the point for most members of the public is the practice of the FOS. If anyone establishes that he or she has been missold product, such as a mortgage endowment policy, whether it is a case of misrepresentation, or non-disclosure, or both, the FOS may order the insurer to pay the complainant a sum that is sufficient to put the complainant in the position he or she would have been in if the proper advice had been received.[58]

Whether the misstatement is that of an insurer or of an applicant, as a matter of general contract law, an operative misrepresentation is a statement of fact by one of them (A) which is one of the considerations that induces the other (B) to make a contract with the misrepresentor (A) or, sometimes, a third party (C).

Fact

A statement of fact is a statement about the present or the past which, as it appears to B, A is in a position (of knowledge, information, or experience) to make.[59] Moreover, a misrepresentation is nonetheless a misrepresentation if it is made innocently and in good faith. So, for example, if a fire insurer advises an applicant to insure the property in the amount indicated by an index of rebuilding costs, even an index prepared by an independent body of surveyors, and that amount

---

[56] Generally see *Bates (Thomas) & Son Ltd v Wyndham's (Lingerie) Ltd* [1981] 1 All ER 1077 (CA); and *The Nai Genova* [1984] 1 Lloyd's Rep 353 (CA).   [57] See Chapter 3, pp. 79–80.
[58] See, e.g., the cases discussed in *Ombudsman News* No. 23 (December 2002). See also Chapter 3, p. 60.   [59] *Bisset v Wilkinson* [1927] AC 177.

turns about to be mistakenly high or mistakenly low, the applicant as policy-holder is entitled to avoid the insurance contract. Insurance is commonly con-tracted on the basis of the insurer's application form, which is completed and signed by the applicant. If, however, applicants answer a question on the form with 'I do not know', it is up to the insurer whether to press for further informa-tion or not. If an applicant's answer to a question is so obviously a blind guess that it should not be treated as a statement of fact, or even as an expression of belief, it is one that insurers should ignore and not rely on, so that, if they contract nonetheless, they cannot later point to the answer as a ground for rescission. These are what general contract law calls 'mere puffs'. If, on the other hand, it is obvious that the statement is the personal opinion of the applicant, it does not follow without more that it is without effect.

In the commercial world even statements of opinion—profit forecasts and the like—may have an influence on those to whom they are expressed, so that in law they count as facts.[60] Equally, outside the world of commerce, a medical 'opinion' that an applicant for life insurance has cancer is a fact, that the specialist holds that opinion, which must not be misstated or withheld: it must be disclosed.[61]

The Value and Importance of Belief: Good Faith

The position is different if the applicant is required by insurers, as they have been exhorted by the ABI in past Statements of Insurance Practice, to answer questions in the application form 'to the best of your knowledge or belief'.[62] Such a form was completed in a leading case, *Economides*,[63] in which a mature student, whose parents were living with him in his flat, insured the flat contents. They included his mother's jewellery, for which he stated a value, which turned out to be a considerable undervalue, on the basis of a figure estimated by his father, a (former) senior policeman. The insurer argued that the policyholder had not gone far enough and that his statement was false, because it was implied that he had reasonable grounds for it, which he did not.

The Court of Appeal rejected the insurer's argument. As a matter of what is meant by 'an expression of belief', the Court accepted the argument that, although a 'blind guess' would not be enough, the test was not whether the belief was reasonable but whether the applicant had 'some basis' for the belief. The requirement is 'solely one of honesty'[64] and 'of good faith which is necessarily subjective'.[65] The student policyholder passed that test. That was not the case, for example, of the complainant to the FOS who offered his own view rather than that of a recent surveyor's report on his house referring to subsidence.[66]

[60] See, e.g., *Bank Leumi Le Israel BM v British National Ins. Co. Ltd* [1988] 1 Lloyd's Rep 71, 75, *per* Saville J. [61] See below, p. 103 ff.
[62] See below, p. 105 ff.
[63] *Economides v Commercial Union Assurance Co. plc* [1998] QB 587 (CA).
[64] Ibid., 598–9. [65] Ibid., 606.
[66] E.g., Case 25/1b, *Ombudsman News*, February 2003.

The requirement to answer questions 'to the best of your knowledge or belief' is most common in consumer contracts. However, the ruling of the Court of Appeal in *Economides* has been applied to commercial contracts even when the word formula was missing, as being the correct view of section 20(5) of the MIA, when the disputed statement concerned the value of property insured.[67]

In any event, insurers are entitled to assume that if an applicant discovers that a belief genuinely held when it was expressed in the application form was mistaken, or that a statement, which although true when made, has become untrue between then and the time of contracting, the applicant will tell them. Otherwise the insurer's consent is flawed.[68] The case can be seen not only as one of a statement which has become false by the time of contract (misrepresentation), but also as a case of non-disclosure.[69] The remedy for misrepresentation, as well as for non-disclosure, discussed below, is rescission of the contract of insurance.[70]

Belief in Value and Importance: Underinsurance

To have a house full of things accumulated over years professionally valued can be expensive to a degree that would be out of all proportion to the matter in hand. Insurers, if so minded, can always require a valuation. In the case of 'high net worth' cover, that is, the house contents of the 'seriously rich', they sometimes do, or else make their own 'walk-through' appraisal; but assessment by a valuer of international repute can cost over £1,000 a day. Even a small local firm may well charge over £500 a day, although updates on previous valuations usually cost less. It is not really so surprising that a market survey in June 2004 indicated that, in spite of popular television programmes such as *The Antiques Roadshow*, 80 per cent of art and antiques collectors were inadequately insured.[71] The seriously rich are not infrequently seriously casual about insurance and seriously ignorant about what 'that ugly vase' that they inherited from Uncle Bill is worth. A few years back the case was reported of an owner who in all good faith sought to insure for £3 million a castle and contents which the insurer found to be worth £25 million. Specific items can be hard to assess, especially in the fine art market. When the painting *Massacre of the Innocents* was bought in 1982 it cost £2.5 million, but, having been reattributed to Rubens, its value in 2002 was put at £49.5 million. Such blessings are unlikely be the lot of Estuary man, but nonetheless most householders are ignorant of the current value of their accumulated possessions, and this is a problem for insurers and policyholders alike.

To require valuation at the expense of applicants would, as insurers well know, put people off buying their insurance. To sell it, insurers take a risk. *Economides*[72] says in effect the estimate does not have to be objectively

[67] *Eagle Star v Games Video Co.* [2004] EWHC 15 (Comm), [2004] 1 Lloyd's Rep 238, para. 118.
[68] *With v O'Flanagan* [1936] Ch 575 (CA).   [69] Below, at p. 103 ff.
[70] Below, at p. 116 ff.   [71] *PM*, 22 July 2004, p. 17.
[72] *Economides v Commercial Union Assurance Co. plc*, op. cit., n. 63, discussed above.

reasonable; that insurers, evidently keen to compete, not only assume the risk of honest but careless policyholders once cover has commenced, but also of similar traits before contract. Moreover, insurers know full well that, if a claim comes in on underinsured property, they are not high and dry. In theory they can, and in practice sometime do, insist on paying the claim 'subject to average', that is, the payment is reduced in proportion to the underinsurance. Thus, if property insured for £20 million is actually worth £30 million, a claim for actual loss of £3 million is paid subject to average (2:3), so the insurer pays only £2 million, two-thirds of the loss. In such cases policyholders are deemed to be their own insurer for the residue.[73] The practice of payment subject to average is not popular with policyholders!

The practice is not often pursued in the high net worth market, where insurers take more responsibility for valuation of the property insured. If the likely value is above a certain level, insurers may pay all or part of the cost of valuation. In practice throughout the market, what insurers are more likely to do is pay the claim in full, less the amount of the difference between the premium paid and what the premium would have been if the property had been fully insured. What insurers cannot do, as long as insurance was contracted and the subsequent claim was made in good faith, as in *Economides*, is refuse to pay at all on the ground of misrepresentation at the time the insurance was contracted.

Non-disclosure

Insurers, on the one side, and applicants for insurance and policyholders, on the other, owe each other a duty described as one of good faith. This is sometimes referred to as the rule requiring 'utmost' good faith,[74] thus to distinguish it from the more general duty of good faith found, for example, in French and German law, or in England in the Unfair Terms in Consumer Contracts Regulations 1999.[75] According to English insurance law, the duty is largely a duty of information, and its main application is the disclosure of information at the time of making or renewing the insurance contract. Moreover, although the duty of disclosure is owed by both parties,[76] it mainly affects the applicant.

Applicants for insurance must disclose all information which, in the language of the MIA 1906, section 18(2), 'would influence the judgment of a prudent insurer in fixing the premium, or determining whether he will take the risk'; this also expresses the common law rule for non-marine insurance. If an applicant does not disclose the required information, the consent of the insurer is flawed and, although not entitled to damages, the insurer is entitled to rescind the

---

[73] *British & Foreign Ins. Co. Ltd v Wilson Shipping Co. Ltd* [1921] 1 AC 188, 214.
[74] E.g., J. Birds, 'Good faith in the reform of insurance law' (2004) 54 Amicus Curiae 3–9, 5.
[75] SI 1999/2083. See Chapter 7, p. 268 ff.
[76] *Banque Financière v Westgate Ins. Co.* [1990] QB 665 (CA), aff'd [1991] 2 AC 249.

contract.[77] Before looking more closely at the duty as it affects the applicant, we shall look first at the duty as it affects the insurer.

The Duty of Insurers

The practical scope of the duty of disclosure to be observed by insurers is unclear, but there is agreement that insurers must disclose to applicants any facts known to them but not to applicants which reduce the risk. Is that all? Cicero, as jurist, might have thought not. Before selling corn in the market when supplies are low and prices high, the seller, he thought, should tell the potential buyer about the imminent arrival of supplies that would lower the price.[78] Pothier agreed.[79] Commerce in England, however, is more pragmatic and less high-minded, and English insurance law takes its tone from commerce; insurers are not obliged to tell applicants that similar cover is available around the corner at a lower premium.[80] Nonetheless, can insurers remain silent about the qualities of the cover itself?

Cover

If the cover proposed does not adequately meet the needs of a particular applicant, the insurer may well want to point this out to the applicant in order to extend the cover and perhaps increase the premium. However, failure to do so does not breach the duty of disclosure or any other duty owed by insurers to applicants, unless an applicant seeks advice about the cover required and the insurer's response falls short of what can reasonably be expected.[81] Giving advice of this kind is not usually the role of insurers. The common law tradition of 'buyer beware', much modified in sales of goods to consumers, appears to remain for those who buy insurance. This, perhaps, is because of the market tradition that applicants, as buyers of insurance, should get advice from a broker about what to buy;[82] if they do not, applicants take the risk of buying inadequate cover. Today, however, this tradition needs to be reconsidered in view of the move, in particular by consumers, to direct contracting with insurers. Unless the applicant is a corporate risk manager, if it is apparent to an insurer that the applicant has no adviser and is not buying cover that really meets the applicant's needs, arguably, the position in law should be different.

The common law rule, that sellers of goods implicitly promise that the goods sold are suitable for the apparent purposes of buyers, became section 14 of the Sale of Goods Act 1979; but there is no corresponding statutory rule for services,

---

[77] See below, p. 116 ff.   [78] *De Officiis*, Book III, XII, paras 50 ff.
[79] *Traité du Contrat de Vente*, Pt II, ch. II, Art. III, 554 (1781), reported by M. Fabre-Magnan *De l'obligation d' Information dans les Contrats* (Paris, 1992), para. 33 ff.
[80] *Laidlaw v Organ* 15 US (2 Wheat) 178.
[81] See, e.g., *Fletcher v Manitoba Public Ins. Co.* (1989) 58 DLR (4th) 23 (CA Ont., 1989).
[82] See Chapter 3, p. 69 ff.

such as insurance. In France it has been argued that a duty of this kind is to be found in all contracts for goods or services,[83] as part of a movement to promote efficient markets and openness in dealings. In Finland, insurers are specifically required by statute to give applicants the information needed to assist them to assess the insurance required and to make a sound choice, including 'such as information regarding forms of insurance, premiums and insurance conditions'.[84] At the very least, lawyers in England should ask whether in this respect sellers of insurance should be in a position different from sellers of bread. Indeed, they will find that increasingly, and from different quarters, sellers cannot retreat in silence behind the old adage *caveat emptor*.

Neither the insurer nor the insurer's agents are obliged at common law to advise on the suitability of the policy, the strategy. In practice they often do advise at this 'macro' level and, in addition, something often overlooked, they may be obliged to advise at the 'micro' level of terms and conditions. As we have seen, they have an obligation of a kind (albeit rarely carried out) to point out restrictions on cover; and there is a rule of general contract law that a contracting party proffering its own contract terms must draw to the attention of the other party any unusual and onerous contract terms.[85] Of course this is the last thing sellers of insurance want to have to spend time on, and the duty has been often 'overlooked'. If, however, a seller does so, or feels compelled to respond to associated enquiries from the applicant, the seller will have to respond with professional competence and in a way that takes account of the applicant's apparent needs. This duty now has statutory backing.[85a]

Not surprisingly, it appears that the FOS is more demanding. One complaint to the FOS concerned household contents cover to a person, who was obviously well endowed with the material things of life, sold without pointing out to the buyer that possessions worth more than £500 were not covered unless itemized. When burglars deprived the policyholder of a number of such items, the FOS required the insurer to pay the policyholder in full.[86]

Scarcely less surprising is that on certain matters insurers are now affected by new rules from Brussels. On 31 October 2004, the UK implemented by regulation the Directive on the Distance Marketing of Consumer Financial Services (EC 2002/65). The Financial Services (Distance Marketing) Regulations 2004[87] set minimum standards for the information that must be provided to consumers before they enter certain financial services contracts, among them contracts of insurance. Distance marketing occurs when there is no personal contact with the consumer but the transaction is conducted through the Internet, or by post, or by telephone. The Regulations also provide the consumer with a right of withdrawal without penalty within 14 days or, in the case of life insurance, 30 days.

[83] Fabre-Magnan, op. cit. above, n. 79, para. 303 ff.   [84] Insurance Act 1994, s. 5.
[85] See above, pp. 90–1; also p. 63.   [85a] See above, p. 69 ff.
[86] Case 23/11, *Ombudsman News* No. 23 (December 2002).
[87] SI 2004/2095. See also p. 61.

Performance

Just as applicants must disclose the 'quality' of the risk, including the 'moral hazard', so also insurers should disclose more than most do about the quality of the 'product'. Indeed, certain insurers have been censured by the Advertising Standards Authority for a misleading presentation of the benefits offered. Among the most important instances in the past was that of life insurance sold as a financial product. In 1993, the *Financial Times* was moved to condemn the 'inadequate disclosure of surrender values' and the 'absurd practice' in the life industry of projecting returns on the basis of industry-wide costs instead of individual life offices' costs. The newspaper complained that lack of disclosure has long prevented investors from comparing the insurance industry's financial products with a straightforward investment in equities, gilts, or building societies; and that many in the insurance industry appear incapable of recognizing that the widespread sale of poor products to the wrong people under the cloak of inadequate disclosure was undermining public confidence.

In the present climate of general hostility to the way insurers have sold products in the past, in particular with the misselling of pension products and the like, it is clear that a more general duty of disclosure about what applicants are getting for the money 'invested' should be imposed. This is the work of the FSA, the source of detailed regulation on such matters which, however, is beyond the scope of this book.

The Duty of Applicants

In *Carter v Boehm*,[88] the landmark case on disclosure, Lord Mansfield said:

Insurance is a contract upon speculation. The special facts, upon which the contingent chance is to be computed, lie most commonly in the knowledge of the insured only; the underwriter trusts to his representation, and proceeds upon confidence that he does not keep back any circumstance in his knowledge to mislead the underwriter into a belief that the circumstance does not exist, and to induce him to estimate the risque, as if it did not exist.

The duty of disclosure is said to be necessary for the protection of insurers. To claim under a policy, the claimant policyholder must prove insurance that covers the loss, to which the insurer has agreed by contract. If it appears that indeed the insurer has made such a contract, that is enough. The claimant does not have to prove performance of the duty of disclosure at the time of contracting. It is for the insurer who wishes to resist a claim (and rescind the contract) to establish non-disclosure by the policyholder. More specifically, the insurer must prove (a) non-disclosure of (b) a material fact (c) known to the policyholder at the time of contract. Even so, having proved this, the insurer's defence will fail if the

---

[88] (1766) 3 Burr 1905, 1909. Generally, see Clarke, ch. 23.

claimant proves that (d) the fact was known also to the insurer, or (e) disclosure was waived by the insurer.

Proof of Disclosure and Non-disclosure

Full disclosure by applicants for insurance is presumed unless the insurer proves otherwise. In the simple case of standard cover and a proposal form, what is decisive is whether the material fact is mentioned in the form; courts are prepared to infer that, if the matter had been disclosed, it would have been done on the form and not in some other way—assuming that there was a place on the form for information of the kind in issue. In a less simple case, it depends on the evidence, on who and what the judge believes. In the past, courts have been more inclined to believe insurers than claimants. In a leading case, the experienced Scrutton LJ found in favour of the insurer, because, he said, it is 'inconceivable to me that the ordinary rate of premium should be charged [as it was] for a cargo as to which an underwriter knew the relevant information'.[89]

Whether a judge of today, who is aware of some of the disastrous underwriting by certain insurers in the recent past, would have quite so much confidence in the judgement of London underwriters we cannot be sure. What is clear is that the FOS is likely to be more sceptical than Sir Thomas Scrutton. If insurers simply assert non-disclosure and refuse to pay an otherwise valid claim, most claimants are poorly placed to dispute the matter and the FOS may well come to the rescue by insisting that insurers prove non-disclosure. In a common case, that of direct insurance contracted by telephone, for example, any insurer who cannot produce a record of the conversation is likely to fail.[90]

Disclosure to Whom

The law requires that disclosure be to the insurer. Applicants may have difficulty identifying the actual underwriter,[91] who assesses the application for insurance, but the law has developed to deal with this difficulty.

First, anyone in business of any kind who has a telephone, telex, or telefax, and who lets the numbers be known, represents to the world that any message that reaches one of those numbers during business hours will be dealt with properly and promptly.[92] The same can be said of a postal[93] or e-mail address. Hence disclosure takes place when the message reaches the recipient's number or address during business hours, or, if out of hours, when business can be expected to resume.

Secondly, in the case of insurance, it is not necessary that the communication be sent directly to the actual underwriter. It is enough to send it to an agent who

[89] *Greenhill v Federal Ins. Co. Ltd* [1927] 1 KB 65 79 (CA).
[90] See, e.g., case studies 13/07 and 13/15 reported in *Ombudsman News*, January 2002; and case study 18/01 reported in *Ombudsman News*, July 2002.   [91] See Chapter 3, p. 58 ff.
[92] *Tenax Steamship Co. v Owners of the Motor Vessel Brimnes* [1975] QB 929, 945, *per* Megaw LJ (CA).
[93] *Holwell Securities v Hughes* [1974] 1 All ER 161, 164, *per* Russell LJ (CA).

has been held out by the insurer as an appropriate line of communication to the insurer; this includes the insurer's local agent. So great, however, is the potential for confusion in the mind of applicants about who is who in the world of insurance, that the Insurance Ombudsman went a step further than the law and treated *any* person who solicits or negotiates a contract of insurance as an agent of the insurer for purposes of this kind.[94] The FOS is likely to follow suit.

In the case of communication via agents, however, disclosure take place not at once, when the information is received by the agent, but within a reasonable time thereafter, that is, the time reasonably required for communication of the information by the agent to the right person, the actual underwriter, within the insurance company.[95] In an age of rapid communication, the time is short; but the rule has not lost all importance because of a tendency to seek to save time, and thus money, by doing things at the last minute.

The Prudent Insurer

The rule of disclosure, the benchmark of the information needed to assess the risk proposed, refers to the judgement of the 'prudent insurer'. The prudent insurer is a hypothetical market figure. With the exception of the Lloyd's marine market,[96] generally applicants for insurance of one kind must disclose if they have had an application refused for another kind. They must tell a prospective fire insurer whether they have been burgled, and vice versa, which is not at all what many applicants expect. Applicants should seek advice; those who do not do so take a serious risk. If the matter is disputed in court, the court receives evidence of market opinion; the court views that evidence with both respect and, occasionally, scepticism. Nonetheless, that is the evidence that determines what is expected by way of disclosure on the part of applicants; this aspect of the disclosure rule is harsh in several respects.

First, applicants may well think that the questions in the application form are the best guide to what prudent insurers need to know and, therefore, to the matters material to the risk which, if possible, must be disclosed. Indeed, if an insurer does ask questions, whether in the form or on the telephone, that is some evidence of materiality, but is that either conclusive or exhaustive of the information required? In some countries, such as Finland,[97] Germany,[98] and the United States,[99] there is a legal presumption along those lines. In most European countries the disclosure duty is qualified in some such way,[100] but not in England.[101] Applicants in England may complete the form with scrupulous care, but still find that there was something else material to prudent insurers

---

[94] The Insurance Ombudsman, Annual Report 1989, No. 2.14.
[95] *Wing v Harvey* (1854) 5 De G, M & G 265.
[96] *Glasgow Assurance v Symondsen* (1911) 16 Com Cas 109, 119, *per* Scrutton J.
[97] Insurance Act 1994, s. 22.   [98] *BGH 25 March 1992*, NJW 1992, 1506.
[99] *INA v US Gypsum*, 870 F 2d 148, 153 (4 Cir., 1989).   [100] See Basedow and Fock, 69 ff.
[101] *McCormick v National Motor & Accident Ins. Union Ltd* (1934) 49 Ll L Rep 361, 363 (CA).

which, apparently, the particular insurer did not think to ask about but which, nonetheless, the applicant was expected to think of and disclose. The Insurance Ombudsman[102] and (now) the FOS, having a jurisdiction that permits decisions on the basis of what is fair and reasonable, have taken a different line; if the insurer does not ask clear questions about something, the insurer has waived disclosure of the matter. That seems fair and reasonable indeed, but it is still not the rule of English law.

Secondly, if the prudent insurer considers information material, it is irrelevant that applicants have no idea that this is so. How many people who have just been allotted a company car and are seeking cover for their family car realize that, because the family car will be more available to be driven by their children, they must tell the insurer? Anyone who ventures into the realm of insurance must take a guide, an adviser, or take a chance. This is a demanding rule, which probably originated at a time when insurers could avoid the contract only by proving that the applicant had withheld information fraudulently; to make that proof practicable, the law adopted an objective market view of what was material. Today, however, the legal boot is on the other foot—the insurer's foot—but, once again, the Insurance Ombudsman Bureau (IOB) and subsequently the FOS have softened the effect on consumers. The IOB dropped the market test nearly twenty years ago in preference for a test of what the reasonable applicant (or reasonable insured) would consider material;[103] if the insurer wants to know more, it is for the insurer to enquire. In the UK this was the (unimplemented) recommendation of the Law Reform Committee as far back as 1957.[104] Since 1984 this has also been the law, for example, in Australia.[105] It is still not the law of England.

Thirdly, material information is any information which would influence the judgement of a prudent insurer when contracting the insurance, in even the slightest degree. In England, information is material if it would have had some influence, although perhaps no more than to confirm a contract of insurance that the particular insurer would have been willing to make anyway. The rule in many other countries is that the information must have been decisive, in the sense that, if the prudent insurer had been told, the insurer would not have made the contract or would have made it on different terms. That is not the rule of law in England.

Lastly, the prudent insurer must be fed 'facts'. Confusingly, however, a material 'fact' sometimes includes opinion. Indeed the appetite of the prudent insurer for opinions has increased in line with that of the public for fatty food. Obviously, a medical 'opinion' that an applicant for life insurance has cancer is a fact, that the specialist holds that opinion, which must not be withheld: it has to be disclosed.[106] The opinion of a gossip columnist that a celebrated singer is anorexic does not.

---

[102] See The IOB, Annual Report 1994, p. 23.   [103] IOB, Annual Report 1989, para. 2.16.
[104] Cmnd 62 (1957), p. 7.   [105] Insurance Contracts Act, s. 21.
[106] *British Equitable Ins. Co. v Great Western Ry* (1869) 20 LT 422.

Less obviously, although applicants charged with a criminal offence remain 'innocent until proved guilty', the opinion of the prosecutor that they are guilty, that is, the fact of the charge, has to be disclosed.[107] The opinion of the *Daily Wail* that immigrants are likely to be thieves does not. Less obviously still, if an applicant has not only been charged but tried and acquitted, nonetheless the fact of the trial and acquittal must also be disclosed. Insurance contract law says that insurers, the grandest of juries, must be allowed to make up their own minds on the matter.[108] That is not all. The latest and, in the view of some, last straw in this cold wind for aspiring policyholders is the disclosure of rumours. It has been held that if a relevant allegation, or even a rumour, has 'some substance' when insurance is contracted, it must be disclosed to the insurer.[109] Applicants about whom outrageous libels have been printed in the tabloid press, thick or thin, will be yet further outraged to be told that, although utterly and correctly convinced of their righteousness, they must repeat the libel to insurers. All must be confessed to the 'priest from the Pru', but without any assurance of either cover or absolution.

Information Known to the Applicant

Although, as we have just seen, English law does not excuse the non-disclosure of information which applicants have but do not have reason to think relevant, the law does not require applicants to disclose information which they do not have at all. However, applicants may well be surprised by what the law expects of the human memory. Ignorance is one thing; forgetfulness another. Applicants must disclose not only information actually in mind when contracting or information which, if prompted, the applicant could recall, but also information which the applicant once knew but has completely forgotten: once known, always known. No allowance is made for age; the person with a bad memory is expected to have a good notepad. Worse, applicants are expected to disclose some matters which they never actually knew at all, matters of imputed knowledge. They are deemed to know what people in their position would be expected to know of their own affairs and of the world immediately around them, as well as what was or should have been known to their agents.

Imputed knowledge of this kind includes the accumulation of past experience, both at work and in the world around them.[110] When insuring a car applicants are expected to know whether named drivers will use it for business or not. When insuring life or health, after being advised to undergo medical treatment, applicants are not expected to know with any precision the name or nature of the condition, but they are expected to know that something is wrong and, when contracting insurance, to tell the insurer. Such matters are easily misunderstood,

[107] *March Cabaret & Casino Club Ltd v London Assurance* [1975] 1 Lloyd's Rep 169.
[108] *The Grecia Express* [2002] EWHC 203 (Comm), [2002] 2 Lloyd's Rep 88, 130.
[109] Ibid., 130–2. Confirmed in *North Star Shipping v Sphere Drake* [2006] 2 Lloyd's Rep 183, (CA).
[110] Such a rule, also applicable to non-marine business, is found in MIA 1906, s. 18(1).

forgotten, or repressed nonetheless; and some insurers of medical expenses have required the completion of an application form with as many as sixty specific questions about present and past medical complaints. Given that the required history may go back many years, the completion of such a form may be difficult. Sensible advice from brokers has been that applicants should add a disclaimer, such as 'in case I have forgotten something, please consult my GP, Dr X'. An insurer that does not do so will be deemed to have waived disclosure of any material information the doctor might have supplied.[111]

Applicants' agents are, first, any agent employed to contract the insurance and, secondly, any agent employed for some other purpose but who receives, collates, or handles material information. An applicant may not know what information has come in; but, knowing that the agent is there to deal with the information, the applicant planning to contract insurance is expected to ask the agent about it. In a particular case there may be more than one such agent. Similarly, when the applicant is a company, the knowledge of the company may be composite. In a leading case,[112] one director contracted insurance for the company, and the other director, who was also the chairman and main shareholder but took little active part in the company, signed the cheques for premium. For the purpose of disclosure, the knowledge of the company was held to be the combined knowledge of both, so the contract was avoidable for non-disclosure of matters known to the chairman but not to the director who contracted the insurance. Exception is made, however, for the knowledge of any senior colleagues when the knowledge is that they were planning to defraud the company.[113] The left side of the corporate brain can plead ignorance of what is known to the right when the right is not right at all but doing wrong!

Information Known to the Insurer

Applicants are not obliged to disclose material information already known to the insurer. They should not expect much. The knowledge of insurers is more diffuse, less focused on the particular risk than that of applicants, whose risk it is. Further, although it might be thought that insurers would have considerable general knowledge of the area of risk covered by their line of business, English law expects very little of them—either as regards what they should know from their agents, or from their own files.

As regards agents, insurers, like applicants, are taken to know what is known, first, by any agent employed to contract the insurance and, secondly, by any agent employed to receive, collate, or handle information of the relevant kind. In this respect, both the points of knowledge and the lines of communication are important.[114]

---

111 *Asfar & Co. v Blundell* [1896] 1 QB 123 (CA); Clarke, 23-13A.
112 *Regina Fur Co. Ltd v Bossom* [1957] 2 Lloyd's Rep 466.
113 *PCW Syndicates v PCW Reinsurers* [1996] 1 WLR 1136 (CA).
114 See above, pp. 102–3.

As regards accumulated data and general knowledge, since the early days of insurance insurers have been presumed to be acquainted with the practice of the trade or context they insure. For example, fire insurers are taken to know that 'corner' shops might stock fireworks in October and early November;[115] and yacht insurers are taken to know that, if yachts are laid up for the winter in Spain, a certain level of theft and vandalism is to be expected.[116]

Generally, however, insurers are not expected to keep up with current affairs in Spain or anywhere else. On the one hand, they are expected to know of important public events at the time of contracting, and to make any connection between those events and the risk proposed. In one case, an insurer doing fire business in Ireland was expected to be aware that there were terrorists there who might well set fire to anything English.[117] On the other hand, the insurer is not expected to recall events reported in the recent past, however prominent at the time, which appeared to have no bearing on the insurer's business at that time but which turn out to be relevant to a risk proposed later. This is the effect of the old, controversial but nonetheless leading case of *Bates v Hewitt*.[118]

The Problem of Information Retrieval

Bates v Hewitt concerned the insurance in London of a merchant ship, *The Georgia*. Previously she had been a notorious warship in the American civil war. This greatly increased the risk to the ship after her conversion to a merchant ship, a matter of great public interest in England at the time. On her very first voyage she was captured by the old enemy. The insurers said that the new owner should have told them about her history and conversion three months before insuring her. The Court agreed. Busy underwriters, keenly focused on the business in hand, may well have short memories; but might they not be expected, as a matter of sound business practice, to have a cutting service (or something of the kind) to collect and accumulate information, which not only is but also *might* be of importance in the future, in retrievable form? Today insurers do not even have to collect much of the information themselves, but can access it, as required, via Nexis or the internet. Indeed, some insurers today do both, but can this be expected of them by the court? In *Bates* Cockburn CJ thought not,[119] and this remains the position of English law. We should, he said,

be sanctioning an encroachment on a most important principle, . . . if we were to hold that a party . . . may speculate as to what may or may not be in the mind of the underwriter, or as to what may or may not be brought to his mind by the particulars disclosed to him by the insured . . . If we were to sanction such a course, especially in these days, when parties frequently forget the rules of mercantile faith and honour which

---

[115] *Hales v Reliance* [1960] 2 Lloyd's Rep 391.
[116] *The Moonacre* [1992] 2 Lloyd's Rep 501, 517.
[117] *Lean v Hall* (1923) 16 Ll L Rep 100.   [118] (1867) LR 2 QB 595.
[119] Ibid., 606–7.

used to distinguish this country from any other, we should be lending ourselves to innovations of a dangerous and monstrous character, which I think we ought not to do.

Mercantile faith and honour may or may not have improved since 1867, but the means of collating, collecting, and recalling information have improved greatly. Still, a similar principle was applied again in 1994 in *Malhi*.[120] *Bates* was not cited, still less challenged. The argument of the life claimant in *Malhi*, that the insurer had imputed knowledge of a medical record submitted to the company, was rejected on evidence that it was not received by anyone who would appreciate its significance to the policy on which the claim was based, and market evidence that it was impractical to expect underwriters to search their records when they had no reason to think they might find material information. Indeed so, not least because, in *Malhi*, the insurer's records were on paper; however, in the last ten years since *Malhi*, science has not stood still.

Modern technology aids enquiry. For example, fire insurers wondering about a corporate applicant can buy an anti-arson financial referencing system. Assuming, as insurers do, that temptation rises when profits fall, this system enables them to check key indicators in published accounts and court judgments affecting the moral hazard of a corporate applicant; and then the same system presents the underwriter with an assessment of the quality of the risk.[121] Today's technology has enabled insurers themselves to store information in vast quantities and to retrieve it at speed. Software is now in use which enables any accredited employee of the insurer to call up the claims history of any policyholder, with images of all original documents and thus without the paperchase through the insurer's different departments that was necessary in the past. Surely, a data mart for the underwriting department is an obvious and easy replacement for the old basement. The *Bates* decision is a precedent from a Dickensian world of paper and pink ribbon, a world which is sold to other countries by the BBC but which, in most matters, they have left behind. In the United States and in Canada, if insurers fail to look in their data files, they are deemed to have waived disclosure of the information which the files contain.[122] So it should be in England today.

The rational rule of law is said to be one that minimizes 'the joint costs of a potential mistake by assigning the risk of its occurrence to the party who is the better (cheaper) information-gatherer'.[123] The inclination against a rule that discourages or impedes the search for information is seen, for example, in modern decisions of the Canadian Supreme Court. The Court has held that a liability insurer should have been aware of the dangers of asbestos at a time when these

---

[120] *Malhi v Abbey Life Assurance Co. Ltd* [1996] LRLR 237 (CA).

[121] See also the Claims and Underwriting Exchange (CUE): below, Chapter 6, p. 209 ff.

[122] Respectively, *Columbia National Life Ins. Co. v Rodgers*, 116 F 2d 705 (10 Cir., 1940), cert. den. 314 US 637; *Coronation Ins. Co. v Taku Air Transport Ltd* (1991) 85 DLR (4th) 609, 623.

[123] A. T. Kronman, 'Mistake, Disclosure, Information, and the Law of Contracts', 7 *J Legal Studies* 1, 4 (1978).

dangers had become a matter of notoriety in the press, both technical and general;[124] and that an aviation insurer should have scanned the public records of accidents that might have a bearing on the risk proposed.[125] The *Bates* rule is inefficient, as it deprives insurers of incentive to acquire available information by investigating risk, because they know that, if a risk turns out to be worse than it seemed when they rated it, they can still fall back on rules of disclosure from 1867 to avoid the contract. Clearly, this is not good for policyholders and, in that insurance is there to spread risk, it is not good for society at large. Nor is it good for insurers in general to plead ignorance in this way, as it does little for the public perception of insurers.

Marine and Non-marine Insurance

A further but distinct reason for reservations about *Bates*[126] is that it was a case of marine insurance. In England, commercial judges have shown respect, almost reverence, for the law of marine insurance, in which until recent years so many of them excelled at the Bar, and to be perhaps rather too ready to pipe its rules ashore to regulate other branches of insurance. Most of the rules of law discussed in this book apply equally to marine and non-marine insurance, but in many other countries, such as the United States, the law keeps them apart. On this particular point, for a number of reasons English law should follow that of the United States.

First, in many respects, the non-marine insurer is in a better position through inspectors and technical expertise to assess the risk and to elicit material information. For the marine insurer, however,

the subject of insurance is generally beyond the reach, and not open to the inspection, of the underwriter, often in distant ports or upon the high seas. Moreover, even today the peculiar perils to which it may be exposed, may well be too numerous to be anticipated or inquired about, known only to the owners and those in their employ; while [the fire risk] is or may be, seen and inspected before the risk is assumed, and its construction, situation and ordinary hazards are as well appreciated by the underwriters as by the owner. In marine insurance, the underwriter . . . is obliged to rely upon the assured, and has, therefore, the right to exact a full disclosure of all facts known to him, which may in any way affect the risk to be assumed. But in fire insurance no such necessity for reliance exists, and, if the underwriter assumes the risk without taking the trouble to either examine, or inquire, he cannot very well, in the absence of fraud, complain that it turns out to be greater than anticipated.

This was the view of a court in Ohio back in 1853,[127] but it was adopted by most courts of the United States in later years, and in substance by the report of the

---

[124] *Canadian Indemnity Co. v Canadian Johns-Manville Co.* (1990) 72 DLR (4th) 478.
[125] *Coronation Ins. Co. v Taku Air Transport Ltd*, op. cit. above, n. 122.
[126] *Bates v Hewitt*, op. cit. above, n. 118.
[127] *Hartford v Harmer* 2 Ohio St. 452, 472 (1853).

Australian Law Commission in 1982. Some risks, such as that of piracy in the Straits of Malacca, are well documented today, but others are not, and in spite of satellites and other tracking devices, the *Bates* rule is less difficult to justify in the law of marine insurance than that of non-marine insurance. Nonetheless, unless clearly inappropriate, courts in England tend to apply the MIA 1906 to non-marine cases, and this is certainly true of sections 18 and 19 on disclosure. In Europe at large it is different.

In Italy the position is similar to that in England, but in reverse. The Civil Code has provisions for non-marine insurance[128] which apply also to marine insurance, except when there is a specific provision on the matter in the Code of Navigation; but the Code dates from the end of the nineteenth century. There is a more recent but more restricted version of the Italian position in Greece, where the Insurance Policy Act of 1997[129] on non-marine insurance also applies to marine insurance when there is no corresponding provision in the Code of Private Maritime Law. Nonetheless, in Europe today, in countries where there is substantial shipping activity, there is something of a trend to have separate legislation, especially as regards the duties of information, for marine and non-marine insurance. The trend is to be seen in France, where the general Insurance Code has a separate and substantial section on marine insurance. In Germany too, marine insurance is separately regulated, albeit not in the general insurance legislation but in a distinct section of the commercial code.[130] That is also the position in Spain, where marine insurance is covered in the commercial code[131] and there is distinct legislation for non-marine insurance.[132] German insurance law is currently under review but, whatever the outcome, marine insurance will be dealt with separately.[133] Perhaps the clearest example is found in the Norwegian Marine Insurance Plan,[134] a modern and comprehensive code of marine insurance, of which the Central Union of Marine Underwriters in Norway is justifiably proud.

Facts that Diminish Risk

Information suggesting that the risk is less great than might otherwise appear does, of course, affect risk; but it has been long established that applicants do not have to mention it to the insurer. An example would be extra security installations in the factory to be insured. Applicants may well choose to do so in order to argue for a reduction in premium, but they are not obliged to.

Waiver

In the 1940s, commentators were concerned about the length of application forms. The chance of innocent but inaccurate answers by applicants increased

---

[128] Civil Code, Arts 1895–1898.   [129] Law No. 2496/1997.
[130] Paras 778 to 900 HGB.   [131] Art. 737 ff.   [132] Ley de contrato de seguro 1980.
[133] Abschlussbericht der Kommission zur Reform des Versicherungsvertragsrecht, para. 1.2.2.1.2.3.
[134] http://exchange.dnv.com/NMIP/.

with the number of questions on the form. Since then, practice in certain sectors such as motor business, where insurers are keen to sell insurance to buyers with a short attention span for such things, has moved from a catechism, in which applicants were asked too much, to quick cover, for which they are asked too little. The move did not quell argument from insurers that the insurance could be avoided later on the ground that an applicant did not provide information—information which the insurer did not ask for and which the applicant did not know was required.[135]

Any practice of this kind was clearly contrary to the Guidance Notes published by the ABI in connection with the General Business Code of Practice concerning to telephone sales and direct marketing, which requires that 'key questions' should be asked of applicants for insurance.[136] Moreover, it is the practice of the FOS to insist on clear proof by insurers of non-disclosure and, in effect, a recording of the exchange between applicant and insurer; so, if insurers cannot prove the negative of non-disclosure, the avoidance argument fails.[137] However, any such argument should fail, even in a court of law, because applicants do not have to disclose information the disclosure of which has been waived by the insurer. Waiver is a frequent and sometimes fertile line of argument advanced for claimant policyholders, which takes more than one form.

Waiver of All Information

One argument is that insurers have waived disclosure of information of a certain type. Cargo insurers, for example, would like to know about the safety record of ships and shipowners carrying the cargo they insure, but, for sound practical reasons, disclosure of this information is waived by the common standard forms for cargo insurance. The main reason is that applicants wanting to send cargo often have no idea which ship will carry the cargo, still less its record, because it is all arranged by forwarding agents whose choice may not be made until the last moment; moreover, carriers often reserve the right to change the appointed ship. Insurers cannot and do not expect applicants to disclose what they cannot reasonably discover. However, if a particular policyholder has a run of 'bad luck' with cargo sent, that may be the result of the policyholder's choice of agents, and the insurer concerned may be inclined to load the premium of that policyholder for that reason.

More contentious is the view of the IOB that insurers who ask no questions at all waive disclosure altogether.[138] The view has been maintained by the FOS,[139] although the established rule of law is quite different.[140] Whether the IOB view can be sustained in a court of law depends on why the insurers did not ask questions. If the reason lies in the way they have chosen to market the cover,

---

[135] See above, p. 103 ff.   [136] Now the FSA regulations; see above, Chapter 3, p. 63 ff.
[137] See above, p. 102.   [138] The Insurance Ombudsman, Annual Report 1991, para. 2.19.
[139] E.g., Case 25/15, *Ombudsman News*, February 2003.   [140] See above, p. 103 ff.

there is force in the view of the IOB and FOS that the insurers have waived disclosure. That would be the case of travel insurers who find it expedient to sell cover through travel agents or post offices; and motor insurers who cover people who rent cars or vans. If applicants were to start to tell assistants in the travel agency about their hernias, they would be unlikely to get much encouragement!

The same can be said of any insurers who sell by telephone to the extent that they cannot produce a record of having asked the key 'questions'. All these sales share the feature that, knowing that the less the formality and fuss the more likely people are to buy, insurers deliberately forgo any real opportunity for enquiry into the particular risk. By contracting in this way, surely, insurers take the risk in an extra sense—they enter the transaction eyes closed. However, although their eyes may be closed, they know what they are doing; expecting a certain percentage of poor risks, insurers adjust the premiums accordingly. The risk is theirs in every sense.[141]

Waiver of Certain Information by Implication

Subject to what has just been argued, the general rule remains that, if insurers omit to ask questions about the risk, that is not waiver on their part.[142] For waiver, the law requires a positive representation. However, if insurers ask questions about some matters but not other, related matters, that may amount to waiver (by omission) of disclosure of the latter.[143] For example, if they ask about fires in the property to be insured over the last five years, that is waiver of information about any fires before that. This appears to be a feature of much direct insurance contracted on the telephone, if insurers do not ask all the usual 'key questions' about the risk. Like fast food outlets, these insurers offer applicants what applicants want, quick and cheap insurance with minimum fuss. Insurers too get what they want, more customers and fewer transaction costs. Who should bear the risks of indigestion? Clearly, the insurers, who are in a better position to spread the risk.

When I go to be checked by my doctor, I want to be in and out of the surgery as quickly as possible, and to be told that all is well. The doctor knows that; it is also what the doctor wants to tell me, not only to make me happy but because the waiting room is full. Yet no responsible doctor would overtly prune the list of patients to cherry-pick the strong and decline the weak. Nor would that doctor cut short the investigation and grant me a clean bill of health, and later, when cancer is found, disclaim responsibility because I did not disclose that I was passing blood. Direct insurance is a marketing method made possible by modern technology, which has been adopted by insurers mainly because it cuts costs and, they believe, gives them a competitive edge. A rule of general contract law is that

---

[141] USA in this sense: see *Uslife Credit Life Ins. Co. v McAfee*, 630 P 2d 450, 454 (CA Wn, 1981).
[142] *McCormick v National Motor & Accident Ins. Union Ltd* (1934) 49 Ll L Rep 361, 363 (CA).
[143] *Roberts v Plaisted* [1989] 2 Lloyd's Rep 341, 347 (CA).

the risks of the medium (e.g., delays in the post) are borne by the party that chose the medium. Although the first telephone call comes from potential applicants, the medium is chosen and publicized by the insurer. The insurer calls the tune and chooses the instrument; and it is the insurer, surely, who takes the risk of information adverse to the risk insured that inquiry would have revealed. In the language of current law, the insurer has waived disclosure.

Waiver of Certain Available Information

If information has been disclosed to insurers, information such that they are put on enquiry, then it can be said that, if they require the rest of the information, they could and should seek it out; and that, if they do not, disclosure of the rest has been waived.[144] This is the case, in particular, if applicants volunteer information, which is evidently incomplete but sufficient to alert the insurer to the possibility that there is more to be had, that might be material.

For example, if an applicant gives the insurer the opportunity to consult specific documents, such as the applicant's records, or refers the insurer to a document to which the insurer has access, the applicant is considered to have disclosed the contents of all the documents concerned.[145] Similarly, if, having been told that the applicant has been ill, the insurer obtains the applicant's permission to consult the applicant's doctor but does not do so, the insurer cannot plead non-disclosure of information which consultation would have revealed.[146] So too, more generally, if health insurers ask about basic factors, such as age, sex, location, occupation, and smoking habits, but do not require medical tests, arguably they waive any material information that normal tests would have revealed. The landmark case, however, concerned a very different world back in 1759. Insurance was contracted on 'Fort Marlborough' which was located, as the insurer was aware, in a potential theatre of war. It was Lord Mansfield who held that it was for the insurer to enquire about the defences, which turned out to be weak, and the likelihood of successful attack.[147]

The Time of Disclosure

The duty of disclosure must be performed at certain points of time during the contractual relationship between policyholder and insurer. These are the conclusion of the initial contract, renewal of that contract, and variation of the contract: the times when the parties, mainly the insurer, have a decision to make and information is needed in order to make that decision. The duty is limited to information which is material to the decision to be taken and which has not already been disclosed or waived. Policyholders often overlook the duty at the

---

144 *Asfar v Blundell* [1896] 1 QB 123, 129 (CA).
145 *Pan Atlantic Ins. Co. Ltd v Pine Top Ins. Co. Ltd* [1993] 1 Lloyd's Rep 496 (CA).
146 *Joel v Law Union & Crown Ins. Co.* [1908] 2 KB 863, 882 (CA).
147 *Carter v Boehm* (1766) 3 Burr 1905.

time of renewal and, when the matter comes before the FOS, the FOS insists that insurers must remind policyholders clearly about the nature and scope of the duty.[148]

Insurers sometimes wish to review the risk while it is running, and perhaps to cancel the cover if it turns out that the risk is greater than expected; generally, English law does not allow this once the insurance period has begun. This is a problematic point to which we return.[149]

Disclosure or Investigation: Whose Line is it Anyway?

Most commentators outside the insurance industry agree that in most cases performance of the duty of disclosure is too difficult for most applicants or policyholders, and that the law is due for reform. Viewed from the perspective of general contract law, the disclosure rule is an unusual one born of particular times and circumstances, which no longer prevail. The time was the middle of the eighteenth century and the midwife was Lord Mansfield in *Carter v Boehm*.[150] The circumstances were those of policies, which contained few warranties, and which were written on marine risks by underwriters who were persons of general business experience; and underwriters who knew much less than the applicants about marine risks, risks which often concerned ships and cargo far away from England. In these circumstances, understandably enough, an effort was made by the judges of a trading nation not only to encourage trade, but also to encourage and develop the business of marine insurance. To a degree this meant protecting the underwriters.[151]

A rule suitable for the insurance of a ship on the other side of the ocean in 1766 is not necessarily the right rule for insurance on the life of a human body the other side of the insurer's desk today. In the United States, by the end of the nineteenth century the Mansfield rule was limited largely to marine risks;[152] and the strict marine rule did not apply to other risks, notably, but not only, fire risks, which the insurer could inspect or investigate.[153] The exception there which 'proves the rule' is reinsurance: applicants for reinsurance are obliged to put before the reinsurer all information on which they wrote the underlying risk, and reinsurers, like marine insurers of 1766, are usually not well placed to conduct an investigation of that risk and are not obliged to do so—that would be a pointless duplication of the activity and expense already incurred by applicants.[154] An element of irony lies

---

[148] *Ombudsman News*, December 2002.   [149] See below, Chapter 5, p. 161 ff.

[150] Op. cit above, n. 147.

[151] J. Oldham, *The Mansfield Manuscripts* (Chapel Hill, NC, 1992) 450–1.

[152] See above, pp. 109–10.

[153] See D. F. Cohen, T. E. DeMasi, and A. Krauss, '*Uberrimae Fidei* and Reinsurance Rescission: Does a Gentlemen's Agreement Have a Place in Today's Commercial Market?' 49 Tort & Ins LJ 602–22, 609 (1994).

[154] See S. W. Thomas, 'Utmost Good Faith in Reinsurance: A Tradition in Need of Adjustment' 41 Duke LJ 1548–97 (1992).

in the point that what we call the 'Mansfield rule' has been shown to be not what Lord Mansfield meant.

In 1867, Chief Justice Cockburn said of the Mansfield rule that 'no proposition of insurance law can be better established',[155] and that, perhaps, is why he cited no other authority. However, his understanding of the proposition was based on a very selective reading of the judgment of Lord Mansfield in *Carter v Boehm*;[156] and the Mansfield rule which Chief Justice Cockburn had in mind was not the rule in the mind of Lord Mansfield at all. The real Mansfield view, excavated by Hasson[157] a century later, is one that puts much more responsibility for obtaining information on insurers. Indeed, Hasson finds that Lord Mansfield eventually developed not just one view but two. The first view, articulated in 1787, was that to vitiate the insurance the non-disclosure must be fraudulent.[158] The second Mansfield view, dating from 1817, is that information *exclusively* known to applicants should be disclosed to insurers, but that information which insurers, 'by fair inquiry and due diligence, may learn from ordinary sources of information need not be disclosed'.[159] Of course, to observe such a rule, applicants will still be well advised to be frank about matters which ordinary sources of information might not reveal and, if in any doubt at all, to presume ignorance on the part of insurers. Nonetheless, the Mansfield rule of 1817 put the main onus of enquiry on insurers and, today, that position is significantly nearer the current rule in the United States[160] than the rule in England.

Today the reality is that health insurers, for example, can expect applicants to know (or to find out) whether their parents had arthritis; but it is insurers who are better placed to discover, for example, whether Fenland farmers are more likely to suffer arthritis than other people. Some years back property insurers started to rate property risks on the basis of the postal code, originally on the basis of the outer postcode sector (CB4), which might contain up to 3,000 houses, and later the inner sector (2AL), which might contain only fifteen houses. This, one might think, was precise indeed and precise enough. No longer. As has been pointed out,[161] within a group of fifteen houses, two might be lower than the rest and next to a river. The trend now among the larger insurers in the UK seems to involve rating on the basis of 'digital mapping', using data obtainable from the Ordnance Survey, the government body responsible for mapping the UK. The drive came from the fear of flooding. A leading company has boasted, justifiably and in public, that is has data that enable it to rate the flood risk at any given address not only in the Fens but elsewhere. In April 2004, it was announced that this would be extended to risks of subsidence, windstorm damage, and crime.

---

[155] *Bates v Hewitt,* op. cit. above, n. 118, 604.   [156] Op. cit. above, n. 147.

[157] R. A. Hasson, 'The Doctrine of *Uberrimae Fides* in Insurance Law—A Critical Evaluation' (1969) 32 MLR 615-37.   [158] See below, p. 124 ff.

[159] *Friere v Woodhouse* (1817) 1 Holt N P 572, 573.   [160] See below, p. 124 ff.

[161] *PM,* 19 August 2004, p. 12.

In 1980, a report of the English Law Commission (ELC) concluded that the law of disclosure was 'inherently unreasonable'.[162] In 1982, a report of the Australian Law Reform Commission recommended that 'a new balance should be struck between the underwriter's need for information and the insured's need for security in relying upon insurance'.[163] In Australia, the law was reformed; in England, it was not.

Remedies

Damages

In general contract law one remedy for misrepresentation is damages, either in tort for deceit, or under the Misrepresentation Act 1967. In insurance contract law the same is true in theory, but such cases rarely appear in the law reports: only when there is a lot of money at stake, a lot of blood on the carpet, and the case is too technical to attract the interest, still less the comprehension, of the tabloid press.[164] Generally insurers prefer not to (be seen to) press points in that way. Moreover, for non-disclosure no claim lies for damages anyway,[165] even in cases of fraud.[166] What insurers usually do is to refuse to pay under the policy and, as the law sees it, rescind (aka avoid) the insurance contract.

Rescission

Effect in Law

For misrepresentation, as well as for non-disclosure, the usual remedy is rescission. Rescission of the contract is achieved by the unilateral election of the party entitled to rescind,[167] without court intervention, and executed by notice to the other party. Once achieved, the effect of rescission is entirely retroactive, restoring the position between the parties to that before the contract was concluded.[168] In the case of insurance contracts, the insurer must return the premium but is discharged from any obligation to indemnify the former policyholder, not only for the future but right back to inception or to the last renewal, if any.

Typically it is insurers that seek to rescind contracts of insurance. The view is widely held that, in many cases, the remedy of rescission is out of all proportion to the flaw in consent that entitles insurers to rescind, notably when the

---

[162] No. 104, *Insurance Contracts*, para. 4–43, Cmnd 8064.   [163] No. 20, para. 175.

[164] See, however, *Hill Casualty Ins. Co. Ltd v Chase Manhattan Bank* [2003] UKHL 6, [2003] 2 Lloyd's Rep 61.   [165] *Banque Financière de la Cité v Westgate Ins. Co. Ltd* [1990] QB 665 (CA).

[166] *Hill Casualty* [2001] EWCA Civ 1250, [2001] 2 Lloyd's Rep 483, para. 163.

[167] *Reese Silver Mining Co. v Smith* (1869) LR 4 HL 64.

[168] *Abram S.S. Co. Ltd v Westville* [1923] AC 773, 781.

misrepresentation was innocent. Whereas in contracts generally rescission is often not much more than a nuisance for an innocent misrepresentor, for a former fire policyholder it may be a disaster. Contracts of insurance are usually rescinded after (fire) loss has occurred. Without cover, the former policyholder insured cannot be restored to the pre-contract, pre-fire position. A business may be left with no premises, no money to rebuild, and, sooner or later, no credit. Indeed, the parlous position of a former policyholder like this has recently been made even worse by the Court of Appeal.

Limits on the Right to Rescind

As we have seen,[169] it has been held that applicants must disclose to insurers relevant rumours, even unfounded rumours.[170] Most people would have thought that if, prior to rescission, it emerged that an undisclosed rumour was unfounded, the insurer would have lost nothing—except the right to rescind. Not so. In *Brotherton*,[171] the Court of Appeal established that the right to rescind is acquired when the contract is concluded, and its exercise is not barred by subsequent revelations. The main reason was that it would be 'an unsound step to introduce into English law a principle of law' which would enable an insured either to conceal a material rumour, or to resist avoidance later by insisting on a trial to decide whether it was true.[172] That is a sensible point, but surely the reason does not apply when the untruth of a rumour has already been established by the time that the insurer seeks to avoid the contract; no real question of costly and troublesome court proceedings can arise. Indeed, it was stated in a lower court[173] that rescission in such a case would be 'starkly unjust' and 'unconscionable' and should not allowed.

This opinion was flatly rejected in *Brotherton*, albeit *obiter*, as being contrary to precedent.[174] The 'mere fact that a right to rescind has an equitable origin does not mean that its exercise is only possible if that is consistent with good faith or with a court's view of what is "conscionable" '.[175] As to precedent, however, the picture put to the court was incomplete[176] and the overall position unclear. As to good faith, fortunately the point will not arise often, not least because insurers know that both their market and the public at large have a more developed notion of good faith than does, it seems, the law of insurance. Insurers were unlikely to assert the *Brotherton* view unless their backs were against the solvency wall or they sniffed fraud. Now it appears that the *Brotherton* view, *obiter* as it was, may not offer even insolvent insurers much protection.

---

[169] Above, pp. 104–5.

[170] *The Grecia Express* [2002] EWHC 203 (Comm), [2002] 2 Lloyd's Rep 88, 130–32.

[171] *Brotherton v Aseguradora Colseguros (No. 2)* [2003] EWCA Civ 705, [2003] All ER (Comm) 298. [172] Ibid., at [31].

[173] *The Grecia Express* op. cit. above, n. 170, 133. [174] Op. cit. above, n. 171, at [27].

[175] Ibid., at [34].

[176] Cf. notably, *Erlanger v New Sombrero Phosphate Co.* (1878) LR 3 App Cas 1218, 1279; and *Spence v Crawford* [1939] 3 All ER 271, 288 (HL).

The issue of principle came more squarely before a differently constituted Court of Appeal in *Drake*,[177] although, once again, the decision did not turn on it. On the question whether an insurer's right to avoid for non-disclosure could be constrained by the doctrine of good faith, the leading judgment of Rix LJ concluded that the doctrine of good faith should indeed 'be capable of limiting the insurer's right to avoid in circumstances where that remedy, which has been described in recent years as draconian, would operate unfairly'.[178] However, he went on to suggest that good faith would not have this effect in many cases because 'once an insured has been found wanting in good faith in the matter of pre-contractual non-disclosure, it is likely to be hard to conclude that the same doctrine of good faith itself prevents the insurer from exercising his right to avoid'.[179] That is true and, it appears, that was the situation before the Court. But it may not be so hard to reach that conclusion if an insurer should seek to rescind when it is clear to all concerned that the applicant's want of good faith was a misrepresentation or non-disclosure which did not prejudice the insurer and was entirely innocent.

Rix LJ also observed[180] that, on the whole, 'English commercial law has not favoured the process of balancing rights and wrongs under a species of what I suppose would now be called a doctrine of proportionality. Instead it has sought for stricter and simpler tests and for certainty.' But certainty is scarcely the most striking attribute of current law on this question. Moreover, the precedent cited in *Drake* came entirely from commercial insurance contract law; and Rix LJ conceded[181] that not all insurance contracts are made by those who engage in commerce and that it 'may be necessary to give wider effect to the doctrine of good faith and recognise that its impact may demand that ultimately regard must be had to a concept of proportionality implicit in fair dealing'.

In England, as long ago as 1980, the ELC thought that insurers should not be allowed the drastic remedy of rescission for non-disclosure unless the insured had been dishonest or unreasonable.[182] In Germany, for example, rescission for non-disclosure is not allowed unless the insured was 'at fault';[183] and in other countries of Europe, too, the right of cancellation for non-disclosure is restricted, albeit in different ways.[184] In England, however, the insurance rule has not been changed. For insurance obtained by innocent or careless misrepresentation, courts must be urged to make more use of their discretion under section 2(2) of the Misrepresentation Act 1967 against the rescission of insurance contracts for non-fraudulent misrepresentation. But there remains the parallel problem for non-disclosure, for which, it seems, section 2(2) gives the court no such discretion. It may well be, of course, that insurers, being aware of all this, waive

---

[177] *Drake Ins. plc v Provident Ins. Plc* [2004] QB 601.   [178] Ibid., at [87].
[179] Ibid., at [88].
[180] Ibid. It seems that the Law Commission of 1980 would have agreed: No. 104, *Insurance Contracts*, para. 4.108, Cmnd 8064.   [181] Op. cit. above, n. 177, at [89].
[182] Op. cit. above, n. 180, para. 4.43.   [183] VVG, Art. 16(3).
[184] See Basedow and Foch, 73 ff.

rescission, but evidence of their practice is not available and this uncertain state of play is a cause for concern.

The Financial Ombudsman Service to the Rescue

The one spot of light in a murky and sometimes dismal legal scenario is that the FOS, which is empowered to adjudicate without having to follow the strict black letter of the law, has consistently upheld complaints from policyholders when insurers have rescinded on the basis of a misrepresentation that was both innocent and of minor importance.[185] In a statement made in April 2003[186] to summarize its approach, the FOS said that, ' if the policyholder's non-disclosure is innocent, the firm should meet the claim in full, regardless of whether, if it had known of the matter that was not disclosed, it would have increased the premium or refused to offer cover', that is, regardless of whether the matter was such as to induce the contract. It will be regarded as innocent when it is 'the result of a genuine oversight or inadvertent error'.[187] An error will be regarded as inadvertent, 'if it seems to have resulted from an understandable oversight or moment of carelessness, rather than from any deliberate act'. It will not be innocent if it is 'reckless'. Thus an innocent non-disclosure is different from what the law regards as an innocent misrepresentation, but more like the kind of carelessness which courts largely refuse to accept as sufficient to trigger a policy exception requiring reasonable care.[188]

The statement stressed that 'much depends on the details of the cases' but set out what the FOS looks for. Of importance are 'the circumstances surrounding the giving of the information' (telephone or travel agency perhaps), 'how clear and concise the firm's questions are'[189] (catch-all questions are ruled out), whether the firm gave a clear warning about the 'the consequences of giving false or incomplete information', and 'the degree to which the policyholder should have been aware of the information he or she was asked to provide, and whether the policyholder was likely to have recognised the significance of this information to the firm' (recent major illness, convictions like dangerous driving or drink-driving, and so on).

Reform

If the English rule, as it is currently understood, is to be changed, what should it become? The possible answers to be discussed here are:

(1) the Australian rule by reference to the reasonable insured;

(2) the Swiss rule, which requires of applicants a reasonable response to the questions from insurers;

---

[185] See, e.g., case studies 13/05 and 13/06, reported in *Ombudsman News*, January 2002.
[186] *Ombudsman News*, April 2003, p. 7 ff.
[187] E.g., Case 25/14, *Ombudsman News*, February 2003.
[188] See below, Chapter 5, p. 166.
[189] E.g., Case 25/17, *Ombudsman News*, February 2003.

(3) the ELC proposal by reference to a reasonable insured such as the applicant;

(4) the French rule based on proportionality; and

(5) the American rule whereby the contract can be avoided only in cases of wilful concealment.

The Australian Rule: The Reasonable Insured

Australia[190] and Belgium[191] have opted for a rule which requires disclosure of what would appear material to the reasonable insured. The rule leaves the onus of information with applicants, but in a more manageable form than the current English rule. However, the ELC thought such a rule too inflexible and preferred a qualified version of the test.[192]

Even so, a test of this kind was for many years the one adopted by the ABI in its Statement of General Insurance Practice for private policyholders: insurers should not refuse claims for non-disclosure of information 'which a policyholder could not reasonably be expected to have disclosed'.[193] Some insurers think that that should be enough to silence critics. Perhaps it should, except that application of this criterion depends nonetheless on the discretion, goodwill, and good faith of the insurer concerned. The experience of lawyers, of course, is that it is rarely satisfactory to put one party in a position to decide whether to use a legal 'rule' to pull out of a contract; and that what is true of most other people is also likely to be true of insurers.

The Swiss Rule: A Reasonable Response to Questions

A related solution is that the duty of disclosure be limited to a full and frank response to the insurer's written questions, as understood by the reasonable insured. A rule of this kind has been in force in Finland since 1994,[194] in France since 1990,[195] and in Switzerland for much longer.[196] In England, such a rule might be enacted as the new reformed rule of law, or as the (main) application of a (wider) rule like the Australian rule (above) which refers to the reasonable insured. Or it might be introduced by the courts as a qualification of the current English rule, whereby applicants still have the current wide duty of disclosure in principle but, in practice, insurers were taken to have waived the duty on matters about which they did not ask questions. When insurers do ask questions, to a

---

[190] Insurance Contracts Act 1984, s. 21(1). See P. Mann, *Annotated Insurance Contracts*, 3rd edn, (Sydney 2001).   [191] Law of 25 June 1992, s. 5.

[192] See below, p. 122.   [193] See above, Chapter 3, p. 60 ff.

[194] Insurance Act 1994, s. 22.   [195] Loi 89-1014 of 31 December 1989.

[196] VVG, Art. 4. The VVG is contained in a federal law of 2 April 1908, as amended by a federal law of 17 December 2004, which will come into force on 1 January 2006.

limited degree this is the law already;[197] however, this kind of solution has been criticized as 'a myriad of exceptions to an unwanted principle rather than an improved principle'.[198] Moreover, the Swiss rule would leave applicants who fail to answer the questions in breach of duty and, unlike, for example, the American rule (below), whereby the initiative lies very largely with insurers to get their questions answered, neither the Swiss rule nor an English rule modified to have the same effect would give any such incentive.

In many instances the effect of the Swiss rule would be that the scope of the duty would be determined by the proposal form. To make any such solution workable, however, first, the 'form' should not be taken literally but should be taken to include any questions put to applicants, provided that, as reasonable people, they should have realized that the questions concerned rating the risk, and that the questions as a whole were such as to lead them to suppose that no further rating information was or would be required. Secondly, applicants would not be permitted deliberately to conceal other obviously material information: to this extent there would remain a residual duty of disclosure. Thirdly, although there would be a presumption that the questions put by insurers were material, insurers would be entitled to rebut the presumption; similarly, applicants would be entitled to ignore questions of such generality that they made a nonsense of the rule—because these give insufficient guidance about the kind of answer required. An extreme example (given by the ELC) is: 'Are there any facts which you, as a reasonable person, consider might influence the judgment of a prudent insurer . . . ?' It is clear today that the FOS would also ignore 'catch-all' questions.[199]

This is the kind of solution originally put forward by the ELC in a working paper,[200] but withdrawn later in the face of objections raised by insurers. One objection was that, if the form were to determine the scope of the duty of disclosure, forms would have to become far more lengthy, detailed, and complex. The retreat of the ELC left some unanswered questions. First, might not applicants prefer a long form to the short shrift they can be given under the present law? Might they not prefer higher transaction costs in the expense of completion and checking of long forms, costs to be shared by all insured persons in the pool, to lower costs at the 'expense' of the few who find out, too late, that they are not covered after all? Might not those aware of the current burden of disclosure like to be relieved of the cost of trying to accumulate all the information required?[201] Is it not possible that more detailed questions would lead to better underwriting and *reduce* the overall cost of cover?[202] The short answer to all these questions seems to

---

[197] Above, p. 110 ff.   [198] C. Wells, 'If It's Broke, Fix It' [1993] 11 Int ILR 355, 356.
[199] *Ombudsman News*, April 2003, p. 8.   [200] Working Paper No. 73, 1989, para. 59 ff.
[201] S. A. Wreathe, 'Economics of Insurance Law', 13 Int Rev L & Econ 145–62 (1993).
[202] See B. Harnett, 'The Doctrine of Concealment: A Remnant in the Law of Insurance', 15 Law and Contemp. Probs 391–414, 410 (1950).

be, not at all. Of course, careful and thoughtful applicants would probably say 'yes'; but this is not the spirit which most applicants bring to buying standard cover.

A further objection to the solution was that the purpose of application forms is to elicit information of a standard nature and not to circumscribe the nature of the risk *in all respects*. Once again, this appears to be an argument partly based on cost: standard questions are cheap; tailored and focused questions are not. The forms, however, have evolved in the context of the current rule requiring a wide range of disclosure; their role is less a practical reason for maintaining the status quo than a consequence of it. In short, this may be one of those cases when second thoughts are not better than first: the retreat of the ELC from a reform that appears to have worked in other countries may have been a mistake.

The ELC's Reasonable Insured of that Kind

The ELC fell back on a qualified reasonable man test: reference to the reasonable man of *that* man's education, etc., so that the standard would depend, for example, on whether the insured was in business or was a consumer.[203] A qualified test of this kind would go some way to providing for those who needed special protection, such as persons whose education, culture, language, and social and commercial experience was different. This point was accepted in principle by the Report of the Australian Law Reform Commission; the Report went on to object,[204] however, that the test would collapse into a subjective inquiry because there might be almost as many reasonable applicants as there were insureds and, consequently, uncertainty. Indeed, from the start, the ELC conceded that, to avoid excessive uncertainty, legislation would have to give 'guidelines'; and later it recommended objective categories of reasonable men.[205]

The effectiveness of a solution of this kind depends on achieving the right balance between fairness, which inclines to particularization, and certainty, which prefers large categories. The ELC was confident that the judges had enough experience of the application of such standards. If, as appears, the categories of reasonable men would be like those inhabiting the tort of negligence, that is true, but not reassuring in view of the amount of litigation generated by the rule in tort. From a commercial viewpoint, the judges are experienced because the law is such that they get practice—too much practice. The very degree of disagreement about the viability of this test is not reassuring either.

Every society has to decide the level of special provision for the handicapped. Ramps for wheelchairs are one thing, but special rules of law for the 'legal legless' another. Even in the United States, the illiterate have not been excused from being bound by their signature. Nor are they in England, where, in general, the law does

[203] Law Commission, Working Paper No. 73 (1979), paras 60–61.   [204] Para. 180–2.
[205] Report No. 104, para. 4.51.

not excuse those with handicaps of which they are aware—if there is something they can do about it. The general rule of contract law is that blind signatories bear the risk that the contents of the document are not what the other party states.[206] In tort, the driver who starts his car and at the same time starts to feel faint must stop; diminished capacity, of which the driver is aware, does not carry a diminished duty of care.[207] Equally, the person asked to fill a form for insurance must also stop and take advice, or take the consequences. The argument that the confused and inexperienced immigrant, whether to England or to English law, should be excused local law is, surely, the thin end of a wedge of confusion of another kind.

The French Rule: Proportionality

In France the rule is that, in the case of *wilful* misrepresentation or non-disclosure of material information, the contract is nullified; but that in other cases insurers must pay that proportion of the claim which the premium paid bears to the premium that would have been paid if the insurer had been given full and correct information.[208] A qualified version of this kind of rule is found elsewhere in Europe, for example in Denmark[209] and Finland.[210] The attraction of the French rule is that it departs from the 'all-or-nothing' approach for which English law has been criticized. It softens the consequences of breach in some proportion to the seriousness of the case.

One objection to the French rule is that the putative premium may be hard to assess in the absence of tariffs or evidence from insurers, evidence which policy-holders would find difficult to contest or to contradict.[211] Moreover, what is the rate for a risk which, had the information been fully disclosed, the insurer would have refused to take at all? Even in less serious cases, as leading American authors have pointed out, moral risk can never be re-rated on a standard basis 'after the fact', that is, once it has emerged that there has been appreciably less than innocent non-disclosure.[212] Nonetheless, in practice, English insurers often apply something very similar to a rule of proportionality: they waive rescission of the contract and pay the claim, but minus the putative extra premium they would have charged if full disclosure had been made.

As for the objection that French law does not allow for the insurer who, if fully informed, would not have accepted the risk at all, in the present climate, will any representative of the UK industry stand up and say that no section of the

---

[206] *Saunders v Anglia Building Society* [1971] AC 1004.
[207] E.g., *Mansfield v Weetabix Ltd* [1998] 1 WLR 1263 (CA).
[208] Code d'assurance, Arts. 113–8 and 113–9.
[209] Insurance Contracts Act 1930, s. 16(2).
[210] Insurance Act 1994, ss. 24 and 25. See also Basedow and Fock, 75.
[211] See ELC Working Paper No. 73, 1989, paras 54–55.
[212] G. S. Staring and G.L. Waddell, 'Marine Insurance', 73 Tul L Rev 1619–96, 1661 (1999).

industry will take the risk? In a few cases, certainly, but only in those of applicants with really bad histories or dangerous occupations. In these cases, the French rule is indeed arbitrary and unfair to insurers. So, if such a case arises in Finland, the version of the rule there allows the insurer to rescind. The objection has most force in respect not of outright rejection but of acceptance subject to conditions. Still, French opinion sees this as the lesser of the evils and favours the retention of the rule. Indeed, if the French rule is seen less as an attempt to guess the terms of the contract, if there has been disclosure, than to be fair to the parties in the face of non-disclosure, this objection loses some of its force.

The American Rule

Although a rule of disclosure of some kind is found in many European countries,[213] for non-marine insurance, the law in some parts of the United States comes close to doing without one. The rule there is that insurers can rescind the contract on account of information undisclosed by applicants on two conditions. The first is that the information was not discovered by the insurer's own investigation of the risk. The second condition is that the odds of discovery were tipped against the insurer by wilful concealment, that is fraud, on the part of the applicant.[214] This rule puts the burden of investigation largely on insurers, except that, unless there is reason to doubt the veracity of what applicants have actually disclosed, insurers are entitled to rely on that without further investigation. There are a number of objections to the American rule; that may be why the ELC, although apparently unaware that such a rule could be found in Canada and the United States, rejected it more or less out of hand.

The first objection lies in difficulties of proof. Proving the applicant's knowledge, and hence fraud, is said to be so difficult that the American rule is for practical purposes one that abolishes the duty of disclosure altogether. Abolition leads to an unacceptable level of 'cross-subsidization', that is, higher premiums for the many to compensate for sharp practice by the few. This, it is said, is unfair and leads to adverse selection, which encourages fraud and increases the number of (bad-risk) fraudsters in the pool, and, as premiums rise as a result, to 'unravelling', whereby good risks leave the pool altogether and efficient insurance becomes impossible. In the United States, however, commentators are more sanguine both about the insurers' ability to prove fraud from circumstantial evidence and the courts' ability to identify states of mind from objective indicators.[215] Whether or not this is a sufficient answer for Americans, it is not self-evidently so for the English ELC, and certainly would not satisfy English insurers.[216]

---

[213] See Basedow and Fock, 75.   [214] See Clarke, ch. 23–8E.

[215] See T. R. Foley, 'Insurers' Misrepresentation Defense: The Need for a Knowledge Element', 67 S Cal LR 659–87, 681 (1994). See also Harnett, op. cit. above, n. 202, 402.

[216] See Chapter 6, pp. 200–1.

Further, the danger of cross-subsidization has been raised again at a second level. Critics argue that the general pool of policyholders should not be obliged to carry those who, when contracting insurance, are not fraudulent but careless about the accuracy or completeness of their disclosure. Defenders of the American rule answer that insurers are better able than insurance buyers to spread the risk of loss caused by non-disclosure and misrepresentation.[217] Just as insurers assume the risk of carelessness during the insurance period, so also they assume the risk of carelessness in their customers before it begins. Just as careful (and lucky) drivers help to pay for the losses suffered by careless (and unlucky) drivers, they also pay for the extra risk posed by applicants who, in response to a question about convictions during the previous five years, overlook that a conviction for speeding five years ago was just inside that period. This is unlikely to lead to adverse selection and unravelling; most insured drivers surely are risk-averse and would prefer to pay a little more to cover careless contracting by the pool than find themselves uninsured.

As it stands, the English rule puts the cost of acquiring information for insurers about the risk on applicants. The American rule saves applicants that as a direct cost and puts it on insurers, together with the cost of the insurers not having the information; insurers then pass these costs on to the pool. Of course, it will cost applicants for motor insurance very little to check indorsements on a driving licence for the exact date of a conviction. It will cost applicants for liability cover a great deal, however, to have an environmental audit to ensure that there is no toxic waste under the property that they wish to insure. Sometimes the cost of requiring applicants to obtain information outweighs the benefits. Even in the less extreme example of fire risks, the American rule, which encourages insurers to combine questions with an inspection of the premises, may be more efficient, as insurers are better able to assess the risk than applicants or anyone that applicants can reasonably be expected to employ for this purpose. In contrast, the English rule is positively inefficient, as it encourages anxious applicants, if aware of the rule, to double-check their property lest one day they have to claim and the insurer pleads non-disclosure.

Another objection to the American rule is that insurance in England is often contracted without questions because insurers rely on the duty of disclosure. But this practice is a consequence of current law rather than a reason for it; and still less is it a justification for it. It is a practice that has served insurers in ways that are not self-evidently good for applicants, or anyone else. As the Report of the Australian Law Reform Commission observed,[218] for 'reasons of cost and competition, proposal forms are often kept to a minimum. Relevant questions concerning the moral risk are not asked in case they should embarrass prospective policyholders. The adoption of direct marketing techniques has increased the pressure for brevity and simplicity.' The practice has enabled insurers to sell more

---

[217] Foley, op. cit. above, n. 215, 660.   [218] Op.cit. above, n. 215, para. 183.

cover at less cost while, for the minority of insurances giving rise to a claim, still having the possibility of using the law of non-disclosure to re-rate the risk with the benefit of hindsight. The practice is scarcely a justification of the present law. Indeed, the objection may prove a little too much. If it is good to save applicants the embarrassment of questions, is it not even better to save them the embarrassment of self-examination and disclosure to strangers, which the current English rule requires?

A third and last objection to the adoption of the American rule in England would be the associated need to change not only the law of non-disclosure but also the law of misrepresentation, in order to maintain the current and important trend to keep them in line.[219] This is true, but, for some, this would be not only a price worth paying but a further gain in the modernization of English law.

Conclusion: More Questions

The ELC with the Scottish Law Commission has the question under review again in 2007. In 1980 the ELC was persuaded that insurers need to rely on disclosure by applicants. But insurers know full well, as the ELC recognized, that applicants have little or no idea what they ought to disclose. Apart from what is said in response to specific questions, do insurers really rely on what applicants tell them? Or, as Lord Templeman thought,[219a] do insurers really rely on being able to raise a defence of non-disclosure if and when a claim is made? Are they really covering themselves against the possibility that later they will not want to cover the insured? And does this mean that the rule discourages investigation by insurers which might have enabled a better evaluation of the risk and, perhaps, better risk management? And is it fair?

As regards effective investigation, the difference between the ELC's solution and the American rule is one of degree. The ELC's solution would allow rescission not only against fraudulent applicants but also against careless applicants, and leave the burden of investigation largely with applicants; in contrast, the American rule puts the burden more squarely on insurers. Where agreement is most evident is in opposition to the current English rule. Typical is the startled reaction of an American court, when a rule like that was put before it. That, said the court, 'would, in effect, be to place the burden of underwriting decisions upon the insured and not the insurer. This would turn the relationship between the insured and its insurer on its head and nullify the duty of an insurer to act reasonably to protect its own interests.'[220] Ultimately, a judgement must be made about the burden of investigation.

The present English rule in favour of insurers, a pragmatic rule born in the common law of commerce rather than in equity as modern judges have assumed,[221] came about because the insurance contract is different: because, as

---

[219] *Pan Atlantic Ins. Co. Ltd v Pine Top Ins. Co. Ltd* [1995] 1 AC 501.
[219a] *Pan Atlantic* (above) at 515.
[220] *Insurance Co. of North America v US Gypsum Co.*, 870 F 2d 148, 153 (4 Cir., 1989).
[221] See Birds and Hird, 102.

Lord Mansfield said, it is a contract upon a speculation.[222] As an economist might say, a prominent feature of insurance contracts is that the characteristics of the buyers affect the costs of the sellers; high-risk customers will cost more than low-risk customers.[223] In some risk situations creditors can take security, or require a performance bond. But insurance is one of the situations in which heavy measures of that kind are not viable. Still the question remains whether insurance is really *so* different from many other kinds of contract in which there is a risk of non-performance, in which one party is depended on for payment or other kinds of performance—the factory that will grind to a halt without the flow of cash or components—that the current rule of disclosure is justified for the protection of insurers. Is the insurance industry so important to society, as it was perhaps at the time of Lord Mansfield, that it merits special protection—not only from the fraudulent in society, but also from the careless and the ignorant?

As information is valuable, generally the law does not oblige people to hand it over without compelling reasons. The insurance rule of disclosure is totally exceptional. Perhaps it can still be justified today for risks about which too little is known; environmental damage liability comes to mind. But if, as appears for better-known risks such as that of fire, the difficulty of investigating risks is much less than in the maritime world of Lord Mansfield, and if, as this book argues, the present law undermines the sense of the security which people rightly seek when buying insurance, it is for those who would retain the present law to make a convincing case for its retention.

The case for retention might run like this. Although insurers are better equipped to investigate risks, it does not follow that insurers should bear the entire burden of investigation, as that is not the cheapest approach; and if indeed insurers must bear that burden, it will be passed back to policyholders in higher premiums. For many aspects of the risk, the best and cheapest investigator is the honest applicant who already has the information in head or at hand. Currently insurers are saying, 'you tell me about the risk, and I shall give you cheaper insurance but you must take the risk of non-disclosure'. The trouble with this arrangement, of course, is that the insurance is cheap, at least for the majority who make no claims, because applicants are largely unaware of the risk of non-disclosure or, if they are, of what they should disclose, and therefore they do not incur the full cost of compliance with the duty. Moreover, the cost to society is not kept down because the arrangement provides insurers with less incentive to manage risk and with a route of escape if there is a claim.

Better, it is submitted, would be a change in the law which allows applicants to reply, 'all right, I'll be your investigator but you must tell me exactly what you need to know'. This, of course, is something not unlike the Swiss rule, and the American rule. Significantly, it is submitted, it is also close to recent practice

---

[222] *Carter v Boehm*, op. cit. above, n. 147, 1909.
[223] See S. A. Rea, 'The Economics of Insurance Law', 13 Int. Rev. of Law & Econ. 145–62, 153 (1993).

here in England;[224] applicants are alerted to the duty of disclosure, and the risk of non-disclosure is limited to what insurers have asked about, together with any other information that is 'palpably material'. Palpably material is the American description of information, which is in the applicant's possession and which an applicant should have known was material, but which the insurer had no reason to suspect and thus did not ask about. The famous example, that of the man who contracts life insurance without telling the insurer that he is about to fight a duel, tells us that it will not arise very often.

Contracting Through Agents

The Problem of Persona

Commonly, insurance contracts are concluded through agents (aka intermediaries) on each side. On the insurers' side, the agent's role should be straightforward and unproblematic; often it is not. In principle, whether insurers are bound by the acts or omissions of such persons is a question governed by the law of agency. An outline of relevant rules is as follows.[225]

Authority

Insurers are bound by all the acts of their agents within the scope of an agent's actual authority as agent. Actual authority may be express or implied. If an insurer instructs an agent to conclude a contract with a particular person on particular terms, the agent has express authority to make that contract. If an insurer appoints an agent to a particular job or position in the company, the actual authority of the agent depends on the actual relationship between the agent and the insurer—about which the average member of the public knows and can learn next to nothing. If an agent has a standard sort of job with an insurer, however, applicants are entitled to assume that the agent is authorized to do what is *usual* in a job of that kind: that the agent has implied authority to make any contract of the kind usually made by a person in that position. Further, if the agent does not have actual authority, express or implied, to do an act, the insurer in question will still be bound by the act if the insurer has let it appear that the agent had authority, and an applicant reasonably relied on the appearance of authority. In other words, if there is disparity between actual authority, on the one hand, and implied or apparent authority, on the other, it is the latter that counts.

Evidence of what is usual has been found in the past in the codes of practice for intermediaries. The underlying common law position is that applicants are entitled to assume that agents, through whom everyday insurance is contracted,

[224] See above, pp. 119, 120.
[225] See Clarke, ch. 8.

are usually authorized to issue interim cover and to receive premiums, but not to make the main contract of insurance: that is decided by someone higher up in the insurer's organization. The agent may be the one to inform the applicant of the decision, but it is not the agent's decision. Importantly, however, such agents are authorized to pass communications to and from the insurer: to 'receive the proposal and put it into shape'.[226]

As regards the FSA's Conduct of Business Rules, which came into force in January 2005, in principle insurers are always responsible for the acts and omissions of such agents in carrying on business for which insurers have accepted responsibility, in accordance with section 39(3) of the Financial Services and Markets Act(FSMA) 2000.[227] Section 39(3) provides that:

The principal of an appointed representative is responsible, to the same extent as if he had expressly permitted it, for anything done or omitted by the representative in carrying on the business for which he has accepted responsibility

This appears to extend the common law, for example, to the (unlikely) situation in which an agent purports to conclude not just interim cover but cover for the entire period of insurance applied for.

Split Personality

If the role of insurers' agents is to 'put the application into shape', reasonable applicants may well think that, as the form is the insurers' own form and has been put in front of them by the insurers' agent, it is part of any such agent's job to help applicants to complete it—as it undoubtedly is with forms in other walks of life and, as regards insurance, in other countries, such as Germany[228] and the United States.[229] Indeed, in Germany, contract terms purporting to change this position have been struck out as unfair.

In particular, applicants may well think that, if there is any inaccuracy or omission in what is written on the form of which the agent was or should have been aware, the insurer in question cannot later complain. Such a case was *Bawden*,[230] in which the insured's application for accident insurance did not state that he had only one eye; if he thought about it at all, he would have thought it did not matter, as it was obvious to everyone, including the insurer's agent, that he had only one eye. The Court of Appeal, clearly, thought likewise and rejected the insurer's defence of non-disclosure. But it is not entirely clear that the court would do so today. This is the result of a later case, the troublesome decision in *Newsholme*.[231]

---

[226] *Bawden v London, Edinburgh & Glasgow Assurance Co.* [1892] 2 QB 534, 539 (CA).

[227] See COB, para. 1.7.1; above, p. 61 ff.

[228] E.g., BGH 18 Dec. 1991, IV ZR 271/91, VersR 1992.217. See also M. Müller-Stüler, 'Broker *v* Tied Agent: Some Aspects' [1996] IJIL 151-7.

[229] *Union Mutual Life Ins. Co. v Wilkinson*, 13 Wall 222 (1872).   [230] Above, n. 226.

[231] *Newsholme Bros. v Road Transport & General Ins. Co. Ltd* [1929] 2 KB 356 (CA).

In *Newsholme*, the applicant gave the agent the right information, but the agent wrote it on the form incorrectly. The Court of Appeal held that the agent completed the form as agent indeed, not as the agent of the insurer but as the agent of the applicant; that, therefore, the agent's knowledge of the correct information was not attributable to the insurer; and that the insurer was entitled to rescind the insurance contract on grounds of misrepresentation. This decision is confusing, impractical, and out of line with principle.

The decision is confusing because the outcome is out of line with the reasonable expectations of those involved in contracting insurance, especially applicants. It is impractical because it envisages an agent with a revolving head, whose role changes from one moment to the next. If *Newsholme* is right, what, for example, of the agent who first notices the inaccuracy in the form an hour or two later back at the office? Is the agent's knowledge to be attributed to the insurer because the agent has left the applicant and is back in the place of employment? *Newsholme* is out of line with principle in that it has left this bit of insurance law high and almost dry, out of the general course taken by the rest of the law of agency. General agency law, as we have just seen, takes a different view of the apparent authority of agents. The appearance to the world of applicants, surely, is that the agent is acting for the insurer, who is bound by all that the agent does for the proper completion of the insurer's form in the furtherance of the insurer's business. To eliminate any trace of doubt left by *Newsholme* in New Zealand, a statute there now spells out that 'as between the insured and the insurer' an agent like this is 'at all times during the negotiations' the agent of the insurer.[232] That, surely, should also be the law of England.

Given, however, the decision in *Newsholme*, if the agency reasoning is ignored, the decision itself can be accommodated on different grounds. The proper place for all these cases is under the established rule that signatories of documents which are part of a contract, or lead to one, are bound by the contents of the document signed, unless that person has made a reasonable mistake about contents of the document of which the other party is, or should be, aware. Although importance is attached to the certainty of transactions based on signed documents, courts also seek to protect those who, without being careless or gullible, have acted reasonably in trusting those with whom they deal. If the relevant cases are seen in the light of these rules, both *Bawden* and *Newsholme* can be made to fit the mould and to make sense. Mr Bawden was entitled to think that his form was in order, because he was entitled to assume that the agent had taken his handicap into account.[233] Mr Newsholme, who signed his form without reading it, and hence without discovering the inaccuracies, was not.[234] In the unlikely event, however, that the inaccuracy had been such that, if he had read the form, Mr Newsholme would not have realized that

232 Insurance Law Reform Act 1977, s. 10.
233 See *Stone v Reliance* [1972] 1 Lloyd's Rep 469 (CA).
234 *Saunders v Anglia Building Society* [1971] AC 1004.

anything was wrong with the form, he would have been in the same legal position as Mr Bawden: entitled to rely on the agent and to assume that full and accurate disclosure had been made to the insurer.[235]

The Problem of Advice

If people are sold unsuitable insurance, it may not cut their finger or crack their mirror but it can make a large dent in their fortunes. One problem recognized by the insurance industry in general is the variable quality of the insurance advice offered by those employed on the front line at the point of sale to the public. Currently, more and more insurance is sold through outlets mainly concerned with something else, places such as banks, whose staff are likely to lack the knowledge to explain in full the products being sold. Front line sellers are now of three kinds.

Brokers, as they used to be called, can recommend insurance products from any source, and are regarded by the FSA as a part of a wider class referred to as independent financial advisers (IFAs). At the other end of the scale are agents who can recommend the insurance from one source only. These are the agents apparently in the employment of the insurer concerned who sells insurance 'across the counter'. Since January 2005 there has been an intermediate class, called multi-tied agents, such as those working for banks and building societies, but which also includes some self-employed advisers. Multi-tied agents can recommend a limited range of sources[236]—more than can tied agents, but fewer than brokers.

One form of government 'interference', as they have called it, concerns the way that insurance, in particular life insurance, is sold. The industry's fight to retain the right of self-regulation was undermined by its poor public image after the pensions 'scandal' in the 1990s. A survey published in 1994 indicated that 76 per cent of those who dealt with them do not expect complete honesty from sellers of financial products. It is not clear that the public perception is much better today. Be that as it may, the *Financial Times* has been calling for government regulation for years, and it has now come in the form of rules with statutory backing[237] drawn up by the FSA.

The detail is beyond the scope of this chapter, however, the rules, Rules on Conduct of Business,[238] require, as regards designated investment business,[239] for example, that information must be communicated to customers 'in a way which is clear, fair and not misleading',[240] and that insurers ensure that any

---

[235] See Clarke, ch. 10-3.

[236] The position has been described in clear and accessible form in *Which?*, November 2004.

[237] The Financial Services and Markets Act 2000.   [238] See above, p. 61 ff.

[239] The 'definition' of this, to be found in a glossary of terms running to 217 pages, takes the form of a list of activities covering more than a page of the Glossary.   [240] COB 2.1.3; above p. 63.

persons acting on their behalf do not 'offer, give, solicit or accept any inducement . . . if it is likely to conflict to a material extent with any duty that the firm owes to its customers'.[241] Moreover, any agent selling insurance as an investment or as part of a pension arrangement is now required by FSA regulations to provide buyers with certain documentation.

Moreover, running a parallel course of regulation we find the Code of Ethics and Conduct drawn up by the Chartered Insurance Institute for its members.[242] These comprise anyone, including corporate members, 'mainly employed or engaged in work connected with insurance' and including, therefore, insurers, advisers and intermediaries. Among the 'key values' stated at the beginning of the Code are 'responsibility and integrity' in professional life, 'taking into account their wider responsibilities to society as a whole', and 'respecting the confidentiality of information'. In their relations with customers, members should 'provide suitable and objective recommendations', 'avoid conflict between personal interests . . . and their duties to customers' and, specifically, they should not 'provide or accept money, gifts, entertainment, loans or any other benefit or preferential treatment from or to any existing or potential customer or provider', other than occasionally 'as part of accepted business practice, and which are not likely to conflict with duties to customers'.

As for advisers, people no longer take their losses on the chin. Applicants for insurance, who have employed an adviser, may well sue that person, for example, if the adviser failed to warn them of what the law of disclosure required. Thus they recover from the adviser what they have failed to recover from their fire insurer.[243] In such cases, the chicken has come home to roost, but in a different sector of the insurance market. There is some satisfaction in the irony of this, but it is also wasteful.

Premium

Payment

What policyholders are contracting for is cover. What insurers are contracting for is money, usually called premium, which they usually insist on receiving at or before the beginning of the period of cover. Like any other debtors, in principle, policyholders are obliged to seek out their creditors and, in the case of companies, pay them at their place of business.[244] Strictly speaking that would mean head office, which would be a nuisance of a kind that insurers seeking to sell their products would not want to inflict. In practice, the proper place of payment may be indicated in the policy, or past practice may indicate payment to a particular

---

[241] COB 2.2.3.   [242] http://www.cii.co.uk/thecii/code_ethics_conduct_04.pdf.
[243] See Chapter 3, p. 76 ff.   [244] *Rein v Stein* [1892] 1 QB 753, 758 (CA).

agent of the insurer concerned.[245] For this purpose the agent may be the person in other respects the agent of the policyholder, the insurance intermediary.

Not only is payment of premium the *quid pro quo* of cover, but also the duty to pay premium is closely related to the commencement of cover, or vice versa. On the one hand, it is not uncommon to find that the contract of insurance stipulates that there shall be 'no cover till premium paid'.[246] On the other hand, an old adage of insurance law is 'no risk no premium', or, as Lord Mansfield famously put it:

... where the risk has not been run, whether its not having been run was owing to the fault, pleasure or will of the insured, or to any other cause, the premium shall be returned: because a policy of insurance is a contract of indemnity. The underwriter receives a premium for running the risk of indemnifying the insured, and whatever cause it be owing to, if he does not run the risk, the consideration, for which the premium or money was put into his hands, fails, and therefore he ought to return it.[247]

Late Payment

Premium must be paid at the time stipulated in the contract of insurance. If no time has been stipulated, the premium must be paid within a reasonable time.[248] In the event of waiver of the policyholder's obligation to pay on time, the insurer may call for payment at any later time, subject to the ordinary rules about revocation of waiver; or the insurer may deduct it from any payment of insurance money.[249] Late payment entitles the insurer to repudiate the cover, but only if it is a condition of the contract of insurance that payment be on time, that is, in the language of general contract law, if time is 'of the essence' of the contract. Whether that is true of premium payment is less clear than it should be.[250] When the contract states that there is no cover until premium has been paid, that factor reduces the importance of the question.

Days of Grace

Days of grace refer to an extra period of time to pay premium allowed by the contract after the date on which payment is due. This kind of arrangement is found mainly in life policies. The effect is that the policy remains in force during the days of grace, although the premium has not been paid on time: time is not of the essence of the contract until the days of grace have expired. After that the insurer is entitled to repudiate the policy and if, in the language of the industry, the life 'drops', the insurer is entitled to refuse to pay. That seems fair enough until

---

[245] *Wing v Harvey* (1854) 5 De G M & G 265.
[246] See, e.g., *Canning v Farquhar* (1886) 16 QBD 727 (CA). See also, above, p. 91.
[247] *Tyrie v Fletcher* (1777) 2 Cowp 666, 668.
[248] *Kirby v Cosindit SpA* [1969] 1 Lloyd's Rep 75.
[249] *Roberts v Security Co. Ltd* [1897] 1 QB 111, 115 (CA).   [250] See Clarke, ch. 13-8.

one thinks about elderly persons, who have paid premium for many years, who become forgetful and disorganized, and who do not pay on time. In principle the law is clear: no cover. At one time in England it appeared that rescue was in sight for such people, but that now appears to have been a delusion.

Contrast Arkansas, where forfeitures 'are so odious in law that they will be enforced only where there is the clearest evidence that such was the intention of the parties'.[251] Years earlier, in the Supreme Court of the United States, Justice Bradley stressed that forfeitures 'are not favored by the law' because they are 'often the means of great oppression and injustice'.[252] In the USA the attitude appears to be the same today. In England too, back in 1972, it was affirmed in the House of Lords that 'equity has an unlimited and unfettered jurisdiction to relieve against contractual forfeitures and penalties',[253] and the House applied the rule to late payment of rent due under a lease, as it would today. For a number of years the prevalent view was that the same principle would apply to late payment of premium if, in a particular case, the justice of the case so required.[254] However, doubt has arisen since 1983 when, in a case concerning late payment of hire due under a time charterparty, the House of Lords held that the rule does not apply to commercial transactions because that would undermine the certainty necessary in such transactions.[255]

Many insurance contracts cannot be described as commercial. Moreover, the commercial character of the transaction, although highly relevant as a possible obstacle to the grant of relief, does not automatically rule it out altogether. Even so, it seems that many, if not most, contemporary commentators take the view that the relief does not apply in commercial cases at all. Of course, the case of forgetful old folk who do not pay is not commercial, but for them the law is sufficiently shrouded in uncertainty as to be a source of stress and anxiety such as they should not have to bear. Perhaps the best cloud dispellant is the argument that as regards insurance contracts, unless the contrary can be inferred from language such as 'no cover till premium paid', time of payment is not 'of the essence of the contract' anyway.[256] That has been the effect of some rulings of the FOS, which has persuaded insurers to make concessions or give more time.[257] Nonetheless, a clear decision on the rule of law would be welcome.

Mode of Payment: Direct Debits

Premium must be paid in the manner agreed by the parties to the contract of insurance. In the event of a wrongful refusal by the insurer to accept or retain

---

[251] *Union Life Ins. Co. v Brewer*, 309 SW 2d 740, 744 (Ark, 1958).
[252] *Knickerbocker Life Ins Co. v Norton*, 96 US 234 24, L Ed 689, 692 (1878).
[253] *Shiloh Spinners Ltd v Harding* [1973] AC 691, 726.
[254] *Snell's Principles of Equity*, 28th edn (London, 1982) 530.
[255] *Scandinavian Trading Tanker Co. A/B v Flota Petrolera Equatoriana* [1983] 2 AC 694. See Lord Diplock at p. 699 and p. 704.   [256] See Clarke, ch. 13-11C2.
[257] See, e.g., *Ombudsman News*, October 2003, case 32/12.

proper payment of premium, the insurer cannot repudiate liability on the basis of non-payment of premium. Insurers, like other members of society, are not allowed 'to take advantage of their own wrong'. On the contrary, insurers in such a case would be liable for breach of contract, and the policyholder would be released from the obligation to pay.[258]

Unless by mistake, why would any insurer refuse to accept or retain proper payment of premium? Indeed, what might have been a very occasional question has acquired currency in relation to the numerous policyholders who have agreed to pay premium by direct debit. *Prima facie*, it is up to policyholders to see that premium payment reaches the insurer concerned. Any breakdown in the chosen mechanism of payment is a risk assumed by the policyholder. However, whereas the mandated bank is the bank of the policyholder, the method, payment by direct debit, is usually chosen by insurers and pressed on their policyholders because there are commercial advantages in that arrangement for insurers.

The point arose in *Weldon*,[259] in which the court decided that, if the insurers in the case were to argue that they were entitled to refuse to pay the insurance money on the grounds of non-payment of premium by direct debit and consequent lapse of the policy, the argument would fail. One reason was that the insurers themselves were in breach of implied terms of the contract concerning payment of premium.[260] The implied terms were notably that the insurer 'would use its best endeavours to implement payment of any direct debit mandate with which it had been provided'; and that 'it would properly and efficiently administer that mandate including the receipt of premiums'. Moreover, breach of such terms might also amount to breach of a duty of care owed to the policyholder in tort.[261] Clearly the court strained to reach what it saw as a fair and sensible result. The FOS does likewise, ruling, for example, in one case that both policyholder and insurer should have realized that something had gone wrong at the bank, and apportioning liability between them.[262]

When all goes well and premium is paid in accordance with the contract, what policyholders get in return for payment is cover. Cover is a large subject that requires at least a chapter, which comes next.

---

[258] See *Honour v Equitable Life Assurance Sy* [1900] 1 Ch 852.

[259] *Weldon v GRE* [2000] 2 All ER (Comm) 914. The court allowed an appeal against an order dismissing a claim against an insurer on the ground that the claim had no prospect of success.

[260] Ibid., 920.   [261] Ibid., 923 ff.

[262] *Ombudsman News*, September 2003 case 31/1. See also *Ombudsman News*, July 2004.

5

Cover

Policies of Insurance

A Large Role for Small Print

What policyholders want for their money during the insurance period is cover—the assurance that, if the insured event (the peril) occurs, they will get something 'for' it, and that is usually money. Policyholders want the circumstances and degree of cover to be as wide as possible; people commonly assume that it is wider than it really is. When they are disabused, they complain about the insurer's small print—which they have probably never read. As a leading London solicitor put it in the *Sunday Times*, 'An insurance policy is like old underwear. The gaps in its cover are only shown by accident.' Most people do not read their policies until they want to claim, if then, but the law on that is clear: they cannot plead ignorance of the terms of their insurance contract. If they do not read the contract terms, they cannot plead in a court of law their own self-inflicted ignorance. If they do read the contract terms but do not understand them, they still cannot complain, because the court's response will be that they should have got someone to explain them. If Mondeo man crosses the Channel to replenish his cellar, he cannot plead ignorance of the road restrictions in Calais. So it is with insurance, whether in Calais or Colchester.

What insurers want is a clear idea of their exposure, of the circumstances in which they must pay, and some idea of the likely amount. This is in their hands. Partly it depends on information and research.[1] Partly it depends on the contract cover—the terms and the quality of the drafting. Nonetheless, according to an outspoken Deputy Chairman of Lloyd's a decade ago, many insurers were prone to underwriting business with little knowledge of the subject-matter, and on wording that was unclear.[2] Whether or not that was then true of the market outside Lloyd's, it is not a practice which he or any other underwriter would have condoned. Whether or not it is still true today, many points about contract (policy) wording are still disputed.

For insurers, the role of the contract terms is, first, to mark the boundaries of cover in accordance with established categories of risk and thus with their data on past losses.[3] Secondly, terms are aimed at better risk management on the part of the policyholder. Against 'thieves that break through and steal', for example, discounts are available to those policyholders who fit their vehicles with tracking devices or their premises with CCTV. Moreover, insurers may specify the kind of locks to be fitted on doors and windows; and, to encourage people actually to lock the doors and windows, theft cover may be conditional on forcible entry. Against 'moths and

---

[1] See Chapter 2, p. 48 ff.

[2] I. R. Hiscox, 'Why So Much Insurance Litigation?' (1996) 90 BILA Jo 1–2, 2.

[3] D. S. Slawson, 'Standard Form Contracts and Democratic Control of Lawmaking Power', 84 Harv LR 529, 552 (1971).

rust that doth corrupt', contracts for collectibles, for example, from vintage port to vintage motor cars, may specify the atmospheric conditions of storage, and so on.

A prominent example of all this is motor insurance. To cut claims, like the Government, insurers would like to cut speed. Drivers under surveillance, whether by a police patrol car or by a video camera, slow down. This inspired one insurer to require the installation of a 'black box' data recorder in a fleet of vehicles with a bad claims record; the record improved dramatically and everyone was happy—except some of the drivers. But, when they complained about 'big brother', their employer, the policyholder, could blame the insurer while still enjoying lower premiums. The box also enabled the insurer to apply a low mileage discount without having to trust policyholders to monitor the mileage.

Life insurers, too, would like to fit a black box to human bodies. Neither medical science yet, nor society for the predictable future, would allow this. What insurers have attempted to do is to address 'life style', offering lower premiums on life or health insurance for those who do not drink (alcohol) or smoke; but, as things are, the perception of insurers is that too many policyholders cheat, and that they cannot afford, either in terms of policy administration or in that of public image, to police the policyholder effectively.

A contract condition requiring a box, however, combines effectively the two most common ways in which insurers seek to combat 'moral hazard' in the form of risk compensation, that is, the tendency of policyholders to relax and thus increase the risk. The first is to impose safety measures, in the case of the black box, psychological measures; and the second, with the incentive of lower premiums for less mileage, is to reduce exposure to risk.[4] In any event, whatever the contract condition, clearly, the drafting of the contract is of prime importance.

Standard Forms

Standard-form contracts are important in the control and allocation of risks of all kinds,[5] but never more so than for insurance cover. Indeed, insurance contracts have long been described in both England and the United States as the archetype of 'contracts of adhesion', tantamount to private or delegated legislation.[6] In the United States private legislation is perceived as undemocratic and, therefore, to be made subject in some way to the democratic process—if not to the consent of the people then, the next best thing, to the consent of the courts,[7] the members of which, in the lower courts, are elected by the people. Courts seek to determine what the weaker contracting party could legitimately expect by way of services according to the other's calling, in the present case insurance, and to interpret the contract accordingly.

---

[4] P. Cane, *Atiyah's Accidents, Compensation and the Law*, 6th edn (Oxford, 1999) 369 ff.

[5] F. Kessler, 'Contracts of Adhesion', 43 Col L Rev 629–42, 631 (1943).

[6] E.g., V. P. Goldberg, 'Institutional Change and the Quasi-Invisible Hand', 17 J L & Econ 461–96, 484 (1974).   [7] Slawson, op. cit. above, n. 3, 538.

Although the response of courts to contracts of adhesion has been largely hostile, standard-form contracting has advantages too. It reduces transaction costs and increases the speed with which, in the case of insurance, cover can be made available and the accuracy with which risks can be rated by reference to past records. 'The predominance of standard forms', it was once argued,[8] 'is the best evidence of their necessity. They are characteristic of a mass production society and an integral part of it. They provide information and enforce order.' Insurance policies, Slawson concluded, are the 'extreme illustration' of the standard form. This claim was made back in 1970, and the writer drew an analogy between mass-produced insurance and mass-produced cars. The trend since with cars, however, is for makers to offer varieties of a basic model in order to customize the car and give the owner a sense of individuality. Equally, the use of computers both to calculate risk and to process words has enabled the insurer to customize insurance to a greater degree and at lower cost than before. Moreover, Slawson's claim was made in the United States where, through legislation and the influence of the Insurance Services Office, standardization has been more extensive than in England and other common law countries. In England today, insurance contracts are still in standard form, but there are many forms. In future the cost of training staff to meet higher standards of advice may reduce the variety and discourage innovation; or, on the contrary, the development of software may lead to the rapid production of insurance tailored exactly to the individual, without destroying the pools of risk. This remains to be seen.

Words: The Rules of Interpretation

To construct a clear contract, the insurers' basic materials are the words of the English language. They must understand their materials and, more to the point, they must be aware of how their words will be understood by others: by policy-holders, to whom the chosen words must be intelligible; and by the courts which, in the event of dispute, decide whether they could, and if so, in what sense they should, be understood by policyholders. So, the rules for writing contracts are much influenced by the rules for reading them—the rules of interpretation applied by the courts. When reading contracts, the courts' overriding objective is said to be a search for the intention of the parties. To this end, the courts apply the same rules to all kinds of contract, which, in summary, are applied to insurance contracts as follows:

Rule 1: Words are to be understood in their ordinary sense as they would be understood by ordinary people.[9] The rule assumes that ordinary people use a dictionary and that they know what is going on in the world immediately around

---

[8] Ibid., 530 ff.
[9] E.g., *Hayward v Norwich Union Ins. Ltd* [2001] Lloyd's Rep IR 410, at [10] (CA). For more detail, see Clarke, ch. 15-2.

them.[10] Moreover, the ordinary person is a useful ally who can be summoned to the aid of a court that might have reason to eschew the pursuit of precision and construe words as a matter of impression.[11] Be that as it may, words are to be understood not in isolation but in the context of the contract,[12] and with the aid of certain traditional canons of interpretation, as follows:

(1) If particular words have a generic character, more general following words are construed as having the same character (*eiusdem generis*). Thus 'flood' in 'storm, tempest or flood' means a sudden flood on a large scale.[13]

(2) The express mention of one thing may imply the exclusion of another related thing (*expressio unius est exclusio alterius*). Thus if policy term A is expressed to be a 'condition precedent' to cover but policy term B is not, the inference is that indeed it is not.[14]

Rule 2: In the event of inconsistency in the ordinary meaning of words in different parts of the contract, the court prefers the meaning that best reflects the intention of the parties.[15] For example, preference is given to non-standard parts of a policy, such as the Schedule, to which the parties gave actual attention.

Rule 3: If it appears that the words have been used in a special sense, either (a) as previously defined by the courts, for example 'theft',[16] or (b) the sense used in a particular commercial context, such as 'motor racing',[17] the words will be interpreted in that special sense.

Rule 4: If, in spite of the application of Rules 1 and 2, the meaning of the words is not clear, and Rule 3 is of no assistance:

(1) the words will be read with reference to any evidence of the purpose of the contract, which is not apparent from the contract itself; and

(2) the words will be construed *contra proferentem*, that is, against the insurer and liberally in favour of policyholders.

An example of Rule 4(1) is found in the decision that a policy on 'accidental death' covered a policyholder who carelessly crossed a railway line and was killed by a train.[18] As for Rule 4(2), the policyholder's interpretation of words is preferred if it is a reasonable view, whereas the insurer's interpretation of the words, if different, will not be adopted unless it is the only reasonable view. As an

---

[10] *Investors Compensation Scheme Ltd v West Bromwich BS* [1998] 1 WLR 896, 912 (HL).
[11] *Lewis Emanuel & Son Ltd v Hepburn* [1960] 1 Lloyd's Rep 304, 308.
[12] *The Fina Samco* [1995] 2 Lloyd's Rep 344, 350 (CA).
[13] *Young v Sun Alliance & London Ins. Ltd* [1976] 2 Lloyd's Rep 189, 191 (CA).
[14] *Home Ins. Co. v Victoria-Montreal Fire Ins. Co.* [1907] AC 59, 64.
[15] *Woolfall & Rimmer Ltd v Moyle* [1942] 1 KB 66, 73 ff. (CA).
[16] E.g., *Hayward*, op. cit. above, n. 9.
[17] The words do not include 'sprint events': *Scragg v UK Temperance Inst.* [1976] 2 Lloyd's Rep 227, 233.   [18] *Cornish v Accident Ins. Co.* (1889) 23 QBD 452, 456 (CA).

American judge put it, if the insurer uses a 'slippery' word to describe cover, 'it is not the function of the court to sprinkle sand upon the ice'. If 'the limits of coverage slide across the slippery area and the company falls into a coverage somewhat more extensive than it contemplated, the fault' is its own.[19]

If it is for insurers to say what they 'mean', the next question is: mean to whom? At common law words are not ambiguous or unclear just because they are complex, or because lay people are not sure what they mean; if lawyers can find the meaning of words, those words are not ambiguous.[20] For consumers, however, the rule is different. A consumer of insurance, for the purpose of consumer protection regulations, is a natural person contracting insurance for a purpose 'outside his trade, business or profession'.[21] A consumer benefits from the provisions of an EC Directive,[22] as implemented in the United Kingdom,[23] in that written terms of any contract must be 'expressed in plain and intelligible language' and that, in case of doubt, 'the interpretation which is most favourable to the consumer shall prevail'.[24] The latter is in effect Rule 4(2), however, a term is not plain and intelligible unless it is plain and intelligible not only to lawyers but to the laity.[25] To pronounce on particular cases is the responsibility in the first instance of the Office of Fair Trading (OFT). The OFT has been quick to condemn what it considered to be legal jargon such as 'indemnify', 'consequential loss', and 'events beyond your control'.[26] Such words, not being 'plain and intelligible language', are ruled out.

Somewhere between Rule 3 and Rule 4, the rules begin to look less technical and more like tools for 'creative' interpretation by a court determined to see a particular result. Nonetheless, it should be underlined that, unless the meaning can be described as absurd, the court must give it the interpretation indicated, however much the court dislikes the result. A poignant illustration of sharp drafting requiring painful decisions is found in accident insurance that covers 'dismemberment within 90 days of the injury'; and in American cases in which the surgeons struggled to save a leg and, in one case only after 100 days, gave up and amputated.[27] Courts there ruled in some cases that a clause like that, which compelled the choice between amputation within the insurance period or continuation of the struggle to save the limb, was gruesome, unconscionable, and to be disregarded. English courts, however, would probably agree with the view in other cases that it was not the role of courts to rewrite the contract; that lines have

---

[19] *Jamestown Mutual v Nationwide Mutual*, 146 SE 2d 410, 416 (NC, 1966).
[20] *Higgins v Dawson* [1902] AC 1; Clarke, ch. 15-5.
[21] Unfair Terms in Consumer Contracts Regulations 1999 (SI 1999/2083), reg. 3(1).
[22] 93/13/EEC of 5 April 1993 (OJ 21 April 1993, L95/29).
[23] SI 1999/2083, above, n. 21. See Clarke, ch. 19-5A.   [24] Ibid., reg. 7.
[25] *Unfair Contract Terms*, OFT Bulletin No. 4, December 1997, p. 16.
[26] Respectively OFT Bulletin No. 25 (p. 8), No 5 (p. 72) and No. 25 (p. 8). Bulletins can be read at www.oft.gov.uk.
[27] See K. S. Abraham, *Insurance Law and Regulation* (New York, 1990) 83 ff. The purpose of the clause is to limit disputes over causation: ibid., 86.

to be drawn somewhere and, if clearly drawn, should be respected. However, the line between a meaning which is merely unreasonable and must be applied and one which is absurd and can be avoided, is hard to draw.

Somewhere between Rule 3 and Rule 4, nonetheless, is indeed another rule, Rule 3(a), a rule against absurdity.[28] Rule 3(a) is that, if the application of Rules 1 to 3 produces a result that is so very unreasonable or inconvenient as to be absurd, that result will be ignored. For example, one of the purposes of reinsurance is to protect primary insurers, the reinsured, from exposures which they cannot bear, and which might otherwise imperil their solvency. Against this background, the contention of a reinsurer in a case that went to the House of Lords, that the reinsurer was not liable until the reinsured had 'actually paid', quite literally, many millions of pounds to primary policyholders, was dismissed by the Lords as being without any warrant in common sense or experience, at least in the very specialized form of reinsurance under consideration,[29] and thus absurd. Again, the contention of an accidental injury insurer that literal effect should be given to an exclusion of cover caused by degenerative conditions was rejected, because that would include the normal ageing process and the effect would be substantially to deprive the policyholder of the protection that the insurance was designed to provide, which would be unreasonable to the point of absurdity.[30]

The Importance of Context

The exercise of policy interpretation, as is evident from what has just been said, is one conducted largely within the boundaries of the policy itself, except when, to avoid an absurd result, a court looks beyond those boundaries to ascertain, for example, the purpose of the insurance. Traditionally, courts have also gone outside the policy to hear evidence of trade custom and when, in spite of working through all the rules of interpretation, the words before the court remain ambiguous; but not otherwise. That was the position until a controversial statement by Lord Hoffmann in *ICS*[31] in 1998, announcing that almost all 'the old intellectual baggage of "legal" interpretation had been discarded'.[32] Instead courts could look outside documents, such as insurance policies, at their background. The meaning of a document, he said, 'is what the parties using those words against the relevant background would reasonably have been understood to mean';[33] and, in particular, 'if one would necessarily conclude from the background that something must have gone wrong with the language [of the document], the law does not require

---

[28] E.g., *Smit Tak Offshore Services Ltd v Youell* [1992] 1 Lloyd's Rep 154, 159 (CA). Generally, *Wickman Machine Tool Sales Ltd v Schuler AG* [1975] AC 235, 251.

[29] *Charter Reinsurance Ltd v Fagan* [1996] 2 Lloyd's Rep 113, 118 (HL).

[30] *Blackburn Rovers Football Club v Avon Ins. Co.*, Commercial Court, 15 November 2004.

[31] *Investors Compensation Scheme Ltd v West Bromwich BS*, op. cit. above, n. 10.

[32] Ibid., 912.

[33] Ibid., 913. Lord Goff, Lord Hope, and Lord Clyde agreed with Lord Hoffmann.

the judges to attribute to the parties an intention which they plainly could not have had'.[34]

The background is what Lord Wilberforce had once referred to, 'famously', according to Lord Hoffmann, as the 'matrix of facts'.[35] In the judgment of Lord Wilberforce it reads as no more than a passing reference which did not require explanation, but Lord Hoffmann developed the idea in his own words thus: the background is 'absolutely anything which would have affected the way in which the language of the document would have been understood by a reasonable man',[36] and which a reasonable man would have regarded as relevant,[37] except evidence of previous negotiations.[38] Whether Lord Wilberforce had anything like this in mind seems most unlikely,[39] but the authority of Lord Hoffmann, together with that of others in the House of Lords who agreed with him,[40] has well and truly opened the stable door once formed by the parole evidence rule. The result has been a forensic gallop around the countryside in each case, foraging for background material that might affect the often ordinary meaning of the contract in question.[41]

Decisions reported in England since *ICS* suggest that the impact of the Hoffmann view, at least in insurance cases, has been slight. In *Ham v Somak Travel*,[42] a case of liability insurance arising out of a holiday accident, the Court of Appeal held that a policy exclusion was clear and should apply, refusing to be influenced by background evidence suggesting something different. Subsequently, in *MDIS*,[43] the Court of Appeal did take a step out into the wider world of Lord Hoffmann, but only a very small step. The background in question was, as Clarke LJ pointed out in the case, something 'well known amongst insurance lawyers and indeed brokers for many years and would have been likely to have been in the back of the minds of those negotiating this contract'.[44] Furthermore, the Court was driven out of the boundaries of the insurance policy to safeguard an important element of public policy, namely, transparency in litigation: the Court sought to avoid the possibility that parties might collude to dress a claim in such a way (as negligence) as to bring it within the scope of the policy, whereas on the true facts (fraud) it would have been excluded.[45] The decision sought to discourage well-informed third party claimants from advancing their

---

[34] Ibid., 913.   [35] *Prenn v Simmonds* [1971] 1 WLR 1381, 1384 (HL).

[36] *ICS*, op. cit. above, n. 10, 913.

[37] A qualification which Lord Hoffman said later went without saying: *Bank of Credit and Commerce Int. SA v Ali* [2002] 1 AC 251, at [39].

[38] Ruled out by *Prenn*, op. cit. above, n. 35 above.

[39] C. Staughton, 'How do the Courts Interpret Commercial Contracts' [1999] CLJ 303–13, 307.

[40] Lords Goff, Hope, and Clyde.

[41] It has been cited in ten reported cases a year on average since 1998.

[42] (1998) 10 ILM No. 6 (CA).

[43] *MDIS Ltd v Swinbank* [1999] Lloyd's Rep IR 516, 521 (CA).

[44] Ibid., 522. The same can be said of *King v Brandywine Reinsurance Co. (UK) Ltd* [2004] Lloyd's Rep IR 554, in which insurers were taken to be aware of what was available to them in the reinsurance market. Appeal dismissed: [2005] Lloyd's Rep IR 508, (CA).   [45] See Clarke, ch. 17-4E.

prospects by being 'economical with the truth'. Cinema-going lawyers will recognize the 'matrix' of fact in this case as having little to do with the real world and more to do with the realities of forensic science.

Prominent among the critics of what appeared to be the Hoffmann view are some distinguished judges whose early careers had been at the commercial bar. Sir Christopher Staughton's trenchant comment was that it is 'hard to imagine a ruling more calculated to perpetuate the vast cost of commercial litigation'.[46] That was also the first of two objections made earlier in *Dellborg* by Lord Saville.[47] His second was that

the position of third parties (which would include assignees of contractual rights) does not seem to have been considered at all. They are unlikely in the nature of things to be aware of the surrounding circumstances. Where the words of the agreement have only one meaning, and that meaning is not self evidently nonsensical, is the third party justified in taking that to be the agreement that was made, or unable to rely on the words used without examining (which it is likely to be difficult or impossible for third parties to do) all the surrounding circumstances?

This is a powerful point which affects cargo and transit insurance, where a buyer usually gets an insurance document from the seller who contracted the cover;[48] and also employees, for example, who are insured under a group scheme arranged for them in that example by their employer.

The very possibility of unrestricted enquiry into background creates uncertainty and cost. The Civil Procedure Rules, whereby judges assume responsibility for case management, state in Part 1.1(2)(C) that the handling of a case is to be proportionate to the financial position of the parties. Indeed, in *ICS* itself, Lord Hoffmann did qualify the authorized quest for background information with the requirement that the information must have been 'reasonably available to the parties',[49] and that surely must take account of the resources available to each party.

Today the dust seems to be settling on this controversy. In the words of Lord Bingham, to 'ascertain the intention of the parties the court reads the terms of the contract as a whole, giving the words used their natural and ordinary meaning in the context of the agreement, the parties' relationship and all the relevant facts surrounding the transaction *so far as known to the parties*';[50] or, as previously stated by Sir Christopher Staughton, 'nothing is relevant to the interpretation of a contract, unless it is known, or at least capable of being known, to both parties when the contract was made'.[51] The vast majority of contracts of insurance, those

[46] Op. cit. above, n. 39.
[47] *Nat. Bank of Sharjah v Dellborg*, CA, 9 July 1997, *per* Saville LJ. Thorpe and Judge LJJ agreed with him.
[48] This point was made specifically in *International Multifoods v Commercial Union*, 98 F Supp 2d 498, 503 (SD NY, 2000).
[49] Op. cit. above, n. 10, 912. He repeated the point in *Bank of Credit and Commerce Int. SA v Ali*, op. cit. above, n. 37, at [49].
[50] *Ali*, op. cit. above, n. 37, at [8], emphasis added. See also Lord Bingham in *Dairy Containers v Tasman Orient Line* [2005] 1 WLR 215, [12] PC.
[51] 'Interpretation of Maritime Contracts', 26 JMLC 259–71, 263 (1995).

on more or less standard risks and agreed on insurers' standard terms, will be unaffected by Lord Hoffmann's adventure into the matrix; and so far the impact on the rest has been slight.[52] The stable door may be open but any excursion is likely to go no further than the familiar surroundings of the yard.

Words: The Problem of Comprehension

Comprehension by Courts

The value of reference to precedent[53] is that the insurers drafting a contract can predict the effect of their words—not only particular words, but underlying ideas too. Moreover, if they use 'old' words and phrases, insurers can assume that words interpreted in one sense by one court will be understood in the same sense by another court. When courts come to new words and phrases, however, they tend to employ what psychologists call a heuristic stratagem, by which they strive to relate the new issue to previously established patterns of experience and thought. So, in the task of interpretation, the court looks for an analogy with precedent or, at a conceptual level, with an established concept. A clear illustration of this is provided by the courts' construction of the requirement of many insurance contracts that the policyholder should take precautions to prevent loss.[54]

Comprehension by Policyholders

The rules of interpretation, when they can be applied effectively, work in favour of both parties to the insurance contract in so far as the rules discourage disputes, inhibit wishful or 'creative' argument, and permit the parties to predict the effect of the contract. If such certainty is achieved, however, it may be at a cost to policyholders. The rules of construction being lawyers' rules and some of the language lawyers' language, policyholders may not know exactly what the contract means and, therefore, may have to pay for professional advice to find out. What is plain to insurers and, perhaps, to courts may not be plain at all to policyholders. Regulations deriving from an EC Directive require contract terms for consumers to be 'plain and intelligible',[55] but individual consumers are poorly placed to insist on this in their own insurance policies.[56] Worse still, policyholders may be in the fool's paradise of believing that their policy clearly means one thing when, in law, it means something else.

For example, what could be plainer than a policy with cover 'from 1 January 2005 to 1 January 2006'? Just as a holiday in France booked from 1 July to

---

[52] E.g., *T & N Ltd v Royal & Sun Alliance plc* [2003] 2 All ER (Comm) 939, at [226].
[53] See, above, Rule 3(a), at p. 140.   [54] See below, p. 166 ff.
[55] See, above, p. 141.   [56] Clarke, ch. 19-5A5.

1 August would be from the morning of 1 July to the evening of 1 August, might people not reasonably assume that travel insurance 'from 1 July to 1 August' is for the same period? If they were to check with a competent adviser, however, they would find that the cover does not begin until the *end* of the first day in July—because the law needs a rule about this and that is what the courts have decided.[57] The ignorant may be in a state of bliss but, as the ferry to Calais founders, they may also be in a state of another sort—up to their necks without insurance. It is all very well to say that the policyholders should always check with their adviser, but that is not good enough. First, in these days of direct insurance, many people do not have advisers to consult. Secondly, if they do have advisers to consult, that is scarcely to the point unless people know when they need to consult them.

More might be done by insurers to avoid some of the stranger definitions of English law. If a word has a technical meaning in criminal law, the word is usually interpreted in the same way in insurance contracts.[58] This seems sensible, but the interpretation is based on a presumption and one that should not be applied automatically. For example, when a Boeing 747 aircraft was quietly and efficiently hijacked in the air by two terrorists in radio contact with others on the ground, the insurer argued in New York that the loss of the aircraft was not covered, because the hijacking was a 'riot'. This argument would surely have been laughed out of court, but for an English precedent inspired by the 'troubles' in Ireland in the early years of the twentieth century, that a riot might include a quiet riot of only three people,[59] and perhaps because the court in New York was too polite. Having expressed 'deference' on matters of insurance law to the 'ancestral authorities on the old mysteries', the court dismissed the argument. The 'notion of a flying riot in geographic instalments cannot be squeezed into the ancient formula'. Riot cannot be 'conducted by mail, by telephone, or as in the present case, by radio'.[60] The court preferred what it saw as the commonsense and popular idea of riot, which connoted some degree of tumult. In England, the common law has been changed by section 1 of the Public Order Act 1986. We now need twelve people to have a riot, and although—obviously—tumult is more likely with the statutory dozen than the common law trio, a quiet riot by a disciplined football team is still possible, if not in reality at least in law. In practice, however, some insurers take their line not from the law but from the police: if the police describe an actual event not as a riot but as, for example, 'a series of incidents of disorder', the insurers pay.

Another word which people find strange, and which, in times of climate change, people are more likely to be concerned about than 'riot', is 'subsidence'. Claims by householders have been refused because what occurred, said their

---

[57] *Cartwright v MacCormack* [1963] 1 All ER 11 (CA).
[58] See, above, p. 140.
[59] *Motor Union Ins. Co. Ltd v Boggan* (1923) 130 LT 588 (HL).
[60] *Pan American World Airways Inc. v Aetna Casualty & Surety Co.*, 505 F 2d 989, 1005, 1020-21 (US CA, 2 Cir., 1974).

insurers, was not 'subsidence' but 'settlement'; there is some support for this view in a relatively old decision of the court.[61] Today, however, the dictionary says that 'subsidence' is 'a gradual lowering or settling down of the earth'. Moreover, as long as downward movement is not part of a larger movement of land and is uneven, the IOB was willing to support policyholders' complaints.[62]

Understandable annoyance and anxiety in the public about terms such as these, fanned by the press, have encouraged the selling of 'security of wording', of 'easy-to-read' policies, written in 'plain English'. Indeed, one leading household insurer announced proudly and prominently in 2003 that it had managed to condense its booklet of standard terms from about forty pages (A4) to eight. And is that not how it should be? Should not all insurance contracts be in plain English and easy to read? Unfortunately, it is submitted here, although the language of these policies makes an immediate impression, like music for easy listening, it is unlikely to withstand the scrutiny of time.

The Myth of Ordinary Meaning and Plain English

English contract forms are often used, if not always understood, abroad. 'Perhaps those whose native tongue is not English have been unduly encouraged by the supreme status accorded to the language of Shakespeare to acquiesce in a degree of inaccessibility', which is hard to justify.[63] But are such forms sufficiently understood in the land of Shakespeare itself? Evidently not, but there is nonetheless a widespread belief that they could be and should be; that insurers and lawyers have heeded too much the warning of Oscar Wilde, that to be intelligible is to be found out; and that their documents should be demystified and brought out of the inner sanctum of the few and made both available and intelligible to the many ordinary people in the street. Indeed, the belief is not new. It was St Luke (chapter II, verse 52) who said: 'Woe unto you, lawyers! for ye have taken away the key of knowledge: ye entered not in yourselves, and them that were entering in ye hindered.' Today, there is a movement for demystification, in tandem with the assumption that there is such a thing as 'ordinary' or 'plain' English; and that this English is used and understood by ordinary people, and should be used in their contracts. Even if we accept another assumption, that ordinary English and plain English are the same and refer from now on (hereinafter?) only to the latter, the notion of plain English is a myth in more than one sense of that ordinary (?) word.

English that is plain should be plain to all, but experience soon shows that it is not. Often enough, words are commonplace precisely because they are not precise but contain several shades of meaning. Moreover, to write plain English we must first tame the emotive power of words; and then we must overcome the limits of

---

[61] Appropriately called *Allen (David) & Sons Ltd v Drysdale* [1939] 4 All ER 113.
[62] IOB, *Digest of Annual Reports and Bulletins*, 2nd edn (1999), p. 315.
[63] F. D. Rose, 'Review of O'May, *Marine Insurance*' (1994) 110 LQR 494–6, 495.

words. It may be an impossible task. 'He who knows does not speak, he who speaks does not know.' Silence, of course, is a golden luxury that insurers and, still less, policyholders can afford. English may be treacherous, but it is also indispensable; and what is needed is not so much a new and 'plainer' use of words but better means of controlling the words we have got.[64]

To control the use of words, we must first understand the limits of words as a medium of expression, the scale of the task. In 1994, the most learned judges in the land were divided on the meaning of the word 'influence'.[65] Of all the cases closed by the IOB in 1995, about 50 per cent concerned one category alone, disputes about the meaning and scope of cover. Since then the IOB and (later) the FOS have published the 'Ombudsman view' of what is meant by important wordings, but it is significant that the FOS does this mostly not by offering definitions or paraphrasing in plain Ombudspeak, but by giving illustrations from its files.

The fact remains that policyholders do not read or understand their policies. Travel insurance complaints to the FOS alone rose by 33 per cent in 2003.[66] The potential of insurance contracts to confuse to the point of driving the parties to the end of the disputes procedure seems undiminished. The prose of the recent past provides little encouragement for those who put their faith in plain English. Further, recent American legal history shows that there are 'none so blind as will not see', and that no language, English or American, is plain to the court determined to find ambiguity and thus do its idea of justice. Much depends on the attitude of the reader, and of the court. Be that as it may, courts commonly seek assistance in dictionaries and, of course, precedent. Both have their limits.

The Limits of Dictionaries

First, the dictionary may not give an answer that ordinary people would regard as plain. Dictionaries cannot be trusted blindly; they have to be used with care. Stories abound of misuse; for example, the translation into Russian of 'the spirit is willing but the flesh is weak' which, translated back into English, came out as 'the vodka is good but the meat is rotten'.

Secondly, the dictionary may not give an answer that ordinary people would think ordinary. In the supermarket, tomatoes are found among the vegetables because that is where ordinary buyers expect them to be; but in the dictionary they will find them with fruit, because that is the view of the botanist and, naturally, that is what they 'are'.

Thirdly, language changes faster than the dictionaries on the shelf of the court. One of the virtues of English is that it accommodates changes in the speech of ordinary people and has not been nailed down by any '*Academie Anglaise*', in

---

[64] C. K. Ogden and I. A. Richards, *The Meaning of Meaning*, 10th edn (London, 1953) 19.
[65] In the leading insurance case *Pan Atlantic Ins. Co. v Pine Top Ins Co.* [1995] AC 501.
[66] FOS Annual Review, 2004, p. 53.

Oxford or anywhere else. The plain meaning itself, it has been suggested by a leading authority in the United States, is 'incapable of responding without lag to a world that changes faster than language'.[67] That was why, not so long ago, a court in England applied an 'ordinary' meaning of 'insurance' which differed from that in the current dictionary.[68] Dictionaries are frozen in time and out of date almost before they are published.

Fourthly, words cannot be properly understood without some regard to their context. Simon Hoggart, a well-known journalist, writing about an even better-known politician, John Prescott, said ruefully: 'As we know, his grammar is all over the place, his syntax and vocabulary entirely haphazard, but—thanks to his body language and emotional energy—we always know exactly what he means.' But when his language must be reduced to writing, the 'readers of Hansard don't have that assistance'.[69] Only to a limited degree can dictionaries help with context by listing common phrases. Some words, such as 'building' and 'goods', have such a fringe of meaning, a penumbra of uncertainty, that no technical definition alone will ensure precision.[70] Nonetheless, these words can usually be understood if they are seen in context, in relation to other words to which, in context, they are opposed or with which they are associated. However, that is a process which requires rules, rules of interpretation, lawyers' rules.

The Language of Precedent

When programmers want to give precise instructions to computers, they do not use plain English. This is not to suggest for contracts of insurance the language of mathematics. As a leading jurist of his day once observed, Euclidean geometry 'starts from notions of points and lines which, having no size, are not objects of sense; thus the figures constructed from these notions are not objects of sense either'.[71] Nonetheless, for precise and predictable communication, a technical language of some kind is unavoidable and, of course, problematic. When the language of the law attributes to a clause in a contract a meaning, which it has been held to have by a court in the past, there is a risk of defeating the intention of the parties who, if they thought about it at all, might well have thought that it would mean something else. Against that consideration there is a legitimate desire among lawyers for certainty. It is their duty to their clients, not least to insurers, to draw up contracts that will keep clients out of court and, if they do find themselves in court, which the court can understand. There is a circle, but a circle of understanding from which policyholders may be excluded.[72]

A study of flaws in standard contracts drafted by lawyers in the USA, such as prolixity, concluded by wondering whether the flaws 'might not be the smallest

---

[67] F. Schauer, 'Statutory Construction and the Co-ordinating Function of Plain Meaning' [1990] Sup Ct Rev 231–56, 252. More general objections come from E. A. Farnsworth, ' "Meaning" in the Law of Contracts' 76 Yale LJ 936–65, (1967).
[68] *Re NRG Victory Reinsurance Ltd* [1995] 1 All ER 533.   [69] *The Guardian*, 8 July 1994.
[70] G.- L. Williams, 'Language and the Law' (1945) 61 LQR 293–303, 301; and 384–406, 393.
[71] Ibid., 300.   [72] *Newbury v Turngiant* (1991) 63 P & CR 458, 478 (CA).

price we could pay for the benefit the process offers'.[73] Moreover, in an attempt to explain why in Germany contracts appear to 'work' more efficiently than in the USA, commentators have pointed not only to a commercial climate where there was more trust and less opportunism but also to the greater use of standard contract terms provided for in legislation or drafted by trade associations and thus, of course, not in plain German but in the language of German lawyers.[74]

Like travellers to foreign parts, people who come to the world of insurance must not expect the natives to speak (their) English. The problem has been debated by Australians—not perceived in England as overly respectful of tradition, especially those exported from England. The Australian Law Reform Commission found a fear there among insurers that both parties to insurance contracts 'may be prejudiced by the abandonment of technical wordings which have been subject, in many instances, to a considerable history of judicial interpretation', and observed that while 'this fear may be readily exaggerated, it is not totally without foundation'.[75] Moreover, the proposal that a 'simple summary of the nature of the cover' be given to policyholders was rejected by the Commission as being unworkable and ineffective.[76] In the end the Commission did require insurers to give applicants certain information 'in clear language', but it did not recommend that insurance policies be written in plain English, plain Australian, or anything else.

Qualified support can be found in New York for plain American, where § 3102(c)(1) of the Insurance Law[77] provides that:

[N]o insurance policy . . . shall be made, issued or delivered in this state on a risk located or resident in this state, unless: . . . (B) *wherever practicable*, it uses words with common and everyday meanings to facilitate readability and to aid the insured or policyholder in understanding the coverage provided.[78]

This is perhaps the most that can be achieved.

Planes of Precision

A distinction has been drawn between clarity and precision.[79] Precision is the medium of persons working in the same field and at the same level. Plain English may also be a convenient point of reference or *lingua franca* for such persons, persons of comparable intelligence and training who *want* to agree with each other, such as drafters and, sometimes, judges; but that role does not qualify plain English as a general means of communication between persons of different intelligence, background, and training, who are dealing at arm's length and who may

---

[73] C. A. Hill 'Why Contracts are Written in "Legalese"', 77 Ch.-Kent L Rev 59–81 (2001).

[74] C. A. Hill and C. King, 'How do German Contracts Do as Much with Fewer Words', 79 Ch.-Kent L Rev 889–926, 912 (2004).   [75] Report No. 20, *Insurance Contracts*, 1982, para. 43.

[76] Ibid.   [77] http://public.leginfo.state.ny.us/menugetf.cgi.   [78] Emphasis added.

[79] On this somewhat technical distinction, see J. Stark, 'Should the Main Goal of Statutory Drafting be Accuracy or Clarity?' (1994) 15 Statute L Rev 207–13.

not always want to agree. Clarity is usually a more subjective matter, which cannot effectively be sought without asking: clear to whom? Surely, we all have a kind of wisdom when we know that we do not know. The danger of the pursuit of plain English is the fool's paradise, one for all, in which English policyholders believe that they understand their insurance policies and that they have cover when perhaps they do not. Real and effective understanding can only be achieved at the level of the individual.

If people do not understand the cover proposed, the proper course is not to complain or to blame other people but to seek an interpreter, such as an independent intermediary or even the insurer. If intermediaries get it badly wrong, they may be liable to the policyholder.[80] If insurers get it wrong, they may be estopped by what they said about their contract and the court will make the contract mean what the policyholder was led to believe it to mean.[81] This seems to be the best compromise on offer between certainty and comprehension. The Banking Code 2003,[82] as one of its 'Key Commitments', contained a promise by bankers to help each customer 'to understand how our financial products and services work' by 'giving you information about them in plain English'. The version current in 2007 dates from 2005[82a] and, significantly perhaps, the promise of plain English has been dropped, although 'Key Commitments' to provide 'clear information about our products and services', and 'clear information' about accounts and 'the terms and conditions and the interest rates which apply' remain. But at the same time and in the same 'Key Commitment' they also promise to do this by 'explaining their financial implications' and by 'helping you choose the one that meets your needs'. Insurers want to sell insurance quickly and cheaply. Many people want to buy insurance quickly and cheaply. However, the dangers associated with speed are not confined to the road. The person who drives in a strange land without map or navigator takes a risk.

Unexpected Effects

Some commonplace words associated with insurance cover do not mean quite what most people expect. Some of these are considered in Chapter 6. Our concern here is with some of the policy conditions, for example, conditions about notifying the insurer about loss or damage. If, in such a case, application of the ordinary meaning of the words under Rule 1[83] leads to an unreasonable result, courts have stated that generally they must give effect to that meaning nonetheless. This is generally true, but there are exceptions.

Words that come before the FOS, or before a court applying the EC Directive on unfair terms in consumer contracts,[84] are subject to a test of fairness. Moreover,

---

[80] See Chapter 3, p. 76 ff.   [81] Below, p. 153.
[82] Published by the British Bankers' Association in March 2003.
[82a] http://www.bankingcode.org.uk/pdfdocs/BANKING%20CODE.pdf
[83] Above, at pp. 139–40.   [84] SI 1999/2083, above, n. 21 reg. 5(1).

as we have seen, Rule 3(a)[85] says that, if the application of Rules 1 to 3 produces a result that is so very unreasonable or inconvenient as to be absurd, that result will be ignored. These exceptions apart, the terms of a contract cannot be defeated according to the common law rules of interpretation simply because they are unreasonable. However, the judges, led by Lord Denning, got around this with a rule that did indeed defeat terms because they were unreasonable, by calling them something else—'unusual' or 'unexpected'.[86] Is there any lesson here for insurance contracts?

The enquiry must start from the rules of interpretation, in particular Rule 1, which gives primacy to ordinary meaning. In England in 1991, in *Smit Tak*, Lord Mustill stated firmly that there was no rule, like that found in the United States, that the contract must be construed in line with policyholders' reasonable expectations,[87] unless, of course, their expectations coincide with the ordinary meaning. The American rule is that policyholders are bound by what they did read of the contract, or can realistically be expected to read, and only in conformity with that is the rest of the contract enforced; it is enforced only in conformity with the reasonable expectations of policyholders, together with any other relevant features implicit in the overall transaction. As regards the overall transaction, just as people buy goods in the expectation that they 'work', they also expect insurers to sell them a policy that works as it was meant to.[88]

For example, in *Kievet*,[89] 'accident' cover was sold to a man of 48, who later suffered an accidental blow on the head which triggered latent Parkinson's disease. The insurer defended the man's claim, pleading an exception of 'disability or other loss resulting from or contributed to by any disease or ailment'. This defence failed. The court noted that people would expect this kind of accident to be covered and, moreover, that, if it were not covered, the insurance would be of little use to a man of 48: if the exception were read literally, any disability or death resulting from accidental injury would in all probability be in some sense contributed to by the infirmities of age, and thus excluded. To make the policy 'work', the court construed it in line with the policyholder's reasonable expectation that an 'accident' policy covered what most people would regard as an accident.

Put like this, surely, the argument takes a form that should at least get a hearing in England because, even without ambiguity, the English court construes in accordance with the main purpose of the contract as it appears from the contract itself: Rule 4(1). Where the American form of the argument would run into difficulty in England is the point of focus on the expectations of just one party, the policyholder, to determine the purpose of the insurance, rather than the

---

[85] Above, at p. 140.
[86] *Thornton v Shoe Lane Parking Ltd* [1971] 2 QB 163 (CA).
[87] *Smit Tak Offshore Services v Youell*, op. cit. above, n. 28, *per* Mustill LJ.
[88] Slawson, op. cit. above, n. 3, 546–47.
[89] *Kievet v Loyal Protective Life Ins. Co.*, 170 A 2d 22 (NJ, 1961). See also *Riffe v Home Finders*, 517 SE 2d 313 (W Va, 1999).

expectations of both. The role of the English court is not to rewrite contracts but to expound and apply existing law to contracts as they have been agreed by both parties.

A further difficulty in England is an ingrained belief in gradualism and pragmatism which, according to Lord Goff, tends away from wide generalizations and abstract principles.[90] Argument with reference to reasonable expectations *tout nu* is too stark, too general, too exposed. Our courts feel agoraphobically uneasy with wide rules like that. The argument would also suffer from association with the violence done to insurance contracts with such a rule by some of the more immoderate courts in the United States; and it is noteworthy that in the last ten years many courts there have retreated to a more conservative position.[91] Moreover, it is but a small step from the purpose of the insurance contract before the court to the purpose of insurance contracts generally and, therefore, from the expectations of the parties before the court to the expectations of the court itself. Nonetheless, an argument of this kind is not entirely without 'legs' in England.

The Reasonable Expectations of Policyholders

In spite of what might be called the traditional view, restated in *Smit Tak*,[92] arguments for a rule of reasonable expectations can be made in England today. Two arguments are the effects of more general and established rules of law or of interpretation. The third is based on insurance contract law and the duty of good faith. The fourth is a direct assault based both on general contract law and on insurance contract law.

First, as we have seen in Rule 2 of the rules of interpretation, if there are words of a contract inconsistent with other words of the contract, the court prefers the words that best reflect the intention of the parties. These will be those, for example, that the parties have specifically adopted, rather than printed words in standard form. More to the immediate point, the preference will be for the words which best give effect to the purpose of the contract. Given that a dominant purpose of insurance contracts is to provide cover, if policyholders reasonably expect to be covered for the loss in question, it should not be too hard to persuade courts to uphold that expectation. For example, if one part of a liability insurance contract indicates that the policyholder's negligence is covered, but another part indicates otherwise, the courts have shown a clear preference for the former.[93]

[90] 'The Role of the Judge in England' RabelsZ 58 (1994) 443–8, 446. It was not always so: J. Gordley, 'Comparative Legal Research: Its Function in the Development of Harmonized Law' 43 Am J Comp L 555–67 (1995).
[91] E.g., *Wilkie v Auto-Owners Ins. Co.*, 664 NW 2d 776 (Mich., 2003). Nonetheless, a version of the rule is found in a number of common law countries; see J.- A. Tarr, 'The Insured's Reasonable Expectations' (2001) 12 Ins LJ 258.   [92] Op. cit. above, n. 28.
[93] *Woolfall & Rimmer Ltd v Moyle* [1942] 1 KB 66, 76 (CA). See also *Forsikringsaktieselskapet Vesta v Butcher* [1989] 1 AC 852, 895, 909.

Cover

Secondly, if policyholders' expectations are not only reasonable but actually induced by the insurer, the contract will be construed in line with those expectations. If, for example, policyholders do not understand the extent of the cover, they may well ask the agent of the insurer, whose role it is to explain the terms. General contract law states that if party A tells party B that a term of their proposed contract means X, although it really means Y, it will be treated as meaning X, if B has acted reasonably in relying on what A said.[94] Clearly, applicant B is entitled to rely on what insurer A's agent says about A's proposed contract of insurance with B. So, if the agent tells B that a certain kind of loss is covered by the insurance, whereas on a strict application of the rules of interpretation it is not, the loss is covered because the insurer's agent said so, and the insurer is estopped from denying what the agent said.[95]

Thirdly, the duty of disclosure between the parties to insurance contracts is mutual.[96] Insurers owe applicants for insurance a duty to disclose all matters which would affect their judgement when deciding whether or not to make the contract at the premium demanded. This cannot be taken entirely literally; for example, insurer X is not obliged to disclose that similar cover costs less from insurer Y.[97] More sustainable, surely, is the contention that insurers should tell applicants exactly what they are getting for their premium money, that is, the scope of the cover. In the words of the American *Restatement 2d of Contracts* (1979), § 211(3), which applies to all standard-form contracts, including insurance contracts: 'Where the other party has reason to believe that the party manifesting . . . assent would not do so if he knew that the writing contained a particular term, the term is not part of the agreement.' As we have seen,[98] the FOS requires sellers of insurance to draw to the attention of buyers of insurance the inevitable restrictions and exclusions that the policy on offer contains,[99] and the practice has *obiter* support from the court.[100] Moreover, if the relevant contract term is onerous and unusual, it is inoperative under general contract law unless specifically drawn to the attention of the other party.[101] The argument here is that English law about disclosure indicates a result that should ensure that reasonable expectations of policyholders about the cover offered are not frustrated.

Fourthly, in recent times countless judges in common law countries have said something like what was once said by Lord Steyn: the 'theme that runs through

[94] E.g., *Curtis v Chemical Cleaning & Dyeing Co.* [1951] 1 KB 805 (CA).
[95] E.g., *Kaufmann v British Surety Ins. Co. Ltd* (1929) 33 Ll L Rep 315. See Clarke, ch. 8-3C.
[96] See Chapter 4, at p. 99 ff.
[97] *Banque Keyser Ullmann SA v Skandia (UK) Ins Co. Ltd* [1990] 1 QB 665, 772 (CA); aff'd [1991] 2 AC 249.   [98] Chapter 4, pp. 90–1.
[99] E.g., for the widely misunderstood limits on cover of curtailment of travel: *Ombudsman News*, July 2003, p. 5; see also *Ombudsman News*, April 2004, p. 36.
[100] *Nsbuga v Commercial Union Assurance Co. plc* [1998] 2 Lloyd's Rep 682, 685.
[101] *Interfoto Picture Library Ltd v Stilleto Visual Programmes Ltd* [1989] QB 433 (CA); *O'Brien v MGN* [2001] EWCA Civ 1279.

our law of contract is that the reasonable expectations of honest men must be protected. It is not a rule or a principle of law. It is the objective which has been and still is the principal moulding force of our law of contract.'[102] The case in which he said that concerned not insurance but banking; however, the IOB has approached insurance contracts with these words of Lord Steyn as its 'guiding light'.[103] In *Smit Tak*,[104] in which in 1991 a different view was taken, the situation was very different too: the case concerned liability cover for salvage and wreck removal by large international companies operating off the coast of Dubai. More recently, however, it seems that the notion of reasonable expectations was applied by the House of Lords to an insurance contract in *Cook*.[105] This case concerned disability insurance contracted by a self-employed builder in order to persuade his bank to finance his business. In the course of his judgment Lord Lloyd said that a certificate, which the man had received from the insurer concerned, 'must be construed in the sense in which it would have been reasonably understood by him as the consumer'.[106]

The Use of Words: Terms of the Contract

Policy terms can be grouped according to their function. Suppose motor insurance covering (a) private saloon SI23 JEB against theft unless (b) it is unlocked, provided that (c) reasonable steps are taken to maintain the vehicle in efficient condition; and requiring (d) that any theft be notified to the police and to the insurer within 48 hours.

Term (a) defines cover in positive terms of the subject-matter of the insurance. Term (b) is called an exception (also an exclusion, restriction, or limit); this also defines cover but in negative terms, qualifying term (a). Term (c) also qualifies cover, but in a different way, and is called a warranty. Term (d) has nothing to do with the scope of cover, but is designed, in part at least, to make the contract less burdensome to the insurer; these are called procedural conditions and are considered later.

Term (a) is case-specific as regards the vehicle. If the registration number is changed, the subject-matter remains the same and cover continues. If, however, the vehicle is modified, for example for rallying, or the policyholder replaces it, for the purpose of insurance the vehicle insured no longer exists—just as if it had been destroyed. Cover ends. Theft, on the other hand, is a peril defined by law.[107]

---

[102] *First Energy (UK) Ltd v Hungarian International Bank Ltd* [1993] 2 Lloyd's Rep 194, 196 (CA). See also in this sense the Rt Hon. Lord Steyn, 'Contract Law: Fulfilling the Reasonable Expectations of Honest Men' (1997), 113 LQR 433.

[103] Insurance Ombudsman, Annual Report 1993, para. 6.1.

[104] *Smit Tak Offshore Services v Youell*, op. cit. above, n. 28.

[105] *Cook v Financial Ins. Co. Ltd* [1998] 1 WLR 1765 (HL).   [106] Ibid., 1768.

[107] See above, Rule 3, p. 140.

Term (b) in common with term (c) may be called a condition and operate to defeat a claim. However, they differ importantly in that breach of (b) must be a cause of the loss claimed, whereas breach of (c) defeats a claim regardless. There is an important distinction between them. Moreover, if the policyholder is in breach of (b), the effect on cover is not permanent but only suspensive. But if the brakes are out of order, unless repaired as soon as reasonably possible, their condition is a breach of warranty, term (c), and the effect is that the cover ends immediately and automatically. Breach of term (d), unlike the others, gives insurers a right (semble never exercised) to damages, but generally does not defeat a claim or end cover.[108]

Breach of a warranty terminates cover automatically and forever.[109] To make matters worse for policyholders, a warranty broken slightly is broken nonetheless. In one rather extreme case,[110] Lord Wright held that the policyholder who warranted that he had paid £285 for his vehicle but had paid £271 was in breach of the warranty. The position of policyholders is less precarious in practice, because insurers may still want a policyholder's business and thus 'waive' the nullifying effect of the breach of warranty.[111] Logically, true waiver is impossible here because it involves an election by the insurer not to exercise a legal right, the right to treat the insurance as terminated; but breach of warranty terminates insurance contracts automatically whether that is the wish of insurers or not. Nonetheless, 'waiver' is regarded as a desirable option, and courts have shown themselves willing to help by treating what has been traditionally called 'waiver' as estoppel.[112] Insurers who have 'waived' a breach of warranty are estopped from pleading that the insurance has ended anyway by automatic operation of law. Evidently, to know whether a term is an exception or a warranty, which is sometimes difficult, is always important.

Exceptions

Exceptions to cover, which insurance law sometimes calls exclusions of cover or restrictions on cover, are terms limiting the scope of cover. For example, a house in East Anglia may be covered against damage except damage caused by flooding; or a parent may be covered against (the cost of) cancellation of a wedding caused by illness and the like, unless it is a case of 'cold feet', that is, bride or groom have had second thoughts!

The more complex the case, the more appropriate it is to see exceptions as part of the overall structure of cover. Cover, like any other contractual undertaking,

---

[108] See below p. 216 ff.   [109] *The Good Luck* [1992] 1 AC 233.
[110] *Allen v Universal Automobile Ins. Co. Ltd* (1933) 45 Ll LR 55.
[111] See Clarke, ch. 20-7.
[112] *HIH Casualty Ltd v AXA Corp.* [2002] Lloyd's Rep IR 325 at [23] ff.; aff'd [2002] EWCA Civ 1253; [2003] Lloyd's Rep IR 1 (CA).

may be drafted entirely in positive terms. In a lease, for example, the landlord may promise to let the first and second floors of the house. Alternatively, the lease may be drafted in a combination of positive and negative terms, for example, a promise to let (all of) the house, except the ground floor. In general contract law, it has been strongly argued that the effect of the contract is the same in each case, and that, in the alternative draft, the role of the exception (of the ground floor) is definitional rather than exclusionary of liability for breach of a broader promise.[113] This view has also been expressed in insurance cases.[114] It is the view of such clauses in France, for example, and, it is submitted, it is the better of the two views in England. The sculptor, who chips bits off a chunk of stone, is doing the same kind of work as the potter, who builds up the shape from clay. The drafting of an insurance policy, whether it is done like the potter or the sculptor, should be viewed in the same way, as a whole. The role of exceptions, therefore, is to define the boundary of the risk insured.

In general contract law the main importance of the point is that, if exceptions are classified as terms excluding liability, the court can strike them out under the Unfair Contract Terms Act 1977 to the extent that they are unreasonable.[115] In contrast, that cannot happen to insurance contracts, because insurers persuaded Parliament that policy exceptions should be outside the operation of the Act. Insurers failed to gain the same exemption from the EC Directive on Unfair Terms in Consumer Contracts,[116] however, under which, according to how they are classified, policy terms can be censored.

Warranties

Warranties have a distinct role in insurance contracts but, unless they have learned the language of insurance law, to lay people and lawyers alike the word 'warranty' is confusing. To the one, warranties are some kind of guarantee of the quality of household goods; to the other, they have something to do with obligations under the Sale of Goods Act. But for lawyers the confusion gets worse, because insurance warranties are sometimes called 'conditions', which does alert lawyers to the possibility that they are important, which they are, but may also suggest something like Sale of Goods Act conditions, which they are not.

Sale conditions are such a significant part of any sale contract that, when they are broken, the effect in law is that buyers have both a right to damages and an option to terminate the contract of sale. This is because in law the buyer in question has been substantially deprived of what was contracted for. Insurance warranties are not part of what either party contracted for. What insurers mainly

---

[113] See, e.g., *Photo Production Ltd v Securicor Transport Ltd* [1980] AC 827, 851. Cf. *Smith v Eric Bush* [1990] 1 AC 831, 857.   [114] E.g., *Concrete Ltd v Attenborough* (1940) 65 Ll L Rep 174, 179.

[115] See *Smith v Eric Bush*, op. cit. above, n. 113.

[116] See Chapter 7, p. 268 ff.

want out of the transaction is premium. What policyholders want out of the transaction is cover. Warranties are closely concerned with cover, but they restrict cover rather than enhance it. Hence, insurance warranties are sometimes said to be 'conditional but not promissory', whereas sale conditions can be described as both.

Further, when sale conditions are broken, the effect in law is that buyers have both a right to damages and an option to terminate the contract of sale which, unless that option is exercised, remains in being. When insurance warranties are broken, breach terminates the insurance contract; however, it does so not at the insurer's option but automatically by operation of law.[117] Moreover, breach does not give the insurer any right to damages. Insurers want warranties in their contracts not for any net benefit that insurers may derive from them, but in order to limit the risk and thus to reduce the burden or extent of their promise of cover.

If, then, insurance warranties are not sale conditions, lawyers new to them might take them at 'face value' as being something like sale warranties. Again, that would be a mistake. Sale warranties are promises collateral to the main purpose of sale contracts. When sale warranties are broken, although they are less significant than sale conditions, buyers have still been deprived of one of the things contracted for. Insurance warranties are not at all part of what insurers contract for, which is simply and solely premium. Moreover, when sale warranties are broken, breach gives buyers a right to damages but does not entitle them to terminate the contract of sale. As we have seen, however, breach of insurance warranties terminates the contract of insurance automatically, and does not give insurers any right to damages. So, clearly, insurance warranties are not sale warranties either. With perversity of the traditional English kind that holds Cambridge May Balls in June, English insurance law calls insurance terms of this kind both conditions and warranties, although in the language of the general law they are neither.

In the end, our lawyer will find that insurance warranties are best thought of as a 'condition precedent to the liability of the insurer',[118] but still one that must be distinguished from the condition precedent of general contract law on two counts. First, the latter is one which must be satisfied before a contract comes into existence. In contrast, insurance warranties have no role at all until a contract of insurance has come into existence, a contract of which they are part. Secondly, fulfilment of the condition precedent of general contract law, if challenged, must be proved by the party seeking to rely on the contract. Breach of warranty is a defence to a claim against the insurer, a defence which must be proved by the insurer.[119]

---

[117] *The Good Luck* [1992] 1 AC 233.   [118] Ibid., 262–3.
[119] E.g., *Farnham v Royal Ins. Co. Ltd* [1976] 2 Lloyd's Rep 437, 441.

Exceptions, Warranties, and Causes

As warranties are conditions precedent to the liability of the insurer, breach terminates the contract of insurance automatically, as we have seen. Furthermore, they have this effect even if there is no causal connection between the breach and either the risk to be covered or the actual loss. Thus, in a leading case, an erroneous statement about where the vehicle insured was kept was a warranty, and when it was broken there was no cover, even though it was less at risk where it was actually kept;[120] and in another leading case, Lord Blackburn said that, if a warranty of temperance in a life policy were broken, the cover would be nullified even though the life died in a road accident stone cold sober.[121] Although the purpose of warranties is to circumscribe risk, the assessment of risk is a matter for insurers. If a warranty has been broken, the insurer concerned may well wish to reconsider the particular risk and either offer the policyholder a new contract, perhaps at a higher premium, or drop the risk altogether.[122]

Exceptions differ from warranties in that, generally, excepted events do not excuse the insurer unless they have some causal connection with loss. Thus, a riot exception does not excuse a property insurer unless it is proved that the loss claimed was caused by a riot. As this may be hard to prove, insurers sometimes convert an exception of this kind into a 'temporal exception', by excepting damage 'occasioned by riot': if a riot occurs in the neighbourhood *at the time* of the loss, a connection is presumed and the insurer excused without having to prove that the riot was the actual cause of the loss. To insurers this is reasonable enough. They are less concerned with a causal connection between riot and loss in a particular case than with a statistical connection between riot and loss over a large number of cases. Their records tell them that when there is a riot there is also a lot of damage to property. As insurers see it, once a riot occurs the risk insured has entered a new category.

To policyholders, this may not seem reasonable at all. As casual observers, people tend to assume a causal connection between results and causes that are close in time and space. As insurance claimants, they are more inclined to see the fallacy of the assumption, but, if a temporal exception defeats their claim, the insurers' explanation relating to categories of risk is more likely to lead to enlightenment than to satisfaction. In New Zealand, by section 11 of the Insurance Law Reform Act , the law was changed to require a causal connection. The Australian Law Reform Commission condemned temporal exceptions as harsh; however, it also accepted the insurers' point of view about categories of risk and rejected a proposal for change as an unjustified interference with the market. Indeed, if the exception is to retain a role in the definition of the risk insured, New Zealand may have pruned the common law too hard.

---

120 *Dawsons v Bonnin* [1922] 2 AC 413.
121 *Thomson v Weems* (1884) 9 App Cas 671, 685.   122 See above, p. 158.

Take, for example, the common exception of business use found in motor insurance. If a vehicle is to be insurable (more cheaply) for private use only, common sense suggests that the exception of business use must except damage *while* on business rather than damage caused by business. However, although the business exception may seem reasonable enough, the temporal exception can have unreasonable results. For example, motor cover may cease 'while the insured is intoxicated'. That seems fair enough at first sight, until the case of an accident to Sam's family car, when driven by Sam's wife, while Sam was getting drunk at his local pub. Clearly, in such a case, the court will construe temporal exceptions strictly.[123]

Problem: Distinguishing between Exceptions and Warranties

As we have just seen, it is important to know whether a term of the insurance contract is an exception or a warranty. To distinguish them, the first step is to see if the insurance contract itself classifies the term. Thus, if a fire policy states that it covers fire 'except' fire caused by earthquake, *prima facie* that term is an exception; and a 'warranty', that the building insured will not be unoccupied for more than thirty days at a stretch, is *prima facie* a warranty. However, an unlabelled term, that the insurance does not cover any loss in a building unoccupied for thirty days or more, has been held to be an exception. Generally, the courts respect labels like 'warranty', but of course labels can be confusing. As we have also seen, both exceptions and warranties may be called 'conditions'. The confusion is 'the worse confounded' by the profusion of labels for exceptions: 'terms delimiting risk', 'exclusions', 'temporal exclusions', or 'limitations of risk'. Although labels are important, they are not always decisive.[124]

The second step is to identify the branch by its fruit: if the contract spells out the effect of the term, the effect of exceptions and warranties being quite different,[125] that should indicate which it is. In one case, for example, the policy explanation of a 'warranty' did just that, and it became clear that it was not a warranty at all but a temporal exception.[126] Anyone drafting policy terms is well advised to do this. A case which is controversial for its severity but clear in law nonetheless, is the 'basis clause': courts have ruled that, if any statements made by the applicant for insurance in a form are stated to be the 'basis of the contract', the effect is that those statements are warranties. This is their effect, whatever the intrinsic nature of the resulting warranty and even though the statements are not recorded in any document, of which the policyholder has a copy,

---

[123] See *Kennedy v Smith* 1976 SLT 110.
[124] *Thomson v Weems* (1884) 9 App Cas 671, 682. See below, pp. 266–7.
[125] See above, p. 157 ff.   [126] *The Lydia Flag* [1998] 2 Lloyd's Rep 652.

not even the policy.[127] This rule has been described as an objectionable trap,[128] and a major mischief in the law of insurance. Reform has been recommended by a Report of the ELC,[129] and the use of the basis clause has been contrary to the ABI's Codes of Practice; but the law has not been changed, except insofar as it is countered by the FSA rules.[129a]

Thirdly, if there is still no answer to the question, the enquiry goes behind the way the term is presented to seek the intrinsic nature of the term. Generally, if the term is concerned with circumstances which give rise to a *temporary* increase in the risk, it is an exception. Thus, if a goods vehicle is insured to operate abroad except in eastern Europe, the insurer is off risk when that vehicle is in the Ukraine but cover resumes when it returns. If, however, the term concerns circumstances in which there is or might be a *permanent* increase in the risk, it is a warranty. Thus, if reasonable steps have not been taken to maintain the vehicle insured in an efficient condition (roadworthiness), as the contract requires, that is a breach of warranty. Once the warranty has been broken, the insurance cover ends, even though the vehicle has been restored to a roadworthy condition.

One reason for the last case is that, although the policyholder did attend to the vehicle in the end, the policyholder now appears to be the kind of owner that the insurer may not want to insure—at all, or not without reconsidering the risk posed by what may be an inefficient operator and whether the premium should be raised. The risk may or may not have changed, as the case may be, but the insurer's perception of the risk has changed and, through the warranty, the insurer has contracted for a right to reconsider. From this point of view warranties make sense. From the policyholders' point of view, however, warranties like that undermine the security of cover. The dilemma is the problem of 'moral hazard': how far can policyholders be allowed to 'play Russian roulette' with the risk? This raises more general questions of aggravation of risk and risk management.

The Problem of Aggravation of Risk

Knowing Where You Are

In the past, the role of insurance has been not to rein in human activity and endeavour but to encourage it. Of course, if people put a match to property they

---

[127] *Dawsons v Bonnin* [1922] 2 AC 413; *Joel v Law Union & Crown Ins. Co.* [1908] 2 KB 431 (CA).
[128] E.g., *Zurich General Accident & Liability Ins. Co. Ltd v Morrison* [1942] 2 KB 53, 58 (CA).
[129] No. 104, para. 7.5.   [129a] See above, Chapter 3, p. 61 ff.

have insured, the fire is not covered—not because they have broken a condition or warranty but because, in insurance law, fire deliberately started is not covered. Moreover, society, except possibly immediate neighbours, has nothing against those who burn unwanted articles in the garden unless, of course, they are then the subject of an insurance claim; that is likely to be seen as fraud. But if the fire arises out of a new and experimental process, English law reflects a society which values scientific investigation and entrepreneurial activity; it is reluctant to let the insurer off risk because the insurer had had no warning of the experiment. People applying for or renewing insurance must mention any plans of that kind at the time, but between times they do not have to tell their insurer every time they plan something new. 'If a person who insures his life goes up in a balloon, that does not vitiate his policy. . . A person who insures may light as many candles as he please in his house, though each additional candle increases the danger of setting the house on fire.' Chief Baron Pollock said that in 1849[130] and that is still the law. Then, as now, a policyholder may be a fool but, unless the fool is also a knave, the fool is covered.

Even so, insurers prefer that policyholders do not take up hang-gliding, or start selling camping-gas from a paint shop. English insurers may well prefer the German rule for non-life insurance, that policyholders are not allowed to increase the risk in any way without the consent of their insurer and that, if they do, the cover ends at once in respect of any loss 'influenced' by the increase, as well as any subsequent loss if the insurer so elects.[131] More attractive still perhaps is the corresponding French rule that, if the risk is materially increased during the insurance period (whether or not through any act or omission of the policyholder) by circumstances specified in the policy, the insurer is entitled to terminate it or demand a higher premium.[132] A similar rule is found in Switzerland too,[133] but, in practice, there it is softened by contract terms in favour of policyholders.

The French rule has been attacked in France itself as an unreasonable burden for policyholders. It would also be opposed in England. The ELC Report[134] concluded that it might be appropriate to the relatively long-term cover found at that time in continental Europe where, for example, Germans might contract motor cover for as long as ten years at a time, but not to the shorter periods of cover usually found in the United Kingdom—and nowadays in France and Germany too. Moreover, one of the very reasons for insurance from the point of view of policyholders is certainty, including certainty of cost. They do not want insurance for which the premium may change during the premium period. Further, anything like the French rule goes against the grain of the classical contract, which is distinct and discrete rather than relational.[135] The English tradition is that the rules

---

[130] *Baxendale v Harvey* (1849) 4 H & N 445, 449, 452.   [131] VVG, Arts 23–25.
[132] Code d'assurance, Art. L.113-2-3.   [133] VVG, Arts 28 and 30.
[134] No. 104, para. 5.50.   [135] See below, p. 172 ff.

of engagement must be fixed at the time of contract and observed for the duration of the contract.

Whereas the law does not allow policyholders to gamble with insurers,[136] it does require insurers to gamble to a degree on policyholders—in the interests of the latter, or of society at large, in some degree of certainty of cover and compensation. In the case of compulsory motor insurance, for example this is evident not only in England[137] but also in other countries, for example France:[138] certain defences cannot be raised by insurers against third parties to whom an insured motorist is liable.

Even in England, however, an intermediate situation should be noted when insurance is contracted a relatively long time in advance of the period of cover: an express warranty may be introduced which makes it a condition of cover that the risk has not increased at a specified date between the contract and the commencement of cover. Moreover, with 'candles' in mind, some English policies require notification of change in the risk; for example, motor insurance may require notification of any modification to the vehicle insured. This is the kind of policy specification sanctioned in France. Just what insurers are entitled to do in response to notification is not always clear from the contract, but it is fairly clear from *Kausar*[139] that the English courts will respond unfavourably to any attempt by the insurer in such a case to end or modify the contract before the renewal date.

Kausar concerned insurance on a shop, which required the policyholder to 'tell us of any change of circumstance after the start of the insurance which increases the risk of injury or damage' and stated that in such a case the policyholder would 'not be insured under the policy until we have agreed in writing to accept the increased risk'. The Court of Appeal refused to apply the clause literally because, for example, the appearance of a fire spreading down the street towards the shop would bring cover to an end.[140] Lord Saville reaffirmed the traditional view that 'the insurance bargain is one where, in return for the premium, [insurers] take upon themselves the risk that an insured peril will operate. In calculating that premium it is for the insurers to assess the chances of insured perils operating.'[141]

This decision exemplifies the English tradition against a contract term or rule of law that makes the activity of policyholders during the insurance period dependent on the will and whim of their insurer. The tradition is observed not only by the courts but also by the FOS;[142] however, it stands in contrast with that in France, that the level of risk should not depend entirely on the will and whim of

---

[136] See Chapter 1, p. 36 ff.
[137] Road Traffic Act 1988, ss. 14(1) and 151(1).   [138] Code d'assurance, Art. R211-13-3.
[139] *Kausar v Eagle Star Ins. Co. Ltd* [1997] CLC 129 (CA).   [140] Ibid., 133.
[141] Ibid., 132, *per* Saville LJ. This attitude can also be seen in the leading judgment of Lord Hobhouse in *The Star Sea* [2003] 1 AC 170, at [56] ff.
[142] See, e.g., Case 36/9, *Ombudsman News*, April 2004.

policyholders. Nevertheless, in reality, the difference is less marked than might first appear. To some extent the entrepreneurial freedom of policyholders in England is illusory, because their activities can be hedged in by 'continuing' warranties undertaken at the commencement of the insurance period.

Future Shocks

Continuing Warranties

To stop policyholders 'playing with fire', insurers insert continuing warranties. These are warranties which policyholders must comply with not only at the beginning of the period of cover but throughout. If anyone wanted to insure a theatre in the nineteenth century, there was a ban on illuminated scenery, fireworks, and the discharge of firearms; and today fireworks can still be warranted out of shop insurance in that way. A more common example of a continuing warranty is a warranty that the policyholder has a working fire alarm—at all times. Again, in the 1970s some insured householders discovered that they could raise cash by dropping mirrors; insurers responded with clauses requiring reasonable care during the period of cover. Breach of any such warranty must be proved by the insurer concerned but, although courts construe them strictly,[143] the warranties are applied.[144]

In the absence of a warranty of this kind, insurers may have to shoulder an unexpectedly heavy burden of increased risk for the full course of the insurance period. If policies do contain a well-drawn continuing warranty, however, policyholders may suddenly be without cover without their knowledge—like the fairy tale king without clothes and without awareness of his exposure. Better sometimes the corresponding French rule, which encourages renegotiation and, if new agreement on premium cannot be reached, gives insurers their freedom and policyholders time to find alternative cover. Indeed, the traditional English attitude goes appreciably further in favour of policyholders than that found in other countries of Europe, where there are more qualified rules. There the debate runs as follows.

The main reason for buying insurance from the point of view of policyholders is certainty: certainty of cost and, above all, certainty of cover and associated peace of mind.[145] In that connection, society at large seeks to promote effective compensation and loss spreading. However, society also wants to foster human activity—but potentially useful human activity, and to discourage wanton or wasteful conduct in human affairs.[146] Furthermore, and connected with that, insurers too have an interest in risk management and loss prevention. The latter considerations, risk management and loss prevention, suggest rules that encourage,

---

[143] See, e.g., *Hussain v Brown* [1996] 1 Lloyd's Rep 627 (CA).
[144] See the following pages.   [145] See Chapter 1, p. 2 ff; also Clarke, ch. 30-9C .
[146] Abraham, p. 60.

or at least allow, some degree of intervention or control by insurers over the conduct of policyholders during the period of insurance cover. Meanwhile, it must not be forgotten that insurance is for the foolish as well as the wise; an optimal spreading of risk and loss requires that to a large degree insurers must be prepared to take on unreasonable policyholders. Moreover, too much must not be expected of even reasonable policyholders. In the early days of motoring, a motorist had to be something of a mechanic. Today, anti-skid brake sensors join power-assisted steering and other devices to make it easier to drive without causing harm; and various kinds of assistance on the road are but a cellphone call away.

Law Reform

Currently the traditional English rule is under review by the Law Commission. That was once the position in Australia;[147] however, in 1984, Australia broke ranks on the traditional common law approach. The nettle of aggravation was partially grasped by statute—and people have been stung, mostly in their pockets by the cost of litigation on the meaning of the statute.[148] The Insurance Contracts Act 1984, section 54(2), provides that, subject to the rest of the section, where the 'act of the insured' after the contract was entered into 'could reasonably be regarded as being capable of causing or contributing to a loss in respect of which insurance cover is provided by the contract, the insurer may refuse to pay the claim'. According to section 54(6)(b), an act of the insured includes one 'that has the effect of altering the state or condition of the subject-matter of the contract or of allowing the state or condition of the subject matter to alter'. Moreover, section 60(2) provides that where '(a) a contract of general insurance includes a provision that requires the insured to notify the insurer of a *specified* act or omission of the insured . . . and, after the contract was entered into, such an act or omission has occurred, the insurer may cancel the contract' (emphasis added).

Nearer home, in 2001 the European Parliament urged the European Commission to compile a database 'of national legislation and case law in the field of contract law, and to promote, on the basis of such a database, comparative law and research and cooperation between interested parties, academics and legal practitioners'. The aim of the cooperation should be 'to find common legal concepts and solutions . . . notably in the following fields: general contract law, the law on sales contracts, the law governing service contracts including *financial services and insurance contracts*'.[149] Although this is to be achieved 'while maintaining a balance between civil law and common law traditions',[150] the tradition of civil law countries is one of intervention and rules that promote risk management

---

[147] See K. Nicholson, 'Mid-term Alterations in the Risk' (1991) 4 Ins L J 27, 29.
[148] See, e.g., S. Derrington, 'Marine Insurance Law in Australia' [2002] LMCLQ 214, 218.
[149] 15 November 2001, COM(2001) 398—C5-0471/2001—2001/2187(COS), paras 12 and 14.
[150] Ibid., para. 16. See Clarke and Heiss [2006] JBL 600.

during the period of cover.[151] At the moment this is but a small cloud on the south eastern horizon, but it is one that is unlikely to go away.

The Prudent Uninsured: Unreasonable Care

The Response of Reasonable Policyholders

Insurers sometimes talk as if policyholders have a legal duty to 'act as a prudent uninsured'. If this were true, continuing warranties (above) would be largely unnecessary and insurers' concerns about policyholders who light candles and start fires,[152] literally or figuratively, unfounded. In law, however, policyholders have no such duty unless the contract imposes one in very clear terms. Whether they *should* have a duty of that kind is a matter for debate.[153] What is clear is that, not surprisingly, insurers would like them to have one and try to impose a duty by contract. Equally clearly, the courts have resisted care conditions by interpreting them strictly against the insurer by reference to what they see as the fundamental purpose of insurance.

Suppose that an employer is careless about fencing his machinery so that a worker's hand is trapped in a welding machine. What is the use of the employer's liability insurance if carelessness is an exception or a breach of warranty that defeats cover? As Goddard LJ said in a leading case,[154] that would mean that 'the underwriters were saying: "We will insure you against your liability for negligence on condition that you are not negligent." ' The response of the courts for a long time[155] has been that it is one of the main purposes of insurance to cover the carelessness of policyholders, and so, whenever possible, any condition requiring care by a policyholder is construed so that it is breached only by extreme carelessness, that is, by something close to recklessness. In another leading case, Lord Diplock took up the theme: what is reasonable, he said, 'is that the insured should not deliberately court a danger, the existence of which he recognises'; and that any breach of the condition

must at least be reckless, that is to say, made with actual recognition by the policyholder himself that a danger exists, and not caring whether or not it is averted. The purpose of the condition is to ensure that the policyholder will not, because he is covered against loss by the policy, refrain from taking precautions which he *knows* ought to be taken.[156]

The result, of course, is that the greater the carelessness, the smaller the chance of cover for the employer and of compensation for the employee.

---

[151] See below, p. 170 ff. See further M. A. Clarke, 'Aggravation of Risk during the Insurance Period' [2003] LMCLQ 109–24, 115 ff.; and Basedow and Fock, paras 82–84.
[152] Above, p. 161 ff.   [153] See Chapter 7, p. 255 ff.
[154] *Woolfall & Rimmer Ltd v Moyle* [1942] 1 KB 66, 76 (CA).
[155] E.g., *Shaw v Robberds* (1837) 6 Ad & E 75, 84.
[156] *Fraser v Furman (Productions) Ltd* [1967] 1 WLR 898, 906 *per* Diplock LJ (CA).

From the viewpoint of people at work, the courts' construction achieves a compromise which, it seems, is better than would be the effect of a literal interpretation of the condition. From the viewpoint of the law student, the result is interesting in the way it is achieved. It shows how courts cope with new issues, what psychologists call a 'heuristic stratagem', by which the thinker seeks to relate the new issue to established patterns of experience and thought. In other words, in the task of interpretation, the court looks for an analogy with precedent, or with some familiar or established concept.

The Response of Reasonable Judges

To decide whether a policyholder has 'taken precautions', as required by many of the clauses aimed at making policyholders more careful, the court reasons in the (more familiar) way it does in tort when deciding whether the defendant has been negligent. First, the court sets the standard of care required according to the sort of person the policyholder purports to be, that is, according to the knowledge and skill that can be expected of a person of that sort.[157] When it comes to handling liquid petroleum gas, higher standards will be expected of an employer in a factory than of a holidaymaker in a caravan. Then the court assesses the degree of care to be expected of policyholders of that sort; this depends on the situation in which the risk arose. The more likely the loss, the more care is expected;[158] which in turn will depend, in liability insurance for example, on the danger of the operation or, in all-risks or transit insurance, on the attractiveness of the goods to thieves. The more serious the consequences of loss, the more care is expected;[159] which in turn will depend, for example, on the kind of human injury in prospect or the value of the goods. The more viable (cheap and available) the precautions, the more that can be expected of policyholders in that direction; which in turn will depend on the location and resources of the policyholder concerned. The IOB approached these cases in the same way, and the FOS is likely to follow suit.[160]

In any one case, however, the court's thinking may be influenced by more than one established pattern of legal thought. The 'tort thinking', just described, may be coupled with that of 'overriding breach', sometimes called 'wilful misconduct'. This is conduct which is *prima facie* uninsurable, or which, in other branches of the law, rules out contractual defences.[161] To the English judge, wilful misconduct implies that the person was aware that he or she was taking a risk. If an insurance case is approached from that frame of reference,

[157] In tort see, e.g., *Nettleship v Weston* [1971] 2 QB 691 (CA).
[158] In tort see, e.g., *Bolton v Stone* [1951] AC 850.
[159] In tort see, e.g., *Paris v Stepney BC* [1951] AC 367.
[160] See IOB, *Digest of Annual Reports and Bulletins*, 2nd edn (1999) p. 271 ff.
[161] See, e.g., M. A. Clarke, *International Carriage of Goods by Road: CMR*, 4th edn (London, 2003) para. 101 ff.

policyholders are more likely to be censured, and less likely to be covered, if they deliberately 'court danger'[162] than if they give the danger no thought at all; something of this can be seen in the words of Lord Diplock quoted in the last section. Again, when the court has to decide whether loss was 'accidental' a similar strain of thought is seen. In *Dhak*,[163] the court held that death caused largely by drinking too much alcohol was not accidental, because the deceased, a well-qualified nurse, would have been well aware of the danger and must have taken a calculated risk.

Typical tort thinking is to be seen in the leading case of *Sofi*.[164] A condition in a householder's policy required the policyholder to 'take all reasonable steps to safeguard any property insured and to avoid accidents which may lead to damage or injury'. One January, the policyholder and family set out for the Dover ferry on holiday. In a case measuring about 30 × 15 centimeters, in the locked glove compartment of the car, was valuable jewellery. The reason, as the policyholder had previously told the insurer's agent, was that, having had a burglary at home, he felt the jewellery would be safer with him than at home. Being early for the ferry, the family stopped to have a quick look at Dover Castle. The car park was unattended. What were they to do about their belongings? Having discussed the matter, they took their money and travellers cheques, but left everything else in the car. On their return fifteen minutes later, they found that the car had been ransacked and that the jewellery had been stolen. The insurer argued that the policyholder was in breach of the condition; that the policyholder should either have taken the jewellery with him to the Castle, or left one of the party behind in the car.

In the response of the Court of Appeal, we see something of the 'heuristic' approach and the template of tort. The gravity of the risk (thieves like jewellery) and the triviality of the occasion (a casual, unscheduled visit to Dover Castle) counted against the claimant. However, the small chance of theft (short absence from an empty car park in January) and the difficulty of taking adequate precautions (what to do with the case) counted in his favour. On balance, held the Court, the policyholder may have been careless but had not been reckless; he was not therefore in breach of the condition of care, and his claim against the insurer succeeded. Likewise, in a number of later cases where motor policyholders have left a vehicle with the keys in the ignition, courts[165] and the FOS[166] alike have taken the view that such clauses do not defeat claims unless (affirmative in most of these cases) the claimant has been reckless in the sense of 'courting danger'.

---

[162] *Devco Holder Ltd v Legal & General Assurance Sy Ltd* [1993] 2 Lloyd's Rep 567 (CA).
[163] *Dhak v Ins. Co. of N. America* [1996] 1 Lloyd's Rep 632 (CA).
[164] *Sofi v Prudential Assurance Co. Ltd* [1993] 2 Lloyd's Rep 559 (CA).
[165] *Devco*, above, n. 164.
[166] See *Ombudsman News*, September 2003, May/June 2004, and July 2004.

Premium Incentive

A common belief is that, if the premium charged goes up or down with the claims record of policyholders, that will discourage claims and encourage care by policy-holders.[167] Insurers cannot play with the premium like this, however, when policyholders are in a stronger bargaining position than insurers, or policyholders can pass on higher insurance costs to their customers. Nor will policyholders respond with more care, if they do not think it will make any difference because, for example, the pool in which they are rated is so large that good risk management on their part will have no effect on their premium. A commonly quoted example of premium incentive is the motorists' 'no-claims' discount (NCD), but here too it has been doubted whether the NCD has much effect on how carefully people drive, or even whether 'experience' rating of this kind in general insurance is very scientific.[168]

First, there is too little up-to-date information on particular policyholders to be a guide to future claims. If rating is perceived to be inaccurate, and thus unfair, it inspires in policyholders discontent and a quest for cheaper cover rather than repentance and a mending of ways. Secondly, to match premiums with sufficient accuracy to risk may not be economic. To have a significant deterrent effect, liability insurance premiums must in some way indicate to each policyholder the cost of each activity but, to achieve this, the insurer has to draw insurance categories narrowly; and that is simply too costly.[169]

If and when premium incentive does have an effect on policyholders, it can be used in more than one way. One is to rate, for example, fire risks according to the design and construction of the building insured, and in this way, insurers have long had an influence on the choice of design and materials. Once a building has been built, another way is to reduce premium if policyholders take certain measures to prevent loss, or if they bear the first layer of risk (excess). These 'excess' provisions (also called 'deductibles'), whereby the policyholder pays the first layer of loss, have two functions. First, they reduce insurers' administrative costs because, proportionately, the smaller the claim the larger the cost. Secondly, they are an incentive to policyholders to avoid loss altogether. They must, however, be marketed as such, otherwise people tend to perceive them as a pun-ishment. They are best presented as a self-generated premium discount. Not only does this make them more acceptable to policyholders, but also, as insurers see it, they emphasize the line between the wise and the unwise, between those who regard insurance as a maintenance contract and those who seek simply to protect their assets.

---

[167] Abraham, p. 44.   [168] Cane, 387 ff.   [169] Abraham, ch. 4.

Risk Management

Policy conditions are just one aspect of risk management.[170] Another, more general and 'strategic' form, is planning and advice. That insurers have a role in managing and preventing the risks is now widely assumed. Sadly, it was not—and is not—always so. As far back as 1918, some insurers in North America refused life cover to workers in the asbestos industry.[171] Yet, other insurers were still covering these workers in the 1960s, as if asbestos and its dust made no difference, and later came to court and denied all knowledge of the hazards associated with asbestos.[172] The courts would have none of it and, as we have seen,[173] the long tail of liability for disease associated with asbestos remains one the blackest clouds hanging over the insurance industry.

Today, risk management is a service that many insurers offer to preserve market share. Some of their customers are companies so large that, were it not for their expertise in risk management, insurers would have little to offer them that could not be done by self-insurance. When the contingency occurs, too, modern insurers may provide more than money: services of one kind or another are also supplied—not only a courtesy car while the policyholder's vehicle is under repair, but care and advice concerning the loss itself and future prevention. The late Reimer Schmidt, an economist with a long association with the industry, once famously described insurance as a prism with three sides: risk-transfer, information-exchange, and services.[174]

This picture is striking but imperfect. At one end of the spectrum, insurance is but one aspect of a package of services on offer. For example, a credit package offered to small businesses might include credit information on other companies, debt recovery including the legal costs, and debt insurance for incorrigibly bad debts. At the other end, insurers might offer insurance uncluttered by advice of any kind, except perhaps what is implicit in the policy conditions. Somewhere in between are liability insurers, for example, who offer a twenty-four hour executive helpline, with access to solicitors for advice to executives about their legal obligations; and the life insurer who offers bereavement counselling to the surviving relatives.

The movement of insurers into risk management and services, in particular advice about risk at the point of contracting, raises the question whether, if they give careless advice, they are liable to policyholders for the consequences. Of course, one consequence may be the loss covered by the insurance. However, insurance covers only the immediate consequences of the peril insured, and there

---

[170] See above, p. 161 ff.

[171] J. Stapleton, *Disease and the Compensation Debate* (Oxford, 1986) 133.

[172] See Clarke, ch. 23-9B1.   [173] See Chapter 2, p. 50 ff.

[174] 'Considerations on the Significance for Insurance Law of the Consequences of Economic Studies', *Geneva Papers No. 74*, (1995), 74–82, 77.

remains the possibility of liability in contract or tort for consequences that are more remote.

Liability for Careless Advice

If the inquiry starts from the baseline of general contract law, it seems that there is no duty of care between people negotiating contracts, especially when it is clear that they are negotiating at arm's length.[175] Apparently against that conclusion is the *Esso* case,[176] and although some have dismissed the decision as a quirk of legal history in which Lord Denning anticipated the operation of the Misrepresentation Act, others[177] accept the decision at face value. On that basis it remains a precedent for the proposition that, when the defendant has superior knowledge and experience, he or she may owe a duty of care to an advisee.

If the inquiry starts from the baseline of insurance law, insurers in breach of the duty of disclosure are not liable in damages either on the basis that the duty of disclosure is grounded in good faith, or on the basis of any breach of a duty of care. This was decided in *Westgate*,[178] albeit a case that did not concern risk advice but a very different situation indeed. If the inquiry returns to the baseline of principle governing actions for negligence, however, a claim by the policyholder seems possible. According to the well-known general guidelines for the existence of a duty of care, the loss must be a reasonably foreseeable consequence of the failure alleged. Secondly, there must be 'proximity' between the parties, which, in turn, is often fused with a third requirement that the imposition of a duty of care must be fair and reasonable.[179] If the claimant's damage is physical rather than economic, just as doctors may be liable for careless advice about preventing illness,[180] risk managers—including insurers, surely—should be liable for negligent advice having foreseeable physical consequences; that is fair. Courts, which have held a fire brigade liable for negligence in the heat of a fire,[181] are unlikely to hold back from a similar decision against risk managers in the business of preventing fire, and with plenty of time to investigate the risk and reflect on their advice. If, however, the foreseeable consequences to the claimant are not physical but purely economic, the general rule is that a duty would not be fair, unless it is also a special case called 'negligent misstatement'.

For such a duty, the law requires a voluntary assumption of responsibility by the insurer.[182] In *Westgate* there was none.[183] Generally, however, an assumption of

---

[175] E.g., *Oleificio Zucchi SpA. v Northern Sales Ltd* [1965] 2 Lloyd's Rep 496, 519.

[176] *Esso Petroleum Co. Ltd v Mardon* [1976] QB 801 (CA).

[177] Notably, Treitel, ch. 9.3.2(2)(c).

[178] *Banque Financière de la Cité v Westgate Ins. Co. Ltd* [1990] QB 665, 801, aff'd on other grounds: [1991] 2 AC 249.　　　　[179] See *Caparo Industries plc v Dickman* [1990] 2 AC 605.

[180] E.g., *Stokes v Guest, Keen & Nettlefold (Bolts & Nuts) Ltd* [1968] 1 WLR 1776.

[181] *Capital and Counties plc v Hampshire CC* [1997] QB 1004 (CA).

[182] *Henderson v Merrett Syndicates Ltd* [1995] 2 AC 145.　　　　[183] Op. cit. above, n. 178, 275.

responsibility will be inferred when advice is given by an insurer, knowing why the policyholder wants the advice and that it is likely to be acted on by the policyholder.[184] Given the greater expertise of the insurer in matters of risk management and the mutual concern with controlling the risk, it is not only likely and reasonable that the policyholder will act on the advice, but it may well be a condition of the insurance.

The inquiry from the baseline of principle is confirmed by the analogy of precedent. A duty is owed by the surveyor of a house to the purchaser of that house about the condition and risk, if any, posed by the structure,[185] by an architect who certified the quality of work done on such structures,[186] by a marine surveyor that certified that a ship was fit to put to sea,[187] and by a credit-rating agency about the credit risk posed by a particular debtor.[188] In this state of the law of tort, it would be surprising if a duty were not owed also by insurers who advised a purchaser or an occupier about the precautions to be taken against the risk of fire or theft. In conclusion, surely, insurers who give advice on risk management assume responsibility for the quality of that advice, and thus undertake a duty of care. Moreover, if that advice is part of the service undertaken by insurers from the start, part of what a policyholder is paying for, the advice will be in performance of a contractual duty in which a similar duty of care and skill will be implied. Indeed, if the trend continues, the law should take another look at insurance contracts in such cases and categorize them perhaps as a contract of service, whereby the company advises its customer on provision against certain risks, with an indemnity if nonetheless the risk strikes.

The Insurance Relationship

Nature

The paradigm of classical contract law is the executory contract. Generally, however, most contracts are not executory at all but are performed almost as soon as they have been concluded, or very soon afterwards,[189] and have been compared with 'relational' contracts. Typical relational contracts are franchising, employment, partnership, leasing, management, licensing, research and development,

---

[184] *Caparo Industries plc v Dickman*, op. cit. above, n. 179. See also *Customs and Execise Commissioners v Barclays Bank plc* [2006] UKHL 28, [2006] 3 WLR 1.

[185] *Smith v Bush* [1990] 1 AC 831. For the difficulty in reconciling this case with cases that negligent inspection of building by local authorities does not give rise to liability, see *Markesinis and Deakin*, 134.   [186] *Sutcliffe v Thackrah* [1974] AC 727.

[187] *The Nicholas H* [1996] 1 AC 211.

[188] *Hedley Byrne & Co. Ltd v Heller & Partners Ltd* [1964] AC 465.

[189] See P. S. Atiyah, 'Contracts, Promises and the Law of Obligations', in *Essays on Contract* (Oxford, 1986). As regards the issue in international commercial arbitration, see N. Nassar, *Sanctity of Contracts Revisited* (Dordrecht, 1995).

and time charterparties.[190] Purely as a matter of duration, insurance looks like one of the latter, but duration as such is not what matters. What does matter is whether the period is such that at some point during the period the contract in question changes—changes sufficiently to enter a different 'relational' category for which different rules of law might be appropriate. If a relational contract were simply one involving not merely an exchange but also a relationship, then insurance would be relational. A relational contract in this sense is one performed over a period of time which gives rise to certain problems, notably unexpected changes, which have to be solved as they arise by 'relating' with the other party.

In the element of the unexpected the insurance contract is archetypal: the insured event is not expected. When it comes to the solution, the response to the unexpected change, however, the opposite is true. A key characteristic of the insurance contract is forward-planning and the retention of risk in the way initially allocated by the contract by one party, the insurer. The very purpose of insurance is the transfer of risk of the unexpected from one party (the policy-holder) to the other party (the insurer) and left there, as initially agreed. For insurance, therefore, there is no question of adaptation such as price adjustment mid-term, unless, as is not likely for the time being, English law has to absorb new rules for aggravation of risk.[191] But there is still the question, what is mid-term?

Duration

People may have the same fire insurer for years and years. Nonetheless, a fire insurance contract is usually for a term of one year only, and its terms remain unchanged during that period. At the end of the year, however, English insurance law says that that is not the middle of any longer term but the end of the term, and that, if there is to be a further insurance period at all, that must be the subject of new agreement; and, therefore, there may be any amount of 'adjustment' in comparison with the previous contract.

Within the world of insurance the main exception is life insurance, which continues for a stated number of years or until the life ends, as long the premium is paid on time. Outside the world of insurance, long-term contractual relationships also include those in a series of discrete contracts of a broadly similar kind; into such a category can be placed certain kinds of insurance, such as health insurance. At the end of the year they may be mid-term in the sense of mid-series, but insurance law has no special rule. Insurance law treats them as discrete, like the sale of soap: fixed terms for the fixed period and, after that, a new fix.

In practice, the line between insurance periods is cut less clearly. The contract of insurance may contain some provision for continuity. For example, the

---

[190] R. Macneil, 'Restatement (Second) of Contracts and Presentation', 60 Va L Rev 589–610, 595 ff. (1974). Cf. the view that such contracts can still be explained in terms of traditional 'classical' rules: R. Austen-Baker, 'A Relational Law of Contract?' (2004) 20 JCL 125–44.

[191] See above, p. 161 ff.

contract may provide for renewal on the basis of a relatively objective reference to the 'table of rates then in effect'. In some policies, however, subjective factors have been brought in; for example, a string of factors including 'current loss experience . . . and such other factors as [the insurer] may determine from time to time'. These leave the policyholder with little security. Should anything be done about this? Are there any lessons for insurance law in general commercial law or practice?

Flexible Friends Measures for the Unexpected

To deal with the unexpected during the period of contract performance, a number of measures have emerged for contracts generally. One is the use of implied terms. This seems to have little relevance to insurance contracts; apart from a few basic terms,[192] there is virtually no implication of terms in insurance contracts.

A second measure is to adapt performance without formal or explicit agreement to vary the original contract. Parties simply do it. If the adaptation is unilateral, English contract law has enforced the change by the device of estoppel[193] or waiver. An important example is found at the point of claim, when the insurer relaxes some of the claims' conditions. This also occurs during the insurance period, if and when the insurer waives breach of a continuing warranty.[194] However, this is a matter entirely for the discretion of the insurer and free of influence either of the law, or of the policyholder.

Thirdly, like other contracts, insurance contracts sometimes refer to a 'standard'. An instance of this is the reference to a premium TBA (to be arranged), when commercial cover is extended under a Lloyd's policy; the shipowners who decide to send their ship into dangerous waters are entitled to cover under their existing insurance on payment of an additional premium. However, this is less an initial contract provision for future uncertainty than a standard option that policyholders choose to take and pay for. Still, this might be seen as an instance of the device, more important in contracts generally, of 'planning for flexibility' by reference to standards such as a Consumer Price Index.[195]

Fourthly, as in contracts generally, a provision for arbitration is sometimes found in insurance contracts to settle disagreement about a claim. Such provisions have been enforced, although sometimes they put the insured claimant at a disadvantage.[196] This is what contract theorist Macneil called 'Direct Third-Party Determination of Performance'.[197]

---

[192] See Chapter 4, p. 90 ff.

[193] In particular estoppel by convention; see Treitel, ch. 3.6.3(2)(j).

[194] See above, p. 155 ff.

[195] E. McKendrick, 'The Regulation of Long Term Contracts in English Law', in J. Beatson (ed.), *Good Faith and Fault in Contract Law* (London, 1995) ch. 12, 316.

[196] See Chapter 6, p. 237.   [197] Macneil, op. cit. above, n. 190, 595.

Fifthly, flexibility is seen in the 'rules' for members of clubs. Insurance clubs, like football clubs, have rules of no fixed duration and contain provisions for change. Clubs resemble the 'firm', such as a joint venture or something yet more integrated.[198] The immediate interest of the club form of mutual cover is that, although a degree of provision is sought by carefully drafted rules of association, outstanding matters, which might arise during the period of cover, may be delegated to the decision of some kind of directorate.[199]

Mostly, all these measures are the creation of contract and the work of the parties. Should the law make other or better provision for flexibility in relational contracts? McKendrick is one of several who argue against the thesis that relational contracts require special rules of law, or special resort to the courts to have contracts adapted.[200] The parties must do the best they can with contract terms for forward planning.

The tradition of insurance law and practice is that insurers respond in the way exhorted by McKendrick. Insurers draft their contracts with a view to the immediate insurance period in its entirety. They seek to limit the impact of the unexpected by hedging their commitment with warranties extracted at the time of contracting, warranties 'controlling' the risk[201] and terms of various kinds that seek to influence the conduct of the policyholder.[202] The suggestion made for other kinds of contract, a suggestion of deliberate and allegedly 'productive' ambiguity to permit flexible interpretation later,[203] is unhelpful for insurance in view of the tradition of strict construction *contra proferentem* and the fundamental desire of policyholders for certainty. Sharp edges may be uncomfortable, but people know where they are. So, it seems that, for insurance contracts, there is little to be gained by any kind of framework for flexibility during the insurance period and nothing will change unless change is compelled by moves from Brussels.[204] Until then, those who wish to change or terminate an insurance relationship must await the due date for renewal.

Rights of Renewal

Reality Check

Insurers are bound strictly by the contract and the risk that they have assumed. For them the moment of release comes at the end of the insurance period: they

---

[198] D. Campbell and D. Harris, 'Flexibility in Long-term Contractual Relationships: The Role of Co-operation' (1993) 20 J Law & Soc 166–91, 169.
[199] S. J. Hazelwood, *P & I: The Law and Practice,* 3rd edn (London, 2000).
[200] McKendrick, op. cit. above, n. 195, 312 ff. [201] See above, p. 164 ff.
[202] See above, p. 166 ff.
[203] See H. Beale and T. Dugdale, 'Contracts Between Businessmen: Planning and the Use of Contractual Remedies' (1975) 2 Brit J Law and Society 45–60. [204] See above, p. 164 ff.

are not obliged to renew at all or on terms, or even remind policyholders that the insurance cover is coming to an end.[205] Even in the United States, where courts are more inclined to take the part of policyholders, courts have upheld the 'absolute right' of insurers to reconsider on renewal, and have done so even when refusal was devastating for the policyholder. One is the case of a private investigator who needed a licence to pursue his profession and earn a living, and could not get one without insurance but was refused cover nonetheless.[206] Another is that of health insurance and the insurer who, as the price of renewal, demanded a massive (489 per cent over two years) increase in premium,[207] a kind of 'constructive' refusal. In theory, in common law, each party to the insurance contract is entirely free to negotiate terms for the next period of cover. The reality is not much different. Basically policyholders have no right to renew their policy at all.

Policyholders are more favourably treated by French law. Although, as in England, insurers are not obliged to accept an application in the first place, if they do so, and thus strike up a relationship, and later a limited modification is proposed (period of cover, range of subject-matter, etc.) by a policyholder, insurers in France are bound by the change proposed, unless they reject it within ten days.[208] A similar rule is found in Switzerland.[209]

In practice in England, neither side is entirely free to spurn the other at the point either of contracting, or of renewal. For their part, insurers may be under moral or political pressure to contract. When the Consumers' Association complained about the difficulty some people had in getting motor insurance, it was significant that the industry's defence of itself did not appeal to freedom of contract; on the contrary, there was tacit acceptance that cover ought to be there somewhere, albeit on the industry's terms. The industry accepts a duty to provide compulsory cover, if only to ward off what it regards as government 'interference'. For their part, when considering the renewal offered, policyholders are not entirely free to take it or leave it. Not only do we find the commonplace inequalities of information and skill, but the hands of policyholders are partly tied by fear of the effect of refusal on their 'record' and, therefore, on the willingness of other insurers to grant them cover then or in future. What can the current law do for them?

Duress

For contracts generally, it is arguable that the law of duress has become the principal means of regulating renegotiation or renewal of contracts. Duress may consist

---

[205] See Chapter 4, p. 92 ff.
[206] *Harding v Ohio Cas. Co.*, 41 NW 2d 818, 823 (Minn., 1950).
[207] *Compton v Aetna Life Ins. & Annuity Co.*, 956 F 2d 256 (11 Cir., 1992).
[208] Code d'assurances, Art. 112-2.   [209] VVG, Art. 2.

not only of threats of physical violence, but also of 'economic' duress—something more subtle, which has been described as illegitimate pressure.[210] Commercial pressure, however, is usually legitimate. To end a relationship by non-renewal might amount to commercial pressure, but it is not illegitimate. For what the law regards as economic duress between parties already in a contractual relationship, duress usually takes the form of threatened breach of contract, which gives the victim very little practical choice but to do what is demanded. Moreover, illegitimate pressure requires an element of bad faith, that is, the deliberate exploitation of the difficulties of the other party. In the case of the insurer who threatens non-renewal of insurance, however awkward that may be for the policyholder, there is no illegitimate pressure of the kind that the law calls economic duress. This doctrine is of no assistance.

Good Faith

The relationship between insurers and their policyholders is said to be one of good faith, with reciprocal duties throughout the contractual relationship at a level appropriate to the operation in hand.[211] In particular, the duty of disclosure, most prominent prior to contract formation, revives whenever the policyholder has an express or implied duty to supply information to enable the insurer to make a decision.[212] Hence it applies when insurance is first contracted or renewed. It is, however, no more than a duty to offer information, as required. A party has no duty to receive information or, in any other way, to consider renewal of insurance which that party does not want to renew.

In some legal systems there is a general contractual duty to (re)negotiate in good faith, but this is not even current general contract law in England.[213] Even so, insurance parties do not deal with each other as market duellists at arm's length but in a 'contractual environment' of other extra-legal norms and influences.[214] For insurance, as we have noted, there is some social and commercial 'influence' or pressure to persist. Moreover, whereas in the past policyholders may have been kept at a respectful distance from their insurers by their brokers, today there is the rise of direct insurance whereby insurer and insured come 'face to face' on the telephone. Above all, insurers have more involvement with their policyholders through greater risk management.[215] Even so, not even a qualified duty of renewal can be built on the insurance doctrine of good faith. This doctrine does not help the policyholder either.

---

[210] See M. Furmston (ed.), *Butterworths Law of Contract*, 2nd edn (London, 2003) ch. 4.132 ff.
[211] See Chapter 4, p. 101 ff; and Chapter 6, p. 202 ff.   [212] See Clarke, ch. 27-1.
[213] *Walford v Miles* [1992] 2 AC 128.
[214] S. Deakin, C. Lane, and F. Wilkinson, 'Trust or Law? Towards an Integrated Theory of Contractual Relations between Firms' (1994) 21 J Law & Soc. 329–49, 340 ff.
[215] See above, p. 170 ff.

Automatic Continuation

The expectation not only of initial cover[216] but also of renewed cover may leave policyholders exposed. This is why in some countries there is a rule whereby the cover is renewed automatically unless insurers act positively to terminate the cover, or the policyholder concerned is given time to find alternative cover. In Australia, insurers are required to give policyholders notice not later than fourteen days before expiry whether they are 'prepared to negotiate to renew or to extend cover'.[217] If they do not, and if the policyholder concerned has not obtained alternative cover before the expiry, the insurance continues for an equivalent period on the same terms, except that no premium is payable at all unless a claim is made.

In California, as regards commercial insurance on such things as real or personal property, but excluding matters such as motor or marine insurance and reinsurance, insurers are required by the Insurance Code § 678.1(c), 'at least 60 days, but not more than 120 days, in advance of the end of the policy period' to give 'notice of non-renewal, and the reasons for the non-renewal' or conditional renewal, as the case may be. Moreover, under subparagraph (d), if insurers fail to give timely notice required by subparagraph (c), 'the policy of insurance shall be continued, with no change in its terms or conditions, for a period of 60 days after the insurer gives the notice'. Rules like these are an important improvement over the English common law, not only because they give policyholders breathing space but also because, in so far as insurers are required to give reasons, the rules may help policyholders to explain the non-renewal, which of course they must disclose, to alternative insurers.

In France, there is no such rule of law, but there is enforcement by the courts of contract terms, whereby renewal is automatic unless one party objects.[218] In German law there is a similar rule under which any objection must be made before the end of the previous insurance period.[219] The purpose is both that of the insurer to retain business and that of the policyholder to provide against unintentional omission to renew and a gap in cover. This practice should be seen, however, in the light of the legal obligation of policyholders (not found in England) to notify the insurer *during* the insurance period of a change in circumstances which increases the risk.[220]

In principle, such terms could be enforced in England. No disputed instance appears to have been reported. However, a rule of limited automatic renewal has attractions. It is a theme of this book that, as it is in the nature of Man to be careless, it is (still) an important purpose of insurance to provide for that. One of the most common instances of human carelessness, surely, is to overlook renewal

---

[216] See also Chapter 4, p. 88 ff.   [217] Insurance Contracts Act, s. 58(2).

[218] Y. Lambert-Faivre, *Droit des Assurances*, 9th edn (Paris, 1995) 202 ff. See also Code d'assurance, Art. L.112-2, al. 2.   [219] VVG, Art. 8.

[220] See above, p. 161 ff.

dates—unless reminded by the insurer. People depend on them and, in general terms, insurers encourage dependence. An important situation arises when, for the convenience and advantage of insurers, policyholders have been persuaded to pay premium by direct debit. It must surely be the duty of insurers, if they do not intend to trigger the debit, that is, if they do not want renewal, to inform the insured.[221] Moreover, when there is no debit instruction to the bank, if the usual notice of renewal does not come but neither does any other notice from the insurer, why not automatic renewal, at least for a limited period?

Where Next?

In England, it has been rightly observed that the 'great enforcer of morality in commerce is the continuing relationship, the belief that one will have to do business again with this customer'.[222] But in the case of insurance, as we have just seen, once the insurance period is over it is not so—not in law; the insurers do not have to renew the insurance at the end of the insurance period. What counts, however, is not the state of the law but the state of the insurer: how much an insurer wants to retain a policyholder's business. Generally, there are powerful forces for continuity, which encourage the parties making insurance contracts to see the first period as the beginning of a relationship that may last beyond the next *Which?* report that says another insurer is cheaper.

The first insurance period may have been preceded by 'investment' on both sides. Insurers survey the risk and incur transaction costs greater than those normally incurred on renewal. Policyholders invest time absorbing *Which?* or otherwise looking for cover, as well as money by spending the time and also perhaps by complying with policy conditions, for example, as regards security or fire prevention. The conclusion and performance of any contract may involve 'sunk costs' and, in insurance, as in many other cases, each party to an insurance contract bears the risk of the initial 'investment'. It costs each side, especially insurers, less to continue the relationship into the next insurance period than to look for a new partner. On the one side, some policyholders are beginning to realize that those who are prepared to enter into a longer-term relationship with their insurers will often benefit from fidelity discounts and can expect the service to improve, especially in the case of a claim. On the other side, it is no surprise that one of the larger motor insurers has been advertising that it believes 'in relationships that last'. Like the banks, which have been wondering if the closer 'relational' banking found in Germany might be better than the more conservative and less committed banking practised in England in the past, insurers are taking a longer view that leads to closer relations with the customers.

---

[221] See Chapter 4, p. 132.
[222] M. Mayer, quoted by Deakin et al., op. cit. above, n. 214, at 335.

If there is to be a longer relationship that looks beyond the immediate insurance period, what will it or should it be like? The answer to this question, this book argues,[223] lies less in the law than in attitudes, less in the marketplace tradition of getting a bargain than in mutual trust. The more immediate concern in this part of this chapter has been with renewal. The contention is that: policy-holders want peace of mind about concerns important to them; society wants it for them too; for this, policyholders need to know where they stand; it is but a small service and minor courtesy that insurers should ensure that policyholders are alerted to renewal, whether an insurer wishes to continue the cover or not; and that, in case of default in response, we should have rules of law along the lines of those found in other jurisdictions such as Australia and California.

---

[223] See Chapter 9, p. 341 ff.

6

Claims: Taking the Drama out of the Crisis

The Claim

In the event of certain circumstances stated in the policy, the insurer promises to pay money (or money's worth) to the policyholder. General contract law calls this promise a promise to pay subject to a condition precedent—the occurrence of the stated circumstances.[1] Insurance law calls this promise 'cover', and calls the circumstances 'the insured event' or 'the peril insured'. To get the insurer to pay the money promised, it is for the policyholder to make out a claim against the insurer by showing that the peril has occurred.

First, the policyholder must notify the insurer about the loss, and only later prove the truth of the claim: that loss has been actually suffered, loss proximately caused by an event (or peril) covered by the insurance. When this has been proved on the balance of probabilities, the insurer is liable to pay the claim unless the insurer can establish a defence.

The insurer's defence is likely to be that the real cause was something other than an insured peril (for example, an excepted peril), or that the insurance contract was ineffective (for example, expired or vitiated), or that the claimant has not followed the correct procedure (for example, that notice was too late).

---

[1] *Farnsworth*, sect. 8.1.

Loss

Insurance law distinguishes between indemnity insurance, which pays on the basis of the actual value of what has been lost as a result of the peril insured (for example, fire), and non-indemnity or 'contingency' insurance, which pays a sum on the occurrence of a specified event or contingency (for example, death) on the basis not of any assessment of the value of what has been lost (the life) but of the amount stipulated in the contract. The amount stipulated depends simply on the amount of cover purchased.

In the case of non-indemnity insurance, the law is little concerned with the extent of loss. The claimant widow has 'lost' her husband. That is a general reference to the contingency, in that example the death. In the case of indemnity insurance, the law is very much concerned with the extent and nature of loss. The insured loss is the immediate effect of the peril on the thing insured, that is, the subject-matter of the insurance, the car, the factory. Here, insurers speak of both loss of the car, which has been stolen, as well as loss to the car, which has been dented and which the policyholder retains, but which has been damaged. In this book, unless otherwise indicated, loss refers to loss in both senses.

Insured loss, which is immediate and proximate, must be distinguished from less immediate 'consequential' loss to the policyholder, which is not covered unless the policy says it is. Loss insured under a motor insurance policy covers the dent to the vehicle but not the dent in the policyholder's business profits because he cannot use it while it is being repaired. The dent to his pocket is not covered unless it is specified as the loss insured—usually referred to as 'business interruption' or 'consequential loss' cover—either in the contract of motor insurance or, more likely, in another contract of insurance altogether.

Insured loss must also be distinguished from other less tangible and less predictable effects on the policyholder. Tort damages may be awarded against a wrongdoer in respect of distress and suffering caused to the victim; wrongdoers are in no position to contend that they should pay less because their victim was too soft. Insurers are not wrongdoers. Their position is that they are not bound to pay more than they have agreed to pay; and the usual interpretation of the policy is that they have not agreed to pay for this or any other kind of intangible loss, because it is hard to predict and to rate. Insurance indemnity is confined to 'material' loss.

The exception is liability insurance, under which the insurers cover policyholders' liability to others for their torts, and, of course, that liability may well extend not only to physical damage but also to distress and suffering. The awards in such cases are perhaps more predictable because they depend less on the sensitivity of the victim than on that of the court; as long as the award of the court is made not by a jury but by a judge, insurers have some confidence that they can rate the risk profitably.

Causation

The price of cover depends on insurers' assessment of the likelihood and extent of loss from the peril(s) to be insured. Assessment requires prediction on the basis of present data and past records. Records are useless without consistency in the categories of both cause (peril) and loss. Assessment like that usually requires a close connection between the peril and the loss, to exclude the more remote and more imponderable consequences; and this explains the basic rule that the insurer pays only for immediate or proximate loss. The explanation, however, tells only half the story. Less immediate 'consequential' loss can also be covered and is available on the market, but as a distinct category of loss at a distinct and higher price. So, the tight rule of remoteness, that limits recovery to loss that is proximate, is less a consequence of the requirement of predictability than of the way insurers classify and rate risk.

Rules of Construction

The close connection desired by insurers may be mechanical (cause x always leads to loss y), or statistical (if x, records show that there is a high incidence of y). In any case, whether concerned with perils that they are willing to cover or perils they want to exclude, insurers need a clear rule about the causal connection. The rule of law[2] which seems to meet their needs is that the loss must be proximately caused by the peril covered. If they make a close examination of the decisions of the courts, however, they will find that the law is far from clear on the point.

Insurance law starts from three important premises. First, the entire exercise is one of contract construction; so, only perils or excepted causes actually mentioned as such in the policy are considered as possible causes.[3] Secondly, there is a strong presumption that policyholder negligence is covered, so that, for the purpose of any enquiry about the cause of loss and unless the contract very clearly states otherwise, the policyholder's negligence, whether in the events leading up to loss or in attempts to contain it, is not considered to be a relevant cause and thus does not defeat cover.[4] Thirdly, fraud is not covered. This being so, the next question is: when is a cause mentioned in the policy the proximate cause?

The answer given by one school of thought is an analytical answer in the form of (tentative) rules. Under Rule 1, if the kind of loss that has occurred was the (more or less) inevitable result of a cause, whether a peril covered or an excepted cause, that cause is the proximate cause.[5] Further, in the case of a peril, the insurer

---

[2] The leading case is *Leyland Shipping Co. Ltd v Norwich Union Fire Ins. Sy Ltd* [1918] AC 350. Generally, see Clarke, ch. 25.   [3] *The Miss Jay Jay* [1987] 1 Lloyd's Rep 32 (CA).
[4] *Canada Rice Mills Ltd v Union Marine & General Ins. Co.* [1941] AC 55, 69 (PC).
[5] *Leyland Shipping*, above, n. 2.

is liable for the full extent of the loss, although its extent may not have been inevitable, as long as it was not too remote.[6] The application of this first and basic rule leads to more rules.

Rules 2 and 3 are these. If an insured peril leads inevitably to an excepted cause, and this leads inevitably to the loss, the loss is covered. Thus, if a person covered by a personal accident policy falls heavily from his horse (covered), but gets cold and wet riding home and contracts pneumonia (excepted) and dies, the death is covered by the personal accident policy.[7] If, however, an excepted cause leads inevitably to an insured peril, and this leads inevitably to the loss, the loss is not covered.[8] Thus, if under a fire policy an explosion (excepted) leads to fire, the fire damage is not covered.[9]

Rule 4 is that, if an insured peril operates concurrently (independently or inter-dependently) with an excepted peril, and together they lead inevitably to the loss, the loss is not covered. Thus, if the combined effect of a design defect in machinery on trial (excepted) and careless operation of the machinery by the insured owner (covered) causes a fire in the policyholder's factory, the fire is not covered.

Lastly, it should be kept in mind that as all these 'rules' are rules of interpretation of the contract, they may be changed by the contract so long as the change is clear; but that courts are not well disposed to changes that make the claimant's position even more difficult than it already is.[10]

Or Common Sense?

The solution to the problem of causation, offered by another school of thought led at one time by Lord Denning,[11] is to dismiss rules of law or construction on causation as intellectual abstraction and technicality. Indeed, no less a figure than Lord Blackburn once stated with evident satisfaction that the pragmatic Englishman prefers to avoid the philosophical maze,[12] to cut through to a practical solution. The Denning school does not dispute that there is one rule of causation, that the cause must be the proximate cause, but beyond that insists that the proximate cause is identified simply and solely by common sense. Moreover, it is very largely the test applied by the FOS to common cases such as those in which, for example, storm damage is covered but poor maintenance is not. As long as it can be said that 'but for' the storm the damage would not have occurred, whether the proximate cause was the storm or poor maintenance is resolved as a matter of common

---

[6] *Reischer v Borwick* [1894] 2 QB 548 (CA).

[7] *Re Etherington and the Lancashire and Yorkshire Accident Ins. Co.* [1909] 1 KB 591 (CA).

[8] Accepted (but not applied on the facts) in *The Salem* [1983] 1 Lloyd's Rep 342 (HL).

[9] *Boiler Inspection Co. v Sheerman-Williams* [1951] AC 319 (PC).

[10] See Clarke, ch. 25-9B.

[11] *Wayne Tank & Pump Co. Ltd v Employers' Liability Assurance Corp. Ltd* [1973] 2 Lloyd's Rep 237, 240 (CA). He is not alone in high places: see *Leyland Shipping*, op. cit. above, n. 2, 362.

[12] *Inman SS Ltd v Bischoff* (1881–2) LR 7 App Cas 670, 683.

sense.[13] This position is instantly attractive in its simplicity; however, simplicity is rarely quite as simple and satisfactory as we all might wish.

It is attractive in that it avoids some of the phantasmically fine lines that have to be drawn by the rules. For example, the Accidental Insurance Co. covered people against accidental death, unless caused by epileptic fits or by disease. When Mr Winspear had a fit while crossing a small river and was drowned, the claim against the company failed.[14] But when Mr Lawrence had a fit while standing on a station platform, fell under a passing train, and was killed, the claim against the company succeeded.[15] How can the rules enable us distinguish these two cases, decided within months of each other by the same court? Probably we do not have to, because the rules of construction start from the subsequent decision of the House of Lords in *Leyland Shipping*,[16] in which the House wiped the slate clean.

One objection to the commonsense approach is that the judge does too much or, rather, that there is too much of the judge in the judgment of the court. On the one hand, the approach has been condemned as a remit for judicial discretion without external control;[17] or, less kindly, as Californian: ritual intonation of the rule of proximate cause and then a jump to the conclusion that the court wants to reach anyway with the aid of whatever 'rule' seems most helpful.[18] On the other hand, an appeal to common sense defies challenge or dispute because it is something of a personal statement, and contradiction carries personal undertones.

Another criticism is that the judge does too little. Lord Hoffmann has described the commonsense approach as cover for 'a complete absence of any form of reasoning',[19] whereas Sir John Vinelott condemned it as 'the last refuge of the intellectually idle',[20] or perhaps the intellectually cautious: to explain is to be found out and to offer a hostage to fortune and to criticism on appeal. A more sympathetic *critique* is that common sense is sometimes a cloak for intuition when data are lacking.[21]

An associated objection is that common sense is a fiction. Hart and Honoré, in their seminal work on causation, tell us 'that it is impossible to characterise any principles on which common sense proceeds'.[22] Psychologists tell us that there is little or no consistency in what the ordinary man means by common sense.[23]

---

[13] *Ombudsman News*, May 2003, p. 8 ff.

[14] *Winspear v Accidental Ins. Co. Ltd* (1880) 6 QBD 42.

[15] *Lawrence v Accidental Ins. Co. Ltd* (1881) 7 QBD 216.

[16] *Leyland Shipping*, op. cit. above, n. 2.

[17] D. Howarth, 'O Madness of Discourse, That Cause Sets Up with and Against Itself', 96 Yale LJ 1389, 1391 (1987).

[18] See, e.g., R. Risley, 'Landslide Perils and Homeowners' Insurance', 40 UCLA Rev 1145–78, 1155 ff. (1993).

[19] 'Common Sense and Causing Loss', a lecture to the Chancery Bar Assn, 15 June 1999.

[20] 6 Co Law 31 (1985), speaking, however, of s. 75 of the Companies Act 1980.

[21] J. D. Fraser and D. R. Howarth, 'More Cause for Concern', 4 Legal Studies 131–56, 138 (1984).   [22] *Causation in the Law*, 2nd edn, (Oxford, 1985), 26.

[23] N. J. Mullany, 'Common Sense Causation—an Australian View' (1992) 12 OJLS 431–9, 436 and references cited.

As Lord Mustill once told us: 'Common sense for one person may be uncommon sense for another.'[24] Indeed, the High Court of Australia once agreed that causation was simply a matter of common sense and then divided 3:2 on the common sense of the case before it.[25] In England the epitome of common sense today is the traveller on the Underground, Lord Steyn's twenty-first century substitute for the man on the Clapham omnibus.[26] This figure too has been described as a thin disguise for the judge and his particular philosophical predisposition.[27]

Real people, whether jammed in the Underground or on the roads overhead, tend to attribute events to things closest in space and time; or to select events or features that are out of the ordinary. The former was rejected in *Leyland*. The latter has some resonance with the law of tort but, as we have seen, little with insurance law on causation, which is concerned only with the insurance contract and the causes mentioned in it.

In contrast, the rules of construction do provide lawyers with some assistance which, however, is far from perfect: the rules can sometimes be hard to draw around future cases, as well as hard to explain to present clients, with the kind of confidence needed to go to court. Moreover, to a degree a court can manipulate the rules of construction by the way it chooses to see the facts. In *The Miss Jay Jay*,[28] a leading case, there were two competing causes, the impact of the sea (covered) and a design defect (excepted). The first court saw the defective design as the action of the architect occurring at a point in time before the vessel first put to sea. On that basis, the exception occurred well before the impact of the sea and on the facts it was clearly not the proximate cause under Rule 1. The Court of Appeal differed, and one judge, in particular, saw the design defect as a physical feature of the vessel which operated concurrently and interdependently with the perils of the seas.[29] That brought the case within Rule 4, with the result that the insurance claim failed.

In the end, it seems, the two approaches to causation are best regarded as being less in competition than complementary. The Canadian Supreme Court once observed that the task of doctrine 'is to identify the factors which unite the different applications with a view to formulating emergent principles, recognizing that absolute logical formulations may not in all cases be possible or practical'.[30] The last word comes from Lord Hoffmann, who said that he doubted 'whether the use of abstract metaphysical theory has ever had much support in practice' and, without making his own position entirely clear, he agreed that 'the notion of causation not be overcomplicated', but said that neither 'should it be oversimplified'.[31]

---

[24] 'Humpty Dumpty and Risk Management' [1997] LMCLQ 488–501, 500.
[25] *Chappel v Hart* (1998) 195 CLR 232.
[26] *MacFarlane v Tayside Health Board* [2000] 2 AC 59, 82.
[27] *Markesinis and Deakin*, 128.   [28] [1985] 1 Lloyd's Rep 264, 271.
[29] Op. cit. above, n. 3, 35.
[30] *Canadian National Ry Co. v Norsk Pacific SS Co.* (1992) 91 DLR (4th) 289, 366, *per* McLachlin J (SCC).
[31] *Empress Car Co. (Abertillery) Ltd v National Rivers Authority* [1999] 2 AC 22, 29.

Common Perils

The loss insured must have been caused by an event, a 'peril', covered by the contract of insurance. Although the law assumes that policyholders have read their policy,[32] it is clear that most people do not until they try to claim, and that some do not read it even then; and that those who do read their policy, may not know what it means. Even among insurers there is division; for example, at one time there was controversy among them over whether modems and fax machines could be regarded as 'contents' under a domestic house policy. The meaning of most wording, however, is well settled—among insurers: their understanding of what the words mean may not be quite what their policyholders would expect.

Fire

People who take out fire insurance may think that they will recognize a fire when they see one. The farmer who sees billowing smoke combined with intense heat from his grain store might think he has a fire on his hands, and doubtless the fire brigade would agree, but his insurer might not. The world of insurance, which is built on a mixture of tradition and pragmatism, is one in which there can be smoke without fire and in which some 'fires' are not fires at all.

First, however great the smoke and heat, fire does not include slow conflagrations from spontaneous combustion in vegetable matter, such as grain, caused by too much moisture in the matter. This is explained by the courts' resort to the dictionary, where the definition of 'fire' is ignition, and this requires not only heat but visible light,[33] with the result that some fires, like that of the farmer, are not covered; and by the concern of insurers with causes rather than effects. Yet if the farmer's grain is damaged by the water hosed on the policyholder's fire at the store next door in a bid to stop it spreading, his damage is covered by 'fire'.[34] This is explained by the pragmatic concern of insurers with the best interests of the parties: hesitation with the hosepipe is in the interest of neither.

Secondly, fire does not include conflagration caused by explosion. So, if live coals fall on the farmer's carpet, the damage is fire damage; but if his boiler explodes, the consequent conflagration of his carpet (and perhaps everything else) is not covered unless (as is usual) the cover is expressly extended to explosions of that kind.[35] The reason for the distinction between fire and explosion lies not only with the concern of insurers with causes, but also with the way that insurers have classified risk in the past and compiled the records, which are essential for assessing risks in the future. The risk of explosion in industrial premises was and is

---

[32] Chapter 5, pp. 137–8.   [33] *Everett v London Assurance Co.* (1865) 19 CB (NS) 126, 133.
[34] *Symington v Union Ins. Co. of Canton* (1928) 34 Com Cas 23 (CA).
[35] See Clarke, ch. 17–2E.

such that, for statistical and other purposes, it has always been classified separately. This is an instance of a recurrent feature of cover, that it may be defined less by reference to language and the understanding of the man on the Underground than by reference to the traditional classification of risks by insurers.

Personal Accidents

In law, policyholders have an accident when they sustain an injury which they neither intended nor expected. More precisely, there is an accident, first, when the injury is the natural or probable result to the person of the policyholder of a fortuitous and unexpected occurrence in the life of the policyholder, which is external to the person of the policyholder:

... for instance, where the assured is run over by a train, ... or injured by a fall ... ; or ... drinks poison by mistake, or is suffocated by the smoke of a house on fire; or by an escape of gas, or is drowned whilst bathing.[36]

Secondly, there is an accident when the injury is the fortuitous and unexpected result to the person of the policyholder of a cause that is a natural or probable occurrence in the life of the policyholder, which is external to the person of the policyholder:

... for instance, where a person lifts a heavy burden in the ordinary course of business and injures his spine, or stoops down to pick up a marble and breaks a ligament in his knee, or scratches his leg while putting on a stocking, or ruptures himself while playing golf. In this case the element of accident manifests itself, not in the cause, but in its result.[37]

In law, however, illness or disease is not an accident. If someone swimming in the Thames gets cramp and drowns, that is an accident.[38] If someone swimming in the Thames cuts his or her foot on a snag, and dies from an infected wound, the cases suggest that that too is an accident.[39] If, however, someone swimming in the Thames is infected by untreated sewage and dies later in hospital, that is not accident: that is illness. But what of the sunworshipper on holiday who takes too much sun on the beach and dies later? The Court of Appeal has told us firmly that that is not an accident but a case of disease.[40] Why?

As our expectations of life and everything else rise, we feel more easily let down when life does not come up to scratch. The aches and pains we put up with in the past have become a condition, a medical condition, for which we expect treatment and cure. The man who, in 1900, might have died at sea, aged 40, and who might now reach the calmer but costlier waters of old age, can be kept afloat.

---

[36] A. W. B. Welford, *The Law Relating to Accident Insurance*, 2nd edn (London, 1932), 268 ff., quoted with approval in *De Souza v Home & Overseas Ins. Co. Ltd.* [1995] LRLR 453, 458–9 (CA).

[37] Welford, op. cit. above, n. 36.

[38] *Trew v Railway Passengers Assurance Co.* (1861) 6 H & N 839, 844–5.

[39] See the quotation from Welford (above).   [40] *De Souza*, op. cit. above, n. 36.

The life expectancy of a man in 1900 was 46; now it is about 80. Women can expect to live longer. But with the increase in the expectation of life has come an increase in cost. Medical treatment and medical insurance are big business and, understandably enough, to insurers medical insurance against illness and disease is something quite different from insurance against accidents; it is a risk of a different kind and a different magnitude. Indeed, a line must be drawn; however, it is drawn at a point that makes more sense to insurers than to policyholders. On one side of the line the person who drinks poison by mistake suffers an accident. On the other side of the line the person who drinks water contaminated by typhoid suffers illness. Nonetheless, both persons might well echo the poet, Yeats, who wrote of 'the discourtesy of death'; it is lawyers rather than lay people who speak of death by natural causes.

All Risks

The words of cover, 'all risks', are reassuring on their face but do not live up to people's expectations in law. On the home front, people buying household contents insurance think of their property as possessions, probably prized possessions, rather than as 'household contents'. Few realize that their possessions will not be covered unless they buy 'all risks' cover as a policy extra; and when they do buy it, they may not be aware that it covers certain possessions and not others. Policies vary, but many do not cover laptops or sports equipment, for example, and those covering sports equipment may cover it in transportation but not when in use. All risks cover of this kind is potentially so confusing that the FOS requires insurers to point these matters out when selling the cover.[41]

More generally there is a problem because there is a conceptual ambiguity in the label 'all risks'. To insurers, the emphasis is on the second word, but policyholders are more likely to focus on the first, only to find, however, that they are not covered against each and every risk but only those risks which, in the law's interpretation of the contract of insurance, are regarded as risks. All risks insurance, it is said, covers risks but not certainties.[42]

In law, there is a certainty, and therefore not a risk, first, if loss is caused by the wilful misconduct of the policyholder.[43] Of course, the wilful misconduct of others, such as thieves, is a risk and is usually covered. Secondly, in the case of property insurance, there is a certainty and not a risk if loss is caused by ordinary wear and tear, depreciation, or 'inherent vice'.[44] Inherent vice is deterioration in things as a result of natural processes in the things themselves, and in the ordinary course of events during the period of cover without the intervention of any fortuitous external accident. As one court put it: 'Foods rot; iron rusts; some wines

[41] *Ombudsman News* No.35, February/March 2004, p. 3.
[42] The leading case is *British & Foreign Marine Ins. Co. Ltd v Gaunt* [1921] 2 AC 41.
[43] Ibid., p. 52 and 57.   [44] Ibid., 46.

simply do not travel well'.[45] Whether it is wear and tear or inherent vice, the significant feature is that the loss or damage was going to happen anyway. In this the law is clear, but nonetheless not what policyholders may have expected.

The main surprise is that the insurability of property with reference to inherent vice is assessed afterwards with the hindsight wisdom of the court and, if necessary, of science. If, as the result of some internal and invisible defect, the goods were doomed from the start to damage or loss, that is not covered, whether the policyholder could or should have known this or not. In everyday language, however, a risk is something about to be taken and yet to be resolved. The skater who sets out on thin ice takes a risk, even though with the benefit of hindsight it becomes clear that the skater was always going to fall through. This is true not only of everyday language but also other branches of insurance law: life insurance (all risks of death) usually pays even if the insured dies of a latent condition of which nobody was aware at the time of the contract. In the case of disability insurance, there is even cover for the person disabled at the time of contracting if, although the symptoms are already apparent, the person's condition has yet to be diagnosed as a disabling condition.[46] In the case of personal accident insurance too, the accidental character of what occurs is assessed largely from the subjective viewpoint of the insured.[47] Why not also when the insurance covers the life and health of property?

The inherent insurability of latent defects in property such as ships,[48] or in buildings, is confirmed by the willingness of insurers to offer such insurance—as long as it is described not as all risks insurance but as something else. The law in the United States is more transparent. Courts take a 'subjective' approach, whereby all risks insurance covers loss, however inevitable at the time of contract, if this was unknown to the insured at the time. In the *Bauxites* case,[49] plant defectively designed and constructed collapsed. The Court of Appeals started from § 291 of the Restatement of Contracts, stating that a fortuitous event 'is an event which so far as the parties to the contract are aware, is dependent on chance', and from this perspective it found that, as the policyholder was ignorant of the defect, the claim should succeed.

Once again, the explanation of the English rule appears to be that the exclusion of this risk from 'all' risks is what insurers intend; insurers then know where they stand, even though the policyholder may not. 'The commercial purpose of the use of standard form policies (i.e., [*sic*] legal certainty as to the risk they cover) would be defeated if their construction varied from case to case according to the different circumstances.'[50] With these words, Lord Diplock rejected any reference to the actual knowledge of the particular policyholder. That was, in his view, one variable too many; but it is otherwise in other kinds of cover, so why not here?

---

[45] *Perzy v Intercargo Corp.*, 827 F Supp. 1365, 1370 (ND Ill., 1993).
[46] E.g., angina: *Cook v Financial Ins. Co.* [1998] 1 WLR 1765 (HL).
[47] See above, p. 189.   [48] See, e.g., *The Nukila* [1997] 2 Lloyd's Rep 146, 151 (CA).
[49] *Compagnie des Bauxites de Guinée v INA*, 724 F 2d 369 (3 Cir, 1983).
[50] *Soya GmbH v White* [1983] 1 Lloyd's Rep 122, 125 (HL).

Surely, as we have seen with regard to other kinds of cover, if the number of policyholders is large enough and the points of reference are in all cases the same, the insurers will have enough information in order to rate the risk. For policyholders the certainty that matters is that they have (or have not) cover, and this they need to know at the beginning of their venture and not months later when experts have had their say. The explanation owes less to reason than to the past practice (and accumulated data) of insurers, and also perhaps to a fear of fraud.

Liability

As we have seen,[51] we live in a compensation culture, with the corollary that liability cover has become an essential of life for many people; golfers, for example, are ill-advised to set foot on a golf course without £2 million of liability cover. Of course, insurance may be one of the services offered by their club, but, however obtained, it is essential and not cheap. The pity is that neither is it easy to understand.

As usual, any enquiry starts with the policy. In principle, liability insurance is any insurance protection which indemnifies policyholders against liability to third parties. In practice, cover extends only to certain heads of liability to third parties, those indicated by the policy. In particular, there is a presumption based on practice and the likely intention of the insurer that cover does not extend to breach of contract.[52] Indeed, the policy may well contain a 'business risk' exception. The underlying factor is insurers' concerns about adverse selection and moral hazard, and the associated premise that policyholders are the persons best placed to remedy defective products or shoddy work and should not lack incentive to do so.[53] If, however, the claim against a policyholder is based on negligence (covered) and also breach of contract (neither expressly covered nor excluded), the claim is covered.[54]

Liability insurance indemnifies policyholders against liability to third parties, thus providing policyholders with cover against a consequent depletion of their assets. Liability insurance is therefore a contract of indemnity and, in principle, the insurance does not oblige the insurer to pay until the policyholder has suffered loss.[55] When does this occur?

Loss

As the cover is against a depletion of policyholders' assets, one view is that no loss has occurred until a policyholder is 'out of pocket', that is, until the policyholder has actually compensated the victim. This was the original common law rule.

---

[51] Chapter 1, p. 6 ff.

[52] *Jan de Nul (UK) Ltd v NV Royal Belge* [2001] Lloyd's Rep IR 327, 359 ff.; appeal dismissed: [2002] 1 Lloyd's Rep 583 (CA).

[53] See *James Longley & Co. v Forest Giles Ltd* [2002] Lloyd's Rep IR 421 at [17] (CA).

[54] *Capel-Cure Myers Capital Management Ltd v McCarthy* [1995] LRLR 498, 503.

[55] *West Wake Price & Co. v Ching* [1957] 1 WLR 45, 49.

The obvious objection to such a rule is that policyholders may not have enough money to pay the liability and thus trigger cover, which would defeat the purpose of the cover.[56]

A second view is that property subject to a claim is worth less than property that is not, and similarly policyholders are 'worth less' as soon as the claim is made against them, albeit by an amount less than the amount of the claim. This is self-evident when the policyholder is a quoted company and, for example, an English pharmaceutical company facing a class action in the USA. Moreover, the view is reflected in standard accounting practice, which takes into consideration not only actual loss but also risk of loss.[57] According to this view, therefore, insurers become liable to their policyholders when a *prima facie* case has been made against them. The policyholder becomes liable to the victim in the sense that the victim has a *prima facie* cause of action against the insured. Moreover, a practical argument for this view is that, if insurers are not liable until later, insurers are not obliged to take a view of the claim and, until they know that view, policyholders may find it difficult to reach a wise decision about whether to settle or fight the claim.

English law, however, is different and takes a cautious middle position between these two views. According to the Court of Appeal in *Post Office v Norwich Union Fire Ins. Sy Ltd*,[58] 'the insured only acquires a right to sue [the insurer] for the money when his liability to the injured person has been established so as to give rise to a right of indemnity . . . either by judgment of the court or by an award in arbitration or by agreement'. Agreement with the third party does not trigger the liability of the insurer unless there appears to have been a genuine claim.[59] Insurers and policyholders may not agree about this, or, if the claim seems genuine, whether to settle it or fight; their interests in this may well conflict. To resolve such differences policies often contain a 'QC clause', whereby the issue is referred to the opinion of a Queen's Counsel.

The Event

The court judgment, arbitration award, or agreement is what establishes the policyholder's loss,[60] but not necessarily the insurer's liability to pay that loss. It must have been preceded by the event (liability) covered by the policy. That event is not the policyholder's loss but something else more or less related to the liability of the policyholder to a third party. The event is usually the occurrence of an act or neglect which gave rise to policyholder liability to the third party. In such cases

---

[56] *Johnson v Salvage Assn* (1887) 19 QBD 458, 460–461 (CA); *Charter Reinsurance Ltd v Fagan* [1996] 2 Lloyd's Rep 113 (HL).

[57] Some support for this view of financial loss can be seen in *Nykredit Mortgage Bank plc v Edward Erdman Group Ltd* [1997] 1 WLR 1627, 1630 (HL).

[58] [1967] 2 QB 363, 373; confirmed: *Bradley v Eagle Star Ins. Co. Ltd* [1989] AC 957, 966.

[59] *McDonnel Information Systems Ltd v Swinbank* [1999] 1 Lloyd's Rep IR 98.

[60] The *Post Office* case, above, n. 58.

we speak of an 'occurrence' policy. Sometimes, however, it is difficult to identify a particular act or neglect, or to pin it to a relevant point in time. This is one of the reasons for the emergence of 'claims made' policies, whereby the insured event is not the original occurrence but the making of a claim by a third party against the policyholder. 'Claims made' polices are more controversial and, in the case of professional indemnity insurance, more common today. The background has been explained by Staughton LJ thus:

One could say that any liability incurred during the policy period by the [policyholder] should be covered. That would have the result that claims might be brought home to roost months or years after the policy had expired. The insurer would have no way of determining within reason when their liability had ended, or what reserves ought to be made after they thought that they had paid all claims. A second method is that adopted in this case of providing that claims made during the year in question are covered by insurance . . . The third method would be to provide that a policy would only cover claims which were actually paid in the years of insurance . . . That would be a disaster, because it would mean that the insured would have to disclose on renewal if a claim was threatened. It does not seem very likely that he would then be able to renew his policy until the time came when the claim was actually paid.[61]

The controversial aspect of 'claims made' policies has been explained by the Canadian Supreme Court:

The difference between the two kinds of policies is that the insurer bears the risk of an uncertain claims future under an occurrence policy a claims-made approach shifts much of that risk back to the insured. For instance, the discovery by a manufacturer, by reason of the claim of even a single consumer, that it has produced thousands of units of a product that is hazardous raises enormous implications for future insurability of that manufacturer.[62]

The problem is mostly associated with the prospect of mass claims. One or two claims against a solicitor or an accountant do not usually pose the same problem. Nonetheless, the French Supreme Court, the *Cour de Cassation*, declared 'claims made' policies to be illegal, although it was later overruled by the legislature in respect of certain kinds of liability such as medical malpractice.[63]

Occurrence

A single act of negligence, for example that of a surgeon in the operating theatre, is likely to be easy to ascertain. However, in other cases it may be difficult to pin the event to a point of time, for example neglect may involve continuous inadequacy. That is also a problem when policyholder liability does not accrue until there has been damage to the victim, notably in the important case of disease

---

[61] *Robert Irving & Burns v Stone* [1998] Lloyd's Rep IR 258, 260–61 (CA).
[62] *Reid Crowther & Partners Ltd v Simcoe & Erie General Ins. Co.* (1993) 99 DLR (4th) 741, 749.
[63] L. 2002-1577 of 30 December 2002.

caused by contact with asbestos.[64] The time of damage may be important for the victim to target the right defendant, and for the defendant to target the insurer on risk at the time. The American experience has been that there are four possibilities.

The first possibility is the time of exposure: loss occurs when the victim is exposed to the activity or circumstance which gives rise to the claim against the insured.[65] One objection to such a rule is that these are 'long tail' cases. For claimants the problem is that by the time the exposure has become manifest and a claim can be got together, the claim may be time barred. For insurers the problem is that, until claims are barred, they do not know for how many claims they must make provision.

The second possibility is the time of 'injury in fact': the time when injury or damage actually occurs to the victim.[66] An obvious objection is the difficulty of proving when it occurred. Another is that its application requires a case by case study of the particular injury and the particular victim, which, in the end, has little value as precedent for settlement or for future calculations.

The third possibility is the time of manifestation: when the injury becomes manifest.[67] A major objection to the manifestation rule is that it is a 'cut-and-run concept': '. . . insurers would refuse to write new insurance for the insured when it became apparent that the period of manifestations, and hence a flood of claims, was approaching.'[68]

Given the imperfections of these rules, which mostly worked against victims in the end, courts came up with a fourth rule which was designed to assist the victim. The fourth possibility is the 'triple trigger' or 'multiple trigger' rule, whereby liability attaches to *any* insurer whose policy was in force at the time of initial exposure, during continued exposure, or at the time of manifestation.[69] Eventually the indemnity cost is apportioned between the various insurers on risk. Apportionment carries the corollary that the insured is treated as an insurer for any periods in which he did not buy cover for the risk in question.[70]

In England it is the fourth rule that is favoured. In *Fairchild*[71] the House of Lords held that the claimant could recover damages in a case of mesothelioma, even though it could not be established on the balance of probabilities when it was that he inhaled the asbestos fibres which caused the disease and, hence, which of various companies that had employed him was liable at the relevant time or which insurer was on risk.

The House took the view[72] that the injustice that arose from the liability imposed on a particular employer (and its insurer) was outweighed by the injustice

---

[64] See Chapter 1, p. 10; and Chapter 2, pp. 50–1.

[65] *Insurance Co. of North America v Forty-Eight Insulations Inc*, 451 F Supp 1230 (ED Mich, 1978), 633 F 2d 1212 (6 Cir, 1980), cert den 454 US 1109.

[66] *Dow Chemical Co. v Associated Indemnity Corp*, 724 F Supp 474, 480 (ED Mich, 1989).

[67] *Eagle-Picher Industries Inc. v Liberty Mutual Ins. Co.*, 682 F 2d 12 (1 Cir, 1982).

[68] *Dow*, op. cit. above, n. 66, 485.   [69] *Keene Corp. v INA*, 667 F 2d 1034 (Col, 1981).

[70] *Owens-Illinois Inc. v United Ins. Co.*, 650 A 2d 974, 993 (NJ, 1994).

[71] [2003] 1 AC 72.   [72] [2003] 1 AC 72, at [33].

of denying redress to the victim. Then in *Barker v Corus*[73] the House held that each employer was liable only for the amount of damage it caused, the amount to be settled by apportionment between the employers. However, the Compensation Act 2006, s. 3(2), made each jointly and severally liable for all the damage and provided for contribution and apportionment later between all those responsible.

Loss Arising out of One Event: Highjacked Aircraft

If someone is negligent over a period of time, is that a single event or occurrence giving rise to a number of losses (a hydra of negligence with heads of loss), or are there as many events or occurrences as there are losses? In England, the question has arisen in its most complex, even philosophical, form under reinsurance contracts, in which the reinsurer is obliged to pay in respect of 'each and every loss and/or occurrence arising out of one event', or 'in respect of any claim or claims arising from one originating cause or series of events or occurrences attributable to one originating cause'. To those outside the arcane world of reinsurance the decisions are complex and hard to follow. An analogy canvassed in argument was that of a war, which is an event in history, while a battle is an event in the war and there are many events in the battle; but which is the relevant level when the event is the focus of an insurance contract? Fortunately, these cases are outside the scope of this book, not least because to a degree each decision turns on its own wording and background.[74]

The question 'one or more' has arisen in its most spectacular form in the USA, as the 'Twin Towers' problem. Specifically, the question is whether the collision of two aircraft, one after each other, into each tower of the World Trade Center in New York in September 2001, was one event or two. It is still being litigated, not least because huge sums of money turn on the outcome. In England this is a question of more than academic interest. On the one hand, some of the risks were reinsured in London. On the other hand, some analogous cases have come before English judges in the past.

Argument usually starts from the Dawson's Field arbitration by Michael Kerr QC (later Lord Justice Kerr). In 1970, four aircraft were highjacked by the Popular Front for the Liberation of Palestine. One was taken to Cairo, where it was soon blown up. The other three were taken to Dawson's Field, an airstrip in Jordan, where they were later blown up in a space of five minutes. The opinion of Michael Kerr, that what occurred at Dawson's Field (but not Cairo) were losses arising out of one occurrence, and his reasons for it, were later adopted in the courts.

The first point, always one of construction of the contract, was that an occurrence 'is not the same as a loss, for one occurrence may embrace a plurality of losses'.[75] This point was adopted later in litigation that arose out of the

---

[73] [2006] 2 AC 572.

[74] The hardy inquirer may wish to look at Clarke, ch. 17-4C3.

[75] *Kuwait Airways Corp. v Kuwait Ins. Co.* [1996] 1 Lloyd's Rep 664, 686; see also *Scott v Copenhagen Re* [2002] Lloyd's Rep IR 775, at [64].

destruction of fifteen aircraft on the ground when Iraq invaded Kuwait. That was true of Dawson's Field and it has been accepted in the USA, where it is referred to, not surprisingly perhaps, as the 'Pearl Harbor Concept'.[76]

The main point, again one of construction, in the opinion of Michael Kerr and adopted by the courts, was that the decision in each case should turn on the 'degree of unity in relation to cause, locality, time and, if initiated by human action, the circumstances and purposes of the person responsible',[77] but the most important of these are locality and time.[78] Clearly, therefore, an English court would see what happened at the World Trade Center in 2001 as a single event, and so far that has also been the decision of the court in New York.[79]

Claims

The argument advanced by the insurer in one case, that the issue of a writ without communication such as service amounted to a claim, has been rejected.[80] For a claim under a 'claims made' policy, the writ must have been served; and imperfections in the writ are irrelevant as long as the recipient is put on sufficient notice of the claim.

Evidently policyholders might be concerned about claims that they know are on the way and which, therefore, they will have to disclose on renewal. This concern is usually met by claims made cover that extends to 'claims notified'. More specifically, cover of claims actually made is commonly extended to claims made later, provided that the insurer has been notified during the insurance period of circumstances suggesting that a claim might be made, for example, notice in writing as soon as practicable of any 'circumstance of which the insured shall become aware during the Period of the insurance which may give rise to a loss or claim against them'. The meaning of a relevant 'circumstance' depends very much on the policy and the context.[81] Moreover, commonly, 'such notice having been given, any loss or claim to which that circumstance has given rise which is subsequently made after the expiration of the Period of insurance shall be deemed to have been made during the subsistence hereof'.

Proving the Claim

In law, the claimants must prove the truth of their claim on the balance of probabilities. In practice, many claims, usually small claims, are paid without the

---

[76] D. Derrington, 'The Terrorist Threat: Australia's Response', 13 Ind Int L & Comp L Rev 831, 832 (2003).   [77] *Kuwait Airways*, op. cit. above, n. 75, 686; *Scott*, ibid., at [64].
[78] *Mann v Lexington Ins. Co.* [2001] Lloyd's Rep IR 179 (CA).
[79] *S.R. Business Ins. Co. v WTC Properties*, 222 F Supp 2d. 385 (SD NY, 2002).
[80] *Robert Irving & Burns v Stone* [1998] Lloyd's Rep IR 258, 264 (CA).
[81] See *Hamptons Residential Ltd v Field* [1998] 2 Lloyd's Rep 248 (CA); and *Layer Ltd v Lowe* [2000] Lloyd's Rep IR 510 (CA).

required degree of proof. For example, a claimant may manage to convince the insurer that the claimant's wallet was lost on holiday, but to prove, as the law requires in a case of indemnity insurance, the amount of money in it at the time may be all but impossible. Nonetheless, the insurer may well pay the claim. Why?

According to one insurer, a sponsor of cricket at the time because it was associated more than other major sports with fair play and honesty, the most important thing in the insurance business is trust. If the insurer pays an unproven claim, however, this may or may not be because he believes or trusts the claimant. Although insurers commonly invite the trust of the public,[82] it is a trust that is not often reciprocated. Suspicion of claimants among insurers and adjusters, their agents, seems to be a recognized occupational hazard. If insurers do pay an unproven claim, it may be because they trust the intermediary, if there is one, handling the claim; or because the claim is small and to reject it would be at the cost of too large a loss of goodwill. Even routine investigation costs money; the cost may be out of proportion to what, if anything, may be saved.

When there is no intermediary on the scene, generally, as the sum claimed increases so does the insurer's distrust and the degree of proof required of the claimant. Moreover, occasionally insurers crack the whip by fighting small but suspicious claims, regardless of cost, *pour encourager les autres*. Distrustful insurers can usually do this because, whether the claim is large or small, the whip hand of the law and the tactical high ground of litigation are theirs.

First, insurers can defend the claim simply and 'cheaply' by doing nothing. They can sit back, sit on their cheque book, and wait for the claimant to prove the claim in full. In one instance a contents insurer demanded receipts for all 147 CDs claimed to be stolen. In another, a travel insurer, faced with a claim that a wallet had been stolen fifteen minutes before the claimant boarded the coach to catch the plane back to England, insisted on the local police report required by the policy. In another, a disability claim arising out of psychiatric illness was rejected, because the contract required diagnosis by a 'relevant registered medical specialist' but the claimant had been diagnosed by his general practitioner. However, faced with a claim for over £10,000 in respect of the accidental death of a prize parrot, the insurer pointed to a policy condition requiring a vet's report certifying the cause of death, which the claimant failed to provide; but the FOS decided for the insurer.[83]

Secondly, for a more active defence, insurers have various moves to test the strength of the claim or of the claimant's resolve. Against a fire claim, for example, the insurer may subpoena documents relating to the claimant's financial affairs;

---

[82] See Chapter 2, p. 46 ff.   [83] *Ombudsman News*, September 2003.

policies often allow insurers to do this. In Australia, the Ombudsman once found, on the part of claims investigators, 'a seductive show of concern for the policy-holder, painting a frightening picture of litigation and costs, with no hope of success, in order to discourage the policyholder from pursuing the claim and persuading him to sign a release'.[84]

Thirdly, as well as money, the insurer has time on his side. Often the claimant has neither. In the 1990s a conference on policy wording disputes was advertised to enable insurers and their lawyers to 'rigorously scrutinise all claims'. This led to an outcry in a wide range of newspapers. Understandably, insurers did not like this kind of press. When a particular claimant issued a press release with allegations of this kind, the insurer sought and obtained an injunc-tion to stop him issuing further press statements of his version of his claim. However, newspaper stories do not run for ever; insurers minded to block claims have time on their side. In some common law countries, insurers slow to pay without just cause risk liability to pay large sums of punitive damages for 'bad faith'; but there is little or no legal sanction against insurers slow to pay in England.[85]

Lastly, insurers have the advantage of experience and expertise. In the past the insurers' practice was to have claims investigated by their own claims inspectors, or, if the claim was large or difficult, by 'independent' loss adjusters.

Loss Adjusters

Loss adjusters are self-employed specialists in the handling and investigation of claims and, formally, are independent of the insurers that employ them. Adjusters say that they 'take care' of the claimant. Indeed, the industry view is that the avail-ability of independent third parties to negotiate and settle claims is one of the great strengths which has been displayed by the UK insurance market; and that without loss adjusters it would be only the very largest companies that could afford to retain such expertise on their own staff. This traditional and rather rosy image of the adjuster is one which the insurance industry would like customers to share. But the independence and objectivity of the adjuster are open to question on at least two points.

First, it has been doubted whether adjusters come to claims with an open mind. Secondly, why, when the adjuster's investigation is complete, is the report drawn up by the 'independent' adjuster available to the insurer but not to the claimant? The answer is that, in reality and in law, adjusters are the agents of the

---

[84] General Insurance Claims Review Panel, Annual Report 1993 (Canberra, 1994), 12.
[85] See below, p. 244 ff.

insurer. The perception of many claimants, who view adjusters with resentment and distrust, is that adjusters are brought in only to beat the claim down.

The Reality of Fraud

Insurers believe that they are paying out more than they have to. This belief has been encouraged by loss adjusters, who talk to them of 'leakage', including above all fraud, and of the need to 'audit' leakage—with the help of adjusters. Fraud, they say, is 'a national sport', in which insurers are 'fair game'. 'A decade ago, fraud was not something insurance companies were willing to talk about. It was hushed up, hidden away and often accepted as a necessary evil—bad debts that were regrettable, but part and parcel of working in insurance. Over the past five years, however, things have changed dramatically'.[86] Insurance companies are appointing 'anti-fraud teams' and insurance fraud has become a subject for serious study.[87] But is fraud really the big business they would have us believe?

Telling lies, we are told, is normal behaviour, an inseparable part of social intercourse.[88] Cultural attitudes affect the tendency and Germans, for example, are less likely to tell 'white' social lies ('What a lovely dress!') than the English. A survey of English students in 2004 indicated that four out of five thought it acceptable to lie in job interviews. So insurers require little convincing that we are prone to tell them lies and, indeed, a number of surveys suggest a widespread willingness to exaggerate insurance claims. One adjuster of household claims was quoted as referring to the 'pub effect': if policyholders go to the pub before we arrive on the scene we are in trouble.[89] In late 2003, a survey of social attitudes in England indicated that 48 per cent of the British public 'would not rule out' making an exaggerated claim, partly because, in spite of efforts by the ABI to educate them to the contrary, most still see such behaviour as 'victimless'.[90] In this the British are not alone. In the same year a survey in the USA indicated that one in three believed it permissible to exaggerate claims to make up for the deductible, and one in four believed it permissible to pad a claim to recoup past premiums paid.[91] In 2007 a conservative estimate of the cost to the UK of all kinds of fraud was said to be £20 billion.[91a]

Added to this are newspaper accounts of striking scams: stories of staged car crashes in certain parts ('hotspots') of England and of 'phantom' ships in certain

[86] Foxwell, PM Management Briefing, 12 October 2006, p. 3.

[87] See, e.g., D. Morse and L. Skajaa, *Tackling Insurance Fraud: Law and Practice* (London, 2004); and in the USA the Insurance Fraud Bureau of Massachusetts, *Insurance Fraud Research Register* (Boston, 2002).   [88] Research reported by F. Harvey, *Financial Times*, 28 May 2004.

[89] *Professional Broking*, February 1998, p. 17.   [90] *PM*, 13 November 2003, pp. 28–29.

[91] D. L. Nersessian 'Penalty by Proxy' 38 Tort & Ins LJ 907–31, 915 (2003), with reference to www.insurancefraud.org/stats.htm.

[91a] Report (7 March 2007) by Burrows and Levi commissioned by the Association of Chief Police Officers.

parts of the wider world that vanish with real cargo; even the stories of a man in Brazil who chopped off a finger to support a claim and of the suicide in France staged by killing a vagrant and leaving the body in the burned out wreck of the life assured's car. Mercifully, events such as the last are rare. Commonplace, however, in the perception of the insurance industry, is insurance fraud of various kinds in the motor, household, commercial contents, and fire sectors. Another concerns the liability of highway authorities: some pay more on claims than they do on highway maintenance. Frauds are often assisted by third parties who spot an 'insurance job'. Garages stretch repairs to cars, and there are private hospitals which have reportedly charged as much as £1 to administer an aspirin.

The Importance of Fraud

Whether or not fraud is really widespread, what is clear and what really counts is that insurers believe that it is widespread, and often approach claims in a spirit of suspicion. In view of the position of strength from which he considers a claim,[92] the insurer's perception of the claimant and his claim is crucial to the outcome. The legal framework for claims assumes good faith and trust on both sides. Society is reluctant to believe that claimants are fraudulent, and the law makes it hard for insurers to prove that they are, but it also assumes the good faith of insurers, with the result that, if so minded, it is easy for them to drag their feet over payment. In the early 1990s, certainly one measure of commercial 'success' applied by insurers was the reduction of 'leakage', especially perceived fraud. The handling of claims was such that it was perceived by the public as slow and hostile.[93] Little has changed. In December 2003, a BBC advertisement for a forthcoming Radio 4 programme on the insurance industry referred to it as commonly held to be 'greedy, ruthless, bureaucratic' and as having claims procedures of 'Kafkaesque complexity'. In the same month the FSA imposed a fine of £675,000 on a leading insurer for poor handling of complaints about endowment mortgages and systemic weakness in complaints procedures. According to the ABI's General Insurance Claims Code,[94] however, policyholders could expect insurers to respond promptly, handle their claims fairly and promptly, and settle them promptly once they have agreed to pay. Policyholders did not appear to have got the message.

Whereas some claims departments are blamed for being too slow to reach a decision, others are blamed for taking a 'stance' on a claim too soon, more on instinct than information. Many investigators of claims believe that they did not need proof of fraud as they have a 'nose' for it. Do they? One reason for the

---

[92] Above, p. 197 ff.
[93] M. Clarke, 'Insurance Fraud' (1989) 29 *Brit J of Criminology* 1–20, 4.
[94] The Code has now been replaced; see Chapter 3, pp. 60–1.

importance attached to oral evidence in the courts of common law is the belief that the experienced observer can indeed tell from the demeanour of witnesses whether or not they are telling the truth. Studies in the 1990s suggested, however, that this assumption is questionable,[95] although more recent research gives experienced policemen a better than average rating in this respect.[96] Is there sufficient reason, however, to think that insurance investigators, even though many of them are former policemen, are better judges of human nature and honesty than the courts?

A negative and suspicious stance on the part of claims departments is in the interest of neither insurers or policyholders; not policyholders because they get paid late and perhaps less than their due, not insurers because it is doubtful that the suspicious insurer really saves money. By stopping leakage in one place insurers may spring a leak elsewhere. On the contrary, in other industries it is accepted that retaining a customer costs about one-tenth of the cost of getting a new one. The message has still to reach some insurers[97] that money saved in the claims department may well be lost in the marketing department seeking new customers to replace those that have left in disgust at the way their claims were handled. Other insurers, however, have had second thoughts and are seeking to put service before suspicion. Traditionally, this is the Japanese model: insurers who measure the success of the claims department by the amount of goodwill generated with the public, by courtesy and speed of settlement.[98]

The Meaning of Fraud

The duty of good faith between insurers and policyholders is sometimes specified as the foundation, although not the only foundation, of the rule that a fraudulent claim by a policyholder defeats the claim and terminates the underlying contract of insurance. This will surprise nobody; on the contrary, the point of claim is where people might expect the law to make the greatest demands of the honesty and good faith of policyholders. What is surprising, however, is that the same rule of good faith which demands so much of their memory when people apply for insurance,[99] demands so little of their scruples when they make a claim. Inflated claims and economy of truth are often overlooked.

If the claim includes a statement which the claimant knows to be false, that is (common law) fraud;[100] but if a false statement is made inadvertently or carelessly it is not.[101] Between these points there is the statement made recklessly, not caring

---

[95] W. A. Wagenaar *et al.*, *Anchored Narratives* (Hemel Hempstead, 1993), 188 ff.
[96] Research reported by Harvey, op. cit. above, n. 88.   [97] See *PM*, 30 October 2003.
[98] J. Itoh, 'The Challenge to the Future', *Geneva Papers on Risk and Insurance*, 72 (1994), 334–56.   [99] See Chapter 4, p. 95 ff.
[100] *Derry v Peek* (1889) 14 App Cas 337. In March 2007 a Fraud Bill was before Parliament. See C1.2(1).   [101] See *The Star Sea* [2003] 1 AC 469.

whether it is true or false: that too is fraudulent.[102] In a recent trust case,[103] the House of Lords rejected tests of fraud which were, on the one hand, entirely objective and, on the other, entirely subjective (the 'Robin Hood test'), and preferred what Lord Hutton called a 'combined test': that is, a standard 'which combines an objective test and a subjective test, and which requires that before there can be a finding of dishonesty it must be established that the defendant's conduct was dishonest by the ordinary standards of reasonable and honest people and that he himself realised that by those standards his conduct was dishonest'. Certainly insurance cases require that element of subjectivity, as can be seen in decisions which tolerate claims which can be charitably characterized as 'wishful thinking'; but some difficulty is encountered in the objective part of the standard for, as we have seen, many people do not regard deliberate exaggeration as dishonest. Moreover, in contrast to common law fraud, an insurance claim is not regarded by insurance law as fraudulent unless it is not only wilfully (subjectively) false but also false in a material respect.

Material Falsehood

The falsehood must be material. If, for example, a claimant presents false evidence to bolster a valid claim, that is dishonest but not material: he is not seeking to get from the insurer more than he is entitled to, and many, including the FOS, do not generally regard that as fraud.[104] But when we say 'more than he is entitled to', what exactly does that mean? Until recently, we would have probably said 'a bigger cheque from the insurer', and so, it appeared at the time, would the Court of Appeal.[105] But a later decision of the Court referred to a 'fraudulent device'[106] and, clearly, this is broader because it takes in not only a bigger cheque but also any falsehood designed to embellish a claim and thus get money sooner and with less argument than might otherwise have been the case. Indeed, if time is money, in effect the claimant is getting quicker money, and thus more money, than would otherwise have been the case. That was a heavily commercial case, and the view that fraud is fraud whether material or not is welcomed by many insurers. Thus the standard cover for ships, the Institute International Hull Clauses of 2002, spells this out to avoid all doubt. However, it remains to be seen whether the FOS will also take the broader line; to date it seems not.[107] Indeed, even if we agree that strictly speaking the broader line is logically correct, does it follow that the consequences[108] should be the same in all cases? In particular, does it mean

---

[102] *Lek v Mathews* (1927) 29 Ll LRep 141, 145 (HL).
[103] *Twinsectra Ltd v Yardley* [2002] 2 AC 164, at [27]. With one exception, the other members of the House concurred. [104] *Ombudsman News*, October 2002, p. 4.
[105] *The Mercandian Continent* [2001] 2 Lloyd's Rep 563, at [35].
[106] *The Aegeon* [2002] Lloyd's Rep IR 191, at [4], [30], and [45(c)].
[107] E.g., FOS, *Annual Review 2003*, p. 36. [108] See below, p. 206 ff.

that the claim fails? As Lord Mustill once observed of such a case, 'to enable an underwriter to escape liability when he has suffered no harm would be positively unjust and contrary to the spirit of mutual good faith'.[109] Moreover, as pointed out by an American court, that 'would encourage an insurer, after the loss, to continually attempt to question its policyholder in the hope of obtaining misstatements'.[110]

Wishful Thinking

Fraud requires a state of mind, but it is one which is hard to prove. Moreover, in view of the serious nature of an allegation of fraud, claimants are given the considerable benefit of quite small shreds of doubt. Wishful thinking may be foolish, but in law it is not fraudulent.

Accounts of accidents, for example, are notoriously unreliable, and no less so when they come from the persons most affected. Most people tend to believe that the cause of an event was what they would like to think it was, or was one consistent with some preconceived idea of what the cause ought to be or to be likely to be.[111] If an event is charged with emotion, this affects recall, not least that of claimant policyholders who have suffered injury or loss. Moreover, most people forget a great deal about events in the first few hours after they occur; this may well be marginal detail of little importance, but it may lead to manifestly inaccurate accounts later which may make the investigator suspicious—even though the substance of the story and of the claim may well be true.

Wishful thinking is no less widespread where money is concerned. So insurance law overlooks the over-valuation of cherished possessions in a contents claims. Over-valuation is scarcely discouraged by the practice, less prevalent today than in the past, whereby the insurer accepts the value put on stolen property such as jewellery by a retailer who was chosen by the claimant and may reasonably hope for replacement business. Once upon a time, claims exaggerated in amount were regarded as fraudulent, but by 1937 we find no less a pillar of rectitude than Goddard J, later to be the Lord Chief Justice, saying that 'mere' exaggeration 'is not conclusive evidence of fraud, for a man might honestly have an exaggerated idea of the value' of his goods.[112] Moreover, there are many cases in which there is real uncertainty about value and the claimant plucks a figure out of the air, such as that of the inflatable fairground rabbit![113] The claim may be fanciful, but it is not for that reason fraudulent.

---

[109] *Pan Atlantic Ins. Co. Ltd v Pine Top Ins. Co. Ltd* [1995] 1 AC 501, 549.

[110] *Longobardi v Chubb Ins. Co.*, 560 A 2d 68, 83 (NJ, 1989).

[111] See, e.g., R. Nisbett and L. Ross, *Human Inference: Strategies and Shortcomings of Social Judgment* (Englewood Cliffs, NJ, 1980), 205 ff.; and Wagenaar et al., op. cit. above, n. 95, 151–3.

[112] *London Assurance Co. v Clare* (1937) 57 LlL Rep 254.

[113] *Dawson v Monarch Ins. Co. Ltd* [1977] 1 NZLR 372.

Exaggeration

On the one hand, in some instances, such as claims for personal injury, where the real extent of the loss will not be clear for some time, it is in the interests of everybody that the initial estimate should be pessimistic and err on the high side so that adequate money can be reserved—subject, of course, to the recent possibility of provisional payment and periodic payments thereafter. On the other hand, a culture has developed in which a degree of calculated untruth and exaggeration is regarded not as wicked but as wise, a bargaining position from which to start discussion. Some insurers see in this support for their handling claims with suspicion. But if, indeed, calculated exaggeration is an aspect of the endemic evil of fraud, it is one which has been partly sown by the insurers themselves: many claimants feel that they have to inflate their claims because they will be beaten down by the insurer. An eminent commercial judge once referred to the 'commercial reality that people will often put forward a claim that is more than they believe that they will recover . . . because they expect to engage in some form of "horse trading" or other negotiation"' and concluded that it would not be 'right' to regard this alone as fraud.[114] In practice, a line has been drawn between knowingly claiming too much for things that have been lost or damaged, which is bargaining or 'mere' exaggeration, and knowingly claiming for things that have not been lost at all, which is fraud.

The first problem about this practice is that in some cases, such as the stamp collection with thousands of items, it may be a very difficult line to draw. The second is that, arguably, the line drawn in practice is different from that drawn by the law. Both law and practice agree that people who claim for the loss of things that they know have not been lost at all commit fraud. But if, as seems to be the law as well as the view taken by the FOS,[115] any claim made with intent to recover more than the claimant is entitled to is fraudulent, the exaggeration, which insurance practice does not regard as fraudulent, may be fraudulent in law. If claimants take a bargaining position by deliberately exaggerating the loss, hoping that they will not have to bargain at all, that to keep goodwill and cut costs the insurer will not dispute the claim, that, surely, is fraud. Even if they really do expect to have to bargain, it seems that it is still fraud. In the Court of Appeal, Staughton LJ recognized that 'some people put forward inflated claims for the purpose of negotiation, knowing that they will be cut down by an adjuster' but, he said, in an insurance claim he 'would not condone *falsehood of any kind*'.[116]

If, indeed, it is a 'commercial reality' that people do not see an exaggerated claim as fraudulent, it may be undesirable to enforce law that is so far out of line with the *mores* of the time. This is the kind of conclusion that commentators have

[114] Thomas J, as he then was, in *Nsubuga v Commercial Union Ass. Co. plc* [1998] 2 Lloyd's Rep 682, 686. [115] *Ombudsman News*, October 2002, p. 3.
[116] *Orakpo v Barclays Insurance Services* [1995] LRLR 443, 450 (emphasis added). For discussion of other judgments in the case, see Clarke, ch. 27-2B3.

drawn from the consequences of the prohibition of the sale of alcohol in the United States in the first part of the twentieth century and the use of marihuana in the twenty-first, as well as the reluctance of English juries in the age of the private motor car to convict reckless motorists of 'manslaughter' rather than a 'lesser' offence: in each case the law was out of line, did not work, and damaged the moral fabric of society. However, no unassailable empirical research in England shows that exaggerated insurance claims are of this kind. When convictions have been obtained, sentencing has been severe. Recent opinion polls suggest that most people would agree. The honest majority have begun to see a connection between increases in premiums and the rise in fraud.

Proof of Fraud

Fraud is hard to prove. The imputation and the consequences for claimants are serious. So, the burden of proof on the insurer, although not the burden 'beyond reasonable doubt' of the prosecutor of crime, is somewhere on a descending scale between that and the 'balance of probability' required in ordinary civil cases. The precise point on the scale varies from case to case. If the allegation of fraud is that the policyholder fired his own property, that is serious and the burden is close to that of the prosecutor in a criminal case on the same facts, involving a high degree of probability.[117] The more serious the allegation, the higher the degree of probability to be established.

Understandably, insurers are reluctant to take on this task and often seek another ground, perhaps a technical ground, for refusing to pay what they believe to be a fraudulent claim.[118]

The Effect of Fraud

The Effect on the Claim

To make a fraudulent claim is a breach of the duty of good faith on the part of the claimant. Clearly, the claim itself is not one the insurer has to pay. Moreover, if a single claim is honest in part and fraudulent in part, the entire claim fails, the honest with the dishonest.[119] As Lord Hobhouse once pointed out, the 'fraudulent insured must not be allowed to think: if the fraud is successful, then I will gain; if it is unsuccessful, I lose nothing'.[120] As a point of public policy against fraud, fraud in any part of the claim corrupts the rest of the claim. This

---

[117] *Hornal v Neuberger Products Ltd* [1957] 1 QB 247, 258 (CA).
[118] See below, pp. 215–16.   [119] *Galloway v GRE* [1999] Lloyd's Rep IR 209 (CA).
[120] *The Star Sea* [2003] 1 AC 469, at [61].

reflects the maxim applied in contract law in general: *fraus omnia corrumpit.* Less clear is the effect of the fraud on the rest of the cover and on the insurance contract as a whole.

The Effect on the Contract

If the duty of good faith is broken by non-disclosure at the time of contracting, that breach entitles the insurer to avoid the contract altogether.[121] If the duty is broken by a fraudulent claim, the consequence is the same for the future. There is force in the view,[122] however, that sometimes the consequence is out of all proportion to the breach. Moreover, if fraud is to be strictly defined and strictly censured, there may be a temptation for the claims inspector to scour large claims for small sins with which to end the contract, although, as we have seen, this kind of crusade is in the best interests of neither claimant nor insurer.[123]

In other kinds of contract, discharge does not occur unless the relevant event, breach, or impossibility is objectively serious and substantial.[124] However, an exception has always been made in general contract law for contracts which can only work properly if trust and confidence are maintained, such as contracts for personal services.[125] Insurance, surely, is not unlike these, and therefore the current rule of insurance law, that *any* fraud in making the claim goes to the root of the contract and entitles the insurer to be discharged, can be justified on that ground. Fraud puts a new but darker light on the moral hazard posed by the policyholder and entitles the insurer to reconsider his position. On the other hand, can insurers really put hand on heart in court, or elsewhere, and affirm that this is true of the policyholder who seeks to bolster a valid claim by fabricated evidence? The insurance relationship is also one of good faith at all stages of the insurance period to which the insurer is committed, unless and until the parties go to court; and it is hardly an act of good faith to cut the claimant loose without insurance before the end of the insurance period without good reason. In other matters, such as an insurer's contractual discretion to accept or reject evidence supporting a claim,[126] or a reinsurer's contractual discretion to approve a settlement,[127] courts have asserted a control on the exercise of that discretion by requiring that it be exercised in good faith.[128] Moreover, that is now the position of the insurer who wishes to avoid a contract of insurance on the ground of non-disclosure.[129] So too, it is submitted, good faith should be observed in the exercise of the discretion in cases of minor fraud.

---

[121] See Chapter 4, p. 116 ff.
[122] E.g., Staughton LJ in *Orakpo*, op. cit. above, n. 116, at 451.
[123] See *Longobardi*, op. cit. above, n. 110.
[124] *Hong Kong Fir Shipping Co. v Kawasaki Kisen Kaisha* [1962] 2 QB 26 (CA).
[125] *Malik v BCCI* [1998] AC 20.   [126] *Napier v UNUM Ltd* [1996] 2 Lloyd's Rep 550.
[127] *Gan Ins. Co. Ltd v Tai Ping Ins. Co. Ltd* [2001] Lloyd's Rep IR 667 (CA).
[128] Ibid., at [67].   [129] See Chapter 4, p. 117 ff.

The Effect of Rescission

Rescission is legal terminology generally associated with turning the clock back and avoiding the contract *ab initio*, notably in cases of misrepresentation and non-disclosure,[130] and for that reason it is more accurate to speak not of rescission of the contract but of its termination.[131] For the future, the effect of 'rescission' is to terminate the insurer's primary duty to pay the current claim, but any secondary duties, such as a duty to arbitrate or settle an earlier honest claim, remain. For the past, if honest claim A is followed by fraudulent claim B, the contract is terminated from the time of the 'rescission' but claim A remains enforceable; and the insurer cannot recover insurance money paid in respect of earlier loss,[132] but can recover payments on account of present loss made prior to the fraud.[132a]

The Case of Joint Insurance

A problem arises when the insurance has been contracted by more than one person, and one is in breach of the duty of good faith but the others are not. The fraudster cannot sustain a claim, but what of the others? In the case of composite cover, a fraudulent claim by one policyholder does not affect an honest claim by the others.[133] In the case of joint cover, however, the traditional view has been that their interests are inseparably connected, so that loss or gain necessarily affects them all, and that, therefore, the fraud of one contaminates the whole insurance and bars a claim by the others.[134] The partnership claim is polluted by the fraud of one partner. The wife's fire claim is defeated by the arson of her estranged husband, even though she was the intended victim of the fire and the defeat of her claim is victory of a kind for him.[135] As with the claim by one single person, which is part honest and part dishonest, the traditional view was formed from the high ground of policy and principle, leads to some hard cases, and has been abandoned by courts in the United States and in Canada.[136] There the rule has become that the success of a claim by the innocent joint policyholder depends on the construction of the contract. No English court would argue with that, but, free of the constraints of policy and principle, courts over there have found more freedom to do what is thought fair and reasonable in the particular case. One can but hope that the English court would now follow suit.

---

[130] See Chapter 4, p. 116 ff.

[131] *Kazakstan Wool Processors v NCM* [1999] Lloyd's Rep IR 596, 602, affirmed [2000] Lloyd's Rep IR 371 (CA).   [132] *The Star Sea*, op. cit. above, n. 120, at [50] and [66] ff.

[132a] *Axa Gen. Ltd Ins. v Gottlieb* [2005] Lloyd's Rep IR 369, (CA).

[133] *General Accident Fire & Life Assurance Corp. Ltd v Midland Bank Ltd* [1940] 2 KB 318, 417 (CA). On this distinction see also *State of Netherlands v Youell and Hayward* [1997] 2 Lloyd's Rep 440, 449.   [134] *Samuel & Co. Ltd v Dumas* [1924] AC 431, 445.

[135] *Hedtcke v Sentry Ins. Co.*, 326 NW 2d 727, 740 (Wis, 1982).

[136] E.g., *Scott v Wawanesa Mut. Ins. Co.* (1989) 59 DLR (4th) 600 (Sup. Ct of Can.).

Countering Fraud

Image Problems

The insurance industry agrees that the public image of each insurer is geared very largely to the public perception of how that insurer settles claims. The industry is divided, however, on the best approach to take to claims that smack of fraud. In the past, insurers have tended to believe that to allege fraud by one policyholder goes down badly with the rest, even the honest majority; and that, if one insurer took a tough line, brokers would steer clients to another insurer who would not. Indeed, in 1994, the claims manager of a leading company warned a conference of loss adjusters of the harm done to the industry by claims handlers who, as he put it, 'look for a spine to shiver down' every time they pick up a file.[137] Moreover, a Gallup poll commissioned by the ABI and published in 1994 indicated that nearly 90 per cent of the public realized that frauds on insurers were a fraud on the honest majority of policyholders. That conclusion is surprising today, as it seems that the public of 1994 was more aware than the public a decade later. Be that as it may, it encouraged some insurers to take a harder line on claims, but they did so at a time when an iconoclastic press had left behind the age of deference and was looking for any chance to champion the cause of consumers, and insurers became fair game. Their image suffered. One newspaper described insurers as 'twisters',[138] and another as 'crooks in bowler hats' who were 'in danger of taking over from the banks as the scourge of British society'.[139] Since then newspapers have sought and found other targets for the public wrath, and the evils of the insurance industry are chronicled more soberly in the consumer columns. Even so, the occasional story does great damage to the image of insurers. In July 2004, it was widely reported that insurance taken out, as required by a lender, to pay the claimant's mortgage while he was off work, refused to pay for the period the claimant spent in hospital so that he could donate a kidney to his son, because he had brought the 'calamity' upon himself. The image was not improved by the most popular film of Christmas 2004. One of the villains was the hero's boss—an insurance claims manager. Still less in April 2005, when a prominent television programme (*Tonight* with Trevor McDonald) devoted 30 minutes to 'dread loss' insurers and income protection insurers and accused them of seeking 'excuses to wriggle out of paying'.

Although nonetheless in some degree the heat of the press is off insurers, in other respects little has changed. Insurers concerned with their image face the same dilemma. They settle small claims with little investigation because of the cost and lest a newspaper sees a small victim worthy of large print. They resist mostly large claims, of which they are suspicious. They are more likely to pay

---

[137] *PM*, 5 May 1994, p. 6.   [138] *Today*, 28 March 1994.
[139] *Sunday Times*, 27 March 1994.

£500 for an elderly Fiesta than £5 million for a vintage Ferrari. Also unchanged is a general atmosphere of distrust. Claimants who believe that they are being manipulated or outdone are hostile claimants. If, as they see it, one claim is beaten down, they are resentful and more likely to exaggerate the next time. The Treaty of Versailles, which ended the First World War, was one of the causes of the Second World War. Rubbing noses in dust is no way to make peace, or to maintain in the future a relationship based on good faith. In the language of social psychology, when people find themselves in an inequitable relationship, they become distressed and, by one means or another, attempt to eliminate their distress by eliminating the inequity.[140] Be that as it may, it seems that in too many cases the distrust between insurers and policyholders was and still is mutual, and is impeding the equitable and efficient settlement of claims. If confirmation were needed, it was provided by a survey of consumer attitudes to personal finance conducted in 2004. The survey, which covered 13,000 people in six countries (China, France, Germany, India, UK, and USA), found a 'high level' of distrust of the insurance industry as a whole, in particular its response to claims, and, among the countries, the highest level of distrust was in the UK.[141] Studies by economists confirm the intuitive view that trust is earned over time by experience.[142] Sadly, it seems that the UK insurance industry still has a long way to go.

Better Information at the Underwriting Stage

Detection requires information. Among the measures to combat fraud, for some years there have been registers of stolen property. For example, a central European register of stolen yachts was set up by the Marine Intelligence Exchange (MIX), a mutual association of loss adjusters formed to disseminate information about marine theft. Another is MIAFTR, the Motor Insurance Anti-Fraud and Theft Register, a central UK record of stolen cars, as well as a register of plant stolen from building sites. Adjusters once found a virtual graveyard of stolen plant in Portugal guarded by a herd of fighting pigs. Loss registers, however, are but a catalogue of the horses that have bolted. More attention is now being paid to information at an earlier stage, in particular information about the 'stable'.

The key to underwriting profitability, whether it be private or commercial, is often the moral and other standards of the policyholder. Fearing that interrogation of the proposer puts people off and is no way to sell insurance, the tactic has been one of oblique or entirely discrete inquiry. For example, there is a database that allows insurers to determine an individual's financial status and personal lifestyle classification, the assumption being that there is an established connection between 'financial stress' and extravagant spending, on the one hand, and fraudulent or inflated claims on the other.

---

[140] R. Korobkin and C. Guthrie, 'Psychological Barriers to Litigation Settlement' 93 Mich L Rev 107–67, 143 (1994).   [141] *PM*, Global Report, 9 September 2004.
[142] Economic Focus, *The Economist*, 17 February 2001, p. 116, and references cited.

A further but related measure aimed both at the recovery of stolen property after the event, as well as moral hazard at inception, is this. Insurers offer discounted cover on valuable goods, such as fine arts and antiques, on condition that they are registered with photographs. For more mundane property, such as televisions, videorecorders, computers, fishing tackle, bicycles, and caravans, selected items can be tagged with a barcode and a postcode, and registered on a central database. Tracking devices are also used on motor vehicles, and this has proved so effective that the equipment and policing to carry out tracking now extends as far as Spain. The idea, of course, is not only that the record or tag aids recovery of property lost, but that the sort of person who is willing to take time and trouble to comply is a better risk. Nonetheless, a survey in 2003 reported that, to counter fraud, most insurers still adopted a reactive claims investigation strategy rather than proactive prevention at the underwriting stage, whereas many experts recommend both.[143]

Better Information at the Claims Stage

Interrogation at the claims stage was perceived in the past as no way to keep a customer, not least when former policemen were in the front line of investigation. Claims handlers are now being trained in 'cognitive interviewing' and 'conversation management techniques'. Rather than asking reams of questions, they are trained to ask the right questions, to be polite but probing, not by rote but by recognizing suspicious replies and responding accordingly. An underlying premise is that, within reason, honest policyholders do not mind answering questions, whereas fraudsters want a quick turnaround with as few questions as possible, and the trained interviewer can sense a negative response. An associated measure is voice-stress analysis (VSA), although insurers appear to be divided on its efficacy.

Insurers can call on information services. For example, insurers can check claims for storm damage by accessing a database that records weather data at specific locations across the country. Against exaggerated claims insurers can call on validation services, which value property accurately. This is aimed at exaggerated claims, but also reduces the cost of handling claims: it replaces the former practice of meeting a claim for consumer durables, for example, by ringing around the local shops and making guesses. One validation service has a database of over 50,000 items, such as (thousands of) models of television sets. For a fee, the insurer can access the database on-line and check the figure submitted by a claimant or, if the claimant is vague about the model or item lost, work out what it was. Then the same validation service can be used to replace the item from a network of chosen and reliable retailers. This works well for household cover, but less so for offices and factories, where commercial policyholders, have their own sources and are likely to need and to make replacements quickly lest business be unduly interrupted.

[143] J. Bernstein, *PM*, 25 March 2004, p. 23.

A measure of a different kind, a high-profile reaction *pour encourager les autres*, is to prosecute a fraudulent claimant. The Consumers' Association and the police have urged insurers not to absorb the cost of fraud and spread it, but to fight it; but insurers are slow to spend the time and money required.[144] Moreover, they are mindful of their own image with the public, and of the perception of people in the past that insurers are there to pay them and not to police them. So, many prefer to grit their teeth and pay; or if they do bare their teeth and refuse, it is usually on some ground other than fraud,[145] notwithstanding criticism from the FOS[146] and calls from some police forces, notably the regional fraud squad for London and the South-East, to tackle insurance fraud directly. Nonetheless, some insurers do prosecute. Eyebrows were raised in both surprise and approval in 2002, when an exaggerated claim was prosecuted and the outcome was that, having described the fraudster as 'industrious in his forgery of false documents', and in spite of evidence that he was of previous good character and good standing in the community, the court sent the fraudster to prison for three months. The sentence was upheld on appeal.[147]

An associated response, when an insurer is confident of its facts, is to 'name and shame' a fraudster in local newspapers. Proponents of this measure point to the success of the Government in a similar campaign against benefit fraud. It is too soon to say whether the same success has been achieved by insurers, not least because some insurers believe that exaggerated insurance claims do not arouse the same opprobrium in middle England[148] as benefit fraud.

Perhaps the best protection against fraud, not least because it does not need the cooperation of policyholders, is the Claims and Underwriting Exchange (CUE) of information on the household, motor, and personal injury sectors. This database was set up in 1994 by the ABI to check statements made in claims against what a claimant said in the proposal. The CUE also records the claims, so that past claims can be scanned for any patterns that arouse or justify suspicion. To the extent that the public is aware of the CUE, it has a deterrent effect on fraudulent claims. Initially, one of the newspapers attacking the industry complained about 'black lists of black sheep',[149] but since then newspapers appear to have lost interest, or seen the sense of the database. Coupled with the CUE is the advice of experts that insurers should share claims data, as serious fraudsters do not confine their attention to a single company; but at this suggestion many insurers have been coyly dragging their feet: of such data is composed the sandstone that they use to maintain a competitive edge. Nonetheless, a database of shared information aimed at effective fraud prevention, sponsored by the ABI, is expected to be up and

---

[144] It may be more practical in future. The Government is proposing a new offence of fraud, which could be committed either by a false representation or by non-disclosure. In each case the defendant's behaviour must have been dishonest and aimed at securing a gain, but, unlike current offences, it would not be required that the gain had actually been obtained: www.homeoffice.gov.uk/docs3/fraud_law_reform.pdf. The proposal is based on the Law Commission Report on Fraud, 2002 (Cm 556).   [145] See below, p. 215 ff.
[146] *Ombudsman News*, October 2002, p. 3.   [147] *R v Mahfooz* [2002] EWCA Crim 2194.
[148] See above, pp. 200–1.   [149] *Sunday Times*, 27 March 1994.

running before the end of 2005. A mundane but effective feature is that it will track changes, and thus discrepancies, in the addresses given by policyholders.

Surveillance and Human Rights

Such is the difficulty of proving fraud that some investigators have resorted to covert surveillance to obtain evidence. Many in the insurance industry expected that, when the Human Rights Act (HRA) 1998 came into force, covert surveillance would have to stop. Now it seems not necessarily so.

The European Court of Human Rights, in a case concerning persons at a public demonstration where offences might have been committed, has decided that covert photography of persons in public places does not infringe their human rights.[150] Further, on the one hand, even photography in a private place, such as a garden or a swimming pool, is not ruled out altogether. Its legitimacy is likely to depend on balancing the policy element (the likelihood of fraud and perhaps the amount) and the degree of intrusiveness.[151] On the other hand, in *Perry*[152] the European Court of Human Rights said that 'a person's private life may be concerned in measures effected outside his or her home or private property'. The case concerned a person who was arrested in connection with a series of armed robberies and released pending an identification parade. When he failed to attend that and subsequent identification parades, the police took video film of him covertly on police premises, which they used in a pictorial identification parade, at which he was identified as the robber. He was later convicted and imprisoned.

The Court said that the monitoring of the actions of an individual in a public place by the use of photographic equipment and the recording of the data, may give rise to 'an interference with the individual's private life' under Article 8 of the Human Rights Convention, particularly in the event of 'publication of the material in a manner or degree beyond that normally foreseeable'. Whereas the 'normal use of security cameras *per se* in the street or on premises, such as shopping centres or police stations where they serve a legitimate and foreseeable purpose, does not raise issues under Art. 8', here 'there is no indication that the applicant had any expectation that footage was being taken of him for use in a video identification procedure and, potentially, as evidence prejudicial to his defence at trial. This ploy went beyond the normal or expected use of this type of camera'.[153] The Court held that there had been a violation of Article 8.

The lack of any expectation might well be enough to distinguish cases of insurance fraud. In *Jean Jones v University of Warwick*,[154] film evidence showing that a claimant's disability had been exaggerated was obtained by entry to the claimant's home by deceit, conduct amounting to trespass. Potter LJ was quoted

---

[150] *Friedl v Austria*, judgment of 31 January 1995, Series A No. 305-B.
[151] See Grosz, Beatson, and Duffy (eds), *Human Rights* (London, 2000), paras C8-11 ff.
[152] *Perry v United Kingdom* (2004) 39 EHRR 3, at H4.   [153] Ibid., at H5 to H6.
[154] [2003] 1 WLR 954 (CA); cf. *Campbell v Mirror Group Newspapers Ltd* [2004] 2 AC 457.

by Lord Woolf[155] as saying that where such evidence 'undermines the case of the claimant to an extent that would substantially reduce the award of damages',[156] it would usually be admitted in the interests of justice. The argument that unless it was *necessary* for insurers to do what they did, the evidence obtained would be inadmissible, was rejected by Lord Woolf.[157] The FOS admits video evidence and views it with considerable caution. If it convincingly demonstrated 'serious inconsistencies' in the complainant's evidence of disability, the outcome will be affected, although it will not necessarily lead to failure of the complaint.[158]

Reinstatement

If, instead of paying cash in response to a claim, the insurer can insist on replacement or reinstatement of property, fraud is less of a temptation to the policyholder. For buildings, insurers have a right to insist on reinstatement under the Fires Prevention (Metropolis) Act of 1774 on mere suspicion, without proof, of arson; but, in practice, few insurers insist on reinstatement, and few policyholders are aware that they may. A right of this kind is now found as an express term of contents cover, however, and, it seems, insurers are enforcing it. For other property, insurers can insist on replacement only if the policy provides for this. By 2003, this was the pattern and practice in about 70 per cent of household claims. An exception concerns what is sold as 'high net worth insurance', what the market calls contents insurance for the very rich. These are customers to be accommodated and, to all appearances at least, trusted.

A related measure is to ensure that the repairer or supplier of property is chosen by the insurer rather than the policyholder. This can cut the cost to the insurer in two ways. First, if the things or services are required often enough, insurers can arrange a discount with the suppliers, thus 'paying', let us say, an insurance indemnity of £500 with something that only cost £400. An all-round benefit is that ordinary items can sometimes be delivered to the policyholder within 48 hours of the insurer receiving the claim. Secondly, as regards repairs, in the past insurers felt at the mercy of the conspiratorial wink by the claimant to the repairer. Evidently, insurer now choose repairers who, they believe, do not do this, and in the motor sector the 'insurance job' is now said to be a thing of the past. Further, some insurers monitor the repairers, or even run their own repair centres. Indeed, in some cases, a video camera in the garage of an approved repairer enables the insurer's own engineers to monitor the extent of damage and the progress, nature, and quality of repairs. If the work is not done properly, the insurer may be liable to the policyholder.[159]

---

[155] [2003] 1 WLR 954, at [24].   [156] *Rall v Hume* [2001] 3 All ER 248 (CA).
[157] *Jones*, op. cit. above, n. 154, at [25].   [158] *Ombudsman News* No. 24, January 2003, p. 5.
[159] See below, p. 228.

Technical Defences

Insurers convinced that a claim is suspect but unable to meet the difficult task of proving fraud, may block the claim on other more 'technical' grounds. Indeed this is notorious, so much so that in conservative Germany the common insurance market was once described as an open gate through which the German consumer would be pillaged by Celts and Angles with cut-price insurance—cheap, it was said, because under English law, insurers who do not want to pay do not have to pay.[160] This picture was heavily exaggerated, but even now cannot be lightly dismissed. Although it is contrary to the tradition, if not also the letter,[161] of English law that one party to a contract should have a large measure of discretion about whether to perform the contract or not, an English judge with considerable experience in the field once described English law as 'probably the most favourable to insurers of any in the world'.[162] The two most tried—and trying— of the technical defences available to the distrustful insurer are non-disclosure at the time of contract and late notice of loss.

Non-disclosure

Usually, non-disclosure is not discovered until a claim is made and, for example, the claim form is checked against the original proposal. Checking has been greatly facilitated by modern methods of storing and retrieving data. If the insurer decides to raise a defence of non-disclosure, it may be as a provisional tactic to test the good faith of the claim: a formal letter is sent, which refers to the non-disclosure and refuses payment. If no more is heard of the claim, that is that. If the claimant protests, some insurers see that protest as suspicious, a sign of guilt, and maintain refusal; but, in the past at least and probably still, others see it as a sign that the claim is genuine, reconsider, and negotiate.[163] In any event, it is clear that insurers used the defence to refuse payment when they suspected fraud but could not, or did not want to, prove it. Indeed, at one time the advice given to insurers by the Arson Prevention Bureau, in a booklet entitled *Fraudulent Arson*, was that where 'confirmatory evidence is not available or may not be available without incurring substantial expense always bear in mind other defences', such as non-disclosure and misrepresentation. This possibility is undoubtedly beneficial to insurers but not at all to the policyholder. It gives insurers what Lord Templeman once called,

---

[160] H. E. Gumbel, 'Neue Vertriebswege und das Beispiel des britischen Versicherungsmaklers' [1992] VersR 1293–1336, 1301.

[161] In an extreme case the contract would lack consideration or cease to be a contract at all: *Suisse Atlantique Société d'Armement SA v NV Rotterdamsche Kolen Centrale* [1967] 1 AC 361, 432.

[162] J. Mance, 'Insurance Brokers' Negligence' (1993) 82 BILA Jo 32–53, 40.

[163] I. Cadogan and R. Lewis, 'The Scope and Operation of the Insurance Practice Statements' (1992) 2 Ins. L & P 107–11, 109.

'*carte blanche* to the avoidance of insurance contracts on vague grounds of non-disclosure supported by vague evidence'.[164] The very possibility is damaging to the certainty and security of cover that honest policyholders are entitled to expect from their insurance. The FOS does not allow insurers to plead avoidance of the contract if it is clear that, had they known the full picture at the time, they would have contracted nonetheless, albeit on different terms such as higher premium.[165]

Late Notice

As we have seen,[166] one type of insurance 'condition' is that which confers no direct benefit on the insurer but is mainly designed to make the rest of the contract work. Prominent among these are 'procedural' conditions, such as that requiring notice of loss, usually notice to the insurer via his local agent. A term like this will be implied as a matter of common sense as well as common law, but, in any event, it is common for the contract to contain an express term about notice of loss. Such terms pose problems of construction.

Reasonable Notice

If the term requires something like 'immediate' notice or 'notice as soon as possible', these words are construed not literally but sensibly, in favour of the claimant, as meaning 'reasonable' notice. Whether notice is reasonable or not depends on striking a balance between the interests of the parties.

On one side, claimants may need time to discover that the loss has occurred at all, that there may be insurance cover, and, if so, what to do about it. In *Verelst*,[167] for example, the policyholder knew she had life cover, but she did not tell anyone else. When she died, she was not in a position to notify the insurer and neither was anyone else, so it was a year before her family discovered the policy and gave notice. In spite of the delay, the notice was held reasonable. On the other side, the insurers want notice as soon as possible. Their legitimate concerns are to test the claim before the evidence disappears, to mitigate the extent of loss, and, if the claim is very large, to make appropriate financial arrangements to effect payment in due course. Notice is reasonable or not according to the comparative weight of these considerations. In *Verelst*, the effect of late notice on the insurer was slight, but the effect of non-payment on the family would have been serious.

Seven Days' Notice

If the term requires notice within a specified period, for example seven days from the loss, the court's hands are tied: it cannot construe seven days as eight days or more. This can be hard when a policyholder is caught up in the trauma of the insured event and thinks more of survival or salvage than insurance—not least

---

[164] *Pan Atlantic Ins. Co. Ltd v Pine Top Ins. Co. Ltd* [1995] AC 501, 515.
[165] E.g., case 18/02 *Ombudsman News*, July 2002.   [166] Above, Chapter 5, p. 155 ff.
[167] *Verelst's Administratrix v Motor Union Ins. Co.* [1925] 2 KB 137. See Clarke, ch. 26-2E.

when the policy is somewhere in a drawer back home. Hard it was in *Evans*,[168] where disablement cover required notice of any disabling event within ten days. The policyholder was seriously ill in hospital throughout the notice period, but the court held nonetheless that notice later was too late. This was an early Canadian case, but English courts are unlikely to decide differently today, unless the policyholder is a consumer and a case can be made against such a term under the Unfair Terms in Consumer Contracts Regulations.[169] In other cases, it is still likely to be the English court's perception of its role to apply contracts as they are written; it is for the parties to write the contract, not the court.

Contrast Swiss law, for example, which provides that late notice has no adverse effect on the claim unless the claimant was at fault or the insurer can prove that the delay in notice was fraudulent, and only in the latter case of fraud does the claim fail altogether.[170] Thus Swiss law appears to be concerned with judging the conduct of the claimant rather than responding to the concerns of the insurer. In other countries a rule is found that is more flexible than the English rule and perhaps more balanced than the Swiss. In these countries the argument runs that terms like this should be construed in the light of their purpose; and that, therefore, late notice should not defeat the claim as long it causes the insurer no prejudice. The argument is supported by considerations of fairness and such a rule is found, for example, in Australia,[171] Belgium,[172] France,[173] and Germany.[174] In the United States, there appears to be no legislation on the point, but the courts have addressed it nonetheless and are divided; for late notice to defeat the claim, prejudice is required in California, for example, but not in New York.

Breach: Prejudice

In England the prejudice argument was rejected in the *Pioneer* case.[175] Bingham J was not bound by precedent, but he thought that a requirement of prejudice would not be in accord with 'general contractual principle'. Indeed, if, as in that case, notice in time is expressed to be a 'condition precedent', words well known to the law, traditionally the condition is likely to be applied strictly and prejudice is irrelevant.[176] Not necessarily so in the USA, where some courts have nonetheless asserted a 'modern view' that such a term, 'although denominated by the policy as a condition precedent, should be construed in accord with its purpose and with the reasonable expectations of the parties'.[177] As to its purpose:

... the function of a notice requirement is to protect the insurance company's interests from being prejudiced. Where the insurance company's interests have not been harmed by a late notice, the reason behind the notice condition in the policy does not apply, and it

---

[168] *Evans v Railway Passengers* (1912) 3 DLR 61.   [169] Chapter 7, pp. 273–4.
[170] VVG Art. 38.   [171] Insurance Contracts Act, s. 54.   [172] Act of 1992, s. 19 ff.
[173] Code d'assurance, Art. L113-2 al. 4.   [174] VVG Art. 6.
[175] *Pioneer Concrete (UK) Ltd v Nat. Employers Mut. Gen. Ins. Assn Ltd* [1985] 2 All ER 395.
[176] See Chapter 5, pp. 160–1.
[177] *Great American Ins. Co. v Tate Construction Co.*, 279 SE 2d 769, 771 (1981).

follows neither logic nor fairness to relieve the insurance company of its obligations under the policy in such a situation.[178]

Purposive rather than literal construction has some appeal even in England, but in commercial cases it is still likely that the label 'condition precedent' will be taken at face value and applied literally. As regards insurance contracted by a consumer and thus within the scope of the Unfair Terms in Consumer Contracts Regulations,[179] however, in *Bankers Ins. Co. Ltd v South*[180] the court underlined that a notification clause, although expressed to be a condition precedent, would be unfair if it operated as such notwithstanding that no prejudice had been caused to the insurer by its breach, and was thus *pro tanto* invalid.

If the notice term is not described as a condition precedent, its effect is a matter of construction[181] and there may well be ambiguity enough to give room for argument,[182] as follows. The more outrageous or absurd the effect of a literal construction of words, the harder the court will strive to find ambiguity—even when the only evidence of ambiguity is the absurdity itself—because the less reasonable the effect, the less likely it is that the parties intended it.[183] True, this kind of argument was rejected in *Pioneer*, but the decision is not a binding precedent and, anyway, the case was one in which there was some prejudice to the insurer; it is hard to believe that the argument will not be better received by a court today.

In practice, insurers usually relax the notice requirement. They are likely to insist on its terms only when they have reasons other than prejudice to refuse payment, such as suspicion of fraud, and such cases rarely get as far as a hearing in court. The practice is sensible no doubt, but, it being a matter of discretion, once again we find a needless source of uncertainty in the practice of insurance.

Conceptual coherence, and thus a measure of certainty, was brought back to the law by Colman J in *McAlpine*,[184] where he said that to resolve the question

involves some but not all of the considerations material to deciding whether a term of a contract is a condition any breach of which will amount to a repudiatory breach or an innominate term breach of which will only give rise to a right to treat the contract as terminated if the consequences of the breach are such as substantially to deprive the innocent party of the whole benefit of the contract.

This, of course, is the principle and language of the well-known *Hong Kong Fir* case[185] in general contract law. Subsequently, in *The Beursgracht*,[186] Tuckey LJ, who gave the judgment of the Court of Appeal, said[187] that the question was

---

[178] *Brakeman v Potomac Ins. Co.*, 371 A 2d 193, 197 (1977).   [179] SI 1999/2083.

[180] [2004] Lloyd's Rep IR 1, at [31].

[181] *Stoneham v Ocean Ry & General Accident Ins. Co.* (1887) 19 QBD 237, 239.

[182] See Clarke, ch. 26-2G.   [183] See Chapter 5, p. 139 ff.

[184] *Alfred McAlpine plc v Bai Ltd* [1998] 2 Lloyd's Rep 694, 699; aff'd [2000] 1 Lloyd's Rep 437 (CA).

[185] Op. cit. above, n. 124. See also *Friends Provident Life Ltd v Sirius Int. Ins.* [2005] 2 Lloyd's Rep 517, (CA).   [186] *Glencore Int AG v Ryan* [2002] 1 Lloyd's Rep 574 (CA).

[187] Ibid., at [44].

whether the breach (a notice called a declaration had been given late) 'was so serious in respect of the *Beursgracht* risk that [the underwriters of the risk] are entitled to avoid liability, not for the whole cover, but for that risk: see *Alfred McAlpine v BAI* . . .'. He then quoted with approval part of the judgment in the court below in *The Beursgracht*, which answered the question by asking two further questions:

As to the quality of the breach, can it be said that the delay was so long . . . that it would offend common sense to say that Underwriters might be bound? As to effect, can it be said that the lateness of the declaration was such as to be liable to cause real or serious prejudice to Underwriters?

Recoverable Loss

Under the rules about causation,[188] the insurance indemnity, the recoverable loss, is restricted to loss which is a more or less inevitable result of the peril covered. The indemnity differs from damages in that the insurer does not pay 'consequential' loss, that is, does not pay for types of loss suffered by the claimant which, although not inevitable, were consequences that the reasonable person would foresee (the tort rule) or contemplate (the contract rule). In *Theobald*,[189] for example, the claimant's accident insurance covered medical expenses but not his loss of earnings. If the railway had been sued, whether for negligence or breach of contract, its liability would have extended to both, but insurance indemnity does not normally extend to consequential loss of this kind. Consequential loss cover is available, but it is categorized and rated differently by insurers and costs more. As in tort, however, the object of insurance indemnity is to restore the fortunes of policyholders—to put them in the position in which they would have been if the loss had not occurred—with the following reservations.

The amount of the insurance indemnity, the recoverable loss, is a sum less than the actual loss suffered by policyholders not only in cases of consequential loss like *Theobald*, but also if:

(1) they cannot prove the amount of their loss; or

(2) their loss is greater in amount than the ceiling on recovery stated in the policy; or

(3) they have agreed, reluctantly perhaps, to be their 'own insurer' for part of the loss.

A commonplace example of (3) is the 'excess' in motor insurance. Both (2) and (3) remind us that it is mainly the contract of insurance that determines the loss assumed and distributed by the insurer, and that the contract is likely to indicate a sum less than policyholders' actual loss. What a contract of indemnity cannot

---

[188] Above, p. 184 ff.   [189] *Theobald v Railway Passengers Assurance* (1854) 10 Ex 45.

do, however, is to promise policyholders more than their actual loss: there is a substratum of public policy that policyholders should not recover a sum manifestly greater than their actual loss.[190]

In some exceptional cases policyholders may get more, say in the case of the 'valued policy', where the nature of the subject-matter is such that it is difficult to put a value on it so the policy fixes an agreed value, which may turn out to be less or more than the actual value, although *ex hypothesi*, they may never find out which. The next question, evidently an important question, is how actual loss is assessed or measured.

Measure of Loss

The object of indemnity, like that of the law of tort, is to put policyholders in the position in which they would have been if the loss had not occurred. So, if a claimant policyholder has been deprived of property, for example a car has been stolen, the measure of the claimant's loss is the cost of replacing it. If the car is recovered soon but damaged, and if the claimant had been planning to sell it, the measure of loss is the difference between its market value before and after the damage. If the claimant was not planning to sell it but to use it, the measure of loss is the cost of making it usable—the cost of repair.[191] In all cases the measure is monetary and based on market values where sentiment has no place. The claimant for the much-loved, much-polished, and customized Cougar Continental has trouble understanding this, but even the FOS, which takes a more flexible view of vehicle value than the courts and which sometimes compensates for distress, does not compensate for loss of pride and joy in possessions.[192] When the cost of repair is high, it may be cheaper to abandon what remains of the car and for the insurer to pay the cost of purchasing a similar car. This is the rule of marine insurance law, the rule of 'constructive total loss'. It is not the rule for other branches of insurance.[193] However, a contract term to that effect may be inserted and, if it is, will be enforced. In any event, it is sometimes the sensible course to take.

In *Dominion Mosaics*,[194] the claimant's business premises were severely damaged by fire. The normal measure of indemnity would have been the cost of rebuilding, but if the claimant company had waited for that, it would have lost a lot of business; so, the company took the quicker course of purchasing alternative premises, and recovered the purchase cost. In that case the action was against the wrongdoer responsible for the fire, but the recovery would have been the same against its fire insurer. In *Dominion Mosaics*, as it turned out, the cost of the alternative purchase

---

[190] See Chapter 1, p. 26 ff.

[191] *Leppard v Excess Ins. Co. Ltd* [1979] 2 Lloyd's Rep 91 (CA); *Dodd Properties (Kent) Ltd v Canterbury CC* [1980] 1 All ER 928, 938 (CA).

[192] See *Ombudsman News* No. 22, November 2002, p. 15. Also below, p. 247.

[193] *Moore v Evans* [1918] AC 185, 193 ff. Cf. Marine Insurance Act 1906, s. 61 ff.

[194] *Dominion Mosaics & Tile Co. Ltd v Trafalgar Trucking Co. Ltd* [1990] 2 All ER 246 (CA).

was less than the cost of rebuilding. If, however, the cost of alternative premises had been greater than the cost of rebuilding, the award might well have been the same against a wrongdoer, but would it have been the same against the insurer?

One argument against recovery is that, when the cost of the alternative factory is higher than that of rebuilding the original factory, the insurer is paying more than it has to. The force of this argument depends on what has to be paid, which turns on the contract and on what exactly is insured. If it is the loss to the policyholder, then the policyholder may well reply that the indemnity is the sum that puts him or her in as near as can be the same position as if the loss had not occurred; and that this is the sum that restores the policyholder as soon after the damage as possible, even if that is more costly for the insurer. Speed has its price. If, however, as is more likely, what is insured is not the loss to the policyholder but the property loss, the insurer's argument surely has force, that the measure of loss insured is the cost of repairing the actual property in due course (later) and not that of buying a similar but different property (sooner).

A further argument against recovery is that, if the insurer paid the (higher) cost of the alternative factory, in *effect*, fire cover would have been extended to business interruption cover which, *ex hypothesi*, was not the risk insured. The logic of a contention like this is equally sound, although perhaps less palatable, in the mouth of a medical insurer who declines to pay for costly medical treatment which would shorten the time that the policyholder was unable to work. There is no reason why property insurance should not have the effect of preventing loss of business, as long as it is incidental. This is the incidental effect of many kinds of insurance indemnity, about which there is no dispute, such as the payment for the stolen van which also prevents (further) loss to the van owner's business. However, the vehicle should be repaired or replaced in due course, not any sooner because the policyholder is anxious to get (business) back to normal.

Cutting Losses: Policyholders

Duties

Insurers sometimes require policyholders to take steps to prevent loss as a condition of cover: 'We shall insure your house, but first you must mend the hole in the roof.' Insurers sometimes speak of policyholders as having a legal duty to act as prudent uninsured, but they have no obligation to take care to prevent or avoid insured loss unless the contract says so in clear terms (and if they do, with the occasional exception of the insurers of large fleets of motor vehicles, insurers will not help with the cost of these measures). On the contrary, as a matter of contract interpretation, there is a strong presumption that insurance is intended to cover policyholder negligence.[195]

[195] See Chapter 5, p. 166 ff.

Once the storm is about to break the position is no different. To rule that policyholder negligence in leaving windows open when going out is covered, but not policyholder negligence in failing to close them when the storm has begun, is to draw a difficult line. Indeed, given the purpose of insurance, it is difficult to see a justification for drawing the line at all. There can be 'no logical difference between preventing damage in the first place (pre-event) and preventing further damage (post-event)'.[196]

Once loss is no longer just imminent but has actually occurred, however, policyholders are said to have a duty to mitigate—not a high level of duty, but nonetheless a duty to respond in a way that implies some degree of care. Nero may fiddle while Rome burns, but once the fire has reached his palace he must down his fiddle and put his hand to the pumps. The duty is not a rule of insurance law as such but 'the corollary of the principle that losses which are reasonably avoidable are not recoverable in the law of contract, and is thus expressed as "the duty to mitigate"'.[197] Moreover, breach of the 'duty' is not actionable in damages but breaks the chain of causation between the liability of the other party (contract breaker or insurer) and the loss suffered by the party who has failed to mitigate.[198] The duty is not onerous. 'Where the sufferer from a breach of contract finds himself in consequence of that breach placed in a position of embarrassment the measures which he may be driven to adopt in order to extricate himself ought not to be weighed in nice scales' at the instance of others blessed with the wisdom of hindsight.[199] The received position, therefore, is that policyholders have a duty to mitigate loss, albeit a duty that is not unduly demanding; but is it really a duty that should be required of them in all cases or even at all?

Assumption of Responsibility and Risk

Mitigation today is still seen by some as an aspect of causation,[200] but now the trend is rather to ask whether the defendant was 'assuming responsibility for the risk of the type of loss in question'.[201] This approach reflects cases in the 1990s on the contract/tort borderline, concerning duties of advice, and a trend there to align contract and tort on questions of causation.[202] When insurance contracts

---

[196] *Yorkshire Water Services Ltd v Sun Alliance & London Ins. plc* [1997] 2 Lloyd's Rep 21, 24 (CA); see also *Quinta Communications v Warrington* [1999] 2 All ER (Com) 123, at [132] (CA).

[197] These words of the judge in the court below were quoted with approval in *Yorkshire Water*, op. cit. above, n. 196, at [32]. The law of marine insurance is the same: *State of Netherlands v Youell* [1998] 1 Lloyd's Rep 236, 245 (CA).   [198] *The Soholt* [1983] 1 Lloyd's Rep 605, 608 (CA).

[199] *Banco de Portugal v Waterlow* [1932] AC 452, 506. See also *The 'Superhulls Cover' case* [1990] 2 Lloyd's Rep 431, 461.

[200] E.g., *Cheshire, Fifoot & Furmston's Law of Contract*, 14th edn (London, 2001) at 684. See, e.g., *Monarch SS Co. v Karlhmans Oljefabriker* [1949] AC 196, 227–8.

[201] *Chitty on Contracts*, 28th edn (London, 1999) 27-050. See also Cartwright [1996] CLJ 488, at 492.

[202] E.g., *South Australia Asset Management Corp. v York Montagu Ltd* [1996] 3 All ER 365, 372 (HL).

are approached like this, it is far from self-evident that insurers, having accepted the risk of policyholder negligence during the insurance period until an insured loss occurs, have not also 'assumed responsibility' for the moral hazard involved in mitigation. Moreover, there are many cases in which it is difficult to draw factual lines between the points at which damage is possible, imminent, or actual, and thus to mark the point at which the 'duty' to mitigate begins. These difficulties undermine the certainty that policyholders seek when buying insurance and insurers seek when rating risks, and suggest another reason for not trying to draw such lines in a particular case—or at all. So, the contention here is that, for insurance, there remains in each case the question whether the consequences of a policyholder's failure to mitigate is not part of the insured risk, the risk assumed by the insurer.

Cost in the Absence of a Duty to Mitigate

The cost of taking steps to protect property against the mere possibility of loss, however sensible on a medium- or long-term view of the risk and however bene-ficial to both insurer and policyholder, is not normally covered by insurance. When policyholders spend money to avert imminent loss, however, there is more than one possible basis for recovery.

An express term that the insurer covers the cost will be enforced. Moreover, if a person undertakes something in the reasonable expectation of payment—an agreed sum or a *quantum meruit*—English law fulfils that expectation. Thus, if a policyholder takes measures to avert loss with the consent of the insurer, there is authority that the insurer must bear the reasonable cost.[203] But what if there is no consent? What if the storm or the burst pipe occurs on a Saturday night when the insurance office is closed? On the one hand, Nero may well be fond of his palace and keen to save both palace and fiddle collection from the flood. He may well recall that part of the service offered by some insurers is emergency work, and may not see why insurers should be prepared to pay for that but not for the local plumber who comes more quickly and perhaps costs less. Both common sense and common interest, he might say, suggest he should 'do something', and that, provided that he does not do something patently silly, the insurer should cover the cost of his action. On the other hand, insurers want to control the degree of risk they assume and may well be wary of extravagant expense authorized by a distraught policyholder seeking to save cherished possessions. There is a conflict of expectations here and English law is less than clear.

Damage done by pouring water on property insured in order to prevent imminent[204] or further[205] fire damage is covered, but that is regarded as a special case. Moreover, it seems that the cover is limited to indemnity for the physical

---

[203] See the judgment of Bankes LJ in *Scottish Metropolitan Assurance Co. v Groom* (1924) 20 Ll L Rep 44 (CA). [204] *Symington v Union Ins. Sy of Canton* (1928) 34 Com Cas 23 (CA).
[205] *Stanley v Western Ins. Co.* (1868) LR 3 Exch 71, 74.

damage caused by the water and does not extend to expense, which, as a head of loss, is usually classified differently.[206] A fire policy covers damage to policyholders' property and not their pockets.[207]

Otherwise, if policyholders spend money to avert loss, the only possible basis for recovery lies in the doctrine of 'imminent peril'. In a leading case, the *Yorkshire Water* [208] case, the Court of Appeal held that the £4.5 million spent repairing an embankment to stop sewage sludge escaping into the adjacent river did not come within the cover of 'legal liability for damages in respect of accidental loss or damage to material property'. But that sum was spent 'to prevent or reduce the *possibility*'[209] of claims: neither liability (the peril insured) nor even flooding was imminent. On that ground the case was distinguished in New Zealand in *Bridgeman*,[210] in which the court awarded the cost of preventing a landslide by reference to the doctrine of 'imminent peril' in *Pyman*.[211] In *Pyman*, a decision not cited in *Yorkshire Water*, indemnity was promised not by insurers but by the charterers of a ship for damage caused by war risks. From this the Court of Appeal inferred a promise to pay the cost of averting such risks—*in casu*, the cost of having the vessel towed away from a minefield, because, said Scrutton LJ, it is 'a commonplace in mercantile law that sums paid to avert a peril may be recovered as upon a loss by that peril',[212] provided that the peril was imminent.

Cost in Performance of a Duty to Mitigate

In some countries there are rules of law obliging policyholders to take preventive action and obliging insurers to pay the cost. For example, German law imposes a duty to mitigate loss and also stipulates that expenses, which the insured was justified in regarding as 'necessary under the circumstances', shall be paid by the insurer.[213] A similar rule is found in Switzerland.[214] These are statutory rules, but in at least one common law country the trend of case law is the same. In the United States, expenses 'necessarily incurred in the course of mitigating damages are recoverable by a policyholder'.[215]

In England, if the contract provides that the insured or insurer is obliged to pay the cost of minimizing loss, so be it.[216] As regards contracts in general, however,

---

[206] *Yorkshire Water Services Ltd v Sun Alliance & London Ins. plc* [1997] 2 Lloyd's Rep 21, 27 (CA).
[207] *City Tailors Ltd v Evans* (1921) 126 LT 439, 443.   [208] Above, n. 206.
[209] Ibid., at 23 (emphasis added).
[210] *Bridgeman v Allied Mutual* [2000] 1 NZLR 433 (liability). But cf. *King v Brandywine Reinsurance Co. (UK) Ltd* [2004] Lloyd's Rep IR 554, at [147].
[211] *Pyman Steamship Co. v Admiralty Commissioners* [1918] 1 KB 480, aff'd [1919] 1 KB 49 (CA).
[212] Ibid., at 55.   [213] VVG Arts 62 and 63.
[214] Loi fédérale sur le contrat d'assurance (LCA), Art. 70.
[215] *Curtis O. Griess & Sons v Farm Bureau Ins. Co.*, 528 NW 2d 329, 334 (Neb., 1995). See also *INA v US Gypsum Co.*, 870 F 2d 148, 154 (4 Cir, 1989); and *Downey v State Farm*, 266 F 3d 675, 683–684 (7 Cir, 2001).
[216] An unusual example is *Jan de Null (UK) v NV Royal Beluga* [2002] 1 Lloyd's Rep 583 (CA).

the mere fact that an obligation is imposed upon one party to a contract for the benefit of the other is not *in general* sufficient to support the implication of a term that the latter should bear the cost of performing the obligation.[217] A term of this kind can be implied only if it satisfies the 'business efficacy' test. This test is found in two senses.

Business efficacy, in a strict sense, means that implication of the term must be necessary to make the agreement work. It is not enough that that such a term would be desirable or reasonable.[218] That was the test of business efficacy applied in certain insurance cases.[219] Moreover, courts are generally reluctant to imply a term of any kind 'where the parties have entered into a carefully drafted written contract containing detailed terms agreed between them'.[220] That was also the position in the insurance cases, reinsurance contracts,[221] and liability contracts written carefully for a large company,[222] but must the same strict test be applied to standard contracts of adhesion?

The business efficacy test is also found in another sense which has not been squarely addressed in the insurance cases in the past. According to Lord Bridge, a clear distinction is drawn 'between the search for an implied term necessary to give business efficacy to a particular contract and the search, based on *wider considerations*, for a term which the law will imply as a necessary incident of a definable category of contractual relationship'.[223] In such cases, the court will 'look to see what would be reasonable in the general run of cases . . . and then say what the obligation shall be'.[224] Arguably, this was not only the basis of the implication of the insurer's obligation to pay the cost of mitigation in one of the marine insurance cases,[225] but it also allows such a term in insurance contracts at large when the policy is in standard from. That would bring the policyholders' duty to mitigate in line with the rule found in the general law of contract (and tort).[226] According to Chitty, the claimant 'may recover damages for loss or expense incurred by him in reasonably attempting to mitigate his loss following the defendant's breach, even when the mitigating steps were unsuccessful or in fact led to greater loss'.[227]

---

[217] *Netherlands Ins. Co. v Karl Ljungberg & Co. AB* [1986] 2 Lloyd's Rep 19, 23 (PC); *Baker v Black Sea and Baltic General Ins. Co. Ltd* [1996] LRLR 353, 363 (CA).

[218] *Liverpool City Council v Irwin* [1977] AC 239.

[219] *Yorkshire Water Services Ltd v Sun Alliance & London Ins plc*, op. cit. above, n. 196, 30 (CA).

[220] *Shell UK Ltd v Lostock Garages Ltd* [1976] 1 WLR 1187, 1200 (CA).

[221] *Baker*, above, n. 217.   [222] *Yorkshire Water*, above, n. 196.

[223] *Scally v Southern Health and Social Services Board* [1992] 1 AC 294, 307. See also *Mahud v BCCI* [1998] AC 20, 45.

[224] *Shell*, op. cit. above, n. 220, 1200. See also *Liverpool City Council v Irwin*, op. cit. above, n. 218, 258.

[225] *Netherlands Ins. Co. v Karl Ljungberg & Co. AB*, op. cit. above, n. 217; see M. Clarke, 'Wisdom after the event: the duty to mitigate insured loss' [2003] LMCLQ 525–43, 541.

[226] P. MacDonald Eggers, 'Sue and labour and beyond: the assured's duty of mitigation' [1998] LMCLQ 228–45, 235.   [227] Op. cit. above, n. 201, 27-098, citing a number of decisions.

Cutting Losses: Insurers

If insurers pay too much insurance money, they can recover it. Mostly the rules of recovery are rules of the general law of obligations, the law of contract, and the law of restitution.[228] A better way of cutting losses is to get in first by reducing the extent of the loss once it has occurred, or preventing its occurrence altogether: by means of salvage, or by advising or educating policyholders, or by cost-efficient replacement of property lost or destroyed.

Salvage

Salvage activity by insurers and others has a long history. A Dutch ordinance of 1769 prohibited the populace from prowling on beaches at night or during storms, with axes, hammers, and saws.[229] The London Fire Brigade, formed in 1861 after the catastrophic Tooley Street warehouse fire, was partly financed by the fire offices. These offices also formed the London Salvage Corps to conserve property threatened by fire. More recently, when theft of cars in the United Kingdom reached epidemic levels, one measure to assist recovery and, incidentally, detection was the installation of a chip that enabled a stolen vehicle to be located rapidly. Another chip the size of a grain of rice is available for a range of property from bicycles to jewels. Such measures have been actively supported by insurers. Speaking of jewels, one of the services offered by insurers of 'high net worth' property is to transfer such items to secure locations after the policy-holder's residence is rendered insecure by, for example, fire.

   As a legal doctrine, the law of salvage applies only to marine insurance, but the non-marine insurers too may want to pick up any pieces and save what they can. Insurers have a right to the pieces as a matter of 'equity', whereas policyholders do not. On the contrary, the idea of indemnity is that policyholders get enough insurance money to buy or build something new to replace the old. This being so, they must give up what is left of the old lest, contrary to the basic principle of indemnity, they end up better off than if the loss had not occurred. In practice, an insurer may let the policyholder have the thing back, but the policyholder may have to pay for it.

   If what is left is a poisoned chalice that nobody wants, what then? Is the insurer obliged to take it? If a lorry is leaking toxic chemicals, whose responsibility has it become? In early cases some judges indicated that ownership of abandoned policyholder property vested automatically in the insurers. But the law, as restated in the MIA 1906, section 63(1), was that the insurer was 'entitled' to the property. One judge thought that section 63(1) meant that the property belonged to

---

[228] See Clarke, ch. 30-5.
[229] J. S. Ignarski, *The Underwriter's Bedside Book* (Colchester, 1987) 10.

nobody, but the balance of opinion now is that, if the insurer does not take the property, the property and the responsibility for it remain those of the policyholder.[230]

Advice to Mitigate Loss

Some insurers have anticipated the situation by pressing their policyholders to work out a plan for contingent action after the insured event, for example, a business continuity plan for the aftermath of a bomb or a fire. In other cases, there is little doubt that insurers give advice and assume some degree of responsibility after loss has occurred. Indeed, to distinguish their cover from cheap direct insurance, some insurers speak of 'assistance insurance', of providing 'immediate help to remedy the immediate problem, even to save life'. To the extent that an insurer has assumed responsibility for the situation, that insurer owes the policyholder a duty of care actionable, if not in contract, in tort.[231]

Disincentives and Discounts: The Insurer as Supplier

Generally insurers pay (insurance) money in order to indemnify their policyholders; but sometimes, as we have seen,[232] the insurer is entitled to have the thing repaired or rebuilt, or to see that the thing lost is replaced. One of the reasons for this is to deter policyholders who want to convert their video cameras into cash for something else by leaving the cameras behind in Tenerife. But this practice on the part of insurers also affects honest claimants—the majority—many of whom find it annoying. First, the belief is still widespread that claimants have a 'right' to cash. Secondly and more to the point, is the feature of a consumer society that many of the items claimed for are no longer manufactured at all or in quite the same form. Many claimants have a very particular idea—and often a more informed idea than their insurer—about what kind of replacement, if any, is equivalent and would best meet their needs. Such claimants resent being given no say in the matter—not least because, in the campaign against 'leakage', some insurers have arranged discounts with certain suppliers and, inevitably, this limits the range of replacements available to the insurer for this purpose. Moreover, the arrangement faces the claimant with a supplier who has an interest in insisting that chalk can be replaced by cheese, because the supplier happens to sell cheese. Worse, some insurers have used the threat of unwanted replacement to ensure a discounted cash settlement. The insurer's right to insist on a particular supplier or repairer is open to abuse, and therefore it has been prohibited in some states in the USA.[233] Not so in England, where insurers' gain in cutting costs in this way loses them goodwill.

---

[230] G. H. Jones (ed.), *Goff and Jones, The Law of Restitution*, 6th edn (London, 2002), ch. 3–039 ff.
[231] See Chapter 5, pp. 171–2.   [232] Above, p. 214.
[233] E.g., in the Mississippi Code Annotated, § 83-11-501.

Insurers may lose more than goodwill. If they insist on replacement or repair, whether from their 'own' supplier or not, they assume the role of supplier under the insurance contract and are liable for the quality of the goods or services provided. First, in the case of repair, they guarantee, collaterally and implicitly, that the chosen repairer is competent. Secondly, although it seems that insurers are not liable as one who 'agrees to carry out a service' under section 12 of the Supply of Goods and Services Act 1982, common law states that, when insurers decide that a policyholder's property should be repaired, the contract of insurance becomes a contract 'for reinstatement' and an insurer is obliged not just to appoint a competent contractor to do the work, but also to assume responsibility for the quality of the work itself. More than that, common law regards it as a contract to complete the work, however difficult or expensive it becomes,[234] within a reasonable time.[235] Further, by analogy, if insurers replace old goods with new, they assume the responsibility of a seller under the Sale of Goods Act 1979, and of a supplier under Part 1 of the Consumer Protection Act 1987.

If for any reason their claims against their insurer in the insurer's role as supplier are ineffective, do claimant policyholders have a contract enforceable against suppliers? Suppliers are chosen not by policyholders but by insurers. Some sort of guarantee may be offered, expressly or impliedly, by suppliers, but what (consideration) do they get in return from policyholders? The answer may lie in the fact that, if the practice is to work for the benefit of all concerned, including suppliers, it is one in which it takes not two but three to tango. The consideration lies in policyholders' cooperation in the process of replacement or restatement and the commercial triangle involved, without which suppliers will not get potentially lucrative business from insurers.[236]

Compromise and Settlement of Claims

When an insurer 'settles a claim', that usually refers to the process whereby the insurer considers and pays an insurance claim. Distinguish that from the settlement of a disputed insurance claim, whereby insurer and claimant, who cannot agree about what is payable under the contract of insurance, make a new contract of compromise to settle the amount payable. The distinction matters because, if the insurer later thinks that by mistake too much was paid out, the insurer will find it harder to get money back in the second case than in the first. Equally, if the claimant thinks later that the insurer paid too little, the claimant may well find it harder to get more in the second case of compromise than if the claimant

---

[234] *Brown v Royal Ins. Co.* (1859) 1 El & El 853.
[235] *Davidson v Guardian Royal Exchange Assurance* [1979] 1 Lloyd's Rep 406 (Sc Ct).
[236] See *Shanklin Pier Ltd v Detel Products Ltd* [1951] 2 KB 854.

had held out and refused the insurer's first offer. Settlements, which we refer to here in the second sense of the contractual compromise of claims, are subject to a principle of public policy, the principle of finality.[237]

The concerns of society to avoid litigation and strife, reflected in the principle of finality, are not always compatible with its concern to see that its citizens are fairly compensated.[238] To avoid strife, society encourages the settlement of disputes and is slow to set aside a settlement—as long as it is fair. Fair settlement is promoted by the rule of good-faith disclosure. The claimant must be open and frank about his or her loss. The insurer, at the very least, must explain the terms of the settlement proposed.

Generally, the interests of all concerned are in finality. The insurer, however, wanting to close the file and minimize the cost of handling the claim, may pay too much. The claimant, worn out by a process that took longer than expected, and perhaps being in urgent need of the insurance money, may accept too little.[239] In some few but ill-defined circumstances the settlement may be set aside. Three instances are discussed below: undue influence, abuse of bargaining power, and duress. If a case is made on any one of these grounds, the contract of compromise and settlement is set aside (avoided). Although few of the cases decided so far have concerned insurance, these circumstances have been much litigated recently in connection with other kinds of contract, and this has had an unsettling effect on the settlement of insurance claims.

Undue Influence

The Nature of Undue Influence

When contracting parties are induced to make a contract (of insurance or settlement) by a misrepresentation or under a mistake, they do so with a free and independent will, albeit on the basis of untrue facts or assumptions. When, however, one party makes a contract under duress or undue influence, they may have no such illusion about the relevant facts but in both cases their consent may have been vitiated nonetheless because they did not exercise a free and independent will. Duress and undue influence differ markedly, however, at their extremities, where duress is the power and influence of the big stick but undue influence is the more subtle power of personality.

The law distinguishes two person cases and three person cases. Influence may be exercised directly by A on B with whom A contracts; or it may be exercised indirectly (collaterally) by A on B, with the result that B contracts with C on terms that benefit A.

---

[237] See N. H. Andrews, 'Mistaken Settlements of Dispute Claims' [1989] LMCLQ 431–49.
[238] See P. Cane, *Responsibility in Law and Morality* (Oxford, 2002) para. 7.2.2 ff.
[239] Note, however, under the Courts Act 2004, the court may order periodic payments to a victim, the amount of which in certain circumstances is reviewable.

Direct Influence and Indirect Influence

Direct influence cases in the insurance context are best considered as being of two types, in order to respect the typology of general contract law.[240] The first type of direct influence arises, for example, in Case 1: an insurer handling a fire claim discovers discrepancies in the claimant's account and threatens to report the discovery to the police fraud squad unless the claim is settled on the (disadvantageous) terms proposed by the insurer.[241] The second type of direct influence would arise in Case 2: an aggressive claims handler, knowing that claimant B desperately need the insurance money, says in effect 'settle on our terms or sue'. No insurance case of this kind has been reported in England,[242] but they have been reported in Canada.[243]

Indirect influence would arise in Case 3: A presses dependant B to settle B's claim against insurer C on quick but disadvantageous terms, because A is bent on enjoying the large motor car that would have to be purchased with the insurance money for the benefit of B, but which would be driven by A.[244] Indirect influence would also arise in Case 4: solicitor A influences B to accept a (disadvantageous) offer from (defendant or insurer) C, because for A a rapid turnover of such claims is profitable.[245]

The influence in Cases 1 and 2 of direct influence is in the nature of a threat. For that reason cases of this kind are sometimes classified today as cases of economic duress[246] (see further below). For influence in Cases 3 and 4 of indirect influence, it suffices that in the particular case B 'reposed trust and confidence' in A.[247] Proof 'that the complainant placed trust and confidence in the other party in relation to the management of the complainant's financial affairs, coupled with a transaction which calls for explanation, will normally be sufficient'.[248] Moreover, the degree of influence required for the doctrine to operate is not great: A does not have to dominate B; and the law is content with proof of the existence of the influence and does not demand direct proof of its effect, which in the circumstances will be presumed.

In all four Cases the motives of A are, to say the least, questionable. However, A's motives do not count.[249] They may even have been wholly benevolent as

---

[240] To be found in *Barclays Bank v O'Brien* [1994] 1 AC 180 and *Royal Bank of Scotland v Etridge (No. 2)* [2002] 2 AC 733, at [13].

[241] The point in general contract law is found in *Williams v Bayley* (1866) LR 1 HL 200.

[242] The point in general contract law is found in *D & C Builders v Rees* [1966] 2 QB 617 (CA).

[243] E.g., *Pridmore v Culvert* (1975) 54 DLR (3d) 133 (BC).

[244] The leading cases of this kind in general contract law are *Barclays Bank v O'Brien* and *Royal Bank of Scotland v Etridge (No. 2)*, above, n. 240. A related case is that found in *Horry v Tate & Lyle* [1982] 2 Lloyd's Rep 416, in which a person settled a claim against his employer under the influence of a representative of his employers' liability insurer.

[245] Solicitors are presumed to have an influence on their clients in such matters: *Goldsworthy v Brickell* [1987] Ch 378, 404 (CA).   [246] *Atlas Express v Kafco* [1989] QB 833, 839.

[247] *O'Brien*, op. cit. above, n. 240, 189–90.

[248] *Etridge (No. 2)*, op. cit. above, n. 240, at [14].

[249] *Bank of Credit v Aboody* [1990] 1 QB 923, 969–70 (CA).

regards B, but if the result is unfair the agreement may be set aside.[250] In law what counts is the effect, a disadvantageous settlement: a transaction that 'cannot readily be accounted for by the ordinary motives of ordinary persons in that relationship, and all the circumstances of the case'.[251] An exception is made for direct influence Case 1. In practice the agreement is likely to be disadvantageous, but the law takes the view that A's conduct is so bad that B should not be bound anyway.[252]

Notice

In Cases 1 and 2 of direct influence, A, the person who exercises undue influence on B, usually does have at least some awareness of the influence; it is not entirely clear if awareness is a necessary element for the 'inequity', but in practice the point is unlikely to be an issue. In contrast, in cases of indirect influence, Cases 3 and 4, that may not be so. If B is to be granted relief it is essential that C had some kind of awareness of A's undue influence on B. Otherwise relief would be unfair on C: if C is to be affected by the undue influence of A on B, with whom C contracts, it must be possible to implicate C. C is implicated if C was sufficiently aware of the possibility of that influence and did not do enough to negate it. The 'true question is not how [B] regarded the transaction, but how it appeared to [C] and whether [C] should have taken further steps'.[253] In short, C must be on notice.

In the cases most commonly before the courts, of lenders of money to husbands, loans secured by wives, the possibility of influence is usually obvious. In practice, this is a point that distinguishes the insurance cases from the common (joint advance and surety case) cases: in Cases 3 and 4 the insurer may have no awareness of the existence, still less of the influence on B, of third party A.

Independent Advice

If insurer C is on notice of the possibility that, when agreeing the settlement with C, B was influenced by A, B will be entitled to relief unless it can be shown that, nonetheless, B contracted with 'the free exercise of an independent will'.[254] Although not the only way of showing this, the most common evidence of independent will is that B took independent legal advice: that B made the contract only 'after the nature and effect of the transaction had been fully explained to [B] by some independent and qualified person so completely as to satisfy the Court that [B] was acting independently of any influence from [A] and with the full appreciation of what he was doing'.[255]

---

[250] *Allcard v Skinner* (1887) 36 Ch D 145 (CA).
[251] *Etridge (No. 2)*, op. cit. above, n. 240, at [15].
[252] *CIBC v Pitt* [1994] 1 AC 200. 209.
[253] *Banco Exterior v Mann* [1995] 1 All ER 936, 944 (CA).
[254] *Inche Noriah v Shaik Allie Bin Omar* [1929] AC 127, 135 (PC).
[255] Ibid. See also *Etridge (No. 2)*, op. cit. above, n. 240, at [50]. *Crédit Lyonnais v Burch* [1997] 1 All ER 144, 156 (CA).

In practice the advice should be given to B by a solicitor 'at a face-to-face meeting, in the absence of [A]. . . The solicitor should obtain from [C] any information he needs. If [C] fails for any reason to provide information requested by the solicitor, the solicitor should decline to provide the confirmation sought' by C.[256] At the meeting the solicitor should first explain to B the purpose of the solicitor's involvement and that, should it ever become necessary, insurer C will rely upon that to counter any suggestion that B was unduly influenced, or that B did not properly understand the implications of the settlement. The solicitor must then obtain confirmation from B that B wishes the solicitor to act for B in the matter and to advise on the legal and practical implications of the proposed settlement.[257] On this and everything else, 'the solicitor's explanations should be couched in suitably non-technical language'.[258]

Effect in Law: Rescission

The effect of undue influence in law is that the contract in question can be set aside at the request of B. The nature of the relief is rescission; it is an equitable right and, as such, liable to be defeated by equitable defences.[259] Thus rescission for undue influence may be barred by affirmation,[260] impossibility of restitution (but it would have to be a significant impossibility),[261] the interposition of third party rights,[262] and, possibly, delay.

Abuse of Bargaining Power: Victimization

In 1974, Lord Denning advanced a general principle of unconscionability,[263] based on 'inequality of bargaining power', to sweep up undue influence and other related rules. A similar doctrine is to be found today in Australia,[264] as well as the USA,[265] but it was rejected in England in 1985 by the House of Lords in *Morgan*.[266] The *Morgan* view was that the Denning extension was undesirable because what justice requires is not interference by the court but that people who have negotiated at arm's length be held to their bargains unless, as English law already provides, their consent is vitiated by fraud, mistake, or duress; and that a general extension of these exceptions by reference to inequality of bargaining power would render the law uncertain: it would introduce what an American court called 'the serpent of uncertainty into the Eden of contract enforcement'.[267]

---

[256] *Etridge (No. 2)*, op. cit. above, n. 240, at [66]–[67].   [257] Ibid., at [64].
[258] Ibid., at [66].   [259] *Goldworthy v Brickell* [1987] Ch 378, 409 (CA).
[260] *Moxon v Payne* (1873) 8 Ch App 881, 885.
[261] *Cheese v Thomas* [1994] 1 All ER 35, 40 (CA).
[262] *O'Sullivan v Management Agency* [1985] QB 428, 459–60 (CA).
[263] *Lloyds Bank v Bundy* [1975] QB 326, 339 (CA).
[264] *Commercial Bank of Australia v Amadio* (1983) 151 CLR 447.
[265] The basis is in § 3-302 of the Uniform Commercial Code.
[266] *National Westminster Bank v Morgan* [1985] AC 686, 708. Cf. D. Capper, 'Undue Influence and Unconscionability: a Rationalisation' (1998) 114 LQR 479–504.
[267] *Klos v Polskie Line*, 133 F 2d 164, 168 (2 Cir, 1997).

However, this line against uncertainty is under some threat from a development as regards 'victims' of their own inexperience.

The 'victims' of their own inexperience are not new; they were to be found in an old line of cases which has been resurrected and newly recruited to the campaign against the use of unequal bargaining power. The typical case in times past was that of B, an expectant and vulnerable heir 'at the mercy' of the superior knowledge or judgement of A, with whom B made a contract (usually to borrow money for wild living). If A had taken advantage of the situation, equity saw that as fraud and intervened.[268] Then, more than a century later, Lord Brightman appeared to take up the cause. He spoke of 'contractual imbalance' and unfairness and, the statement that caught the attention of commentators, said this: 'Equity will relieve a party from a contract which he has been induced to make as a result of victimisation.'[269] This encouraged one writer to rebrand these cases as cases 'of an unconscientious use of bargaining power arising out of the necessitous circumstances of the weaker party'.[270] More recently still, in 2000, the Court of Appeal said that for such victimization to exist there must be more than inequality of bargaining power. The victim must be at a 'serious disadvantage', the transaction must be not just improvident but 'overreaching and oppressive', and the situation must have been 'exploited' by the other party in 'a morally reprehensible manner'.[271] The principle was accepted on this basis, but the facts of the case did not come up (or come down) to this standard.

Duress

The general law also allows agreements to be set aside if they are the result of economic duress by one party on the other. Duress, however, is more than just pressure. Many claimants may settle under the pressure of their need for the money, but the settlement will be set aside only if the pressure comes from the insurer, it is strong enough to suggest absence of true consent, and it is in some significant sense 'illegitimate'. What is 'illegitimate' is a matter of some debate.[272]

On the one hand, it would not be illegitimate for an insurer to indicate that, unless a policyholder stopped making absurd claims or otherwise being 'unreasonable', the insurance would not be renewed; or that, unless a claimant accepted the insurer's final offer, it would be withdrawn and the claimant would be left to remedies at law. On the other hand, it has been argued that the well-known case of *D & C Builders Ltd v Rees*[273] is really an instance of economic duress and authority for something like this: if insurers, aware of claimants' urgent need of money, 'beat them down' and offer relatively low amounts on a take it or leave it

---

[268] *Earl of Aylesford v Morris* (1873) 8 Ch App 484, 489.
[269] *Hart v O'Connor* [1985] AC 1000, 1017–18 (PC). See also *Boustany v Pigott* (1995) 69 P & CR 298, 303 (PC).   [270] H. Collins, *The Law of Contract*, 3rd edn, (London, 1997) 140.
[271] *Portman v Dusingh* [2000] 2 All ER (Comm) 221, 229.
[272] See Treitel, ch. 10.1.   [273] [1966] 2 QB 617 (CA). See also Chapter 5, p. 176 ff.

basis, a low settlement may later be set aside and the question of the amount payable reopened. Insurance decisions to this effect can be found in Canada[274] but not yet in England. In principle, however, the possibility is there. Cash in hand may well be better for some claimants than the jackpot in the bush, but insurers who point this out, especially to claimants lacking professional advice, must pick their words carefully. A related and more controversial contention on behalf of unrepresented claimants is that low settlements may be set aside if, whatever the insurer says, they have settled for too little because of their own ignorance, the case of significant information imbalance.

The Power of Information: Information Imbalance

In general, it is 'unconscionable', it has been argued many times, for one party consciously to take advantage of the other's ignorance or lack of advice to close a contract on terms unfair to the latter; and that terms are unfair if one party is 'sold short'.[275] Although not an argument with much appeal in an ethos of enterprise and bargain hunting, it deserves serious consideration within the confines of a contract of settlement between parties in a relationship of good faith. The argument in the context of insurance is that settlement contracts will be set aside unless the terms are fair or, at the very least, insurers do what is necessary in particular cases to save the claimants from their own ignorance; and that this may require insurers to see that claimants are sufficiently informed and, to some extent therefore, to help them with their claims.

The rule of general contract law for settlement of a disputed claim is that the claim must be bona fide or 'honest'. The focus of that rule has been on the openness and 'honesty' of claimants.[276] As regards insurance claims, however, the rule indicates that settlements may be bona fide and honest, even though agreed between parties without knowledge of all the facts. Indeed, there is force in the argument that one of the objects of settlement is to avoid the time and expense involved in pursuit of the full facts: the production and assessment of all the accounts, documents, and other evidence required to decide whether the claim would succeed in a court of law. 'Honesty' does not require disclosure of all information which, regardless of trouble and expense, might have been obtained. However, the rule of contract law assumes that *neither* party has the full facts, a mutual lack of information rather than a significant information imbalance. For court intervention on account of the latter, there must be some kind of 'dishonesty' or unconscionability, albeit not amounting to common law fraud, on the part of insurers.

---

[274] *Pridmore v Calvert* (1975) 54 DLR (3d) 133 (BC) and *JFB v MAB* (2001) 203 DLR (4th) 738 (CA Ont.).

[275] E.g., H. Beale, 'Inequality of Bargaining Power' (1986) 6 OJLS 123–36, 126. See also above; p. 233.

[276] D. Foskett, *The Law and Practice of Compromise,* 5th edn (London, 2002) ch. 5.

Insurance law requires good faith that continues until a policyholder's claim has been definitively rejected by the insurer concerned.[277] Insurance good faith takes the form of a requirement that parties must disclose to each other any information in their possession that the other may need to make a decision.[278] As long as the parties are in dispute but are still seeking a settlement, the duty continues and insurance law requires that disclosure. For their part, claimants must 'lay the cards on the table', the weak suit as well as the strong, knowingly conceal nothing about the claim, and disclose all. Moreover, the duties of good faith and of disclosure being mutual, for their part too, insurers must be frank and forthcoming about claims—frank and fair: it is worth repeating that the claims handlers who are too 'frank' about the weakness of a claimant's hand may find that a settlement is set aside on grounds of economic duress.[279] Be that as it may, insurance contract law is coloured here by the more general patina of good faith that is currently being developed in general contract law. In a banking case,[280] the leading case in England on the Unfair Terms in Consumer Contracts Regulations 1999,[281] Lord Bingham said that the requirement of good faith 'is one of fair and open dealing' and that fair dealing requires that a supplier of services, banker or insurer, 'should not, whether deliberately or unconsciously, take advantage of the consumer's necessity, indigence, lack of experience, unfamiliarity with the subject matter of the contract, weak bargaining position or any other factor listed' in the legislation concerned.[282] This, of course, is reminiscent of the common law background, including abuse of bargaining power and victimization, discussed above. Some of the implications for settlement of claims are as follows.

First, insurers are not obliged to undertake a factual investigation to ensure that claimants have not *under* stated the amount recoverable under the policy, but insurers are obliged to make appropriate suggestions if an understatement is obvious. Secondly, however, insurers can and do check a claim against the cover, and are required to point out any respects in which the merits of a claim have been understated. The American decision,[283] that a claimant who was unaware of a change in the law in her favour should have been informed by the insurer, may well be followed here: some English decisions point in the same direction.[284] Thirdly, the English court is also likely to adopt the spirit of the American decision,[285] that an insurer was obliged to advise a claimant about the existence of

---

[277] *The Star Sea* [2003] 1 AC 469. [278] See Chapter 4, pp. 113–14.
[279] See above, p. 234.
[280] *Director General of Fair Trading v First National Bank* [2002] 1 AC 481.
[281] SI 1999/2083, giving effect to EC Directive 93/13EEC.
[282] Op. cit. above, n. 280, at [17]. In truth this is a rather narrow view of good faith: see Chapter 7, p. 268.
[283] *Dercoli v Pennsylvania Nat. Mut. Ins. Co.*, 554 A 2d 906, 909 (Pa., 1989).
[284] *Scally v Southern Health and Social Services Board* [1992] 1 AC 294; but cf. *Reid v Rush* & *Tompkins Group plc* [1990] 1 WLR 212.
[285] *Davis v Blue Cross*, 158 Cal. Rptr 828, 835 (Cal., 1979).

arbitration for claims of that kind. The reasoning was that, in general, when policyholders submit or discuss claims with insurers, they rely on insurers for information about their rights under the policy. Arbitration is not a step favoured by
claimants in England, but the spirit of the case does suggest, at the very least, that
insurers may be required to ensure that claimants are aware of the possibility of a
complaint to the FOS.[286]

Enforcement of Claims in the Courts

If the insurer does not pay, the claimant can bring court proceedings to enforce the
contract.[287] Equally obviously, right-minded claimants do not want to do this unless
they have to. With the advent of contingency fees, a similar pause for thought may be
imposed on the claimant's solicitor, as solicitors' chances of payment will also depend
on the outcome of the case. At the same time, American experience of contingency
fees suggests that the insurer is more likely to test the nerve of the claimant and to
refuse a settlement until all have reached the door of the court. Something of a surge
in claims was seen in England initially, fuelled in part, ironically perhaps, by the
inventiveness of insurers who designed and offered 'after-the event' (ATE) insurance
to cover the costs of litigation in such cases. The trend slowed down when it emerged
that only part of the premium for the cover, which might be as high as £25,000, was
recoverable in the end, even by the successful litigant.[288] This gave both client and
solicitor pause for thought. Consumers representatives, however, while doubting the
value of claims management companies that push consumers and their claims forward, concluded that there had been a radical change in this part of the legal system
and that 'much of that change has been for the good'.[289]

As claimants now see the situation, they are likely to think twice or more before
going to any court, but some believe that they hesitate less than they did ten years
ago.[290] Litigation is stressful. It takes time and trouble and, whether or not it also
takes money directly, it always costs money in lost time. Whether or not it costs
money in the end, according to whether claimants win and recover costs or not, it
still costs time: more than required by the alternative methods of settling disputes
discussed in the following pages. Moreover, litigation is usually an unequal contest.
For example, unless the amount claimed brings the case within the jurisdiction of
the High Court in London, in theory at least, insurers can insist on being sued in
their local court, which may be far off from middle England in deepest Dorset.
Insurers have easy access to experts, one of the many advantages enjoyed by 'habit-
ual' litigators. Any settlement insurers offer is made from a position of strength.

---

[286] See below, p. 239 ff.   [287] See below, p. 244.
[288] See *Callery v Gray* [2002] 1 WLR 2000 (HL). Aspects of the matter have been before in the
courts many times since; see e.g. *Garrett v Halton BC* [2006] EWCA Civ 1017, [2007] 1 All ER 147;
and *Rogers v Merthy Tydfil CBC* [2006] EWCA Civ 1134, [2007] 1 All ER 354.
[289] *Which*, February 2004, p. 16.   [290] See Chapter 1, p. 7 ff.

In the reform of the rules of civil procedure instituted by Lord Woolf, which came into operation in April 1999, he sought *inter alia* to make litigation more focused, more cooperative, and more user-friendly. The changes helped not only potential claimants, but also insurers defending claims. If a reasonable pre-trial settlement offer is refused by a claimant, the claimant risks extra costs and enhanced interest payments.[291] Thus a pre-trial offer of this kind has been described as the 'weapon of choice' for claims handlers seeking to reduce the overall amount of claims settlement, not least against persistent and stubborn claimants. However, it does not appear that the cost of claims has been significantly reduced by the Woolf reforms. On the contrary, as regards employers' liability claims, in the immediate future an increase of 15 per cent has been predicted.[292] Whereas the Woolf reforms have met with qualified approval by some on the insurers' side of the court,[293] approval on the other side is harder to find.

Whether claimants are legally represented or not, uncertainty about the outcome of litigation provides the conditions in which delay and cost pressures push them towards settlement rather than trial. In one respect, of course, this is desirable. But uncertainty, delay, and cost pressures can also be consciously manufactured or exacerbated by the strategies of defendants, who are themselves relatively insulated from the effects of these pressures. Claimants are not in a good position to counter strategies of this kind. Except in extreme cases amounting to duress,[294] there is not much they can do about it, and any settlement agreement reached with an insurer is likely to be upheld by a court.

Claims Arbitration

Legal aid is not available for arbitration. If an insurance contract requires claimants to go to arbitration before going to court or any other place, a claimant, who may have been granted legal aid to go to court but who is disadvantaged by being unable to afford legal representation in the arbitration, must submit to arbitration first. If the claimant goes to court nonetheless, the insurer can have the proceedings stayed.[295] The court's discretion, however, allows it to refuse the stay if it would result in a 'denial of justice',[296] in particular, if the claimant's poverty is the consequence of the defendant's breach of contract. So, if the claim is that the fire insurer has not paid on the claimant's only business premises, the stay will be

---

[291] Civil Procedure Rules 1998, Part 36.10.

[292] *PM*, 23 September 2004, 'Strategic Focus', p. 4, with reference to the Government report 'Better Routes to Redress', published in May 2004.

[293] E.g., G. Reed, 'Review of the Civil Procedure Rules from the Perspective of a Defendant Personal Injury Lawyer' [2000] JIPL 13–18.   [294] See above, p. 233 ff.

[295] *Smith v Pearl Assurance Co. Ltd* [1939] 1 All ER 95 (CA).

[296] *Fakes v Taylor Woodrow Construction Ltd* [1973] QB 436 (CA).

refused. A stay might also be refused if the insurer were to make tactical use of the general rule in a way unfairly prejudicial to claimants. An example is that of the insurer who did not exercise his option for arbitration until the policyholder had incurred expense preparing an action in the courts. Although arbitration of insurance disputes was referred to with evident approval in the Statement of General Insurance Practice, in actual practice, arbitration is not a hazard to which claimants are often exposed, as most insurers take disputes through whatever in-house procedures are in place and then, if that is the wish of a claimant, to the FOS.[297]

According to the Ackner Report,[298] a report on complaints procedures at the time of the Insurance Ombudsman, who was the forebear of the FOS, ombudsmen procedures have the following advantages over arbitration. They are more accessible, cheaper, and quicker; one reason for this is that most, if not all, of the requisite information has been gathered during the prior attempt at conciliation. They are less formal, and thus, if any kind of hearing is needed, more 'user friendly'. The Insurance Ombudsman is not bound by the strict black letter of the law and can sidestep what the Ackner Report (paragraph 78) called well-recognized defects in insurance law. The Insurance Ombudsman produced annual reports which set standards for the industry. The Ombudsman is in a better position than an arbitrator to develop a relationship with the industry and with the media, as well as a consistent line on regular issues in his sphere of adjudication. To the claimant, some of these advantages make the Insurance Ombudsman a forum more attractive than the court.

Ombudsmen

Occasionally in the past, dissatisfied claimants have banded together, for example those with subsidence claims brought together through the columns of a newspaper, for mutual assistance and encouragement in the unequal struggle against the insurers concerned. Most claimants, however, are lone claimants and need help. Informal dispute resolution, also called by some people alternative dispute resolution, has been developed in a number of countries as far apart as Norway and Australia for insurance disputes. For disputes in the United Kingdom, the Insurance Ombudsman Bureau (IOB), with an Ombudsman and later a Deputy Ombudsman, who of course might have been women but in the event were not, was set up by the insurance industry. The IOB was to deal with most general business and, for much of its life, long-term investment products such as life insurance. Jurisdiction was limited to complaints by consumers and, something consumers found it hard to understand,[299] did not extend to claims against

[297] See below, p. 239 ff.
[298] Lord Ackner, *Report on a Unified Complaints Procedure* (Personal Investment Authority, London, 1993), para. 66.   [299] See Chapter 3, p. 58 ff.

brokers. A generic picture of ombudsmen emerged from the first UK Ombudsman Conference in 1991. The essential features were independence from those under investigation and a scheme that is 'effective, fair and publicly accountable'.

In the past some complainants, usually when they discovered that the IOB had rejected their claim and was funded not by the Government but by insurers, questioned the independence of the IOB. The budget of the Bureau was ultimately settled by a body appointed by insurers and, as the Ackner Report pointed out,[300] 'he who pays the piper almost invariably calls the tune'. In practice this was not true, but it did not look well to the outside world. To counter this perception the Ackner Report insisted,[301] *inter alia*, that the jurisdiction, the powers, and the method of appointment—and, we might add, the existence of the Ombudsman—should be matters of public knowledge; that those who appoint ombudsmen should be independent; that appointment should be for a sufficient period not to undermine the independence of the Ombudsman, and not be subject to premature termination other than by an independent body and, then, only for incapacity, or misconduct, or other good cause; that an Ombudsman should have power to decide whether a complaint is within his jurisdiction; that an Ombudsman should be required to report to an independent body; and that the organization should be sufficiently staffed and funded to enable effective and expeditious investigation and resolution of complaints. The IOB satisfied all these criteria.

The FOS, which is much larger than the IOB ever was, currently has 400 specialist staff called adjudicators who work under the general direction of ombudsmen, some of whom are women, who are answerable to a Chief Ombudsman. The FOS, which came fully into operation in 2001, is the successor of the successful IOB, and the person currently in post as Chief Ombudsman was formerly Ombudsman of the IOB. One important question that the Ackner Report does not address was who should appoint the appointers. This was one reason for the subsequent replacement of the IOB by the FOS, which was set up by the Government and was staffed by well-qualified persons appointed by the Government.

The Financial Ombudsman Service (FOS)

Perceptions from Within and Without

The role of the IOB was to act as counsellor or conciliator, to facilitate the satisfaction, settlement, or withdrawal of the complaint, and, failing that, to act as investigator and adjudicator in order to determine the complaint; and to do this in an independent, impartial, cost-effective, efficient, informal, and fair way. The FOS continues that role. The public perception of the IOB was less clear. The public picture was obscured by ignorance—many insurers which had undertaken to tell claimants about the IOB did not do so—and by a proliferation

---

[300] Op. cit. above, n. 298, para. 76.   [301] Ibid., para. 77.

of ombudsmen. A survey reported in the *Financial Times*[302] found that for someone with a complaint about an insurance policy or an investment product, there were no fewer than eleven 'ombudsmen', from whom the complainant could not simply choose but among whom the correct choice had to be made. In practice, the 'wrong' ombudsman referred a complainant to the 'right' one, but best practice, surely, would be for insurers to tell the complainant in the first place. One of the reasons for setting up the FOS was to open a single door for the settlement of all disputes in the financial sector, insurance disputes among them.

Nonetheless, public awareness of the IOB increased through the 1990s, and with it the number of complaints. However, although the overall increase in cases might be seen as an increase in dissatisfaction with insurers, it was probably more a reflection of increased public confidence in insurance and in the insurance industry.[303] The trend has continued with the FOS. Between 1 April 2005 and 31 March 2006, the number of enquiries received from consumers rose from 614, 148 in the previous year to 672, 973, and the number of complaints referred to FOS adjudicators, whose role is described below, from 110, 963 to 112, 923.[304] This suggests that the number of realistically framed complaints brought to the FOS had risen substantially in that period.

As in previous years among the new complaints referred for adjudication in the year ending 31 March 2006, by far the largest category concerned endowment policies linked to mortgages; much smaller in number were, in third place on the full list of complaints, endowment policies not linked to mortgages and whole life policies and, in fourth place, personal pension plans. Types of insurance not associated with investment were lower down the list, the most significant categories being motor insurance, buildings insurance, and travel insurance—as well as insurance of credit cards, a new and growing category in this group. Lowest in the order of those justifying specific mention were (in order) private medical insurance, legal expenses insurance, and personal accident insurance. This being so, it will be no surprise that in the entire financial sector the kind of business receiving the most complaints was life insurance.[305] In between the bottom and the top, mention must be made of critical illness insurance, evidently an increasingly troublesome category.[305a]

Today public awareness is clearly greater than in the past. Over 125,000 hits are now registered on the FOS website[306] each month. Clearly, many complainants hear about the FOS from newspapers and broadcasts. The FOS routinely asks complainants which newspaper they read and found that in the year ending 31 March 2006, a quarter of them read the *Daily Mail* or *Mail on Sunday* and another quarter the *Times* or *Telegraph*.[307] Under the IOB scheme insurers were obliged to mention the scheme in the insurance contract, and many did not.

---

[302] 17 June 1995.

[303] As the Ackner Report (para. 66(5)) pointed out, 'the better the service which is provided to the public, the more use is made of it'.

[304] FOS, *Annual Review and Report 1 April 2005 to 31 March 2006*, p. 15.   [305] Ibid., p. 32.

[305a] See p. 19 of the *Review*.   [306] www.financial-ombudsman.org.uk.

[307] FOS, op. cit. above, n. 304, p. 46.

What would have been better would have been an obligation to mention it to the claimant at the time that a claim is disputed. This is what they are now obliged to do by the FOS Rulebook.[308]

Jurisdiction

A complaint to the IOB had to be one against a member of the Bureau. Most insurers were members, but not intermediaries. The public often does not appreciate the difference between makers and retailers of insurance. This limit was reconsidered, and eventually it became a clear aim of the Financial Services Authority (FSA) to bring intermediaries within the scope of the FOS. From 14 January 2005, those advising on the sale of general insurance had to be authorized by the FSA, become an appointed representative of an authorized firm or, if already authorized, apply for a variation of permission. The FOS covers complaints against all general insurers based in the UK. Insurers based outside the UK but within the European Economic Area may voluntarily submit to the jurisdiction of the FOS, and some have done so. Consumer credit activities come within the remit of the FOS in 2007. It now covers most FSA-regulated firms, about 26,000 in all.

Another limit on the IOB was that complainants could complain only about their own insurer and not about someone else's. Thus the victim of tort could not complain about the wrongdoer's liability insurer, from whom payment was overdue; and employees, who had group health or life cover arranged by their employer, could not automatically complain about that, although the employer might well be persuaded to do so and to do so more effectively. This was a serious limit which does not restrain the FOS, because the category of 'eligible complainant' includes persons 'for whose benefit a contract of insurance was taken out or was intended to be taken out'.[309] Moreover, the FOS can take such complaints even though the employer that contracted the cover has a group annual turnover of over £1 million, that is, larger than the 'small' firm within the jurisdiction of the FOS.[310]

Even small firms were not within the jurisdiction of the IOB, which was limited to policies which the complainant had taken out as an individual in a private capacity. Even then, back in the early 1990s, other ombudsmen—such as the counterpart of the IOB in Denmark and Australia, and the Banking Ombudsman in England—could deal with small commercial claims, but this the general insurers in England, who funded the IOB, resisted. However, the FOS has taken a small but significant step into commerce. Those eligible to bring a complaint are now not only private individuals but also small businesses, that is, 'a business, which has a group annual turnover of less than £1 million at the time the complainant refers the complaint to the firm'.[311] It had already held, for example, that the professional indemnity insurer of a forestry consultant must observe the ABI's Statement of General Insurance Practice, even though strictly

---

[308] See above, Chapter 3, p. 63 ff.
[309] Ibid. See also *Ombudsman News* No. 32, October 2003.
[310] *Ombudsman News* No. 32, October 2003, p. 7.   [311] Ibid.

the latter applied only to non-commercial policies. The FOS took the view that a sole trader such as the complainant was effectively in the same position as a private policyholder.[312] The FOS takes this line when complainants in business are self-employed, lacking experience in financial matters, and without easy access to expert advice on insurance matters such as a broker.[313]

In many instances, the reluctance of insurers to pay comes from the conviction that the claim is fraudulent. If the evidence against the complainants was sufficient to raise an issue of fraud, the IOB exercised a discretion not to take the case further: the Bureau was not the appropriate forum in which to resolve questions of fraud. The FOS takes the same view. Moreover, the jurisdiction of the IOB was limited to complaints concerning 'a claim under the policy or the marketing or administration, but not the underwriting of the policy', notably the amount of premium charged. This limit does not apply to the FOS, however, it is a matter which the FOS may well decline to take up in a particular case.[314]

Claims Procedure

Complaints are out of time six years after the event complained of, or, if later, three years after complainants became aware or should have become aware that they had cause for complaint. A condition of reference to the FOS, as it was with the IOB, is the 'exhaustion of local remedies': complainants must first 'exhaust' the insurers' complaints procedure, not least to allow insurers to show that they process claims fairly and fully. The time rules are extended for complainants who can establish that they complained to the insurer concerned within the time limits. Meanwhile the FOS does offer advice on the telephone,[315] as well as by leaflet and on-line, on how to complain to insurers. Other schemes, such as those in Australia and Denmark, always had a default rule of some kind, limiting the time for which the matter could be held up in-house with the insurer, and after which the ombudsman could take the complaint up, which the IOB could not. Under the FSA Rulebook, however, insurers are required to send a written acknowledgement of a complaint within five business days of receiving it; a 'holding response' within four weeks, if unable to make a 'final response'; and, in any event, a 'final response' within eight weeks.[316] The last must refer the complainant to the FOS. In practice, once an insurer knows that the FOS is awaiting the outcome of a complaint, it is likely to keep the matter moving.

Once a complaint has come back to the FOS, the first stage is that an adjudicator seeks to achieve 'mediation', that is, settlement by agreement without detailed investigation of the facts of the complaint. If that does not work, the adjudicator

[312] *Ombudsman News* No. 31, September 2003, p. 4.
[313] *Ombudsman News* No. 39, August 2004, p. 11.
[314] *Ombudsman News* No. 32, October 2003, p. 7.
[315] In the period ending 31 March 2004 the FOS consumer helpline handled enquiries in 23 languages other than English.
[316] See http://www.fsa.gov.uk/pubs/nb-releases/rel35/rel35disp.pdf.

looks more closely at the facts and makes an 'adjudication', indicating how, in the adjudicator's view, the dispute should be resolved. At this stage most disputes are indeed resolved on that basis but, if not, the case is then reviewed by one of the ombudsmen, working closely with the adjudicator handling the case. The ombuds-man then reaches a final 'decision', which is binding on the insurer concerned but not on the complainant, who may still go to court but not to another ombudsman. In practice resort to the court is rare.

Most of the process is done in writing, without formality and without a hearing of any kind, thus saving costs, although, in certain circumstances, either side is entitled to demand one. Such cases tend to take nine months to clear. In the year ending 31 March 2006, the FOS resolved 119, 432 complaints (completed cases), to be compared with 90, 908 in the previous year. The unit cost of each case was £433, a slight drop on that for previous years. The FOS has published targets of resolving 45 per cent (47 per cent) of complaints within three months, 80 per cent (79 per cent) within six months, and 90 per cent (91 per cent) within nine months.[317] The FOS reports publicly on how well it has met these targets in its annual review, and the numbers in brackets are the latest published achieve-ment figures. This is impressive considering the difficulty posed by an unexpect-edly large increase in the period concerned in the number of relatively complicated complaints about mortgage endowment policies. An Independent Assessor handles complaints about the performance of the FOS.[318] In the year ending 31 March 2006, the Assessor received 322 complaints, and found reason to investigate further in 186, 0.125 per cent of the total caseload of the FOS.

Law and Market Practice: Justice Certain and Justice Seen

When adjudicating complaints, the IOB was mandated to have regard not only to the contract and to the law, but also to the codes of insurance practice and to 'gen-eral principles of good insurance, investment or marketing practice'. Strikingly, if in a particular kind of case these principles were considered to be inconsistent with rules of law and were more favourable to policyholders, the principles were to prevail. In the early days of the IOB good market practice was equated with actual practice. Over time, however, good market practice was interpreted as what good practice ought to be, whether it actually was or not. This allowed the IOB the flexi-bility required to sidestep sharp edges of the law, such as the law of non-disclosure. In terms of current contract theory, the IOB could pursue a less 'formalist' and more 'realist' approach to insurance contracts, one touched by 'consumer-welfarism'.[319] Hitherto there had been little sign of such an approach in the courts

---

[317] Ibid., p. 6.

[318] See FOS, op. cit. above, n. 304, p. 54. See further http://www.financial-ombudsman.org. uk/news/speech/fair-reasonable.htm.

[319] See, e.g., J. N. Adams and R. Brownsword, *Understanding Contract Law*, 4th edn (London, 2004) 36 ff.

and, although students of contract law could take the change in their stride, it came as something of a surprise to the insurance industry, with which it led to differences, as well as attracting unfavourable comment from Lord Ackner.[320]

One of Lord Ackner's objections was that to make awards on what practice ought to be was to allow the IOB to act 'as the embodiment of the conscience of the industry', involving 'a wholly subjective perception subject to no appellate process', and thus an outcome that was a 'hostage to fortune of uncertain and therefore unpredictable liability'. This, however, betrays the thinking of a person who had had a distinguished career in the Commercial Court, a court which the IOB did not purport to be. Although obliged to have regard to previous awards, the IOB was not bound by them in any sense that an English lawyer would see as precedent. But this did not make the IOB any more unpredictable than, for example, those tribunals of other countries that have no rules of binding precedent. The IOB published a selection of its decisions every year in its annual report, and twice published a digest of decisions in conjunction with the Chartered Institute of Insurers. The second, in 1999, updated the first and ran to nearly 400 pages. The task has been continued by the FOS with an almost monthly bulletin containing notes of awards in banking and insurance cases, interspersed with in-house analyses of trends. Thus, more consistency and predictability has been achieved than is possible among arbitrators, for example, who are entirely their own masters, whose mission may differ from case to case and who do not systematically collate and publish their awards. This is important because, as has been powerfully demonstrated in the United States, adjudication is more than the settlement of particular disputes. It is also a form of 'social ordering', which in some degree enters 'into the litigants' future relations and into the future relations of other parties who see themselves as possible litigants before the same tribunal'.[321] The FOS faces the challenge of any tribunal, to balance justice in the particular with certainty in general. In 2007, for example, it was criticized for inconsistency on the extent of insurers' responsibility for the conduct of tied and multi-tied agents. In the following pages we consider some hard rules of black letter insurance contract law which have been softened by the IOB and FOS without, it is submitted, sacrificing certainty.

Compensation for Late Payment

In the past insurers sought to sell their services as rescue services which 'take the drama out of the crisis'. One advertisement for professional indemnity cover showed the insurer in a rescue helicopter pulling the sinking professional from a sea of liability. This image of urgency and speed is justified in practice. Most of the primary cover at Lloyd's on the World Trade Center in New York, for example, responded within a few days of the events of September 2001, and thus much more quickly than most of the other insurances in place. Out in the High Street,

---

[320] Op. cit. above, n. 298, para. 93.
[321] L. L. Fuller, 'The Forms and Limits of Adjudication', 92 Harv L Rev 353–409, 357 (1978).

however, is a business culture of non-payment or, at least, slow payment. In 1994, a leading article in the *Financial Times* [322] concluded that business in the United Kingdom had one of the worst records in Europe for late payment. The position has not much improved since, and this culture seems to have rubbed off on some insurers. Some insurers, it should be said, whose insurance has been sold through a policyholder's bank, have been known to pay claims on household contents the same day they received the claim. That, however, is very much the exception. In the United States, if insurers drag their feet over payment without justification, that is said to be bad faith and insurers may be liable for large sums of 'punitive' damages.[323] Not so in the United Kingdom, where, with a few reservations, insurers can delay payment indefinitely and with impunity.

One reservation concerns contingency (non-indemnity) insurance. Actions against the insurers are regarded as actions for debt. Although the court has a discretion to award interest against debtors who pay late, potentially two kinds of loss are left uncompensated. First, the court has no power to award interest if the debtor pays late but before proceedings for recovery have been begun; and, secondly, interest as such does not compensate special damage over and beyond loss of the normal use of the money.

In general contract law, any special damage is compensated simply by resort to the rule of remoteness of damage and the second limb of *Hadley v Baxendale*:[324] the defaulting debtor is liable for any loss that should have been in his reasonable contemplation as resulting from late payment.[325] Thus, the debtor who knows that unless the debt is paid on time the creditor will suffer a loss of business is liable for that loss. It appears that this rule also applies to contingency (non-indemnity) insurance contracts. So the accident insurer who knows that the victim needs the money for a domestic lift will be liable for extra private nursing needed until the lift can be installed.

In the case of indemnity insurance, people might well expect a similar rule to apply. Owners of heavily mortgaged business property, who suffer a substantial fire loss, may be unable to meet mortgage payments, and may thus be in jeopardy of losing the property and going into liquidation. A major reason why firms buy fire insurance is to guard against such eventualities. Moreover, if a roof is damaged by fire and the insurer elects to have it repaired but the work is done badly, that insurer is liable for consequent rain damage to contents; so, if insurers elect to pay the money for repair instead, but pay late with the same result, because the firm cannot afford to have the roof repaired, the claimant may reasonably expect the insurer to be liable for the rain damage. That is the law in other common law jurisdictions, such as Australia and New Zealand[326] and California,[327] as well as some civil law countries such

---

[322] 28 March 1994. [323] See, e.g., Mayerson, 38 Tort & Ins LJ 861 (2003).
[324] (1854) 9 Ex 341. [325] *President of India v La Pintada Cis. Nav. SA* [1985] AC 104, 127.
[326] See Campbell (2004) 15 Ins L J 185.
[327] *Reichert v General Ins. Co.*, 428 P 2d 860, 864 (1967).

as France.[328] That is also the decision likely in England from the FOS—but not from the courts.[329]

The reasoning is curious. In other jurisdictions, including Scotland,[330] actions against indemnity insurers are actions for breach of contract subject to the usual rules of remoteness. In England, however, the insurer's obligation to pay insurance money is regarded not as a contract debt but as an obligation to pay damages.[331] Pearson J once pointed out that in the insurance context 'the word "damages" is used in a somewhat unusual sense', which could be explained, however, by old forms of pleading.[332] Fifty years later, this seems to have been forgotten and the word 'damages' has been taken at face value. Current orthodoxy is that as soon as the fire occurs the insurer is in breach of contract for failure to prevent the insured suffering loss,[333] although the duty actually to pay the policyholder may be postponed, both in reality and in law, until loss has been quantified.[334] Is this really the intention of the parties? Of English insurers aware of English law perhaps, but English policyholders?

If we assume that, unlike in apparently every other developed legal system, that is indeed party intention in England, the English rule begs a further question—a question less of law than of precedent. The question of law is whether there can be an action in damages for the non-payment of damages. In an insurance case the Court of Appeal has said not 'in the light of previous House of Lords decisions'.[335] What the Court had in mind, however, is a dictum of the redoubtable Lord Brandon that there is 'no such thing as a cause of action in damages for late payment of damages'.[336] The dictum was unsupported by citation. Moreover the context was very different, a decision that there could be no action for damages for non-payment of a liquidated damages clause. Given the purpose of such clauses to allocate the risk of loss in an arbitrary but fixed way, Lord Brandon's statement has little logical impact on the insurance indemnity question. So, the Court of Appeal reached what appears to be a plateau of certainty which is but the top of an inverted pyramid of precedent standing on a slim base: a dictum of Lord Brandon in a distinguishable case.

Meanwhile, first, the general law of obligations has moved on. If, as we have also been told more than once by Lord Diplock,[337] the obligation to pay damages is a secondary contractual duty, it is not immediately obvious why (at a tertiary

---

328 J. Kullmann, *Rev. Gén. Du Droit d'Assurance* 1998.662. But cf. Germany; Basedow and Fock, p. 400 ff.
329 *Sprung v Royal Ins. Co.* [1997] CLC 70 (CA); cf. *Grant v Co-operative Ins.* (1983) 134 NLJ 81.
330 *Scott Lithgow Ltd v Sec. of State for Defence* (1989) 45 BLR 1, 8 (HL).
331 *Sprung*, op. cit. above, n. 329, 80.
332 *Jabbour v The Custodian of Absentee Israeli Property* [1954] 1 WLR 139, 144.
333 *The Italia Express* [1992] 2 Lloyd's Rep 281, 286.
334 *Virk v Gan Life Holdings plc* [2000] Lloyd's Rep IR 159 (CA).
335 *Sprung*, op. cit. above, n. 329, 76.
336 *President of India v Lips Maritime Corp.* [1988] AC 395, 424.
337 E.g., *Photo Production Ltd v Securicor Transport Ltd* [1980] AC 827, 848.

level) damages should not be payable for breach of the secondary duty. Alternatively, if we approach the same question as Lord Goff might have done,[338] can we say that both parties, not least the policyholder, understood that the risk and responsibility for late payment was to be the burden of the policyholder rather than the insurer? Secondly, the ABI General Insurance Claims Code[339] required insurers to pay out within ten working days of the amount of indemnity being agreed between claimant and insurer. The FOS is likely to insist on this as regards complaints within its jurisdiction.[340]

Distress

In the general law of England, damages for distress are now recoverable for breach of a contractual undertaking, the object of which was to secure peace of mind or freedom from distress.[341] As we have seen,[342] peace of mind is one of the objects of most consumer and many commercial insurance contracts. Research shows that, for some people, losing property causes as much distress as losing a friend. The corollary in many cases must be that distress is a likely consequence if the insurer delays payment and, unless the delay is justifiable, the insurer should be liable in damages. Decisions to that effect can be found in other countries of common law.[343] No insurance decision of this kind has been reported from the courts in England, but the IOB won praise from the press for awards of that kind and the FOS has continued to follow that line.[344]

Insolvency

Between 1844 and 1883, no fewer than 519 new insurance companies were formed, but 471 failed or were wound up, and this became a matter of concern to government. Laissez-faire ended first for life companies. The idea of floating a company to receive large sums now (premium) against the mere possibility of payment on policies at some time in the future was most attractive, sometimes to the wrong people. So, intervention began in the first half of the nineteenth century and became marked with the Life Assurance Companies Act 1870, which required life companies to submit accounts, actuarial valuations of their businesses, and a substantial deposit. Society has an interest in the solvency of its insurers.

[338] See *The Pegase* [1981] 1 Lloyd's Rep 175, 183.
[339] See above, Chapter 3, pp. 60–1.
[340] As to which, see above, p. 241 ff.
[341] *Johnson v Gore Wood & Co. (No. 1)* [2002] 2 AC 1, 37.
[342] Chapter 1, p. 3 ff.
[343] Australia, Canada, New Zealand, and the USA; see Clarke, ch. 30-9C.
[344] E.g., case 13/06 and case 13/08, *Ombudsman News*, January 2002; and, in particular, the statement of the FOS view in *Ombudsman News*, February 2002, p. 8 ff.

Society has an interest because of the importance of insurance, and because of the size of the insurance industry's investment in other industries: the importance of the insurance industry in connection with pensions, for example, is all too apparent. It was once described by a critic of the industry 'as the guardian of the country's nest-egg'.[345] The business of insurance, however, to which society is increasingly committed, has become increasingly difficult. The number and cost of natural catastrophes—usually defined by insurers as those costing over $5 million—has been rising. Insured losses caused by Hurricane Charley in Florida in August 2004, according to the United States' Insurance Information Institute, are likely to exceed $7 billion.[346] Moreover, whereas four hurricanes in the USA and the two typhoons in Japan cost the London insurers £20 billion, it was announced in February 2005 that the cost of the Boxing Day tsunami would be no more than £100 million.[347] However, the latter reflects more the poverty of the victims than the benevolence of the climate. 2006 was a relatively 'good' year for hurricanes but there is little reason to expect such good behaviour in future years. Moreover man, too, has got 'better' at causing damage. The cost of events at the World Trade Center in September 2001 is enormous and even now yet to be fully quantified.[348] Resulting litigation rumbles on.

Watchdogs that Bark too Late?

Insurers must be licensed to commence business. After that, the Secretary of State has wide powers of intervention under sections 38 to 52 of the Insurance Companies Act 1982. A more rigorous assessment of insurers has been demanded of intermediaries seeking cover for clients,[349] but, if assessments raise doubts about an insurer, can intermediaries really be expected to raise the alarm rather than lower their sights and look elsewhere? And, anyway, how reliable or useful is the information on which assessments are based?

Under the legislation, the financial health of insurance companies is measured by their solvency margin, the detailed regulation of which is the responsibility mainly of the FSA. The FSA states its role to be, *inter alia*, to secure the right degree of protection for consumers by vetting firms, including insurers, at entry in order to allow only those firms and individuals satisfying the necessary criteria to engage in regulated activity. The criteria include financial soundness.[350] Once firms are authorized, the FSA monitors how far firms meet the particular standards set by the FSA, among them standards aiming to ensure solvency. To do this the FSA is currently 'revisiting prudential supervision', for example, by participation in the amendment of the EC directives governing the capital

---

[345] *Sunday Times*, 13 March 1994.   [346] *The Economist*, 21 August 2004, p. 70.
[347] *Financial Times*, 3 February 2005.   [348] See Chapter 2, p. 50 ff.
[349] See Chapter 3, p. 71 ff.   [350] http://www.fsa.gov.uk/what.

framework for banks, investment and insurance firms, and 'by creating a consistent and coherent European regime for financial conglomerates'.

In the past this work was the responsibility of a different sector of government in the Department of Trade and Industry (DTI). It sought to ensure that the volume of business underwritten was not excessive in relation to the insurer's capital base. The assumption was that there is a close relation between premium income and the degree of risk to which the insurer is exposed, an assumption that dates from the days of tariffs and standard rates. In recent years, of course, rates have not been standard. Insurers compete on price. When they try to push into new areas of underwriting they often undercut rivals, with the result that the risk profile of one insurer is quite different from that of another insurer, although their premium income may be the same. It is true that each company must submit accounts. But accounts do no more than present a picture of a company—a picture of a time that is past and a picture painted by the company managers and auditors, some of whom may be more inclined to the school of Monet than Canaletto. By the time the alarm has been raised, the company may have collapsed. Consistency and coherence of regulation in what is becoming a European marketplace evidently makes sense, but is there any reason to think that the FSA will be significantly more effective than the DTI?

The Financial Services Compensation Scheme

If insurers are insolvent, protection in respect of UK policies was offered in the past under the Policyholders Protection Act 1975 (as amended in 1997). With effect from 30 November 2001, the scheme under the Act was replaced by the Financial Services Compensation Scheme established under Part XV of the FSMA 2000. It applies where certain insurers are 'unable, or are likely to be unable to satisfy claims against them'.[351] As well as marine, aviation, and reinsurance, credit insurance is also excluded altogether. Also excluded are policies taken out at Lloyd's, for which a separate compensation scheme applies. The Scheme is focused on small policyholders—private individuals and small businesses, that is, partnerships with net assets of less than £1 million and companies with a called-up capital of £1 million. Moreover, it is clearly confined (unlike the previous arrangement) to risks located within the UK (including the Channel Islands and Isle of Man) and the EEA. For this purpose property insurance is located where the property is situated, motor insurance where the vehicle is registered, and travel insurance where the contract of insurance was concluded.

As under the Policyholders Protection Act, the Scheme will pay 100 per cent of a claim or unexpired premiums in the case of compulsory insurance, and at least 90 per cent of the value of the policy in the case of long-term insurance. However,

---

[351] Section 213(1).

in other cases, the Scheme will pay more than before: 100 per cent of the first £2,000 of a claim or the unexpired premium, and 90 per cent of the rest of a claim over £2,000. As regards the operation of the Scheme, the FSA is required to make rules. The FSA's Consultation Paper 86, entitled 'Financial Services Compensation Scheme Draft Funding Rules', was published in March 2001 and the period for consultation responses closed on 4 June 2001. However, at the time of writing the rules have not been implemented.

7

Insurance and Society

The Role of Insurance

The main issues in this chapter are whether insurance should be left entirely to the insurers, and insurance law to the lawyers. We start from the position that people should be free to contract insurance, like other services, as they wish, and that insurers should be free to write what terms they please. We ask whether, when, and how that freedom is, or should be, restrained.

The main role of insurance in society is to spread risk and, if the risk materializes, to spread the resulting loss. Thus, the few who need it can be compensated from the contributions paid by the many who do not but might: people who are risk-averse and buy insurance can be assured that, if they were the ones in need, they too would be compensated; so that, in the words of an Act of 1601, there 'followeth not the undoing of any man, but the loss lighteth easily upon many than on few'. Incidental to this role but, increasingly, an important ancillary role of insurance in itself is the management of risk and the prevention of loss.[1] When insurance carries out these functions effectively, the consequences are, first, to encourage useful activity and enterprise that might not otherwise have occurred. Insurance has been called the 'hand-maiden of industry'. A second consequence is the reduction of loss, damage, and stress in society to more acceptable levels.

But is it necessary to stop kids playing conkers in the school playground in case others are allergic to them? Surely life without any risk at all would be simply dull, and there is something of this in contemporary complaints about the 'Nanny State'. As an American scholar put it some years back, without risk, much of 'what makes life challenging, complex, and satisfying would be missing. The right to take risks is very much part of our political tradition and social compact. Indeed, the availability of a rich variety of risky endeavours is part of what is special about our culture.'[2]

Some people would ban walkers from the Highlands of Scotland in winter— but not many. Nor are there many who would suggest that walkers should walk there without any insurance at all, of one kind or another. They can meet the concern of society at large, and of their nearest and dearest in particular, by contracting to cover life and limb, and their liability to others too. But sometimes, not perhaps in the Highlands but back at home, the comfort of insurance cover may make policyholders careless; and this a concern of all of these, insurers among them. This is the main instance of what insurers call 'moral hazard'.

Moral Hazard

From time to time anxiety surfaces that insurance encourages behaviour that is, in some sense, undesirable or even objectionable. Top of the list in the past was the concern that life insurance would encourage death—that the beneficiaries of a life policy would be tempted to hasten the event. The concern was reflected as early as 1774 in the Life Assurance Act of that year.[3] Today a more subtle form of the temptation, on which the statute is silent, might face the family in a position to have a life-support system switched off before the next premium is due. Today, however, as every reader of detective fiction knows, the prime beneficiary is the prime suspect, and it is a very cool or very foolish beneficiary who kills the person whose life is insured.[4] Today, the most common concern about the insidious effects of insurance, if any, is more mundane: that insurance makes people more careless.

---

[1] See Chapter 5, p. 161 ff.   [2] Abraham, p. 2.   [3] See Chapter 1, p. 27 ff.
[4] See Chapter 1, pp. 37–8.

Carelessness

From early days, one of the stated purposes of insurance was to provide cover against human frailty[5] and, therefore, to cover human negligence; fire insurance that does not cover fires started by carelessness is of little use. Indeed, psychologists tell us that everyone makes mistakes, and that mistakes are a normal and necessary part of the human cognitive function. If possible, the response of society should be to correct people rather than to punish them, whether by loss of liberty or loss of insurance. Society expects insurers to play a parental role. On the one hand, both effective loss prevention and accurate underwriting are better promoted not by 'punishing' people for mistakes—that just encourages them to suppress information or blame others—but by seeking a climate of openness the better to assess the extent of the risk. This is at least part of the thinking that motivates the parent who picks up the careless child and comforts it; as well as those who set up the system of anonymous reporting of 'near misses' by airline personnel. However, the parent may punish the child that is careless too often. So, the more claims made, the more it costs the claimant in premiums, or the higher the excess.

The strong arm of technology has strengthened the hand of human beings to a degree that marks it out from the past. On the one hand, technology has increased people's potential for inflicting damage, and with it the need for compensation. The motor vehicle comes quickly to mind. Road 'accidents' in England, according to the Audit Commission reporting in February 2007, cost the United Kingdom over £8 billion a year, although according to the World Health Organization, England and Wales have the lowest level of road deaths in Europe, apart from sparsely populated Sweden and the Netherlands. The World Health Organization has predicted that by 2020, road accidents will kill more people worldwide than HIV, tuberculosis, or war, being exceeded only by heart disease and depression.[6] On the other hand, technology has given people a sense of power over events, so that what was once accepted with resignation as an act of God is now seen with anger as the actionable act of others. Before dialysis machines, people with kidney failure simply died. Now some do not die, but whether they do or not, machines have to be paid for. The search is on for a human being who might be negligent and be sued.[7] Negligence as inadvertence or forgetfulness is inevitable. Insurance to cover all concerned against the consequences of negligence, their own or that of others, has never been more necessary.[8]

---

[5] E.g., *Shaw v Robberds* (1837) 6 Ad & E 75, 84. Generally, see Clarke, ch. 19-2.
[6] *Financial Times*, 11 February 2003.   [7] See Chapter 1, p. 7 ff.
[8] M. F. Grady, 'Why Are People Negligent? Technology, Nondurable Precautions, and the Medical Malpractice Explosion' 82 NWUL Rev 293–334 (1988). See Chapter 2, p. 50 ff.

Risk taking, however, may be more than inadvertent; it may be 'strategically intentional'. This is so when the cost of precautions against it is relatively high and a deliberate decision is taken not to buy the precaution, to take the risk of negligence and to buy insurance. An example is the decision of the railways in the UK not to install an advanced and expensive system (ATP) against driver error. Risk taking may also be 'stubbornly intentional'. There are still people like the man who answered his call of nature in a dangerous place because it was the only place where he could be sure that he would not be seen; or the man who went back into the burning building to save his dog. Whether or not our courts would find, as did courts in the United States, that the dog-owner was negligent, the very least he might reasonably expect would be to be covered by his insurance. We may not tolerate rashness or non-conformity in people as much as we did once, but at least we allow them to seek to insure against it.

Somewhere between stubborn negligence and strategic negligence comes the more casual negligence of policyholders who relax their guard, who do not think about the likely consequences of their actions. Indeed, the relaxation may be something of which they are more or less aware. With 'the passing of time the insured have increasingly come to look on the premium as a payment that gives rights. People took less care and personal responsibility made way for the shifting of responsibility onto society as a whole. Higher claims led to higher premiums, thus reinforcing this behaviour.'[9] This is the observation of a Dutch sociologist; however, a similar view can be taken of attitudes in England. Concern about moral hazard of this kind is justified in varying degrees according to context. As regards liability insurance, for example, there is little ground for this concern,[10] with the possible exception of insurance against health hazards exemplified by viruses in hospitals,[11] but it remains a concern for property insurers. This is what concerns insurers most as 'moral hazard'.

As regards extreme cases of moral hazard, the law helps insurers with the rules requiring that applicants for insurance have an insurable interest,[12] and rules against wilful misconduct[13] but not rules against more casual carelessness. In recent times some insurers sought to cut claims and costs with policies that excluded loss caused by negligence altogether. From the perspective of insurance history, the tail in the claims department was wagging the underwriting dog. In Switzerland the current code effectively prevents insurers from excluding ordinary negligence.[14] English legislation does not go that far, but the English courts have largely reached the same position by means of strict interpretation of the policy terms.[15]

---

[9] C. J. M. Schuyt, 'The Paradox of Welfare and Insurance', *Geneva Papers* 77 (1995), 430–8.
[10] See, e.g., S. W. Gallagher, 'The Public Policy Exclusion and Insurance for Intentional Employment Discrimination', 92 Mich L Rev 1256–1326, 1267, 1291 (1994) and refs cited.
[11] Earlier research suggests that this kind of problem is not new: J. Stapleton, *Deterrence and Health Hazards* (1986) 128.   [12] Chapter 1, p. 26 ff.
[13] Below, at p. 255 ff.   [14] LCA, Art. 14-4.   [15] See Chapter 5, p. 166 ff.

Uninsurable Loss: Intentional Injury

Deliberate Damage

Deliberate damage done by third persons, such as malicious damage by neighbours, is insurable by the potential victim; but, generally, loss or damage inflicted deliberately by policyholders themselves is not. That is a rule of law in some countries, such as France and Germany,[16] or, as in common law countries, it may be either a rule of public policy or the effect of insurance policy interpretation by the courts.

Obviously, society is concerned to discourage me from deliberately damaging the gnomes in my neighbour's garden. Equally obviously, the right to destroy my own property is an incident of ownership and, if I could not burn my garden rubbish, both my neighbour and my gnomes would be overwhelmed. However, my insurer's concern with me and my gnomes is that, if I have insured them and have 'nothing to lose' by destroying them, I might be tempted to do so. To allow a policyholder's whims to affect risk makes it unpredictable and hard to rate. So in England there is a rule against the insurability of deliberate loss,[17] a rule based on the presumed intention of the parties, that is the insurer, as well as public policy.[18] The court asks, first, whether the loss is covered by the insurance policy and, if so, whether recovery under the policy would be contrary to public policy. So, there is a rule of a kind against the insurability of deliberate loss, but also exceptions to the rule.

For example, cover is available in respect of consequences of certain events that policyholders might have always wanted to bring about, indeed, events that they strive and drive daily to bring about, such as the golfers' 'hole in one': golfers, who succeed in hitting the ball into the hole with just one shot must then observe the potentially ruinous custom of buying drinks for everyone in the clubhouse. They can cover the cost by insurance, because the chances are sufficiently small for insurers to rate and to cover the possibility, usually as part of a larger package of cover for golfers. So can the manufacturers of golf clubs who offer a large prize—a kind of contingency insurance called 'prize indemnity'. Although premiums for golfers have risen on the suspicion of collusion with caddies, and one golf course has installed CCTV cameras to monitor 'claims', insurers still offer cover of this kind.

Deliberate Injury

Deliberate injury inflicted by third persons, such as that suffered in street violence, is insurable by the potential victim; but, generally, injury inflicted deliberately by

---

[16] Respectively Code d'assurance, Art. 113-1; VVG, Art. 61 and Art. 152.
[17] *Beresford v Royal Ins. Co.*[1938] AC 586, 604. Generally, see Clarke, ch. 19-2E, 24-5 and 24-6.
[18] *Charlton v Fisher* [2002] QB 578, at [17] (CA).

policyholders themselves is not. An important exception is that life insurance can cover suicide. If it does, however, usually it covers not suicide straight away but suicide after, say, one year: the chance, at the time of contract, of suicide a year later (or of the applicant planning that far ahead) is small and thus insurable.[19]

Expected Loss

Liability cover usually extends to liability for 'accidental' loss (death, injury, or damage to property); or, to the same effect, cover extends to liability (generally) perhaps with an exclusion of liability for loss which is 'either intended or expected', or which is 'intended or expected from the standpoint of the insured'. For the exclusion to apply, loss must be more than just foreseeable. It is only when loss is probable that it is not accidental but to be 'expected', and thus not insured. What the drafters had in mind is clear enough. What courts in the common law world, notably in the United States, have made of their words is anything but.

Very few cases on these clauses have been reported from the English courts, but a survey of cases in the USA shows three markedly different interpretations of the exclusion of what is intended or expected.[20] First, an objective interpretation, sometimes called the 'objective tort standard', is that policyholders are taken to have intended the natural and probable consequences of their intentional acts. Secondly, a purely subjective interpretation is based on what, on the evidence available, policyholders seem to have intended in fact. Between these two interpretations is a third, 'semi-subjective' interpretation: the loss is not insured either if the evidence is that policyholders actually did intend the loss, or, although actual intention is unclear, if intent can be inferred because the loss was practically or substantially certain to follow from their (intentional) acts or omissions.

To complicate the picture further, each of these three interpretations comes in two versions—according to whether the perceived intention is to inflict *any* loss, or (the narrower version) to inflict loss of the kind or to the extent that actually occurred. A court might require, for example, not only purely subjective intent to injure but also intent to inflict the more or less precise injury that occurred.[21] Most courts, however, do not see punching people in the face as an exact science, and that kind of limit is usually found only when the court wants to rule against the exclusion and in favour of cover.

Attempts to relate the cases to more general concepts must be made with caution. Although, for example, the objective test has been referred to as the 'tort standard', it would be facile to suggest that the less stringent tests of accident,

[19] *Ellinger v Mutual Life Ins. Co.* [1905] 1 KB 31 (CA).

[20] M. A. Clarke, 'Insurance of Wilful Misconduct: The Court as Keeper of the Public Conscience' (1996) 7 Ins LJ 173–96; Clarke, ch. 19-2E.

[21] E.g., *Breland v Schilling*, 550 So. 2d 609 (La, 1989).

notably the subjective test, resemble a 'criminal law standard'. Sometimes principles of criminal law are overtly applied, but, in other cases, courts have been careful to distinguish them. Equally, inability to distinguish right and wrong, which may be a defence to a criminal charge, does not make something an accident; for an accident the decisive element is not moral awareness but intention or capacity for effective choice of action, so that, for example, an attempted suicide may be accidental. Cross-reference to concepts of criminal law is made, but not consistently.

Public Policy

One explanation of this diversity of interpretation is that courts' construction of the contract is randomly affected by elements of public policy. The court may or may not mention the public policy in mind. When it does, the emphasis depends on the decision that the court wants to reach. The court that wants to enforce cover usually stresses the importance of compensation. The court against cover stresses the seriousness of the act of the insured and the importance of discouraging that kind of behaviour. Clearly, the courts' perception of public policy has a role, but that role is not clearly defined or articulated.

In England today, however, the role of public policy is limited but relatively clear. Faced with unacceptable conduct in *Tinsley v Milligan*, Nicholls LJ spoke of a 'public conscience test', whereby the court weighed the adverse consequences of granting relief against the adverse consequences of refusing relief. He admitted that this called for a value judgement.[22] The test was rejected on appeal by Lord Goff,[23] apparently unaware that a test of this kind has long been applied to insurance cases by courts throughout the common law world, including the House of Lords itself,[24] and his opinion should be kept in context: an action to recover an interest in land in spite of an illegal transaction to which the plaintiff was party in the past.[25] Nonetheless, the role of the public conscience test is currently very limited in English law.[26]

In England, the impact of policy factors, when they are applied at all, depends on the kind of cover in question, and when there is express reference to them, it should not be taken entirely at face value. For example, in practice the weight given to the importance of compensating victims is rather different in liability cases from that in personal accident (PA) cases. In PA cases the urge to compensate the main victims, the policyholders themselves, or their dependents, is less strong than in liability insurance cases, where the victim is a third party.

Liability Cover

The apparent importance attached to deterrence in cases of liability cover should not be taken too seriously. The idea that people who do wrong in spite of the

[22] [1992] Ch 310, 320 (CA).   [23] [1994] 1 AC 340, 358–9.
[24] *Gardner v Moore* [1984] AC 548.
[25] See M. Clarke, 'Air Rage: Businessmen Behaving Badly: Civil Liability for Uncivil Air Passengers' [2001] LMCLQ 369–82, 380 ff.   [26] See below, pp. 259–60.

possibility of other sanctions, such as imprisonment, will be deterred by the thought of losing insurance cover, is not overwhelmingly convincing. In reality, however, deterrence is often associated with retribution. Even when deterrence alone is mentioned, there is some suggestion that it is really a proxy for punishment and retribution directed at wrongs which the judges find most objectionable. Anyway, deterrence, in whatever sense, and compensation are not the only values that affect the decision. These values, more than one of which can be seen in judgments in the leading and controversial case of *Gray v Barr*, discussed later,[27] are as follows.

First, courts have clearly been influenced by the form of wrong. On the one hand, court decisions (found mainly in the USA) show no sympathy for policyholders guilty of sex offences, and in effect, therefore, remarkably little practical sympathy for victims. On the other hand, even in sex cases there, courts sometimes enforce cover if it is not the offenders' own insurance but their employer's—in respect of the alleged vicarious liability of the employer, or, more likely, the negligence of the latter in the employment or supervision of the offender—especially if the court can be persuaded that the offence is 'inextricably intertwined' with professional activity, such as medical treatment or psychotherapy. One ancillary factor in these decisions appears to be that for professionals (but why not others?) there are other uninsurable deterrents, such as loss of reputation in the community and loss of livelihood.

Secondly, courts have been influenced by the means of harm: the weapon. Courts are most reluctant to indemnify policyholders who use guns,[28] even in self-defence. In contrast, when guns have not been involved, although deliberate injury in self-defence is not likely to be held to be an accident, an instinctive reflex reaction, such that the policyholder did not have the time to form the intent required for the exclusion, may well be an accident. By the same token, however, policyholders are not likely to be covered if, in a deliberate and calculated way, they seek to take the law into their own hands.

Somewhere between the reflex and the Rambo response comes brawling, about which courts have been more ambivalent. On the one hand, even on the purely subjective approach most favourable to policyholders, neither a one-sided beating nor a man hitting a woman in the face is likely to be seen by the courts as accidental. On the other hand, brawling on the sports field is more likely to be tolerated and covered.[29] So is violence on the roads. Even in cases of utter recklessness on the roads, people still speak of motor 'accidents' and, on the whole, courts dealing with insurance in the past have seen events in a similar way. Another important example, at least in the USA, is the enforcement of cover for liability for 'calculated' pollution poisoning of the environment.[30] In England, however, enforcement of

---

[27] [1971] 2 QB 554 (CA), discussed below, p. 277 ff.

[28] E.g., *Gray v Barr*, above, n. 27.   [29] E.g., *Breland v Schilling*, above, n. 21.

[30] M. A. Clarke, 'Liability Insurance on Pollution Damage: Market Meltdown or Grist to the Mill' [1994] JBL 545–65, 553. V. Fogleman, *Environmental Liabilities and Insurance in England and the United States* (London, 2005).

liability cover in respect of deliberate environmental damage now seems unlikely unless such insurance is compulsory. Indeed, in England, when policyholders' liability to others is also a crime, it now seems that the insurance will not be enforced unless the cover was of a kind that Parliament has made compulsory.

Compulsory Liability Cover

Until relatively recently, one might have expected a flexible response by the courts in all cases along the lines of the 'public conscience test' by reference to the values discussed above. The court might have been expected to weigh the adverse consequences of granting relief against the adverse consequences of refusing relief; this was the test debated in *Tinsley v Milligan*.[31] The test is indeed a source of possible uncertainty, because effective application assumes that the court has sufficient information[32] and because the outcome depends on a judgment that is unlikely to be entirely objective. This may be why English courts have now shrunk from the task and retreated to a perfectly reasonable but cautious position, where they cannot be attacked either for ignorance, or for subjectivity. Their position is that the only cases in which liability cover will be enforced in spite of unlawful behaviour on the part of the policyholder are those where Parliament has made the cover compulsory and thus emphasized the importance in such cases of compensating victims.

In *Charlton v Fisher*,[33] the policyholder deliberately rammed another car parked in a hotel car park, not only damaging the car but also injuring an occupant, of whose presence the policyholder was unaware. The policyholder was liable to the victim nonetheless, but the Court of Appeal held that he was not covered by his motor insurance. The reason was that at that time the motor cover required by the law, which has changed since, was limited to use of a motor vehicle on a public road which the hotel car park was not.[34]

The question whether liability insurance is enforceable in respect of unlawful behaviour now has a clear answer. However, as is often the case with clearly drawn legal lines, it may give odd results. For example, if a driver overcome with road rage in a motorway service area runs me down with his Chelsea tractor, his insurance responds. If, having failed to hit me with the vehicle, however, he takes his shot gun from under the seat and finishes the job with that, his insurance, if any, does not. Nonetheless, it is difficult not to have sympathy with the judges and the position they took in *Charlton v Fisher*. They may have recalled the plea of Lord Devlin forty years or more ago, that, if Parliament wants to make the enforcement of a contract illegal, why can it not say so? Lord Devlin went on:

Need judges, as if they were sycophants who have to anticipate their masters' wishes even before they are uttered, be so zealous in smelling out new victims and devising further

---

[31] Op. cit. above, n. 22.   [32] See below, p. 277 ff.
[33] Op. cit. above, n. 18.   [34] Ibid., at [9].

punishments? Yet for a hundred years and more the judges have been grappling with the task of trying to find out what Parliament meant by what it did not say; and not unnaturally have left a confused trail of cases behind them.[35]

For the judges in *Charlton v Fisher* the task is over; as regards the enforcement of liability insurance, Parliament has spoken or not, as the case may be.

Personal Accident Cover

If Socrates, with (compulsory) employers' liability cover, poisons his staff with hemlock in the office coffee machine, the cover is likely to be enforced. If Socrates poisons himself, the enforceability of his life or accident insurance, if any, is not so easy to predict. In modern life there are many poisons and many different attitudes to them.

In the USA, most likely to be compensated is an 'accidental' overdose of drugs obtained from a doctor on prescription, such as sleeping pills. Indeed, a hard line of this kind is drawn by some insurance contracts, which exclude injury or death by drug use unless used on the advice of a licensed medical practitioner. However, in a leading English case, where the victim was a qualified nurse, the Court of Appeal seemed to take the line that 'she should have known better', and declined to enforce the cover.[36]

Alcohol is a drug to which courts in the past have been less hostile than other 'street' drugs. As recently as 1990, a federal court in the United States declined to apply an exclusion (of death occurring 'during the commission of a crime') because, although the insured was drunk and driving fast when his car hit a tree, the court considered that people would not regard drunken driving as a crime.[37] On the whole, however, in recent years courts there have taken a harder line on hard drinking,[38] but have indicated nonetheless that they are still likely to enforce cover if it enures to the benefit of a surviving dependant.[39] Be that as it may, it may have been significant that in Canada[40] and in the only reported insurance case involving drunken death on the road in England,[41] the courts applied the subjective test most favourable to the insured. These decisions were given nearly thirty years ago when judges, for whom coke was something that came in a can from the corner shop, might well have been less sympathetic to users of illegal drugs than to alcohol drinkers when things go wrong. That may be different today.[42]

A major point, about which there is less doubt, is that courts are more likely to favour insurability if what policyholders were doing at the time of the 'accident' is

[35] P. Devlin, *The Enforcement of Morals* (Oxford, 1965) 56.
[36] *Dhak v INA (UK) Ltd* [1996] I Lloyd's Rep 632 (CA).
[37] *Chen v Metropolitan Ins. Co.*, 907 F 2d 566 (5 Cir, 1990).
[38] *Mullaney v Aetna Healthcare*, 103 F Supp 2d 486 (D RI, 2000).
[39] *West v Aetna Life Ins. Co.*, 171 F Supp 2d 856, 884 ff. (ND Iowa, 2001).
[40] *Mutual of Omaha v Stats* (1978) 87 DLR (3d) 169 (Sup Ct).
[41] *Beller v Hayden* [1978] QB 694.   [42] *Todd v AIG Life Ins. Co.*, 47 F 3d 1448 (5 Cir, 1995).

considered useful, such as keeping the peace, than if it was foolish, such as playing Russian roulette. So, in Canada, the death of a person demonstrating his 'nerve' to his companions by walking a parapet thirteen floors up after drinking vodka will not be an accident;[43] but clearly, if he is trying to rescue a person trapped in a building on fire, the assessment is likely to be different.[44] English courts may well take a similar view if analogy can be drawn from decisions on the tort of negligence.[45]

Certainties

The question, was the leg broken accidentally or not, is usually answered by the law in the same way, whether it is the policyholder's leg or that of a Chippendale chair. In principle it is only when the injury or damage was the intended or probable result of policyholder conduct that it is not accidental but to be 'expected', and not therefore covered by the insurance.

An exception is found in all risks (AR) transit insurance on goods, an exception not easily explained. AR insurance does not normally cover loss due to ordinary wear and tear, which of course is hardly surprising, but neither does it cover what the law calls an inherent vice.[46] Inherent vice 'means the risk of deterioration of the goods shipped as a result of their natural behaviour in the ordinary course of the contemplated voyage without the intervention of any fortuitous external accident or casualty',[47] that is, a potentially defective condition in the goods, which was present at the time cover commenced and which materialized during transit, that is, the period of cover. It may be that the food went 'off', or the metalwork rusted. The most common explanation of the absence of cover, both for inherent vice and indeed for ordinary wear and tear, is that, in the particular case, the deterioration was going to happen anyway; and that, as AR insurance 'covers a risk but not a certainty',[48] the AR insurance does not apply. But that does not answer policyholders, who object that in many cases of inherent vice the damage might have been expected by an omniscient God but not by anyone like them down on Earth, and that therefore inherent vice should regarded as accidental.

Like it or not, English law takes a different approach to AR transit insurance; and, incidentally, in some other countries, like France, which may have been influenced by the London insurance market, the rule is the same.[49] The event is objectively assessed, that is, it is assessed not with the knowledge of policyholders when cover commenced but with that of the court with the benefit of hindsight.

---

[43] *Candler v London Accident Co.* (1963) 40 DLR (2d) 408.
[44] *American Int. Life Co. v Martin* (2003) 223 DLR (4th) 1 (Sup Ct) at [28].
[45] Decisions such as *Watt v Herts CC* [1954] 1 WLR 835 (CA).
[46] The leading case is *British & Foreign Marine Ins. Co. Ltd v Gaunt* [1921] 2 AC 41.
[47] *Soya GmbH v White* [1983] I Lloyd's Rep 122, 126 (HL). See also *Noten BV v Harding* [1990] 2 Lloyd's Rep 283 (CA).   [48] *Gaunt*, op. cit. above, n. 46, 57.
[49] Codes des Assurances Maritimes, Art. 172-18.

If it proves later, perhaps after a close examination of the goods, that all along the goods suffered from an inherent vice, even one which was latent in the sense that it could not possibly have been discovered earlier by the policyholder, the loss is not covered. The question remains, why? Policyholders, to whom the defect came as an unpleasant surprise, may well feel the same about the law and object as follows.

First, in everyday language and experience, taking risks concerns the risk of something about to happen or not. People step out onto the icy surface of the lake not knowing if they will fall through; they take a risk even though the die has already been cast, even though with right equipment and sufficient time they could predict the outcome. So, argue the policyholders, an insurance risk too should be seen in the same way and assessed at the corresponding moment, before the risk has been run. When transit cover commences, it may appear that the weather will be mild, that the goods are in good condition, and that, even if the true state of the goods were known, the inherent vice would not develop while cover lasted; or that the defect would be dealt with in time to arrest its progress or to prevent loss. If the eventuality of loss is not apparent to reasonable policyholders when transit and cover commence, surely the loss is not a certainty but a risk.

Secondly, policyholders may ask why life and health insurance contracts are different. True, policies sometimes exclude expressly the effects of 'pre-existing conditions', but that is not universal and not a rule of law. A person may enforce disability insurance in respect of angina which, at the time of contracting the insurance, was there but had yet to be diagnosed.[50] Life insurance is the same. If an exporter's life insurance covers a latent defect in that person's liver, why does AR transit insurance not cover a corresponding defect in the exporter's meat?

Thirdly, when people buy 'white' goods like refrigerators, they can also buy insurance that will 'guarantee' the fitness of the refrigerator, so why not also the fitness of refrigerator contents in transit? The talk of covering a 'risk but not a certainty' implies that latent defects are inherently uninsurable, but that is evidently untrue. Although goods in transit are not covered against inherent vice, the vessels in which such goods are carried are commonly insured against a 'latent defect in the machinery or hull'.[51] Moreover, in England,[52] as well as other jurisdictions such as the USA,[53] people can also insure latent defects in buildings, although in England it is described not as AR insurance but as something else.

When defects in buildings are insured in the USA, courts start from first principles and apply a test of latent defect that English policyholders may well wish to import. In the *Bauxites* case,[54] plant defectively designed and constructed collapsed. The lower court held against the insurance claim, taking the kind of

---

[50] *Cook v Financial Ins. Co.* [1998] 1 WLR 1765 (HL).

[51] See *The Nukila* [1997] 2 Lloyd's Rep 146 (CA). *Idem* in France: Codes des Assurances Maritimes, Art. 173-4.

[52] See, e.g., *Kier Construction Ltd v Royal Ins. (UK) Ltd* (1992) 30 Con LR 45.

[53] *Compagnie des Bauxites de Guinée v INA*, 724 F 2d 369 (3 Cir, 1983).   [54] Above, n. 53.

view to be expected in England, that the loss was not accidental because 'it was predictable and certain that a defectively designed building such as the one involved here would fail and collapse'.[55] The Court of Appeals reversed. It applied § 291 of the Restatement of Contracts (1932), that 'a fortuitous event . . . is an event which *so far as the parties to the contract are aware*, is dependent on chance'.[56]

The real explanation of the legal presumption in England, and perhaps in other countries like France, that latent defects are not included in AR transit insurance, lies, it is submitted, not in the realm of concepts or principles, but in two largely historical features of AR cargo insurance. First, insurers were unwilling to assume that kind of risk on account of moral hazard. The conjecture is that, as a result of past experience of transit risks, the real concern, as with the kindred exclusion of wear and tear, is that people might be tempted to dump defective goods on their insurer. Currently there is plenty of evidence of this hazard in the household insurance sector, for example, although whether it is still true of AR transit insurance is hard to say. The effect of covering inherent vice would be that insurers would be guaranteeing the quality of meat when delivered, and this is not a risk that insurers are willing to assume. So, it being hard to prove that consignors knew the goods would not last the journey, insurers protected themselves simply by ruling out altogether cover of risks of this kind, and this became a presumption of interpretation which has hardened into something like a presumption of law. Secondly, once the law had been established in this sense, as it has now for about 100 years, there is a strong case against change because that might undermine the value of the historical data on which each new application for transit insurance is assessed.

Wilful Misconduct

The intentional act exception,[57] hitherto found mainly in the USA, is now found in England. In England, however, whether as a contract term or an overriding public policy, and whether concerned with property damage or personal injury, a similar result has been sought by excluding cover of 'wilful misconduct'. This is hardly surprising, but the point merits mention because of the way that courts have construed the phrase and because the meaning attributed to the phrase is different from that of courts in other countries when the same phrase is used, as it is, in international conventions.[58]

In the interpretation of 'wilful misconduct' by the courts we find again[59] what psychologists call 'heuristic' patterns of analysis, that is, cautious use of analogy with more general legal concepts, categories with which the court is more familiar.

[55] 554 F Supp 1080, 1 084 (WD Pa, 1988).   [56] Op. cit. above, n. 53 (emphasis added).
[57] Above, p. 256 ff.
[58] See M. A. Clarke, *Contracts of Carriage by Air* (London, 2002) 160 ff.
[59] See Chapter 5, p. 167 ff.

In this example, the concepts and categories belong mainly to the tort of negligence. The outcome for insurance contracts, in which 'wilful misconduct' is excluded, is that, in general, what lawyers understand as negligence is covered, but that recklessness is not.

By rephrasing the question, however, the courts have also affected the likely answer. Whereas the question asked, for example in personal accident cases,[60] whether an injury is to be expected, is essentially one of probability or likelihood, in English law the question whether the policyholder was reckless is more subjective and more relative. In its latter form, the question gives the court licence not only to refer to 'pure' probability but, like the court seised of an action in tort, to consider the social impact, the usefulness or otherwise of the policyholder's conduct. The result is that, as we have seen,[61] the fireman who falls from a parapet suffers an accident but the exhibitionist does not, although the probability of falling may be the same in each case. Again, the heatstroke suffered by the stoker of a steamship is an accident,[62] but the heatstroke suffered by the holidaymaker on the beach is not.[63] This form of enquiry, although appropriate to a claim in tort which concerns the liability of the actor and affects the duties of the community at large, is rather less appropriate to an insurance claim, which is concerned with the liability of the insurer and the interpretation of a particular contract.

Regulating Contract Terms

Contracting insurance, it is said, does not meet the optimal standards of economic efficiency (whatever that is) because applicants lack the information needed to bargain efficiently. It is argued that, as regards consumers, the cost of obtaining and evaluating information about the terms of insurance contracts will tend to direct competitive forces away from this exercise and towards broad price-quantity comparisons. The result may then be 'harsh-term-low-price policies, whereas many consumers, in the absence of information and transaction costs, may have preferred an easier-term-higher price combination'.[64] In other words, consumers take one look (if that) at the small print, their eyes glaze over, and they go for what appears to be adequate cover at the lowest premium.

Of all the more important transactions made by consumers, insurance stands out as the one that has been clear of outside control, or, as the insurance industry sees it, free from regulatory 'interference'. For many years the hazards of employment

---

[60] Above, at p. 256.   [61] Above, pp. 200–1.

[62] *Ismay, Imrie & Co. v Williamson* [1908] AC 437.

[63] *De Souza v Home & Overseas Ins. Co. Ltd* [1995] LRLR 453 (CA).

[64] V. P. Goldberg, 'Institutional Change and the Quasi-Invisible Hand' 17 JL & Econ 461–96, 483 (1974); cf. M. J. Trebilcock, 'The Doctrine of Inequality of Bargaining Power' (1976) 26 U Toronto LJ 359–85, 375.

have been regulated largely by statute. If consumers buy a car or borrow money, the terms are controlled by statute, as they have been for more than a century. If they buy a house the terms are standardized to similar effect. For other hazards of life not covered by social security, which is regulated by statute, they can or must buy insurance by contract. Until very recently, however, when they bought insurance, there was no such control at all. When Parliament passed the Unfair Contract Terms Act 1977, insurance contracts were excluded from the Act because Parliament had been persuaded by the insurance industry that it would be enough if the ABI issued guidelines in the form of voluntary codes of practice. When the EC was considering the matter, however, it was not so persuaded, and the Unfair Terms in Consumer Contracts Directive now applies.[65] In the 1990s the perception that the industry could be trusted to regulate itself was doubted as never before, and the trend was to some kind of regulation or control of policy terms. This might have been done, as it has been sometimes in the past and still is, piecemeal by courts called on to interpret particular policy terms. Some people think that in future the terms of certain insurance contracts will be regulated by the Financial Services Authority (FSA). Meanwhile the European Commission has mandated work on a draft directive to cover default rules of insurance contract law.[65a]

Validation

A future possibility is that firms will not be authorized to carry on insurance business, unless the terms of certain insurance contracts have been approved by a body such as the FSA. If so, there would be precedent abroad. In some countries in the past, and others still today, insurers cannot use terms unless they have received prior approval by a State supervisory agency of some kind. The advantage for the public is that, just as buyers of licensed drugs can have some confidence that the right drug will do some good, it can have confidence that the insurance will provide some cover. However, licensing has some disadvantages too.[66]

The first is the cost of having all the policy terms examined. Secondly, the expertise of the validating agency can never be comprehensive, so its scrutiny will be slow, incomplete, or both. Thirdly, insurers will tailor the policy terms to the perceived views of the agency, and this discourages innovation. Fourthly, if the agency is sensitive to the first two drawbacks, it is likely to be restrictive of unfamiliar insurance terms, so this too inhibits innovation. Lastly, the cost and trouble of getting new terms approved discourages insurers from tailoring contract terms to the needs of minority groups of customers. In Europe, the current view is that the disadvantages outweigh the advantages to a degree that is anti-competitive, so State validation is not a sensible option.

---

[65] See below, at p. 268 ff.   [65a] See http://www.restatement.info/.
[66] See P. -O. Bjuggren et al., 'Should a Regulatory Body Control Insurance Policies Ex Ante or is Ex Post Control More Effective?', *Geneva Papers* No. 70 (Jan. 1994), 37–45.

Interpretation by the Courts

Relative Truth

Insurance contracts exemplify the tradition of courts' interpreting contract terms in a way that makes them less unfair. As we have seen, the effect of a breach of warranty is so serious for policyholders that courts construe strongly both against the argument that a term is a warranty at all[67] and, if it is, that it is a warranty continuing throughout the insurance period or that it has been broken by a policyholder.[68]

One example is the ruling that policyholders warrant belief rather than truth. Although something is true or not regardless of what people believe, warranties are interpreted not absolutely in this sense but relatively, relatively to the honest belief and intention of the particular policyholder at the time. So, when a policyholder promised that 'the vehicle will not be driven by any person under 25', the court limited the undertaking to a statement of what he intended at the time.[69] When applicants for cover warrant but understate the value of property to be insured, what counts is not the view of a professional but the honest belief of the applicants.[70] Again, when applicants state that they are in good health, that refers not to their actual state of health but to what they honestly and reasonably believe at the time of contract.[71]

Health, moreover, is relative to expectations of time and circumstance. When once an insurer complained that an applicant had not disclosed venereal disease, Lord Mansfield retorted that with such common complaints, 'if such objections were admitted, there would be no end of insurance litigation'.[72] Not so today no doubt, but health is nonetheless relative to what is expected of the body concerned. In London, for example, the porter who opens taxi doors at the Savoy Hotel, and still less the non-executive director who emerges from the taxi, may not be fit to work as a porter shifting carcasses in the early hours of a winter's morning in the meat market at Smithfield.

Safety Practice

Insurers have strongly argued that the safety practice of policyholders at the time of the contract is of little value to the insurer without a promise that it will continue throughout the insurance period.[73] The courts have rejected the argument. Even as a promise confined to the present, it still has value to insurers

---

[67] Chapter 5, p. 159 ff.   [68] Chapter 5, p. 161 ff.

[69] *Kirkbride v Donner* [1974] 1 Lloyd's Rep 549. See Clarke, ch. 20-5.

[70] Jewellery: *Economides v Commercial Union Ins. Co. plc* [1998] QB 587 (CA); a ship: *Eagle Star Ins. Co. Ltd v Games Video Co.* [2004] 1 Lloyd's Rep 238.

[71] *Thomson v Weems* (1884) 9 App Cas 671, 683.

[72] *Smith v Mather* (1778), reported in J. A. Park, *A System of the Law of Marine Insurances*, 6th edn (London, 1809) 482.   [73] See above, p. 252 ff.

as an indication of the sort of person the policyholder is (then) and is likely to remain (thereafter during the insurance period); so, warranties about efficient fire and burglary alarms, for example, have been interpreted as being limited in application to the state of affairs at the time of contract.[74]

Again, a clause requiring precautions or reasonable care during the period of cover conflicts with the supposition that it is a normal and proper purpose of insurance to cover people against their own negligence. The conflict has been resolved by restrictive interpretation of such clauses. In most instances, the court scales down what is required of policyholders so that there is cover, unless policyholders have been more than negligent, that is, grossly negligent or reckless.[75] Note, however, that the court must be able to justify its decision as a matter of interpretation of the policy before it. If the policy specifies precautions clearly, policyholders must comply. For example, some travel policies specifically exclude theft of personal possessions from unattended motor vehicles, unless stolen from a locked boot in a vehicle in which all doors and windows have been secured. Such clauses, being clearly drawn, have been applied, even by the IOB and FOS.

The Effectiveness of Reliance on the Courts

Although the attitude and approach of the courts is clear, the decisions they will reach are not; at least, they are not so clear that policyholders can always be advised with confidence about the effect of their policies. The courts' duel with the drafters in years past has left scars and jagged edges. This is what a leading American jurist once called the 'juridical risk'.[76] Courts have made it difficult for insurers to tailor premiums closely to narrowly defined risks:

Insurers capable of making estimates of the probability of natural occurrences are far less able to determine the inclinations of individual judges. Thus, companies must overestimate premiums to reflect not only the primary risk, but also the secondary risk that courts will extend coverage beyond a policy's intended scope.[77]

The cost of the court's interpretation in favour of one claimant must be paid for by the rest of the risk pool. Risk spreading of a kind, perhaps, but is it efficient? To preserve their clauses from restrictive interpretation by the courts, the drafters' device is to write them into the description of risk covered, the insuring clause, or to spell out the consequences of breach in unequivocal terms.

As a principal means of controlling insurance contract terms, strict interpretation by the courts is not satisfactory, because it is of only marginal assistance to most

---

[74] *Woolfall & Rimmer Ltd v Moyle* [1942] 1 KB 66, 70, 71 (CA); *Hussain v Brown* [1996] 1 Lloyd's Rep 627, 629 (CA).   [75] See Chapter 5, p. 166 ff.

[76] F. Kessler, 'Contracts of Adhesion—Some Thoughts about Freedom of Contract', 43 Col L Rev 629–42, 631 (1943).

[77] D. S. Miller, 'Insurance as Contract: The Argument for Abandoning the Ambiguity Doctrine', 88 Col L Rev 1849, 1862 (1988).

consumers. To get help they must go to court, which, they know, is expensive; and, moreover, success in court cannot be guaranteed. Insurers know this too, so they have little incentive to remove unenforceable terms from their contracts. More satisfactory, in theory, is institutional intervention of the kind envisaged by the EC Directive, whereby bodies representing consumers might have clauses declared unfair on their behalf, and to which we now turn.

The EC Directive 1993

The Scope of the Regime

The EC Directive on Unfair Terms in Consumer Contracts, implemented in the United Kingdom by the Unfair Terms in Consumer Contracts Regulations 1999,[78] applies to certain terms in certain insurance contracts within the scope of the regime. As to the contracts, the first question is whether one party is a consumer; if not, the regime does not apply. If one is a consumer, the next question is whether the contract was individually negotiated; if it was, and this is for the insurer to prove,[79] the regime does not apply. If, as is most likely with insurance for consumers, it was not individually negotiated, the regime applies to the contract.

The first main thrust of the regime is that terms must be 'plain and intelligible': regulation 6(2).[80] The second addresses terms, which are not core terms but which have the effect of creating a 'significant imbalance', 'contrary to the requirement of good faith': regulation 5. Such terms are to be regarded as unfair and, although other terms of the contract remain in force, such a term 'shall not be binding on the consumer': regulation 8.

Plain and Intelligible

The regime requires terms to be plain and intelligible—but to whom? At common law, if words are plain and intelligible to lawyers, that is enough and terms are applied as lawyers would understand them. Under regulation 7, however, the terms must be plain and intelligible to consumers. Whether insurance contracts can ever be drafted in language plain and intelligible to people in general, such as consumers, is doubtful,[81] but that is what the regulation requires.

Many, if not most, insurers reacted to the regime by reviewing their current contracts. Subject to the pitfalls of plain English, this is likely to be beneficial because, at least, insurers have been compelled to take a new look at some old clauses. Moreover, the Office of Fair Trading (OFT), whose role it is to police consumer contracts in accordance with the regime, has published its findings.

---

[78] SI 1999/2083, implementing Directive 93/13/EEC of 5 April 1993 [1993] OJ L95/29.
[79] Reg. 5(4).
[80] Quaere whether this provision gives effect to the Directive; Clarke, ch. 19-5A.
[81] See Chapter 5, p. 147 ff.

It has ruled out as unintelligible jargon what lawyers regard in some instances as ordinary legal terminology. Examples include 'indemnify', 'consequential loss', and 'events beyond your control'.[82] The repercussions in practice are hard to assess, but over time the impact is likely to be extensive.

Core Terms

Core terms in consumer contracts must be plain and intelligible,[83] but they are saved from the other main thrust of the regime, fairness, so the meaning of core terms is important. Regulation 6(2) states that 'the assessment of fairness of a term shall not relate—(a) to the definition of the main subject matter of the contract, or (b) to the adequacy of the price or remuneration' for the services supplied. Moreover, for insurance contracts the Directive specifies that 'the terms which clearly define or circumscribe the insured risk and the insurer's liability shall not be subject to such assessment since these restrictions are taken into account in calculating the premium paid by the consumer'.[84] No such provision is found in the UK Regulations; however, regulation 6(2) is required to be interpreted in the light of the Directive.[85]

Terms which 'define or circumscribe the insured risk and the insurer's liability' appear to include terms defining the peril covered, as well as exceptions and warranties. The inclusion of warranties has been doubted, but since the House of Lords has characterized them as conditions precedent to cover,[86] it is difficult to escape the conclusion that they are core terms, which means that the difficulty of identifying warranties reappears here in another role.[87] Further, as insurers' liability has a dimension in time, core terms beyond scrutiny include some potentially unfair clauses such as cancellation clauses. Further still, controversially, the OFT has taken the view that 'other insurance' clauses, whereby a policy does not cover risks covered by other insurance contracts contracted by a policyholder, are also core terms.[88]

Whereas the attack on legal jargon has been undertaken by the OFT, the task of explaining the concept of unfairness has fallen to the House of Lords. Its interpretation has been conservative, coming from English common law rather than any essay in comparative jurisprudence.

Unfairness: Good Faith in English Courts

A term is not binding on consumers if it is unfair: regulation 8(1). A term is unfair if, 'contrary to the requirement of good faith, it causes a significant imbalance in the parties' rights and obligations arising under the contract, to the detriment of

---

[82] OFT Bulletin Nos 5, 23, and 24 respectively.
[83] See Reg. 6(2); and Clarke, ch. 19-5A2.   [84] Para. 19 of the Preamble.
[85] *Axa Royal Belge v Ochoa* [2002] 2 CMLR Case No. 5 (ECJ).
[86] *The Good Luck* [1992] 1 AC 233.   [87] Chapter 5, pp. 160–1.
[88] OFT, *Unfair Contract Terms*, Issue No. 5, October 1998.

the consumer': regulation 5(1). If parties agree a one-sided or unbalanced contract, that is their business and the regime does not apply, unless there is also something about the term, or the way that it was agreed, which is contrary to good faith. The key concept is good faith.

Good faith has been the subject of much speculation by commentators. One criticism of the requirement is that it is too vague, and that it allows judges to exercise discretion without intellectual rigour.[89] However, in *Director General of Fair Trading v First National Bank*,[90] Lord Bingham, with whom the other members of the House of Lords agreed, paid no attention to the literature, because perhaps, in his opinion, the language used in expressing the test was perfectly clear. Indeed, he referred to the influence of Lord Mansfield and proclaimed that good faith was a concept not 'wholly unfamiliar to British lawyers'.[91]

As regards the requirement of 'significant imbalance', that, said Lord Bingham,[92]

is met if a term is so weighted in favour of the supplier as to tilt the parties' rights and obligations under the contract significantly in his favour. This may be by the granting to the [insurer] of a beneficial option or discretion or power, or by the imposing on the consumer of a disadvantageous burden or risk or duty.

He also observed that the illustrative terms set out in Schedule 3 to the Regulations provide very good examples of terms which may be regarded as unfair.

As regards the requirement of 'good faith', that, said Lord Bingham, 'is one of fair and open dealing'. He continued:[93]

Openness requires that the terms should be expressed fully, clearly and legibly, containing no concealed pitfalls or traps. Appropriate prominence should be given to terms which might operate disadvantageously to the customer. Fair dealing requires that a supplier should not, whether deliberately or unconsciously, take advantage of the consumer's necessity, indigence, lack of experience, unfamiliarity with the subject matter of the contract, weak bargaining position or any other factor listed in or analogous to those listed in Schedule 2 of the Regulations.

Lord Steyn said something similar[94]—as had Lord Bingham many years earlier, before the Regulations came into force, in a case well known to students of English contract law, the *Interfoto* case.[95] There he referred to the principle of good faith found in many civil law systems as being 'in essence a principle of fair and open dealing', which he distinguished from English law which had 'developed piecemeal solutions in response to demonstrated problems of unfairness'. Among these piecemeal solutions he specified rules of equity against unconscionable bargains,

---

[89] D. Yates, 'Two Concepts of *Good* Faith' (1995) 8 JCL 145–53, 145.
[90] [2002] 1 AC 481, at [17]. The case concerned a clause about the rate of interest payable if a borrower defaulted on a loan.					[91] Ibid.
[92] Ibid.		[93] Ibid.		[94] Ibid., at [36].
[95] *Interfoto Picture Library Ltd v Stiletto Visual Programmes Ltd* [1989] QB 433, 439 (CA).

disguised penalties for breach of contract, and requirements of sufficient notice of standard contract terms, in particular, the case before the court, notice terms of an unusual and stringent nature. Nonetheless, it is a principle based on openness and fair dealing that emerges as a principle of English law in the passage from *Interfoto* quoted here. Be that as it may, although it is correct to say that the good faith of regulation 5(1) is not intended to be the same as that previously found in civil law systems, which vary,[96] it would not be correct to read Lord Bingham's speech as an invitation to carry on as before on the well-known paths of the common law. In Luxembourg, the Court of Justice of the European Communities held in 2003, not surprisingly, that national courts should interpret national law, that implements Directives, in the light of the purpose of the Directive in question so as to achieve the result intended.[97] This suggests some reference to decisions and doctrine beyond these shores.[98]

The Grey List

In *Director General of Fair Trading v First National Bank*,[99] Lord Bingham did acknowledge the importance of Schedule 3. This is the so-called 'grey list', that is, 'an indicative and non-exhaustive list of the terms which *may* be regarded as unfair': regulation 5(5) (emphasis added). In a particular case, the eye runs down the list in search of a category for the case in hand.

For example, category (i) indicates terms with which the consumer 'had no real opportunity of becoming acquainted before the conclusion of the contract'. English common law expects a certain amount of energy and enterprise on the part of insurance applicants to seek out the terms. They are bound by the insurer's standard terms for standard risks on the basis of constructive knowledge.[100]In some instances, it seems possible that applicants for insurance may have notice under the common law rule, and yet have had no 'real opportunity of becoming acquainted' with them as required by the regime. See, for example, the anodyne summaries of cover offered by some outlets, such as travel agencies selling travel insurance as part of a holiday package. Further, 'acquaintance' interlocks with the requirement of intelligibility.[101] The more complex the terms, the less intelligible they become; and the harder it will be for the insurer to establish that the consumer had a real opportunity of becoming acquainted with the terms.

One more example is to be found in category (n): terms making the insurer's commitments 'subject to compliance with a particular formality'. This includes terms requiring notice of loss within a stated period of time. At common law such terms have been rigidly applied, even to a claimant in hospital and in no position

---

[96] See below, pp. 272–3.   [97] *Axa Royal Belge v Ochoa*, op. cit. above, n. 85.
[98] See J. N. Adams and R. Brownsword, *Understanding Contract Law*, 4th edn (London, 2004) ch. 5.4.   [99] Op. cit. above, n. 90.
[100] Chapter 4, pp. 90–1.   [101] See above, pp. 268–9.

to give notice.[102] Under the regime such a claimant would not be bound. Insurers will be permitted to require no more than 'reasonable notice'.[103] Moreover, the consequences of failure must not be unfair. In *Bankers v South*,[104] it was agreed on all sides that, even if a notice clause were expressed to be a condition precedent to the liability of the insurer, it would be unfair if it were applicable even though late notice had caused no prejudice to the insurer.

Good Faith in English Legal Literature

Although based on German law, the good faith in the regime is not so similar that we can simply import German law. Nor should we. The literature and case law to which it has given rise is vast. Moreover, good faith is also a general and established concept in EC law and in other countries, such as France, and they might have something to say on the matter. Inevitably, good faith as a general principle (*Treu und Glauben, bonne foi*, and so on) means slightly different things in different places, so, to interpret the regulation in a broad and comparative sense, as perhaps English courts will do eventually, sooner or later we shall have to look at the attempts made to synthesize the different versions in language that the common lawyer can understand.

According to one, good faith stands for the principle *pacta sunt servanda* and, in particular, a notion that requires the court to look to the spirit or true intent of transactions and the duty to fulfil expectations engendered by one's promise.[105] Another, which is not at all at odds with the first and which seems to be the most promising, speaks of an 'ethic of co-operation'.[106]

The ethic of cooperation as a version of good faith has attractions. First, it is authentically international in so far as it can be traced in commercial arbitrations at that level.[107] Secondly, it is European in so far as a similar version of good faith can be seen in France. Thirdly, it is anything but alien to the common law. A version of the idea of cooperation was a vehicle for the successful launch of good faith in the United States. Moreover, for some time a limited version of that same idea has been part of English common law, where it has been found in two forms. The first is negative—less a positive duty of cooperation than a duty not to obstruct.[108] The second is more positive: if 'both parties have agreed that something shall be done, which cannot effectually be done unless both parties concur in doing it, the construction of the contract is that each agrees to do all that is necessary to be done on his part for the carrying out of that thing, though there be no express words to that effect'.[109]

---

[102] See Chapter 6, p. 216 ff.   [103] See Chapter 6, p. 216.

[104] [2004] Lloyd's Rep IR 1, at [31].

[105] See, e.g., H. K. Lucke, 'Good Faith and Contractual Performance', in P. Finn (ed.), *Essays on Contract* (Sydney, 1987) 155–82.

[106] R. Brownsword, 'Two Concepts of Good Faith' (1994) 7 JCL 197–243.

[107] N. Nassar, *Sanctity of Contracts Revisited* (Dordrecht, 1995) ch. VII.

[108] *Southern Foundries Ltd v Shirlaw* [1940] AC 701, 717.

[109] *Mackay v Dick* (1881) 6 App Cas 251, 263.

If the ethic of cooperation is to fulfil the 'reasonable expectations' of the parties to the contract of insurance and to 'achieve the goals' of insurance, those expectations and goals have to be identified. For argument's sake, let us say that the main purpose of insurance is both to minimize financial loss to policyholders and to maximize financial gain to insurers: by spreading it when it occurs, as well as reducing it by measures taken both before and after its occurrence. If so, what might the parties expect of insurance carried out in an ethic of cooperation?

First, of course, there is the established common law requirement of 'good faith as disclosure'—mostly that of applicants and policyholders whenever their insurer has to make a decision.[110] Secondly, insurers should, as many now do, offer not only cover but also advice to reduce risk and promote the prevention of loss.[111] Thirdly, when claims are settled, cooperation demands speed rather than sloth because policyholders usually need the money so much more than insurers. The slow and suspicious scrutiny of claims, which occurs sometimes today,[112] is essentially non-cooperative and subtractive, and should cease. This, of course, is what is prescribed already by the FOS. At the same time, the ethic of cooperation does not require insurers to sacrifice the interests of their shareholders. The short-term financial gains from a tough attitude to claims has been at the expense of longer-term interests which, it has been argued, are better promoted by longer-term relationships.[113] Usually it costs less to indulge existing customers and keep them as customers than to save in the short term by savaging claims—but then lose the customer and have to spend more than the money thus saved to attract another customer in place of the first.

Enforcement of the Regulations

Evidently, it is open to consumers to plead the unfairness of their policy terms before a court. Past experience, however, is that those who use unfair terms are not going to tell consumers about their rights under the regime. If they do find out, suppliers, insurers or others, will insist that 'nobody has complained before' and that their terms are fair, thus raising a prospect of litigation that is likely to deter all but the most determined consumer.

With this in view, Article 7 of the Directive provides that Member States shall ensure that 'adequate and effective means exist to prevent the continued use of unfair terms'. What are envisaged are measures to prevent sellers and suppliers ignoring particular decisions against particular terms or bluffing it out with consumers. Measures may include measures of criminal law but, in addition, Article 7 provides that the means of prevention shall include provisions whereby consumers' organizations may start actions in court for decision on whether contractual terms drawn up for general use are unfair.

---

[110] Chapter 4, p. 101 ff; Chapter 6, pp. 200–1.
[111] See Chapter 2, p. 53 ff; Chapter 5, p. 170 ff.   [112] See Chapter 6, p. 244 ff.
[113] See Chapter 6, pp. 209–10.

To implement Article 7 English law has regulation 10(1), whereby it is the duty of the Director General of Fair Trading to consider any complaint that a term is unfair. If he thinks a term unfair, he *may* bring proceedings for an injunction: regulation 12(1). Complaints may also be initiated by 'qualifying bodies' listed in Schedule 1, Part 1 of the Regulations. These are organs of government such as the Director General of Gas Supply. This appears to fall short of the facility for individuals or organizations to initiate proceedings, which the Directive requires.

Self-regulation: Codes

In 1976 it was said with sincerity and conviction that, although a heavy responsibility rested with the intermediary to see that buyers get the type of life insurance best suited to their needs, it 'can be claimed with confidence that there are very few life insurance salesman in this country who fail to discharge this responsibility' and that an applicant for insurance 'can safely entrust his insurance to the representative of whatever company approaches him'.[114] By the 1990s, however, the extensive misselling of personal pensions had become a matter of national concern, because it appeared that many people had been 'advised' to change their pension arrangements contrary to best advice. The *Financial Times*[115] referred to the 'personal pensions fiasco' and pronounced that public confidence in the life insurance companies and banks had been 'severely shaken'. It has not fully recovered since. Even today, some victims of bad advice are still awaiting compensation.

Back in the 1970s, moves to regulate the industry, including the proposal to extend the operation of the Unfair Contract Terms Act 1977 to insurers, were countered with promises of self-regulation. Self-regulation by the industry took the form of various Statements of Insurance Practice (codes) for private lines. Their efficacy has been a matter of dispute. One objection to the codes is that, although the practices as stated are more favourable to policyholders than the general law, they give considerable discretion to insurers and, therefore, create considerable uncertainty in the mind of policyholders about whether, or when, a claim will actually be paid. Another is that, although the industry claims that the codes work well, there is little evidence to support (or contradict) this claim.[116]

Parliament and the FSA

Clearly, insurers do not want more regulation, do not want what they call government 'interference'. Clearly, some people, politicians among them, think that insurers have been left alone too much and for too long. The tradition of many

---

[114] H. Cockerell, *Insurance* (London, 1976) 193.   [115] 25 March 1994.

[116] A small-scale survey some years back suggested otherwise: I. Cadogan and R. Lewis, 'Do Insurers Know Best ?' (1992) 21 Anglo-Am L Rev 123–37. For the position today, see Chapter 3, p. 60 ff.

other countries, the United States, France, and Germany among them, has been one of control: notably, standard terms for domestic fire insurance and premiums which have to be approved by a State authority. In contrast, much 'law' in England is made by the insurer's own standard form, so it is important that it be 'democratic'—with the genuine agreement of both parties—but in practice it is not.[117] In practice, it is a kind of commercial 'subsidiarity', but an imposition of rules nonetheless, a one-sided contract.

Against the possibility of 'undemocratic' abuse, the law has developed rules of interpretation which tend to favour policyholders[118] and, more recently, provided for judicial intervention against unfair terms under the Unfair Terms in Consumer Contract Regulations.[119] Some say that this is sufficient, but others believe that, for example, 'consumer insurance contracts represent the abyss of exploitation permitted by free markets'.[120] On the merits of this debate this book has little to say. However, it does seem likely that sooner rather than later, insurance contract terms will receive at least 'light touch' regulation by the FSA. Any regulation of insurance must have bounds, and one of those must be some kind of definition of insurance, a thorny question with which the FSA has been wrestling for some time, and which this book addresses in the final chapter.[121]

The Role of the Courts

Judges have a significant role in the control of contract terms by the way they interpret and apply them. In so far as the process requires the court to seek the purpose of terms it may be value driven; however, on the whole interpretation is a technical exercise for which judges are well qualified. Judges may also have a more subjective and unscripted role when the words of a contract confront public policy. Insurance can be used for unlawful ends. The main example in the distant past was insurance as a vehicle for gambling, and the law intervened with general rule requiring insurable interest.[122] Then as now, if a wife poisons her husband she should not expect to collect on his life insurance. Other cases are less straightforward. They include those of liability for conduct that is uninsurable, such as brawling or wounding other people with firearms.[123] Courts may be called upon to draw lines in the sands of public policy, and this cannot be done without some sense of direction. Neither can it be done definitively in advance by Parliament; sands and lines shift. Questions arise. What exactly is the role of the court in this connection? What is it trying to achieve? What is it able to achieve?

---

[117] D. S. Slawson, 'Standard Form Contracts and Democratic Control of Lawmaking Power', 84 Harv LR 529–66, 530 (1971); and the Symposium 'Boilerplate Contracts', 104 Mich L Rev 821–1246 (2006).   [118] See Chapter 5, p. 139 ff.
[119] Above, p. 268 ff.
[120] H. Collins, 'Good Faith in European Contract Law' (1994) 14 OJLS 229–54, 242.
[121] See Chapter 9, p. 347 ff.   [122] Chapter 1, p. 36 ff.   [123] Above, p. 255 ff.

Social Engineering

A common assumption is that the court, in its decision whether to enforce a contract, should not lose sight of the effect of enforcement on society at large. For example, if the smuggler of beer from Boulogne crashes his van, the court may ask whether non-enforcement of his motor insurance is an appropriate form of social censure or retribution? An affirmative answer has attractions, but if the van did not belong to the smuggler, or a passing postman was injured in the accident, not enforcing the insurance loses some of its attraction. When the van is his, what the court may well ask itself is whether enforcement of the insurance will encourage bad behaviour of this kind in future? The sooner the smuggler can pay to repair his van, the sooner he can get back on the road to Boulogne, but, even so, it is clear that it will be enforced in favour of the injured postman.[124] If, however, the question is turned around and becomes whether non-enforcement will discourage bad behaviour of this kind, not only by this policyholder but also by others who might use vehicles for breaking the law, non-enforcement by the court becomes more likely.

One objection to all this is that social engineering, whether aimed at retribution or deterrence, is the role of the criminal court in criminal proceedings and not that of the civil court in a civil case about insurance.[125] Generally, the civil courts do not set out to punish people, because litigation in the civil courts lacks the evidential and procedural safeguards developed for the protection of offenders by the law of criminal procedure.[126] The Law Commission questioned whether that really matters when the liberty of the subject is not at risk.[127] However, in a subsequent Report it noted that in the past the availability of the punitive remedy of exemplary damages had been strictly constrained, and recommended that the availability of exemplary damages should be expanded but, at the same time, made subject to significant limitations.[128]

The main objection to social engineering by the court, however, is different: it is that retribution is pointless and that, generally, non-enforcement as deterrence simply does not work. Can it really be supposed that a cheated husband, inflamed by jealousy and half a bottle of wine, when warned that he may lose his liability cover, will be deterred from assaulting the other man?[129] Or that a bank robber who is undeterred by the prospect of ten years in prison for inflicting injury will, given a similar warning, be deterred from endangering the policeman who is clinging to the get-away car?

---

[124] See above, pp. 259–60.
[125] E.g., J. Shand, 'Unblinkering the Unruly Horse: Public Policy in the Law of Contract' [1972A] CLJ 144–67, 154.
[126] The issue was debated in the House of Lords in *Broome v Cassell* [1972] AC 1027.
[127] Consultation Paper No. 132, 'Aggravated Exemplary and Restitutionary Damages' (London, 1993) para. 5.32.   [128] Report No. 247 (December 1997) para. 2.40.
[129] Cf. *Gray v Barr*, below, p. 278.

If deterrence is to be a factor at all, it cannot be a primary objective of the court's decision but just one of several strands of public policy to be considered. When deciding whether to enforce a contract, the enforcement of which may have socially undesirable effects, the court, it has been said, must weigh the gravity of the anti-social act and the extent to which it will be encouraged by enforcement against the social harm which will be caused if the contract is not enforced.[130] On one side of the scales the court puts factors for non-enforcement: the encouragement/deterrence factor and also the gravity of the bad behaviour. For example, murder matters more than most other kinds of mischief. On the other side, for enforcement, first, there is sanctity of contract. Society can function only if promises are kept: a central but sometimes forgotten principle of public policy is that, in general, insurance contracts, like other contracts, should be enforced. Secondly, there are the consequences that non-enforcement may have for third parties. In cases of liability insurance, for example, the court will consider carefully the need to compensate victims which, in many cases, will not be fully achieved unless the insurance is enforced.

Clearly, this is a difficult role for the court to play.[131] To a degree the debate has now lost currency: deterred perhaps by the difficulty of answering questions of this kind, in recent insurance cases the court has declined to enter the debate, and retreated to the wings and sought to push Parliament centre stage.[132] The decision is one for Parliament and not for the court. However, the broader questions remain to be answered. Is this undue modesty on the part of the judges? Are courts qualified and equipped to decide cases raising issues of public policy of this kind? Intellectually, of course, but there are nonetheless some problems to be solved before an affirmative answer can be given.

The Problem of Information

In 1824, Burrough J, in words that have been his memorial, said that public policy is a very unruly horse and that you never know where it will carry you.[133] We do not know whether he meant that judges are not properly trained for the task, or that they lack directions, or perhaps both. In 1971, Lord Denning, another judge of many memorable sayings, said that, with a good man in the saddle, it is a horse that can be kept in control; it can leap the fences put up by fictions and come down on the side of justice.[134] The trick, of course, is to ensure that the judge is 'a good man in the saddle', that he or she knows what he or she is doing.

---

[130] This is the so-called 'public conscience test': see above, p. 257.
[131] See the lament of Lord Devlin, quoted above, pp. 259–60.
[132] See above, pp. 259–60.
[133] *Richardson v Mellish* (1824) 2 Bing 229, 252.
[134] *Enderby Town FC v FA* [1971] 1 Ch 591, 606–7 (CA).

Riding Unruly Horses

If public policy is to be applied by judges, everyone agrees that it must be applied by judges not according to their own views of public policy, but according to precedent, unless, of course, they see no precedent. If indeed there is no precise precedent, in the past that was not perceived as a serious difficulty, according to Lord Roche in 1927, because although 'their applications may be infinitely various from time to time and from place to place', the principles of public policy are no more than 'a branch of the principles of ethics' and 'are themselves unchanging'.[135] But can judges today be so confident? Many values widely held in 1927 have been challenged. Public policy on many issues has been obscured by a penumbra of uncertainty, which is beyond the reach of either precedent or the principles of ethics, and which may have as much to do with economics, for example, as with ethics. The principles of economics are not beyond dispute, neither, like ethics, are they something with which judges can be expected to be fully familiar. How much does this matter?

Neither ethics nor economics are necessary to know that murder is bad for people. Significantly, perhaps, many of the main precedents for the public conscience test concern motor insurance; in these cases, the problem was relatively simple, and in the end the compensation factor was dominant. The main case is *Gardner v Moore*,[136] in which M had a row with G and deliberately drove his van at him. G was seriously injured and would have been uncompensated unless the insurance was enforced, which it was *for that reason*. That was in 1984, but, as we have seen,[137] in 2001 *Charlton v Fisher*[138] declined to address what is sometimes a difficult question to answer. It was enough that Parliament had spoken by making motor insurance compulsory in such a case or not.[139] However, a review of liabilities for which insurance is compulsory reveals some striking anomalies.[140] Insurance is compulsory for mayhem inflicted by motor car or wild animals, but not injury or damage done by speed boats and jet skis or (more common) domestic dogs. The courts have passed the hot potato to Parliament, but Parliament has shown no inclination to deal with it. A coherent social policy does not exist.

Contrast *Gray v Barr*,[141] decided in 1971. The angry policyholder (recklessly) killed his wife's lover with a shotgun, but his liability insurance was not enforced on grounds of public policy. Crimes of violence with guns, said the Court of Appeal, were one of the curses of the age, and the public interest demanded that they should be deterred. Motor insurance, said the Court, was different. Today a court would reach the same conclusion, but not for that reason but for that given in *Charlton v Fisher*: liability insurance to cover shooting neighbours (or anyone else)

---

[135] *James v British General Ins. Co.* [1927] 2 KB 311, 322, *per* Roche J.
[136] [1984] AC 548.   [137] Above, pp. 259–60.
[138] Op. cit. above, n. 18.   [139] Ibid., at [9].
[140] See R. K. Lewis, 'When you must insure' (2004) 154 NLJ 1474.
[141] Op. cit. above, n. 27.

is not compulsory. Be that as it may, what was the evidence of public interest in *Gray*? Why, for example, is the man who spreads his tormentor's brains over the stairs with a shotgun so much more of a threat to society than the man in *Gardner v Moore*, who sought to spread his victim over the pavement with a van? Did the court believe—and if so, on what basis—that deterrence worked better on angry husbands than on angry motorists? Or that women widowed by road rage should be compensated more readily than those whose husbands had been shot? *Gray* gives no answers. We do know from government records of the time—but apparently the Court did not—that for every homicidal shooting at the time of *Gray*, there were about twenty cases of death caused by reckless or dangerous driving.

The judges in *Gray* were condemned by a leading Australian commentator as being 'unequal to the heady challenge' of public policy. The decision in *Gray* may indeed have been unfair to the widow, but the comment from Australia was unfair to the judges. The English legal system is not well geared to getting information, such as government statistics, to the court—not now and even less so then. Judges have to decide cases and do their best with the information that they have got. In the greater legal Europe, it is difficult enough, even with counsel before the court and CD-ROMs on the bench, to trawl current English law for precedent. How much further must the court go? The realms of comparative law? Economics? Sociology?

The answer, it seems, is 'sometimes', when material is accessible. For example, in the past, disputes over restraint of trade have been resolved according to the 'interests of the parties'—but for the simple and sensible reason that the parties get an opportunity to participate in argument to the court about their own interests, and any differences are justiciable. In the result, the judgments carry conviction. Occasionally, however, restraint cases have been grounded less on the interests of the parties than on the interest of the public at large. In 1967, the House of Lords dealt with tied garages, and spoke with the confidence and conviction that came, to a degree at least, from the coincidence of a recent report on the matter by the Monopolies Commission.[142] Later, in a case about restraints in the record industry,[143] however, the House of Lords did not have that advantage; it lacked the relevant data and, it has been plausibly argued,[144] reached the wrong decision. In other areas too, judicial resort to economic arguments has left judges open to the accusation of insufficient learning.[145] This may be why in a later restraint case in the High Court requiring, as the judge put it, the balancing of a mass of conflicting economic, social, and other interests which a court of law might be ill-adapted to achieve, 'interests of the public at large would lack sufficiently

---

[142] *Esso Petroleum Co. Ltd v Harper's Garage (Stourport) Ltd* [1968] AC 269.
[143] *Schroeder Music Publishing Co. Ltd v Macaulay* [1974] 1 WLR 1308 (HL).
[144] M. J. Trebilcock, 'The Doctrine of Inequality of Bargaining Power' (1976) 26 U Toronto LJ 359–85.
[145] E.g., Lord Hoffmann in *Stovin v Wise* ([1996] AC 923), concerning whether liability should be imposed on public authorities for impaired visibility on highways caused by obstructions. See B. S. Markesinis, 'Judicial Style and Judicial Reasoning' [2000] CLJ 294–309, 302 ff.

specific formulation to be capable of judicial as contrasted with unregulated personal decision and application'.[146] As Lord Goff once put it: 'Humility is perhaps too much to ask of judges; but a reasonable degree of modesty, or at least diffidence, should be part of the judicial job specification.'[147] Once on the job, however, can judges be trained to cope? And should they be?

Gone is the golden age in which an elderly law professor did not read new cases but, nonetheless, could say grandly to his Cambridge students, 'you tell me about the cases and I shall tell you about the principles'. Detail can be tedious but, tedious or not, today it cannot be ignored. We cannot, like Canute, order back the tide of information and bury Lexis or Westlaw in the sand. People expect judges to be wise—not only in the law but also in other matters, not only in the generalities but also in the detail. Outside the High Court lurk journalists who know that they can sell copy by knocking judges. Judges are not well placed to answer back, but can they at least get better information on which to reach their decisions?

In the United States, the justices of the Supreme Court have clerks to do research. There are moves to provide judges with legal assistants in Australia, Canada, and New Zealand, but not in England, and not even in the House of Lords until relatively recently. There, it has been for the insufficient reason that there was insufficient space, but there are more serious objections. First, of course, there is the inevitable objection of cost. Secondly, clerks on the American model are trained in law, and that may not be enough. For example, even in the USA it has been claimed that 'the parties to an insurance contract are generally in better positions than courts to determine which party is the better risk avoider'.[148] Thirdly, it is fundamental to the English tradition that any opinion formed by judges from their own research, or that of their assistants, would have to be subjected to the scrutiny and the argument of counsel.

The Role of Counsel

Sometimes, as Lord Mustill once admitted, courts state a principle in terms which conceal the fact that the process of deciding on liability begins with an answer which is largely intuitive, and reasons backwards from it.[149] That is one reason why, according to Sir Robert Megarry, justice requires 'the purifying ordeal of skilled argument on the specific facts of a contested case' as 'a safety measure against the peril of the judge who yields to preconceptions'.[150] Counsel have an essential role in the adversary system, 'in which opposing theories are propounded

---

[146] Ungoed-Thomas J in *Texaco Ltd v Mulberry Filling Station Ltd* [1972] 1 WLR 814, 827. More recently in this sense, see Hoffman J in *Morgan Crucible Co. plc v Hill Samuel & Co. Ltd* [1991] Ch 295, 303. Cf Markesinis and Fedtke, 'The Judge as Comparatist', 80 Tul L Rev 11–167, 127 ff. (2005).

[147] 'The Search for Principle', *Proceedings of the British Academy 1984*, 169–87, 175.

[148] Miller, op. cit. above, n. 77, 1863.   [149] (1992) 5 Supreme Court Journal 1, 10–11.

[150] *Cordell v Second Clanfield Properties* [1969] 2 Ch 9, 16.

and debated by advocates on behalf of real clients in whose interests they act', which 'is more likely to reveal the strengths and weaknesses of conflicting arguments than the solitary ruminations of a scholar in the quietness of his study'.[151]

A second role of counsel is to be the voice of their clients. Many people, two-thirds of the population according to a study published by the Nuffield Foundation in late 1999, believe that judges are out of touch with the concerns of ordinary people. The response of Lord Woolf was to blame 'irresponsible media reporting'.[152] Even so, people go to court, and those who did were more favourable in their answers to the Nuffield research than those who did not. People go to court partly because they think that the judges will listen and reach a decision on the basis of argument—argument chosen and prepared by counsel, their counsel.[153] The decision, any decision, is likely to be more acceptable to those who have had their say than to those who have not. To the extent that the decision is influenced by considerations on which counsel has not been able to comment, whether the influence of bribes (not here an issue) or of the private research or the personal values of the judge, the litigant is excluded from the process of adjudication unless, of course, the research or values are exposed to rational comment by counsel.

At the same time, it follows from arguments of that kind that the court must support its statements with reasons and, when appropriate, with references, and even statistics. Otherwise parties cannot be sure that their involvement in the decision has been real, or that the court has actually understood and taken into account their arguments.[154] This brings us back to the quality of the arguments and of the information on which the decision is based. A third role of counsel, it seems, is that of researcher, the source and channel of the information, legal and more. But, if so, where do they stop? Indeed, where do they start?

In the first century AD, Quintilian said to fellow advocates that they must 'not always burden the judge with all the arguments we have discovered, since by so doing we shall at once bore him and render him less inclined to believe us'.[155] In some ways some things do not change. Counsel can scarcely be blamed for not commissioning research on the economic implications of a case if there is little or no chance that it will be heeded by the court. So, if research is to come through counsel, in some measure, the initiative must come from the court. Indeed, in his report in 1996,[156] Lord Woolf recommended more case management by the court. It is the court that should now indicate what expert evidence should be brought. This brings us back to the judges—not as researchers themselves, but as directors of research.

---

[151] Lord Goff, op. cit. above, n. 147, 184–5.   [152] *Guardian*, 19 November 1999.
[153] See, e.g., L. L. Fuller, 'The Forms and Limits of Adjudication' 92 Harv L Rev 353–409, 364 (1978).   [154] Ibid., 388.
[155] *Institutio oratoria*, Y, 12, 8.
[156] The Rt Hon. Lord Woolf, *Access to Justice* (London, 1996).

Exhorted by successive occupants of the Woolsack to cut the time and cost of days in court, however, judges hesitate to commission research: research takes time and money, and it is often hard to predict how far it must go and how long it will take.

> The information you have is not the information you want.
> The information you want is not the information you need.
> The information you need is not the information you can obtain.
> The information you can obtain costs more than you want to pay.[157]

Moreover, some thoughtful observers have dared to ask whether counsel are the right people to do research of a kind for which some will have no taste and many will have no experience.[158] To that, of course, the answer is that research may be commissioned by counsel and does not have to be carried through by counsel.

In the United States it is common for *amicus* briefs, some of high quality, to be put before the Supreme Court on the initiative not of the Court but of outside bodies concerned about the decision. They are welcomed by the Court not only for their content, but also because of the prominent role of the Court in the democracy of the country, and the associated feeling that briefs allow ordinary citizens to express their views to the Court of what the law should be.[159] A good case has been made for an institutional *amicus* in England,[160] but to date the courts do not have that kind of technical support.

Even if the right advice is available or the right research has been conducted, it must still be put before the court. As we have seen, the expert evidence must be available for comment by counsel. Moreover, expert evidence in writing is rarely intelligible by persons outside the 'knowledge', without the opportunity to ask questions of the expert, without dialogue; it must be distilled, focused, and brought to bear on the case. Concern has been expressed, for example, about the way in which scientific evidence is presented to, and assessed and used by, the courts.[161] However, the European Science and Environment Forum,[162] an independent, non-profit-making alliance of scientists based in Cambridge, is concerned to counter 'junk science'. It states that its mission is to ensure that scientific debates are properly aired, and that decisions which are taken, and action that is proposed, are founded on sound scientific principles, not least (but not only) in the courts. It is particularly concerned to address issues where it appears that the public and their representatives, and those in the media, are being given misleading or one-sided advice.

Since the Woolf reforms the tendency is to appoint single experts in place of the 'hired guns', experts on each side who were there to say what the parties

---

[157] Bernstein, 202.
[158] P. Birks, 'Adjudication and Interpretation in the Common Law: A Century of Change' (1994) 14 LS 156–79, 170; B. S. Markesinis, 'A Matter of Style' (1994) 110 LQR 607–28, 622.
[159] P. L. Bryden, 'Public Interest Intervention in the Courts', 66 Can Bar Rev 490–526 (1987).
[160] D. R. O'May, 'Marine Insurance Law: Can the Lawyers be Trusted?' [1987] LMCLQ 29–42, 36.
[161] G. Edmond, 'Judicial Representations of Scientific Evidence' (2000) 63 MLR 216–51.
[162] www.scienceforum.net.

wanted to hear. Obviously, that makes the right choice of expert more important than before. It is not reassuring to read in the *Financial Times*[163] that with 'persistent and high profile failings, the impartiality and professionalism of expert witnesses—who can often charge up to £1,500 a day—has come into question'. One of the allegations was that experts have yet to understand that their duty is not to one or other of the parties but to the court. Moreover, they must be not only objective and truly expert, but also intelligible. As every teacher knows, the most learned are not always the most comprehensible.

In the United States, the Supreme Court can cope with the volume and quality of information because the information is first vetted and filtered by the clerks paid to assist members of the Court. The English judge has none of this. English judges are mostly men and women who have succeeded at the Bar and are, therefore, among the best of those who show an astonishing ability to absorb new information for the case in hand, to master any brief. If anyone can cope with new information it must be the English judge. Even so, it seems that the volume of information now is such that, whether or not the *amicus* brief is allowed, the judge is faced with what society is now calling 'information overload'. Judges face problems both of time and of training.

The Role of Judges

The training and qualification of a judge 'is to elucidate the problem immediately before him, so that its features stand out in stereoscopic clarity', and that

is why judicial advance should be gradual. 'I am not trained to see the distant scene: one step enough for me' should be the motto on the wall opposite the judge's desk. It is, I concede, a less spectacular method of progression than somersaults and cartwheels; but is the one best suited to the capacity and resources of a judge. We are likely to perform better the duties society imposes on us if we recognise our limitations.[164]

Thus spoke Lord Simon, nearly thirty years ago, but it is still true today.

The duties of care in tort, for example, have been developed in recent years not by reference to broad principles or goals, but 'incrementally' and with strict regard to 'traditional categories' of case. As Lord Goff put it once, England is 'inhabited by a people temperamentally inclined, perhaps climatically conditioned, to a philosophy of gradualism'.[165] In a leading case on property law and contract law,[166] for example, a 'public-conscience test' was rejected by the House of Lords because it was imponderable and because it gave too much discretion to the judge. Lest Homer should nod, it is, as Aristotle observed, best 'that everything should, as far as possible, be determined absolutely by the laws, and as little as possible left to the discretion of the judges'.[167] Most judges prefer, it seems, to fall

---

[163] 1 December 2003.   [164] *Miliangos v George Frank (Textiles) Ltd* [1976] AC 443, 481–2.
[165] Op. cit. above, n. 147, 169.   [166] *Tinsley v Milligan* [1994] 1 AC 340. Above, p. 259.
[167] *The Rhetoric* (trans. Welldon) Bk I, ch. 1.

back on the black-letter rules in which they were trained, with which they feel comfortable, and into which public policy, economics, and the rest do not come. Is that due modesty, or undue caution?

In 1625, Francis Bacon exclaimed that judges should be 'more learned than witty' and 'more advised than confident'.[168] Today, their wit is not an issue; but ours is an age of continuing education. Should something be done about their learning and, at the same time perhaps, even for their confidence? The Judicial Studies Board does excellent work, but is short of money and other resources; and judges are short of time. High Court judges are not obliged to attend sessions arranged by the Board, and not many do. Lord Mansfield developed the law of marine insurance from his own knowledge of Continental practice and custom, much of it acquired by his own personal and professional contact with merchants and underwriters. Something of this tradition survives. In a jurisdiction where most judges once practised at the Bar, the feeling is that judges know what business people want, without having to ask.[169] They have dealt with these people as clients and learned their ways. But even if that is true of the mysteries of commerce and finance, the horse of public policy is not confined to the City, and a wider range of expertise may be required of the court. For many years the court has had power to appoint an expert to carry out investigation and research and to present a report, not only at the request of a party but also on its own initiative; however, the procedure has not proved popular.[170] Moreover, for many years the court has had power to press the parties to agree on a single expert report in writing[171] rather than a brains trust competition in open court. Only recently, under the Woolf reforms, has this been practice rather than theory.

Until judges are given the time and the incentive to learn, and the assistance to marshal the flow of information, the conclusion must be that litigation will not be the best framework for research; the drawings for the social plan must be done somewhere else. Collins has argued that 'contractual behavior' should be seen and ultimately interpreted with not one but three points of reference, the others being sociology and economics.[172] In an ideal world he would be right. However, as critics have concluded, the 'project fails because it demands of judges skills and knowledge that no human could muster' and 'because the information [needed] is not available in the easily accessible form that is required'.[173] Certain

---

[168] *Essays* (1625), LVI, 'Of judicature'.

[169] Staughton LJ, 'Good Faith and Fairness in Commercial Contract Law' (1994) 7 JCL 193–6, 194.

[170] J. A. Jolowicz, *On Civil Procedure* (Cambridge, 2000) 229. The author then considers the more popular institution of *technicien* found in France, a person employed (only) when a case raises technical questions which the judge cannot resolve without assistance, and who is more like a judge, part of the court, than a witness.

[171] Ibid., 237. Notwithstanding the Woolf reforms, Prof. Jolowicz suggests (p. 239 ff.) that we might learn from the French system.

[172] H. Collins, *Regulating Contracts* (Oxford, 1999) 128 ff.

[173] J. Gava and J. Greene, 'Do we need a Hybrid Law of Contract?' [2004] CLJ 605–31, 630.

issues affecting public policy—those with the widest implications for the largest number of people—are often (but not always) those that take the case beyond the proper limits of adjudication. In such cases, it is not reasonable to expect either the parties or their counsel to undertake an investigation and to seek solutions, work best done in, or for, Parliament. Until that occurs, however, the cases will still come to the courts. The judges still have to decide them. What are they to do?

The Response of the Courts

In *Tinsley v Milligan*,[174] the House of Lords rejected the public conscience test, which would have given discretion to judges in matters of public policy, in favour of an older and uncompromising principle of Lord Mansfield: 'No court will lend its aid to a man who founds his cause of action upon an immoral or an illegal act.'[175] This principle offers a more modest and more defined basis for refusing to enforce insurance contracts. The underlying idea is that the court, conscious of the need to keep its hands clean, does not want to be seen to assist policyholders with remedial measures to use their insurance to profit from their wrongdoing. Unlike the public-conscience test, this is a workable rule, which requires the court only to handle lawyers' law, to find the facts, and apply rules of deduction.

If the wrongdoing is murder, for example, the victim's life insurance has always been enforced except to the extent that the insurance money finds its way to the murderer or the murderer's estate. In *Davitt v Titcumb*,[176] the defendant bought a house with a mortgage secured by life insurance on himself and his partner. When he murdered his partner, the insurance money on her life went to the innocent mortgagee. The house was then sold to pay off the small balance due to the mortgagee and other debts, leaving a considerable surplus. But for the murder, there would have been no insurance money and no surplus, to which, held the court, the defendant was not entitled: he must not be enabled to profit from his wrong.

If the wrongdoing concerns property, theft, or smuggling, for example, the principle is the same, although it is sometimes less easy to apply. In *Geismar*,[177] insured jewellery, on which the duty payable had not been paid, was stolen. The insurance claim failed, not because enforcement would assist the claimant to obtain a profit—his profit had been made already when he brought back the jewellery without paying duty—but because the court would not assist him to keep it. As long as he had the jewellery, it might have been seized by the customs authority; but once it was transmuted into insurance money, it was beyond its

---

[174] [1994] 1 AC 340. Above, p. 259.
[175] *Holman v Johnson* (1773) 1 Cowp 341, 343, quoted by Lord Goff, op. cit. above, n. 174, at 360.
[176] [1990] Ch 110.   [177] *Geismar v Sun Alliance & London Ins. Ltd* [1978] 1 QB 386.

grasp. If, however, the claimant had sold the jewellery and used the money to buy jade, insurance on the jade would have been enforced. The lesson of *Geismar* is that the clean hands of the court may have to handle clean money that once was dirty; but the court cannot be expected actually to launder it.

If the wrongdoing is a tort, as we have seen,[178] the court today enforces insurance contracts only in cases of compulsory liability insurance. The court does not assist policyholders to make a profit, but it does reduce their loss. Although they are no better off than they were before their crime, they are still less badly off than they would have been after the crime because, to take a simple case like *Gardner*,[179] the driver's liability to his victim has been discharged by the insurance. What counts is the role of the court, which is less one of assisting a wrongful design than of compensating a victim. Moreover, if the wrongdoer profits, it is not from the crime but from the insurance. Thus, it seems, Lord Mansfield's uncompromising principle against aiding a man whose cause of action is founded on illegality has not been compromised. As regards the courts, consciences are clear and hands are clean.

Even so, in cases like that people might say that the effect of enforcing the insurance was that the wrongdoer 'got off lightly'. In a sense he did, but he did not 'get off' punishment; he went on to prison. The insurance paid his debt to the victim but not his debt to society. That is something that insurance is not allowed to do. A distinction has been drawn between insurance of civil liability to the victim, which may be enforced, and insurance to cover the penalties of the criminal law, whether in money or in kind, which are not.[180]

The distinction is clear in principle, but in practice it may be difficult to draw. Between penalties, on the one hand, and civil damages, on the other, are exemplary damages. The Court of Appeal has held that an award of damages made up both of compensation damages and exemplary damages can be covered by insurance.[181] The Court did not have to decide whether exemplary damages could be covered as a separate item of cover, and that is a question that remains open. Another marginal case is 'mobility cover'. For many motorists the most serious consequence of motoring convictions is the possibility of disqualification. Currently this can be covered as just one part of 'mobility cover', which provides policyholders with a driver or the cost of alternative transport in the event of their inability to drive a vehicle, whether because they have lost a leg or their licence. If the purpose of disqualification is simply to protect the public from a bad driver, the cover is unobjectionable, but if, as it is generally perceived, the purpose is to be part of the punishment, the cover is surely difficult to justify.

---

[178] Above, pp. 259–60.   [179] Ibid.
[180] *Askey v Golden Wine Co. Ltd* (1948) 64 TLR 379, 380; but cf. *Osman v J. Ralph Moss Ltd* [1970] 1 Lloyd's Rep 313 (CA).
[181] *Lancashire CC v Municipal Mutual Ins. Ltd* [1997] QB 897.

Insurance Law and Society

As we have just seen, the law is not well suited to be a negative instrument of public policy. It is more useful in a more positive role, to assist the social aims of insurance, and among the possibilities are fairness (below) and economic efficiency.

Economic Efficiency and Subrogation

The goal of economic efficiency has been called in question, *inter alia*, because maximizing aggregate wealth does not guarantee more aggregate utility,[182] but that is not our immediate concern. Efficiency has been a declared object of the free market economy and the immediate question is the role of insurance law in that context.[183] Even the meaning of 'economic efficiency' is a matter of debate, but it must suffice here to say that it is achieved when people use resources in the way which is most valuable to them. It is often assumed, however, that people bargain with each other in a world of zero transaction costs, where there is no allocation of risks by law, so as to maximize the joint value of their resources. In these terms insurance is efficient at the lowest combined cost of insurance and of loss prevention.

Students in lodgings may well find that it is cheaper, and thus more efficient, to buy a good lock for the door of their room than to pay for contents cover. If a student pays pay £20 for a lock rather than £160 for the lowest level of cover available, that leaves £140 for cakes and ale or the replacement of anything which, in spite of the lock, may be stolen while the student is at the pub. Alternatively, students may find that their parents are seen as a 'better' risk by insurers and are quoted lower premiums; so, in theory at least, they will take a free ride on their parents' insurance, spending some of the notional £160 on locks and alarms.

In both cases, insurance law can assist by seeing that, as far as possible, the parties have the information needed to make an efficient decision. This means, for example, that insurers must have the information needed to rate the risks accurately and cheaply, and that applicants understand the terms available which, of course, usually they do not.[184] In practice, perfectly informed contracting parties do not exist. For students, who spurn insurance, the law can do little. For parents, who do buy insurance, the law can help by reducing transaction costs, notably by offering a good legal framework for contracting and for claims, and by enforcing the relevant contract terms.

---

[182] W. P. J. Wils, 'Insurance Risk Classification in the EC' (1994) 14 OJLS 449–67, 455.
[183] See also Chapter 8, p. 322.   [184] Chapter 5, p. 145 ff.

When insurance is efficient, its function is to spread loss. This is not an immediate concern of the law; however, one problem concerns whether law which allows subrogation actually impairs that function. The function of subrogation is twofold.[185] The first is to preserve the principle of indemnity.[186] If insurer U compensates policyholder A for the damage to A's car by the careless driving of X, but then finds that A has also been compensated by X, the law of subrogation enables U to recover from A to the extent that A has been over-indemnified. The second function is to allow U, once U has compensated A for the damage to the car, to exercise any rights that A has against X[187]—in that case, to claim in A's name against X in tort.

The first function of subrogation, to preserve the underlying principle of indemnity, could be achieved in other ways. For example, A might be required to claim as much as possible from X before claiming from U. This alternative has been rejected because the burden of recovery, litigation perhaps, is one that U is usually better able to bear than A and is something that A wants to avoid; indeed, to avoid having to seek indemnity in court is one of the main reasons for buying insurance at all.

The first function of subrogation, to preserve the underlying principle of indemnity, could also be achieved by reducing the amount that A could get from X by the amount of the insurance money that A could be expected to get from U. This alternative has also been rejected. The courts recoiled from the idea that the providence of victim A, in buying insurance, should relieve wrong-doer X of the burden of damages.[188] Moreover, that would remove any incentive for U to proceed against X, and thus impair one aspect of the second function of subrogation, that people like X should be punished by being made to pay. Perceptions of punishment, however, usually premise that the punishment should match the 'crime'. So, inevitably it must seem a bit bizarre that a wrongdoer's liability varies according to whether victim A is rich or poor, whether A's car is a Bentley or a Brabant; and no less bizarre, surely, if X's liability also depends on the chance of whether A is insured, so that X is let off the hook in the one case (more likely in prosperous communities) but not in the other.

The subrogation rules are regarded as based in equity both in England[189] and in other countries of common law, such as the USA, where one of the federal courts gave 'three equitable reasons' for the doctrine of subrogation:

(1) that the person who in good faith pays the debt or obligation of another has equitably purchased (quasi-contractually), or at least is entitled to, the obligation owed by the debtor or tortfeasor (2) that the third party (tortfeasor) is not entitled to a windfall release

---

[185] Generally, see Clarke, ch. 31.

[186] *Castellain v Preston* (1883) 11 QBD 380, 387 (CA). See Chapter 6, p. 220 ff.

[187] Ibid. See also *Caledonian North Sea Ltd v London Bridge Engineering Ltd* [2002] 1 Lloyd's Rep 553 (HL), at [11].   [188] *Bradburn v GWR* (1874) LR 10 Exch 1, 2.

[189] *Napier v Hunter* [1993] AC 713.

from his obligation simply because the injured party had the foresight to obtain insurance and (3) that public policy is served by allowing insurers to recover and thus reduce insurance rates generally.[190]

Doubt has arisen about the efficiency of the third proposition, that is, the second function of subrogation: to allow U to exercise any rights that A has against X. The loss has been moved in the direction of U and the loss insurance pool, so why redirect it to X and, if X's liability is insured with Y, to Y and Y's pool? To many people, this seems to be a costly and inefficient way of spreading loss. An entertaining illustration is Weir's discussion of a celebrated action in subrogation:

Shortly after Mr Murphy's house in Brentwood settled, so did his insurance company . . . Murphy was happy enough with the £35,000 it paid him, but [the company] went off to court (with which it is much more familiar than Mr Murphy) and claimed the whole of its payment from Brentwood District Council, allegedly at fault in passing plans for Mr Murphy's house. The company won and the public paid. Now it hardly needs saying (any more) that a local authority does not normally have to pay companies which suffer merely pecuniary loss as a result of their carelessness as the [company] did in this case, and it is hard to imagine anybody less deserving than an insurer who profits from taking the risk that houses may collapse . . . But our absurd law as to subrogation to tort claims means that in such cases the public must bail out our private insurers.[191]

True, to enforce the liability of X has the apparent attraction that wrongdoer X may get something of what he deserves, but is that a concern of the law of insurance?

One part of an affirmative answer is that subrogation allocates costs to the activity to which the damage is attributable, and through X to those who might have benefited from the activity.[192] However, if A is a motorist, A is in the same (or a connected) risk pool, and so it remains a costly and inefficient way of spreading loss.[193] The other part of the answer is that subrogation is a tool of social engineering to implement a theory of deterrence. In theory, the cost of accidents is thus placed upon those who can avoid them most cheaply (the X pool rather than the A pool) and who will be spurred (mainly by higher liability premiums) to avoid them; in other words, the insurance is 'perfectly responsive', that it is 'insurance whose premiums are set so as to exactly relate to the level of risk that insured's own conduct occasions'.[194] This part of the answer is open to a number of objections.

---

[190] *Stafford Metal Works Inc. v Cook Paint & Varnish Co.*, 418 F Supp 56, 58 (ND Tex, 1976).

[191] Tony Weir, 'Government liability' [1989] PL 40–63, 43, concerning *Murphy v Brentwood DC* (1988) 13 Con LR 96, later aff'd [1990] 2 All ER 269 (CA); appeal allowed [1991] 1 AC 378. See also in this sense R. Hasson, 'Subrogation in Insurance Law—A Critical Evaluation' (1985) 5 OJLS 416–38.

[192] As regards personal injury, see e.g., J. Stapleton, *Disease and the Compensation Debate* (Oxford, 1986) 121.

[193] E.g., P. Atiyah, *The Damages Lottery* (Oxford, 1997) ch. 6. USA in this sense: e.g., *Breaking the Litigation Habit*, A Statement by the Committee for Economic Development, (New York, 2000); J. O'Connell, *Accidental Justice: The Dilemmas of Tort Law* (with Peter A. Bell) (New Haven, 1997).

[194] G. T. Schwartz, 'The Ethics and the Economics of Tort Liability Insurance', 75 Cornell L Rev 313–65, 320 (1990).

One objection is that it is doubtful that X will be deterred. In particular, it is not all clear that X will (or should) respond to higher premiums by reducing the amount of dangerous activity (drive less), or pursue it with more care (drive better).[195] Deterrence theory assumes that people behave 'rationally', whereas, arguably, motoring is an activity which, under the influence of powerful advertising, is motivated less by the light of reason than by much darker elements in human nature. Further, if A was damaged not by X's car but by X's product, producer X can simply pass the cost on to its consumers, and thus perhaps back to A; in this situation, evidently, subrogation is wasteful, as well as insensitive to the needs of individuals.[196]

A further objection is that, even if X responds rationally, X may well reason that, in practice, recourse in subrogation is not very likely, and has little effect on premiums anyway. Moreover, insurance is rarely 'perfectly responsive' to the risk of particular policyholders.[197] As a deterrent, it seems that subrogation simply does not work[198] and, therefore, that the law does little service to society by allowing it.

Fairness

Most social institutions work better if the people affected perceive them as fair. The fairness of insurance depends in part on the law. One obvious way of promoting fairness between insurers and buyers of insurance is by having rules of law designed to redress any imbalance of information or of bargaining power between them, both at the stage of contracting insurance[199] and at the stage of settling claims.[200] At first sight, the focus of these rules appears to be fairness between particular parties. But unless some attention is paid to their effect on the rest of society, the cost of fairness may be uncertainty, and thus cost to others in the future—especially in grey and value-ridden areas such as moral hazard.[201]

Classification of Risk

Fairness between insurance buyers in general implies that there should be a fair distribution of the risks insured. The problem here is that people do not agree entirely about the existence of unfairness, whether it concerns insurance or other aspects of wealth, or, when they do agree, what to do about it. The issue cannot

---

[195] This is the position with some other kinds of insurance too; some reasons have been discussed by H. A. Cousy, 'Tort Liability and Liability Insurance: A Difficult Relationship', *Tort and Insurance Law Yearbook* (2001) 18–55, 47 ff.

[196] See J. Stapleton, *Product Liability* (London, 1994) 73 ff., 150 ff., and 205 ff.

[197] See Schwartz, op. cit. above, n. 194, 318 ff., and 337 ff.

[198] Abraham, pp. 154–5; R. Derham, *Subrogation in Insurance Law* (Sydney, 1985) 153.

[199] See Chapter 4, p. 98 ff.   [200] See Chapter 6, p. 228 ff.

[201] See Chapter 7, p. 252 ff.

be avoided, however, because insurers cannot insure risks without classifying them, and any classification must distribute risk. Classification, therefore, raises issues of fairness between the people affected.[202] It is not, however, an issue which is as important as instinct suggests.

First, it is difficult to condemn a classification as unfair without being sure about the causes of the loss in question, and often we are not. A merely statistical correlation between loss and a certain risk 'factor' may be a good ground for insurance classification without being sure ground for any judgement about fairness. For example, if, as it seems, there is a statistical correlation between smokers and road accidents, is it fair to charge smokers more for cover? Secondly, fairness may be too expensive to achieve. Insurers choose risk factors not for their fairness but according to how difficult and how costly it is to get the relevant information and to administer the classification. Most people would agree that people who do not smoke should pay less for life and health insurance, but not many insurers offer a discount of this kind because it is difficult to check that policyholders who say that they do not smoke are telling the truth. The same problem arises with 'life style' underwriting in general. Nor do many people demand discounts of this kind, once the administrative cost and associated effect on premiums is explained to them.

For insurers the best classification is one which enables them to sell insurance profitably. If, on the one hand, insurers were able to assess each individual risk with complete accuracy and state a premium for it, they would put themselves out of business—as insurers; they would still be in business as actuaries, and applicants would pay for the assessment and then self-insure on that basis. Of course, complete accuracy is not possible for most risks, some applicants at least will run for cover in a pool of like risks and buy insurance. If, on the other hand, an insurance pool is too large, that is, the classification of the risk is perceived as being too broad, the effect in some cases is that the good risks pay for the bad risks to such an extent that, eventually, the good risks will react to perceived unfairness, leave the pool, and insure elsewhere ('unravelling').[203] If that happens, the insurer in question will be left with a disproportionate share of bad unprofitable risks ('adverse selection') and will go out of (that kind of) business.

The trick is to classify in a way that convinces enough customers that they are in the 'right' pool; and this tends to more precise classification, smaller pools, and 'niche' marketing, but classification nonetheless. The trend has been made possible by the power, speed, and (ultimately) cheapness of the computer. For example, one house contents insurer uses nineteen different rating factors, including exact geographical location. A corollary of niche classification is that some people cannot find their niche—no insurer wants them at all, or not at a price they can

[202] See Abraham, pp. 19, 64, and 83 ff.; Wils, op. cit. above, n. 182, 456 ff.
[203] Marcus Radetzki, Marian Radetzki, Niklas Juth, *Genes and insurance: ethical, legal and economic issues* (Cambridge, 2003), 4.

afford. In some cases, along comes a specialist insurer and the bad risks are swept
up into a niche of their own; but some are left out, and they, or someone for them,
will call this 'unfair' and 'discriminatory'. Is it?

Discrimination

The primary dictionary meaning of 'discriminate' is 'differentiate' or 'distinguish'.
Those who choose to buy from one vineyard rather than another may be compli-
mented as discriminating. If, however, their choice is criticized, it will not be
because it is unfair but because it is ill-advised. Evidently, discrimination is not
judged in the abstract but with reference to context. Nobody will think it unfair if
an insurer (male) chooses to have sex with a woman rather than a man; but if he
chooses to insure women but not men, that may be seen as unfair. In the context
of insurance some degree of discrimination is inevitable—but is it acceptable?

Anti-discrimination law, which is concerned less with the blameworthiness
of the discriminator than with a remedy for the perceived disadvantage to the
'victim', may say that it is never acceptable; this appears to be the position taken
by the European Court of Justice (ECJ) to direct discrimination that infringes the
Equal Treatment Directive.[204] The Sex Discrimination Act 1975, however, is
more like international law, which allows the differential treatment of groups
when exercised for the welfare of the community as a whole, or when 'just and
reasonable'. Insurance classification satisfies these standards, if it results in an
acceptable distribution of risk.

In 2004, the international insurance industry was faced with a draft Equal
Treatment Directive coming from the European Commission, approved by
the European Parliament, requiring insurers to apply 'gender neutrality' in the
calculation of insurance premiums. Implementation of the Directive would
have required changes in the current UK legislation, section 45 of the Sex
Discrimination Act 1975, which allows gender discrimination effected by reference
to actuarial or other data from a source on which it was reasonable to rely.
Implementation would require, for example, abolition of a long-standing differential whereby women are offered lower premiums for motor insurance.[205]
Indeed one or two insurers only cover women. In a society in which more and
more women run their own cars, often in order to get to work, one must wonder
whether female drivers—or, for that matter, male drivers—would regard any such
change as fair. According to the UK Home Office, men commit about 85 per cent
of all serious motoring offences.[206] Probably we shall never know what women

[204] See E. Ellis, 'The Definition of Discrimination in European Community Sex Equality Law'
(1994) 19 EL Rev 563–80.
[205] As regards the likely effect on annuities, see www.eoc.org.uk, follow 'research', and 'pensions'.
[206] In 2004, an 18-year-old man wishing to drive a Vauxhall Astra would have to pay about
£1,620, whereas a comparable woman would pay £600 less. To lower the premium for men, it has
been said with reference to experience in Canada, would encourage 'boy racers': M. Ross,
www.timesonline.co.uk/legalarchive, 19 October 2004.

drivers think because, after widespread protest by the industry and scepticism at street level throughout the Community, the plan was dropped at the end of 2004. In a society in which the cost of motoring is a sensitive issue, the proposal touched a raw nerve.

Insurance Discrimination

Let us suppose that fire insurer Nero believes that fires are more likely to break out in the houses of first-generation immigrants from Arcadia than in those of other people living in the same area, and charges the Arcadians higher premiums. Will that be perceived by society at large as unfair discrimination?

One group in society may value freedom of contract so highly that it defends the 'right' of Nero to load these people as Nero thinks fit, also pointing out that such underwriting practices promote fairness to other policyholders, in not requiring them to bear in premiums the costs of insuring others in higher risk categories, and also the solvency of insurers, which is in the interest of society at large. The law, they say, should not interfere with underwriters' commercial judgement.

A second group, which values risk spreading, might argue that Arcadian immigrants are less likely than other groups to see the importance of adequate insurance and should be encouraged to insure by being offered lower premiums, to the ultimate benefit of society at large as well as the immediate benefit of the Arcadians.

A third group might also argue for lower premiums, but for a different reason, namely, that Arcadians tend to be poorer than other groups and cheap insurance is a way of redistributing wealth. Studies suggest that it is not an effective method of redistribution,[207] nonetheless, the argument cannot be ignored.

A fourth group might argue for higher premiums for Arcadians because they are less likely than other people to install solar heating, which is safer and greener, and which the group wants to encourage.

Lastly, a fifth 'egalitarian' group might rule out consideration of all factors over which applicants for insurance have no control, and thus rule out the (Arcadian) origin of the applicants.

English practice currently takes the position of the first group,[208] qualified, however, with some regard for the second and fifth positions. The interplay of the first and fifth positions can be seen in the operation of legislation against unfair discrimination.

Unfair Discrimination

In the nineteenth century, at least one life office demanded an additional premium if the life insured was Irish. In England today, discrimination on the ground of

---

[207] Abraham, p. 25; Wils, op. cit. above, n. 182, 461.
[208] Also the position adopted in New York: *Health Ins. Assn v Corcoran*, 551 NYS 2d 615, 618–9 (1990), aff'd 565 NE 2d 1264 (1990).

nationality, whether it be Irish or Arcadian, is prohibited by Article 6 of the EC Treaty. So, for example, when German insurers tried to charge certain nationals more for motor cover, the Commission objected and, it is generally believed, the objection would have been sustained by the ECJ.[209] Other instances of particular difficulty concern classification according to sex and, recently, certain aspects of the applicant's medical profile.

Unfair Sex Discrimination

The Sex Discrimination Act 1975 is infringed if a person is treated less favourably than persons of the opposite sex unless, as regards insurance, that treatment is based on 'actuarial or other data from a source on which it was reasonable to rely'.[210] In *Pinder*,[211] it was held that a self-employed woman dentist could be lawfully charged health insurance premiums 50 per cent higher than self-employed male dentists, because the insurer had data suggesting that women in that position were more likely to be 'off sick'. In contrast, men are commonly charged more than women for motor cover, for example, but this has yet to be challenged in the courts—by a man or by a woman.

This may be because, in reality, the perceived evil is not discrimination by sex but discrimination by men against women. Hence the insurance exception has been attacked because, in the past, women were stereotyped as inferior and weak, and the retention of a series of exceptions in anti-discrimination legislation, which is ostensibly designed to eradicate such stereotypes, sends out competing messages. The protected class is said to be further stigmatized as inferior and weak by being singled out for protection.[212] Some critics go further and argue that all classifications encroach on the fundamental right of a person to be treated as an individual.[213]

A further argument might be that data of that kind should not be taken at face value because they may speak for something else, and that there is an unacceptable hidden agenda. Just as insurance classification by colour has been shown in the United States to be really a cheap, convenient, and crude proxy or surrogate for other, usually cultural, risk factors, the same may be true of sex. Even if this is true, it may be, of course, that behind the classification lies another factor to which no objection can be taken; or it may not. If, for example, it emerged that a lower rate is charged for women drivers under 25 because they drive less, that is unlikely to satisfy those who believe that the lower mileage reflects other social disadvantages associated with sex: that women drive less

---

[209] See Wils, op. cit. above, n. 182, 463.   [210] See ss. 1, 2, and 45 of the Act.

[211] *Pinder v The Friends Provident* (1985) 5 EOR 31 (Westminster County Court). See also the Disability Discrimination Act 1995.

[212] M. Thornton, 'Sex Discrimination and Insurance' (1990) 3 Ins. LJ 12, 13. See also Wils, op. cit. above, n. 182, 458–60.

[213] In this sense: *City of Los Angeles v Manhart*, 435 US 702 (1978). Contra: Case C-152/9T *Neath v Hugh Steeper Ltd*; see Wils, op. cit. above, n. 182, 463 ff.

because of lower economic status and because they are afraid to drive at night.[214] Although critics see the avoidance of the historical stereotype as a social goal sufficiently important to require the more costly search for the concealed cultural factors, it is clear that the investigation may be long and complex. Moreover, the more thorough the investigation and the more refined the classification, the more likely that any attempt to match applicants to the classification will infringe other values such as privacy. Finally, some women may be willing to put up with the discrimination if, in the instance already referred to, its elimination leads to higher premiums.

Unfair Disease Discrimination

The interplay of the first and second positions[215] is to be seen in acceptance by the insurance industry that it ought to cover certain groups that most insurers would prefer not to have on their books.[216] An important instance is when the applicant has, or is likely to have, AIDS. For some years insurers asked whether applicants had had 'a negative HIV/AIDS test or counselling', but this practice met a number of objections.

One objection to this question is that it was pointless, because, although a negative HIV test suggests that the subject is more likely to contract AIDS than most people, it does not indicate a probability that that will happen,[217] and many of those likely to have received counselling were in certain professions, such as nursing, or were simply people who were concerned, and were by no means people more likely than others to contract AIDS. Another objection is that the question deters some people from having the test for fear that they will be unable to obtain (affordable) insurance, or that the result will be leaked to third parties. A third objection, based on experience in the United States,[218] is that insurers will be tempted to use the information in a way that discriminates unfairly against homosexual or bisexual men. For example, in 1985, an American reinsurer published an 'AIDS profile' in its 'underwriting guidelines'. This required underwriters to differentiate between 'single males without dependents that are engaged in occupations that do not require physical exertion' and named the occupations in mind: 'restaurant employees, antique dealers, interior decorators, consultants, florists and people in the jewelry or fashion business'.[219]

---

[214] E.g., M. A. Wiegers, 'The Use of Age, Sex, and Marital Status as Rating Variables in Automobile Insurance' 39 U Toronto LJ 149–209 (1989).   [215] See above, p. 293.

[216] See Chapter 4, p. 86 ff.

[217] K. A. Clifford and R. P. Iuculano, 'Aids and Insurance: The Rationale for Aids-Related Testing', 100 Harv L Rev 1806–25, 1811 (1987); B. Schatz, 'The Aids Insurance Crisis: Underwriting or Overreaching?', 100 Harv L Rev 1782–1805, 1784, 1787 (1987). Cf. R. R. Bovbjerg, 'Aids and Insurance' 77 Iowa L Rev 1561–1615 (1992).

[218] Schatz, op. cit. above, n. 217, 1799 and 1800. See also A. Widiss, 'To Insure or Not to Insure Persons Infected with the Virus that Causes AIDS', 77 Iowa L Rev 1617–1735, 1640 ff. (1992).   [219] Schatz, op. cit. above, n. 217, 1787.

A broader objection of a different order is that ignorance of one's bodily condition, if not bliss, is a fundamental human right. The objection assumes the necessity of chance in life and a person's right not to know as an integral part of existential freedom, without which the human personality cannot fully develop. This kind of consideration has been recognized by the British Medical Association. It has even been suggested that any infringement might be contrary to the constitution in some countries, such as Italy, or contrary to international conventions on human rights.[220] Of course, testing might be arranged in such a way that the subject was unaware of the result, but would such a procedure satisfy concerns about human dignity? An associated argument is the view that restriction on testing helps to protect a person's 'personal integrity'[221] because this includes the right to control the dissemination of information about oneself. That restriction might be justified on this basis assumes that the test results are of a nature that most people in society would not wish to be disseminated.

Genetic Tests

Insurers can and do require a general medical examination without provoking public outrage. Objections to testing have been pointed at testing for AIDS and also at genetic tests. In 1993, the Nuffield Council on Bioethics published a report,[222] in which it supported the current practice of the insurance industry of not requiring any genetic testing. The Council also recommended a temporary moratorium on requiring disclosure of existing genetic data except, first, when there is a known family history of genetic disease that can be established by conventional questions about the applicant's family; and, secondly, when the amount insured exceeded a certain figure. The recommendation was based on practice in Holland and not unlike that in Germany.[223] Outright prohibition, it has been suggested,[224] might infringe EC law as inhibiting the free provision of services unless justifiable in the public interest.

In 1996, the Council of Europe adopted the Convention on Human Rights and Biomedicine (ETS No. 164). Article 12 stipulates that presymptomatic and predictive genetic testing may be performed for purposes of health care and health-related scientific research only. Although the Convention came into force in 1999, the UK is one of many States that have not adopted it. Restrictions of this kind run up against the argument that they are incompatible with a free market in services, and are likely to be ineffective anyway in a global market.[225]

---

[220] E. Deutsch and G. De Oliveira (eds), *Genome Analysis: Legal Rules Practical Application* (Coimbra, 1994) 132–3.   [221] See Radetzki et al., op. cit. above, n. 203, ch. 3.4.2.
[222] *Genetic Screening, Ethical Issues*, December 1993.
[223] G. Wiese, *Genetische Analysen und Rechtsordnung* (Berlin, 1994) 77 ff. Further, see Y. Chiche, 'Genetics & Life and Health Insurance: International Aspects', *Geneva Papers* No. 76 (July 1995) 274–8. For the legal position in other countries, as it stood in 2002, see Radetzki et al., op. cit. above, n. 203, ch. 3.2.   [224] Wils, op. cit. above, n. 182, 467.
[225] See Radetzki et al., op. cit. above, n. 203, ch. 5. On commercial aspects see the 'FT Biotechnology Report', *Financial Times*, 10 November 2004.

In evidence to the House of Commons Science and Technology Committee in January 1995, a representative of the ABI stated that, if applicants have had genetic tests that indicate that they might be prone to disease, insurers expect this to be disclosed, and that, if insurers were banned from requiring this information, premiums would have to rise. This was confirmed by a statement in 1997; however, the ABI announced in 2001 that people will not be asked to take genetic tests when applying for life insurance up to £500,000, and for critical illness, long-term care, and income protection policies up to £300,000. The most that is being claimed for this practice is that it is a temporary solution to the problem.

In 1995, genetic tests were thought to have little predictive value, except for a few relatively rare diseases such as Huntington's disease and cystic fibrosis. In recent years Parliament has not directly regulated the matter, but the mapping of the human genome has put the issue back on the agenda. In 1999, the Government set up an independent committee, the Genetics and Insurance Committee (GAIC), to evaluate the genetic test results that insurers might wish to use. It subsequently agreed to testing for Huntington's disease. However, meanwhile, the Government established the Human Fertilization and Embryology Authority. In 2004, the Authority authorized pre-implementation genetic testing of embryos to be used in IVF treatment, where the husband had a rare form of cancer that might be passed on in the embryo.

In 2001, the Science and Technology Committee, a select committee of the House of Lords, reported.[226] Once again it was accepted that insurance consequences must not deter people from submitting to genetic testing, either for clinical or for research purposes. It was also accepted, however, that insurers have legitimate concerns about adverse selection in the form of persons knowing or suspecting that they were diseased taking out large insurance policies. However, the Report considered that, in spite of scientific advances, it was still not clear that the results of testing were sufficiently predictive to be of real use to insurers.[227] It even doubted the usefulness of testing for Huntington's disease. It expressed scepticism about observance of the ABI Code on testing, and recommended that the membership of GAIC be strengthened and its role extended to scrutiny of insurance practice.

Let us suppose, however, that science establishes a high probability that all those with the Arcadian gene will contract AIDS and that all insurers would like to test for the gene. If insurers are allowed to test, the Arcadian AIDS risks are likely to be carried not by private insurance, which might well be too expensive for most Arcadians, but by whatever social security is in place. If insurers are not allowed to test or underwrite on the basis of previous tests, insurers will have to raise premiums against the possibility that there are Arcadians in their pool, and

---

[226] See www.parliament.the-stationery-office.co.uk, under House of Commons/select committees/science and technology/publications.

[227] Cf. the more positive assessment in Sweden: Radetzki et al., op. cit. above, n. 203, ch. 1.

the Arcadian AIDS risks will be carried by the pool.[228] From the viewpoint of wealth distribution, it is not self-evident that the second solution is fairer or more efficient than the first.

Insurers as Licensing Authority

Many collectors, whether of stamps, china, or plastic gnomes, have satisfactory cover for the collection under a household contents policy. Then the time may come when the collection has reached a value that makes the insurers uneasy. Insurers start putting in the policy onerous conditions about the storage of the collection, and insist on safes or start to charge stiff rates, and may even require a schedule that catalogues every item. The message, of course, is that the insurer does not want to lose the policyholder's business but, equally, does not want to cover the collection. Perhaps the collector will find affordable cover with an insurer who specializes in that kind of business. Others may be less fortunate. In one instance, contents cover for (high risk) students and other persons in shared accommodation required that small valuables worth more than £50 be kept in a substantial cupboard with strong internal bolts and a five-lever lock to British Standard 3621. This too is tantamount to saying, 'don't buy these things or don't buy insurance from us'. In this case, however, specialist cover may not be available at all and general contents cover may have become unaffordable. Is that just 'life'?

The question has been the subject of a 'life or death' debate in connection with liability insurance[229], in particular, employers' liability insurance. The availability of affordable employers' liability insurance is such a serious issue that it has been recognized that it can be resolved only by cooperation between the insurance industry and government.[230] The context of essential, or of compulsory, insurance raises again the question whether, by providing, pricing, and withholding cover, insurers would effectively decide which businesses did business at all and, if they did do business, how they did it; in other words, whether that would or should make insurers 'licensors' of industry. Already marine insurers have driven old and unsafe ships to the breaker's yard, and insurers could do something similar in other industries with potential for pollution. Should there be any constraint or control on the insurers? The question has become urgent not only because of the importance of employers' liability insurance, but also because there is no coherent government policy that indicates which kind of cover should be made compulsory and which not.[231] The question is not new. It arises every time there is a conflict of expectations—between insurers, who consider that they

---

[228] Deutsch and De Oliveira, op. cit. above, n. 220, 105.   [229] See Chapter 1, p. 7 ff.

[230] See the various reports published by the Dept of Work and Pensions: www.dwp.gov.uk/publications/.   [231] See R. K. Lewis, 'When you must insure' (2004) 154 NLJ 1474.

have a right to choose their customers, and the public, which believes that, as regards some risks at least, it has a right to cover.

The Public 'Right' to Cover

The 17-year-old in London who cannot obtain, or cannot afford, basic insurance cover to ride a motorcycle cannot (lawfully) ride a motorcycle. True, some will ride anyway, not least the streetwise cowboys who have found that the cost of paying fines for riding without insurance is less than the cost of insurance. However, for most young people the cost of cover is decisive, and if insurance is unaffordable, they do not motorcycle. No doubt this pleases London taxi drivers, except perhaps those who realize that the cost of motorcycle cover is driving the young to buy cheap, second-hand cars instead, with which to make their own contribution to congestion in the capital.

A response of a different kind was heard in an American case.[232] It was that the effect of a clause excluding motor cover was an unacceptable deprivation of the basic necessities of life, a violation of the fundamental right to travel, and thus a violation of the Constitution. The argument failed, but on other grounds; the premises about the necessities of life and the right of travel were not disputed. In England, opinion does not appear to have gone that far, but in the past motor insurers have faced attack not only from newspapers but also from the Consumers' Association, for 'cherry-picking' good risks. The assumption was that there is a 'right' to drive on the roads, hence a 'right' to insurance; and that it was somehow 'wrong' that insurers should pick and choose. Similarly, the newspapers have sought to stimulate public debate over whether property insurers should be compelled to offer affordable cover for homes and business in the inner cities, or in areas at risk of flooding.

The Insurers' Right to Select Risks

If anyone does drive without insurance, it is the industry, through the Motor Insurers' Bureau (MIB) and a levy on policies, that pays for any injury or damage done. To this degree at least, insurers collectively take on drivers, many of whom no individual insurer would insure. This is not, however, in any sense a recognition of drivers' right to drive, but rather of the 'right' of victims on the roads to compensation. The MIB agreement was a special case of collective action—indeed of defensive action, less for the victims than for the industry itself—against the peril of what it sees as 'government interference' that might ensue, if motoring mayhem were uninsured.

The insurance industry is wedded to the ethos of free enterprise and united against 'government interference'. The industry's perception of its role and responsibility in society does not see risk distribution as a primary goal, but rather as a useful by-product of the natural operation of the free market. A natural

---

[232] *Mayo v Nat. Farmers Union*, 833 P 2d 54 (Colo., 1992).

market involves natural selection. Indeed, some insurers are so sure that the cherries want to be picked out from the rotten apples that one has advertised its motor insurance as 'taking careless drivers off your back'. Whether or not that is what the market wants, market forces push insurers in that direction.[233] On the one hand, if insurers do not refine their classification of risks (or raise premiums and cater specifically for bad risks), the book of risks will contain too high a percentage of bad risks, who are being charged no more than the average premium, and the result will be a loss on the underwriting account. On the other hand, one way to gain market share is to offer low risks lower prices. Moreover, except when classification is based on factors outside the control of the insured, such as age and sex, some believe that accurate risk classification encourages people to invest in loss prevention, and thus further differentiate themselves from others who do not. Selection is a natural and normal part of the commercial process.

When the insurance industry was attacked for picking cherries, the ABI defended the practice as good underwriting, but, significantly perhaps, others who speak for the industry did not. There is a conflict of opinions and of interests—between those (usually in the industry) who highlight the risk-assessment or efficiency-promoting features of insurance classification and those (often outside the industry) who stress the risk-distributional function of insurance. Moreover, the latter point out that gains for one sector may mean losses for another, so that there is no net gain for society at large. To offer lower fire premiums to non-smokers may lead to smokers giving up smoking, but the consequence, which is both more likely to occur and to be what the insurer is seeking, is to attract new, non-smoking applicants believed to be better risks. This measure may reduce the losses paid by the particular insurer, but is not likely to lead to a significant overall reduction in loss in society as a whole. Similarly, some kinds of loss prevention, such as Neighbourhood Watch schemes, simply move the hazard to someone else's backyard without reducing the level of crime in the community at large.

The insurers' 'right to select' implies a right to 'deselect'—to refuse renewal, or to change the rules of engagement so radically that the former insured is effectively without cover.[234] In other words, the insured's licence to conduct relevant activity is withdrawn. Recently controversy arose from property insurers refusing to offer flood cover; and before that (and still today), from liability insurers' step back by switching from occurrence cover to cover of 'claims made'.

Occurrences covered are acts (or omissions) of liability policyholders occurring during the policy period, although the consequent claim by their victims may come later. Rating the cover requires prediction of the claims that will be made in the future. The past, however, is not necessarily a very reliable gauge of the future, especially as regards claims such as those arising out of toxic torts or professional

---

[233] Abraham, p. 67 ff.   [234] See Chapter 5, p. 175 ff.

negligence, which may not surface until the distant future—called 'long tail' exposure—and on which courts may have become more severe. At the time of underwriting, it is difficult to anticipate not only the discoveries of science but also the legal and economic inflation over the years to come.[235] So, many liability insurers switched to claims made policies. These cover policyholders against all claims that are made during the policy period, regardless of when the activity giving rise to the claim occurred. Rating this kind of cover is much less difficult, because only the claims that will be made during the imminent policy period have to be predicted.

As regards the risk beyond the imminent period, the effect of claims made cover is to shift significant aspects of the risk back to policyholders. For instance, the successful claim of a single consumer against one tobacco company in respect of the consumer's lung cancer, raises enormous implications for the future insurability of that company (and other tobacco companies). At the end of the current claims made period, in the light of the now known potential for future claims of a similar nature, the company may find itself faced with either enormous rises in premium, or a complete refusal to grant or renew cover at all. Victims with cancer may find that they have fallen through a gap in the company's cover. Consequently, there has been something of a reaction against policies of this kind in certain countries. They were outlawed, for example, in Belgium, but have now been made legal again. Also in France, they were outlawed by the *Cour de Cassation* which, however, was later overruled by the legislature in respect of certain kinds of liability such as medical malpractice.[236] In England, however, claims made cover is widespread[237] and has given rise to little of the concern expressed in other European countries. Nonetheless, the practice has been one factor at least in the demise of certain businesses.

---

[235] Abraham, p. 159.   [236] Loi 2002–1577 of 30 December 2002.
[237] See further M. Simpson (ed.), *Professional Negligence and Liability* (London, 2000) ch. 5-5 ff.

8

Insurance and Law

The Insurer as God?

When drafts of international conventions reach the stage of a diplomatic conference, the 'deus ex machina, the insurer, is not mentioned in the cast'.[1] Thus spake Lord Diplock in 1970. His words echo what has been said about the drama of domestic lawmaking too, both in Parliament and in the courts. However, reticence about the role of insurance and insurers is less the rule now than it was forty years ago, although what is said about it is debatable.

---

[1] Lord Diplock, 'Conventions and Morals', 1 JMLC 525 (1970).

The Effect of Insurance on Rules of Law

Insurers and the Conduct of Litigation

The development of some parts of English law depends to a large extent on litigation and litigants. Recent studies indicate that 98 per cent of tort claims are settled. In most cases settlement requires the concurrence of an insurer, so that it is insurers who allow trial judges to determine only a tiny number of all the claims made, albeit a disproportionately important minority. Of these only a few are appealed, 'with the result that the senior judiciary are left to adjudicate upon a small fraction of what are, by then, very untypical cases'.[2] Once again, whether an appeal court 'is to be given an opportunity to examine a point of law may depend on the insurer for, if it serves the insurer's purpose for doubt to remain, the claimant can be paid in full and threatened with a costs award if the action is continued'.[3] Moreover, as Lord Denning MR, once pointed out, when an insurer 'has obtained a decision of this court in its favour, it will buy off an appeal to the House of Lords by paying ample compensation to the appellant. By so doing, it will have a legal precedent on its side which it can use with effect in later cases.'[4]

Liability insurers can thus stifle the development or refinement of liability law by smothering it with settlement; however, a determined attempt to do that in 2002 in *Fairchild*,[5] a case of liability for the effects of asbestos, doubly failed. The attempt was described by Lord Bingham as 'entirely regrettable',[6] and by one of the victims' lawyers, less politely, as 'a sordid attempt to smother the judicial process'.[7] In spite of the industry, the House of Lords heard the case and gave the landmark decision that many insurers feared. Moreover, the associated publicity generated by the entire affair led to a leader in a prominent industry journal observing that the week was a 'black one for the insurance industry's reputation'.[8]

When insurers choose to fight, it is more likely to be on account of the size of the claim, and of those that might follow, than the importance of the point of law. In more recent times insurers have had less choice about the field of battle on account of an increased taste for a scrap on the part of claimants with the scent of big money in their nostrils, led on by lawyers and conditional fee agreements (CFAs).[9] Such litigation has resulted in some significant decisions against insurers, such as *Fairchild*.[10] In that case, a tort claimant was allowed to 'jump the evidentiary gap': to sustain an indemnity claim without establishing that but for

---

[2] R. Lewis, 'Insurance and the Tort System' (2004), a summarised version of which appeared as 'Insurers and Personal Injury Litigation' [2005] JPIL 1–11. [3] Ibid.

[4] *Davis v Johnson* [1979] AC 264, 278.

[5] *Fairchild v Glenhaven Funeral Services* [2003] 1 AC 22. See above pp. 195–6.

[6] Ibid.   [7] Sir Sydney Kentridge, *Financial Times*, 23 April 2002.

[8] *PM*, 25 April 2002.   [9] See Chapter 1, p. 7 ff.   [10] Above, n. 5.

the act or omission of the defendant the claimant would not have suffered the harm in question. Nonetheless, for the practitioner, who seeks to advise a client about a claim, the 'law' lies less in the pronouncements of judges and the deductions of commentators from the tip of the iceberg that comes out in court, than in the submarine topography of settlement practice. The insurer is the sophisticate of settlement, who therefore still calls most of the shots in an arena in which contestants do not meet on equal terms.[11]

Discovering Whether Insurance Exists

Back in the 1950s, in *Lister*,[12] Viscount Simonds said that, when determining people's duties, 'the fact that one of them is insured is to be disregarded' by the court. As concerns the insurance position of the particular defendant, the substantive formalism of Viscount Simonds, who so scrupulously left stones unturned, is still sometimes found. The result, if not the intention, was that defendants were defended by the court to a degree that left indefensible perils for the plaintiff. Potential plaintiffs could never find out sufficiently in advance whether people who, they believed, had wronged them had adequate liability insurance, or any at all. They had to commit themselves to battle in court to discover whether their adversary was 'worth powder and shot'. In England today this was still largely true until very recently, and in an era of 'cards on the table litigation' this makes little sense.[13]

This is in stark contrast with the USA, where the Federal Rules of Civil Procedure require disclosure of the existence and contents of any insurance contract that may cover a judgment against a defendant. Moreover, insurers are obliged to notify potential claimants of relevant terms of the policy,[14] which has had an effect on settlement practice beneficial for claimants.[15] In other common law countries, such as Australia, the corresponding law seems to have been moving in the American direction for some time.[16] Now, at least when the debtor is bankrupt or insolvent, the claimant can demand the information in England.

In *In Re OT Computers*,[17] a company, liable for its computers' poor performances under extended warranty schemes, was insolvent. Longmore LJ, giving the judgment of the Court of Appeal, stressed that 'a third party claimant needs to know . . . whether the person against whom he is making a claim is insured and, if so, in what terms'. Having examined the language of the relevant legislation, the

[11] H. Genn, *Hard Bargaining* (London, 1987) 163 ff. See also *Davis v Johnson*, op. cit. above, n. 4, 278, *per* Lord Denning.
[12] *Lister v Romford Ice and Cold Storage Co. Ltd* [1957] AC 555, 576–7.
[13] Goldsmith, (1995) 88 BILA Journal 5, 12.
[14] See *Union Automobile Indemnity Co. v Shields*, 79 F 3d 39 (7 Cir, 1996).
[15] Generally, see K. D. Severed, 'On the Demand for Liability Insurance', 72 Tex L Rev 1629, 1634 ff (1994).
[16] See *Gerah Imports Pty Ltd v The Duke Group Ltd* (1994) 68 ALJR 196 (HCA), discussed critically by Sheller in a note: [1994] IJIL 202.   [17] [2004] Ch. 317 (CA).

Third Parties (Rights against Insurers Act) 1930, he concluded that the information about the defendant company's insurance position was 'such information as may be reasonably required' within section 2 of the Act.[18]

The Effect of Existing Insurance: in Theory

In *Davie*,[19] Viscount Simonds, having insisted that insurance in place should be disregarded (above), went on to say, more specifically, that it is not 'the function of a court of law to fasten upon the fortuitous circumstance of insurance to impose a greater burden on the employer than would otherwise lie upon him'. The decision in *Davie* satisfied almost nobody, and was overturned by statute ten years later.[20] The 'pretence that insurance does not exist' in negligence cases has been said to be a 'product of English conceptualism' and over-reliance on vague concepts such as 'proximity'.[21] Be that as it may, by 1989 Lord Griffiths could say without fear of contradiction that everyone knows that all prudent professional men, such as surveyors, carry insurance, and that 'the availability and cost of insurance must be a relevant factor when considering which of two parties should be required to bear the risk of a loss'.[22] Liability and insurance, it has been said, 'are so intermixed that judicially to alter the basis of liability without adequate knowledge (which we have not the means to obtain) as to the impact this might make upon the insurance system would be dangerous and, in my opinion, irresponsible'. These are the words not of the critical legal studies movement but of Lord Wilberforce in 1972, who was thought of at the time as an 'articulate exponent of judicial restraint'.[23] Courts are slow to extend liability unless they believe that affordable insurance can be found to cover it.[24]

Today the emphasis in tort is less on punishing the wrongdoer than on compensating the victim. Influential judges such as Lord Steyn have been outspoken on the importance of compensation and distributive justice,[25] and the significance of insurance in developing the law.[26] Cane is right, surely, to say that

it is misleading to think of tort law as being the primary vehicle for ensuring payment of compensation to accident victims, with liability insurance as an ancillary device to protect the insured. It is more accurate to view insurance as the primary medium for the payment of compensation, and tort law as a subsidiary part of the process. [One] of the chief reasons why the great mass of personal injury claims arise out of road accidents and industrial injuries is that insurance is nearly always available in these cases.[27]

---

[18] Ibid., at [33].   [19] *Davie v New Merton Board Mills* [1959] AC 604, 627.
[20] The Employers Liability (Defective Equipment) Act 1969.
[21] B. A. Hepple, 'Negligence: The Search for Coherence' [1997] CLP 69–94, 81.
[22] *Smith v Bush* [1990] 1 AC 831, 858. Idem: *Caledonian North Sea Ltd v London Bridge Engineering Co.* [2002] All ER (Conn) 321, 44 per Lord Scotte (HL).
[23] R. Stevens, *Law and Politics* (London, 1979) 556 and 557.   [24] See below, p. 319 ff.
[25] E.g., *McFarlane v Tayside Health Board* [2000] 2 AC 59, at 83.
[26] E.g., *Marc Rich & Co. AG v Bishops Rock Marine Co. Ltd, The Nicholas H* [1996] AC 211, 239.
[27] P. Cane, *Atiyah's Accidents Compensation and the Law*, 6th edn (London, 1999) 191.

Indeed, the primacy of insurance in motor claims is reflected in the Road Traffic Act 1988, whereby, for example, late notice, which may defeat a claim by policyholders against insurers, cannot be used in defence by insurers against road victims. Moreover, it is now only when Parliament has kitemarked a particular kind of insurance, such as motor insurance, as important by making it compulsory, that courts will enforce the insurance even though the wrong may amount to a crime.[28]

The Effect of Existing Insurance: in Practice

Clearly insurance is important; courts know that and do not pretend otherwise. Insurance responds to cover a new danger, or a new liability.[29] But is the reverse also true, that new rules of the general law are in some sense caused by insurers and insurance? One perception is that the shift of emphasis in tort from fault to compensation was partly caused by the introduction of compulsory liability insurance.[30] To test the accuracy of this perception we must first be clear about what we are looking for. What is the 'effect' of insurance?

One effect, the effect of the very existence of insurance cover, is that a case is decided in such a way that the insurance pays. This is the magnetic effect of money, the perennial attraction of any 'deep pocket' in a case; it is not special to insurance, but was found, for example, in the liability decisions against railway companies in the nineteenth century. Anyway, the courts have not allowed themselves to be drawn too much. Lord Denning once observed that although

most defendants are insured and heavy awards do not ruin them . . . small insurance companies can be ruined. Some have been. And large companies have to cover the claims by their premiums. If awards reach figures which are 'daunting' in their immensity, premiums must be increased all the way round. The impact spreads through the body politic.[31]

What is special about insurance is that the pocket is not really a pocket at all but a reservoir that is constantly refilled by numerous small streams: the risk is spread. Courts are well aware of this and seek, in the words of Lord Diplock, to 'avoid fixing the scale at a level which would materially affect the cost of living or disturb the current social pattern'.[32] On the other hand, in Australia, while insurance has had virtually no role in expanding duties of care, awareness of the existence of insurance cover has been a targeting flare for those seeking cover,[33]

---

[28] See Chapter 7, pp. 259–60.   [29] See Chapter 2, p. 42 ff.

[30] Cane, op. cit. above, n. 27, 202 ff.

[31] *Fletcher v Autocar and Transporters Ltd* [1968] 2 QB 322, 335–6 (CA).

[32] *Wise v Kay* [1962] 1 QB 638, 670 (CA).

[33] See M. Gill, 'The expansion of liability and the role of insurance—who's the chicken?' [1999] IJIL 27–39.

and may have had a role in the 'tort crisis' there in recent years: the more so there than in England, because in Australia it has been easier for claimants to discover who is insured and what are the terms of the cover.

Nonetheless, the importance of insurers to the tort system 'is reflected in the fact that claims which are brought closely match the areas where liability insurance is to be found. Thus road and work accidents predominate partly because those are the two major areas where tort insurance is compulsory',[34] and, of course, known to be by potential claimants. The incidence of tort liability 'closely mirrors the areas of compulsory insurance'.[35] Then there is a second pull up to the perceived limit in amount of the cover: the higher plaintiffs think it to be, the higher their expectation of indemnity and the harder the bargaining for a settlement. This, it has been argued,[36] affects adversely both fairness and efficiency of a system of tort liability based on fault. Be that as it may, the pull of insurance, when it is known to be in place, is real.

The second and more significant effect attributed to insurance is that the law itself is influenced by insurability. In the well-chosen words of Ehrenzweig, 'Assurance oblige'.[37] Such a thesis has been advanced by some distinguished commentators.[38] Thus Cane, for example, is in 'little doubt that the development of the law has been influenced by the growing prevalence of liability insurance'.[39] The central theme of the argument is that the very imposition of a liability by court or legislature is framed so as to be targeted at a particular kind of insurance. Moreover, the influence, it has been argued, may be particular or general. In the particular case of a particular contract, albeit a standard contract such as a building contractors' form, a term requiring one party to insure may determine and proscribe the liability of the other party: the inference is that the party obliged to insure bears the risk of the event insured against, with the corollary that, even if the event is brought about by the fault of the other, the latter is not liable to the other party, or, therefore, indirectly to the insurer by means of subrogation. Clearly, this does indeed occur.[40] A more general influence is that insurability influences the lawmaker, Parliament, or judge, in the delimitation and development of liability law in general. That this occurs, it is submitted, is not clear at all.

---

[34] Lewis, op. cit. above, n. 2, 5–6.   [35] Ibid., 9.

[36] E.g., E. S. Pryor, 'The Tort Liability Regime and the Duty to Defend', 88 Md L Rev 1-54 (1999).

[37] A. A. Ehrenzweig, 'Assurance oblige: A comparative study' [1995] *Law and Contemporary Problems* 820–45.

[38] E.g., M. Davies, 'The End of the Affair: Duty of Care and Liability Insurance' (1989) 9 LS 67–83; and more recently, but with only passing reference to the UK, H. A. Cousy, 'Tort Liability and Liability Insurance: A Difficult Relationship', *Tort and Insurance Law Yearbook* (2001) 18–55. Professor Cousy rests his case on legislation rather than on decisions of the courts.

[39] Cane, op. cit. above, n. 27, 203. This view is still widely held; see e.g., *Markesinis and Deakin*, ch. 1.1.

[40] E.g., *Scottish Special Housing Assn v Wimpey Construction UK Ltd* [1986] 1 WLR 995 (HL). As regards subrogation in such a case, see Clarke, 31-5D.

This chapter argues that this kind of influence can be seen in the legislature, but, in England, much less in the courts than some of the proponents of the influence view would have us believe. On the one hand, English insurers have a history of innovation and enterprise; they are always looking for new ways of making money by launching new kinds of cover.[41] However, they are not social engineers or industrial enterprise boards seeking to advance the prosperity of the nation. They watch and assess the line taken by the courts rather than lead or cajole the courts in any particular direction. The only current instance of specific influence is negative rather than positive: when it is the legislator that plans a development of the law but first checks with the industry whether it is insurable, and the industry says that it is not.[42] On the other hand, it is contended here[43] that most judges these days do not know enough about the insurance background and are duly diffident about reaching decisions on that basis. Moreover, study has confirmed Stapleton in her 'suspicion that on the very few occasions when courts refer to liability insurance they do so as a "makeweight" factor after it has been decided, having balanced other concerns, to impose liability'.[44] Nonetheless, we shall now consider the arguments for the influence view more closely.

Invisible Effects: Development in the Courts

When they first met, tort liability and liability insurance seemed 'to fit together beautifully and a romance and even true courtship is floating in the air', not least because liability insurance possessed 'the charm of youth'. This view of the theme, which comes from Belgium,[45] has been more mysteriously but prosaically referred to in England as the thesis that the application and development of legal rules 'have been "invisibly" affected by the existence of insurance'.[46] The invisible hand of insurance, runs the argument, is seen less in particular cases than in general patterns of parallel development. Patterns of this kind were charted in the United States in the 1940s and 1950s.[47] Like the 'invisible' hand of God in the world at large, however, where some such as Lord Diplock[48] and Lord Denning[49] see the effect clearly, others think that the effect had been

---

[41] See Chapter 2, p. 42 ff.

[42] An instance at the time of writing is the lack of progress on the Athens Convention relating to the Carriage of Passengers and their Luggage by Sea.   [43] Below, pp. 315–16.

[44] J. Stapleton, 'Tort, Insurance and Ideology' (1995) 58 MLR 820–45, 833.

[45] Cousy, op. cit. above, n. 38, 33.

[46] B. A. Hepple, M. H. Matthews, and D. R. Howarth, *Tort: Cases and Materials*, 5th edn (London, 2000) 1102.

[47] F. V. Harper and F. James Jnr, *The Law of Torts* (Boston, 1956) ch. XIII.

[48] Above, pp. 302–3.

[49] Rt Hon. Lord Denning, *The Discipline of Law* (London, 1979) 280.

overstated[50] and others see only coincidence. This chapter argues, like some of the insurers,[51] that what we shall call the Denning perception, specifically that the availability of insurance has driven the expansion of liability in tort, is not at all apparent; and that, on the contrary, liability insurance is no more than a shadow that follows tort rather than vice versa. Indeed, it is a fearful and apprehensive shadow, as appears from the recent debates about pollution, terrorism, and climate: any big changes in the law or in perceptions of danger create uncertainty, uncertainty is bad for business,[52] and insurers, far from leading the way, draw back and decline business. Nonetheless, according to the Denning perception, the effects of insurance are said to be seen, in particular, in the law of tort, to which we now turn.

Vicarious Liability

The Denning perception is still shared by some distinguished commentators,[53] who point to vicarious liability and cases in which vicarious liability is strict. Specifically, there may be liability although the defendant has exercised reasonable care and skill, and sometimes in a field of activity where liability was not strict before. This, it is said, is an instance of law following available insurance. Similar trends were mapped in the USA in the middle of the last century, but their extent and significance was always disputed.[54] Certainly, the institution of the National Health Service in England at the same period prompted courts, led by Lord Denning, to an extension of vicarious liability; but that may simply have been a sensible response to what was seen then as a gargantuan organization in which the traditional targets of tort could hide, an episode in legal history which is over. Moreover, it was a time when science had made strides such that it was possible, much more than before, to establish that someone somewhere had made a mistake, but not which person where.

Viewed as a whole, the case, it is submitted, proves too much, unless it explains also why the tendency to stricter liability has occurred in some contexts (employment) but not others (contractors and subcontractors).[55] Even as regards employment, the trend to strictness has become less obvious. A feature of work patterns in the last years of the twentieth century was a move away from traditional employment to more flexible forms of relationship, part-time employment, and contract labour. This has been well documented by scholars in the field of

---

[50] W. L. Prosser and R. E. Keeton, *Prosser and Keeton on Torts*, 4th edn (London, 1971) 547 ff.

[51] E.g., H. Schulte-Noelle, 'Challenges for Insurers in the Nineties', Geneva Papers on Risk and Insurance No. 72 (July, 1994), 287–303, 291.   [52] See Chapter 2, p. 48 ff and p. 52 ff.

[53] In this instance B. A. Hepple, 'Negligence: The Search for Coherence' [1997] CLP 69–94, 79.

[54] W. P. Keeton, *Prosser and Keeton on Torts*, 5th edn (St Paul, 1984) sect. 82.

[55] Stapleton, op. cit. above, n. 44, 828–9.

labour law,[56] and the result of the move appears to be that the new relationships have escaped the grip of the law of vicarious liability in tort.

Any recent expansion of vicarious liability seems to have been driven less by desire for loss distribution of the kind perceived by Lord Denning than by the goal of loss prevention (and safety at work),[57] or by respect for the logical development of legal principle.[58] In the area of employer's liability, if one looks back at the century before the National Health Service, it was liability that led to insurance rather than the reverse,[59] so the Denning perception does not fit the facts of the workplace—at least until the present century, when it can be seen to operate in reverse. Employers have found it increasingly hard to get (affordable) liability insurance, as statute requires. Insurance journals have been discussing at length the 'EL crisis'. As to the Denning perception, Lord Pearce once observed that the doctrine of vicarious liability has grown not from any clear logical or legal principle, but from social convenience and rough justice.[60] While cautioning that no basis for the rule can be dismissed altogether, this appears to be the current view held by at least some leading commentators of today.[61]

Nuisance and Pollution

Another instance of the Denning perception is said to be liability for dangerous escapes, toxic torts. As regards dangerous escapes once actionable under the rule in *Rylands v Fletcher*, the trend to strictness appeared to stop in 1946[62] and lie comatose until finally laid to rest in 2003. As regards nuisance, in the second half of the last century nuisance became less strict,[63] and writers began to assimilate nuisance generally with (the less strict tort of) negligence. As regards pollution, in particular, the trend to strictness has mostly come from the legislature. Far from encouraging any such trend by marketing cover, insurers have responded with restrictive drafting and howls of protest. A notable example is liability insurance to cover environmental pollution. English insurers, somewhat aghast at litigation and liability in the USA,[64] have followed the drafting paths marked by American insurers into a cautious defensive position that offers cover only against damage that is both accidental and sudden, ruling out the

---

[56] E.g., E. McKendrick, 'Vicarious Liability and Independent Contractors—A Reexamination' (1990) 53 MLR 770–84; R. Kidner, 'Vicarious Liability: For Whom should the Employer be Liable?' (1995) 15 LS 47–64.

[57] *Lane v Shire Roofing Co. (Oxford) Ltd* [1995] IRLR 493, CA.

[58] E.g., *Lister v Hesley Hall* [2001] 1 AC 215, at [13] ff, *per* Lord Steyn; followed in *Mattis v Pollock* [2003] 1 WLR 2158, CA. See also P. Cane, 'Vicarious Liability for Sexual Abuse' (2000) 116 LQR 21, 24.   [59] Hepple, op. cit. above, n. 53, 74.

[60] *ICI Ltd v Shatwell* [1965] AC 656, 685.   [61] *Markesinis and Deakin*, p. 572.

[62] *Read v Lyons* [1947] AC 156.

[63] See *British Road Services Ltd v Slater* [1964] 1 WLR 498, 504, *per* Lord Parker (HL).

[64] For a recent account, see W. P. Shelley and J. A. Mooney, 'Toxic Torts and the Absolute Pollution Exclusion Revisited' 39 Tort & Ins LJ 55–83 (2003).

long-tailed and enormous serpent of liability for gradual seepage into water-courses and the like.[65]

Res Ipsa Loquitur

According to the Denning view, the 'doctrine' of *res ipsa loquitur*,[66] whereby it can be inferred that the person in control of a damage situation has been negligent, is a strict 'doctrine' that has developed thus in response to the draw of insurance. This, it is said, is because the 'doctrine' is strict, and puts the onus of proof (and thus the cost of unexplained loss) on the better risk avoider, whose control of the situation enables the most precise risk assessment and rating. 'The obvious effect of increasing the procedural disadvantages of defendants is that *res ipsa loquitur* becomes, to that extent, a more effective device for imposing strict liability under the pretence of administering rules of negligence.'[67]

An alternative view of the *res ipsa loquitur* 'doctrine', however, is that it is nothing more than recognition of a reasonable factual inference of negligence, an inference which the court is entitled to draw on the usual basis of what is probable.[68] As long as the defendant is allowed to refute the inference by proof, there is no automatic liability without fault. One may as well say that conviction of crime upon circumstantial evidence amounts to law of guilt without proof of crime.[69] Moreover, the 'doctrine' goes back to the mid-nineteenth century, when insurance clearly did not influence liability in this way; and it is not clear that the 'doctrine' is applied more often today than before, if only because such cases are more likely to settle. Neither is it clear that today the rule is applied much more strictly: the cases reported in the last thirty years appear to conflict,[70] and although the most powerful precedent among them can be construed as support-ing a move in the direction of strictness, some decisions of importance in modern society do not.[71] So, the argument from strictness, this time with reference to *res ipsa loquitur*, is not conclusive.

The Duty of Care

The Denning view is based mainly on developments in the duty and standard of care. As regards the duty of care, one version of the argument is that the duty was expanded, first by Lord Atkin and then by Lord Wilberforce, under the influence

---

[65] See Chapter 7, n. 30.

[66] Once described by Megaw LJ as 'no more than an exotic, although convenient, phrase to describe what is in essence no more than a common sense approach . . . to the assessment of the effect of evidence': *Lloyde v West Midlands Gas Board* [1971] 1 WLR 749, 755 (CA).

[67] J. G. Fleming, *The Law of Torts*, 8th edn (Sydney, 1992) 325. See also Harper and James, op. cit. above, n. 47, vol. 1, p. 764.   [68] See Megaw LJ, above, n. 66.

[69] Prosser and Keeton, op. cit. above, n. 50, 552.   [70] Clerk & Lindsell 16th (1989) 10–140.

[71] See *Ng v Lee* [1988] RTR 298, 302 (PC).

of liability insurance; and that, later, in the last years of the twentieth century, the duty contracted as liability insurance started to dry up. If this is true of the early years, then Winfield, in what has been described even by one who regards the Denning school as the seminal account of the development of the duty of care,[72] missed it.

Dirty Work

In the second half of the twentieth century, expansion of the duty of care went furthest in *Junior Books*,[73] as the decision was understood at the time in 1982. The cause of loss in that case was negligence in work undertaken. Liability for that, as well as insurance, had been available for many years. The novelty of the case lay in the imposition of liability for consequential (financial) loss rather than just for physical damage. Liability insurance for consequential (financial) loss caused by negligent work had been available for many years, however, not as such but as professional indemnity (PI) cover. If this was a case of tort following insurance, it had taken a long time to do it. Insurers saw *Junior Books* as a different risk situation, and almost at once one insurer offered specific cover, bringing PI cover out of the office and into the workshop; but that was a response to the decision in *Junior Books*, not a cause.[74]

In the event, the decision in *Junior Books* seemed to bring on an attack of judicial agoraphobia, a feeling that the scope of the duty had been pushed too far, and the judges retreated some way back in the direction of the trenches dug before 1932, trenches of 'traditional category' from which there could be periodic incremental advances. 'It is not surprising' said Lord Goff in 1987,[75] 'that once again we should find the courts seeking to identify specific situations in which liability can properly be imposed'. But the argument—this time tort followed insurance backwards—that the retreat on duty was a reflection of the withdrawal of unlimited liability cover in the insurance market,[76] is once again unconvincing. First, limits were a feature of liability cover well before 1982. Secondly, the immediate response of insurers to *Junior Books* was not retrenchment and retreat but, as mentioned above, for one company at least, to offer expanded cover for what was perceived as the new and expanded liability for economic loss of that kind. Indeed, the strongest evidence against the argument is in the cases in which the courts declined to find a duty even though it was probable that liability

---

[72] M. Davies, 'The End of the Affair: Duty of Care and Liability Insurance' (1989) 9 LS 67–83, 78, concerning P. H. Winfield, 'Duty in Tortious Negligence', 34 Col L Rev 41–66 (1934).

[73] *Junior Books Co. Ltd v The Veitchi Co.* [1983] AC 520.

[74] Stapleton, op. cit. above, n. 44, 827. A similar situation has been reported abroad: E. Klingmuller, 'Liability Insurance in the Federal Republic of Germany', *Geneva Papers on Risk and Insurance* No. 56 (July 1990) 330–6.

[75] *Smith v Littlewoods Organisation Ltd* [1987] AC 241, 280. Cf *Customs and Excise Commissioners v Barclays Bank plc* [2006] 3 WLR 1, [7] per Lord Bingham (HL).

[76] It seems that this did occur in Australia, where the unavailability of affordable insurance has had a clear but negative effect on the law of liability in tort—its restriction.

insurance was, or would have been, available. Here again, there is no real evidence that the law followed insurance; rather, insurance followed the law.

Dirty Play

A more recent instance of a quite different kind concerned whether rugby referees owe a duty of care to rugby players. Lord Phillips MR, who delivered the judgment of the Court of Appeal,[77] had little doubt that a duty should be owed, concluding thus:

> Rugby football is an inherently dangerous sport. Some of the rules are specifically designed to minimise the inherent dangers. Players are dependant [*sic*] for their safety on the due enforcement of the rules. The role of the referee is to enforce the rules. Where a referee undertakes to perform that role, it seems to us manifestly fair, just and reasonable that the players should be entitled to rely upon the referee to exercise reasonable care in so doing.[78]

As for the impact of insurance, the judgment might be seen as one in which insurance was what Stapleton called a makeweight, for, earlier in his judgment, Lord Phillips quoted and apparently accepted the insurance position described by the judge below,[79] but did not reiterate the point in his conclusion. Indeed, in another such decision of the Court of Appeal insurance counted for even less. That decision concerned the 'noble art' of boxing and a widely reported bout for a world title between Michael Watson and Chris Eubank, in which Watson was seriously injured. In the judgment of Lord Phillips, with which the other members of the Court of Appeal agreed, the value attached to human life and limb was overwhelming, and other considerations such as insurance were swept aside.[80]

The Standard of Care

As regards the standard of care required of those who owe a duty, the Denning view is that the courts have become stricter, being more concerned with compensating claimants and rather less with whether defendants were really at fault; and that this is because a liability insurer stands behind the defendant. In other words, insurance has had what has been described as the magnetic effect of money.

---

[77] *Vowles v Evans* [2003] 1 WLR 1607 (CA).   [78] Ibid., at [25].

[79] Ibid., at [11]. It was this: 'In my judgment when rugby is funded not only by gate receipts but also by lucrative television contracts I can see no reason why the Welsh Rugby Union should not insure itself and its referees against claims and the risk of a finding of a breach of duty of care by a referee where "the threshold of liability is a high one which will not easily be crossed". Amateur rugby players will be young men mostly with very limited income. Insurance cover for referees would be a cost spread across the whole game.' He also noted counsel's submission that 'it was public knowledge that the WRU was heavily in debt and that public liability insurers were considering excluding cover for sporting injuries', but rejected it because no evidence to that effect had been put before the court.

[80] *Watson v British Boxing Board of Control Ltd* [2001] QB 1134, 1163, with reference to a statement in an earlier case by Buxton LJ that underlined the importance of personal safety.

The opposing view is that the trend to strictness was not the result of available insurance but came first.[81] A trend to strictness in the history of tort is certainly there, but it is not an unmistakable line in one direction and it does not appear to follow insurance. Neither is the trend even on all fronts. Away from roads and motor vehicles, the duty of care is often less strict.[82] The move to higher standards of care and to stricter liability on the roads might be explained apart from insurance. The key decision was that learner drivers owe the same standard of care and skill as other drivers—not only to other road users, but also to their own passengers.[83] The reason, however, was less a move for more compensation than the uncertainty that would be created by a variable standard of skill for drivers. Yet a variable standard is found in other contexts, and, once again, one wonders whether the motoring cases are sufficiently typical to tell us anything about the rest.

Perhaps it is not entirely coincidental that Lord Denning, who had so much influence on this part of the law after 1945, had learned to drive in 1941 but disliked it so much that he never drove again! Be that as it may, the driving cases may simply reflect a greater awareness that the jolly roadster of Wodehouse's Bertie Wooster has been replaced by the GT4 of Grahame's Toad of Toad Hall, and that there are a lot more of them. Thus, in a recent case of contributory negligence the judge said that 'in deciding how far to reduce his damages having regard to such responsibility, I think it right to reflect the injunctions of the Highway Code to motorists who drive what, all of us who are drivers should constantly remember, may be lethal instruments. The injunctions are to respect other more vulnerable road users.'[84] Moreover, there is consciousness in some quarters at least that every time someone is killed on the roads, that causes damage to society at large to the tune of more than £1 million a time—and that is a sum which takes no account of the cost of damage to the environment, or (even more than that) cost to the National Health Service when the vehicle does not finish the job, and the victim survives and needs long-term care.

The causal role of insurance, if any, is hard to prove.[85] At best, the argument is like that of epidemiology, the study of the prevalence of specified diseases within a sector of the population: it measures results in that sector, but can only speculate about causes. It was epidemiology that first established the 'connection' between smoking and lung cancer which today is accepted. But while there is currently more heart disease in Scotland than in Japan, it is still a matter of speculation whether, or to what extent, that is because the Scots drink more whisky and the Japanese, while also having a taste for Scots whisky, eat more fish.

---

[81] See Lewis, op. cit. above, n. 2—Also Prosser, op. cit. above, n. 69, 548 ff.

[82] E.g., the 'art' of valuation: *Luxmoore-May v Messenger May Baverstock* [1990] 1 WLR 1009 (CA); R. Kidner, 'The Variable Standard of Care, Contributory Negligence and *Volenti*' (1991) 11 LS 1–23.

[83] *Nettleship v Weston* [1971] 2 QB 691, 699–700 (CA); Cane, op. cit. above, n. 27, 206.

[84] *Russell v Smith* (2003) 147 SJLB 1118, at [15], *per* His Honour Judge Rich QC.

[85] Stapleton, op. cit. above, n. 44.

The degree to which a statistical correlation establishes cause and effect depends in part on whether there are other possible causes and how many. Higher and harder standards of care may have causes other than insurance.

One possibility is that social attitudes have changed and are still changing. One change is that scientific determinism 'has replaced religion and magic as the way in which many ordinary people explain adversities. One consequence is that there is generally a search for causes and an attribution of responsibility or blame.'[86] For that and other reasons, people are looking for scapegoats. So, in the realms of negligence, more liability for doctors, for example, may be the result not of more insurance but of changes in society. First, in the profession there is more understanding of medical cause and effect, and there are more doctors willing to give evidence for claimants. Secondly, among patients there is more consumerism and litigation-mindedness,[87] as well as more social conscience about and sympathy for the victims of our society and its products, and less awe of the men in white coats.

Damages

The belief is widespread that awareness of the existence of cover has an inflationary effect on the amount of damages awarded,[88] especially damages awarded by juries; that juries award too much; and that the awareness has some effect too on the awards made by judges. To a degree this could well be true. It is hard to draw precise conclusions, and an empirical study published in 2002 concluded that the effect on awards had been overstated.[89] Nonetheless, one of the authors of that study has also concluded that, in the absence of insurance, 'it is doubtful whether the tort system would survive at all', and that in one sense insurance 'provides the lifeblood of tort'.[90] Moreover, 'there is a trend in the UK towards preventing claimants obtaining double compensation by reducing damages to take accent of . . . collateral benefits' such as the receipt of insurance money. However, the trend is mainly seen with regard to money from public sources, such as social security, rather than private insurance (unless paid for by the victim's employer).[91]

Another effect altogether has been attributed to the insurance factor in the United States. A popular theory there is that the amount of compensatory damages in a tort case should be assessed according to the 'insurance theory of compensation'. This theory sees a successful action in tort for damages as a 'port of entry' to insurance cover. From this perspective, the damages, it is argued,

---

[86] B. Corby, 'On Risk and Uncertainty in Modern Society', *Geneva Papers on Risk and Insurance* No. 72 (1994), 235–43, 238. [87] See Chapter 1, p. 4 ff.

[88] E.g. Cane, op. cit. above, n. 27, 204.

[89] R. K. Lewis et al., 'Court Awards of Damages for Loss of Future Earnings' (2002) 29 J of Law & Society 406. [90] Lewis, op. cit. above, n. 2.

[91] Ibid., at 36.

should be assessed according to an estimate of the insurance the claimant would have taken to cover the loss or injury, if he, the claimant, had planned for the contingency—the accident or mishap.

According to the theory, a utility-maximizing individual would incur the expense of an insurance premium if, by transferring dollars from the preloss state to the postloss state (via the insurance policy purchase), she would be transferring wealth from a state in which it yields less utility (the preloss state) to one in which it yields more (the postloss state). In fact, she would continue to make such transfers until the marginal utility of money in the preloss state was the same as in the expected postloss state. Once she reached that position of equality, she could no longer increase expected utility by transferring dollars to the postloss state. Hence, she would purchase no more insurance. Insurance theorists then apply these general guidelines to determine the insurance decisions that individuals would make as to specific sorts of potential losses.[92]

In other words, to the extent that (wise and well-organized) victims insured against the loss that occurred, they recover damages—but that is all they get. For example, loss of income will be fully compensated. Loss of wedding gifts, however valuable, will not if, as is likely, the donee would not have chosen to insure them, or to insure them in full. Clearly, the theory is more easily applied to pecuniary losses than to non-pecuniary losses. Indeed, from the perspective of the wheelchair, it achieves heights of objectivity that might be regarded as chillingly remote. People's priorities and perspectives change when disability strikes. The theory is presently just a shadow on the western horizon of English law.

Visible Effects: in Parliament

The Insurers' Voice

In the more distant past, the insurance industry did not speak with one voice and, consequently, was not well heard. Even with the formation of the British Insurance Association (BIA) in 1918, the industry was not greatly active in and around Parliament until shaken by the threat of nationalization in the period of Labour Government commencing in 1945. Since then the BIA and the Association of British Insurers (ABI), its successor in 1985, have taken a lively interest in what is proposed in Parliament, ranging from proposed rules about dangerous dogs to the pension schemes for osteopaths. This the ABI is usually well placed to do. Not only is it geared up to present the views of its member insurers, but the Parliamentary Register of Members' Interests usually reveals a significant number with financial links with the insurance industry. Yet it is not in Parliament, where insurance factors make for dull debate, that the industry is

---

[92] E. S. Pryor, 'The Tort Law Debate. Efficiency, and the Kingdom of the Ill', 79 Va L Rev 91–151, 100–01 (1993).

best able to influence opinion, but in the ministries charged with the legislation concerned; it is there that the ABI has concentrated its fire.[93] The ABI actively lobbies on matters of concern to insurers and can expect a hearing.[94] Moreover, it is government policy to require ministries to make a Regulatory Impact Assessment (RIA) when preparing legislation. The ABI is one of the regular consultees, specifically on the impact of the proposed legislation on insurance costs and insurability. Within the industry there have been complaints that the ABI spends more time and energy representing some insurance sectors than others. Be that as it may, two striking and ongoing features of that fire are concern about limits on liability cover, especially that of employers,[95] and limits on regulation of the insurance industry itself.

The Insurers' Limits

The extent of statutory liability is commonly tailored to the extent of cover that the industry can provide. In some instances what the insurance industry is unable to provide is the enormously large sums required; but more often it is *unpredictably* large sums: in the famous 'flood' warning of the American Justice Cardozo, it is 'liability in an indeterminate amount for an indeterminate time to an indeterminate class'.[96] So, when people say that a liability is uninsurable, this usually means 'indeterminate to a degree that makes actuarial assessment by the insurer too imprecise for cover to be marketed at a price that will appeal to the relevant pool'. If insurers know the extent of their exposure, although the applicant may not like the rate, the insurers can nearly always quote.

In commerce, a clear example of the influence of insurance on legislation is provided by the evolution of the legislation, known originally as the Hague Rules, that dictates the balance of risk and the burden of insurance between the parties to contracts for the carriage of goods by sea. The insurance factor has been central to the debate[97] and, although it is not beyond doubt that the prevalent view of insurability was correct,[98] the view did have a significant impact on the regime and the limit on the amount of carriers' liability. The availability of what was believed to be affordable insurance cover is also the premise behind certain other

---

[93] ABI, *The Political Process: The Art of Representation* (London, 1995) 2.

[94] See, e.g., R. K. Lewis, 'Lobbying and the Damages Act 1966' (1997) 60 MLR 230.

[95] However, Lewis *et al.*, op. cit. above, n. 89, quote from the Government's 'Review of Employers' Liability Compulsory Insurance' (2003) that, whereas high risk construction companies (scaffolding and roofing) may pay up to 15 per cent of pay roll, the average cost is only 0.25 per cent of payroll.

[96] *Ultramares Corp. v Touche*, 255 NY 170, 179 (1931). In English law see, e.g., *Cattle v Stockton Waterworks Co.* (1875) LR 10 QB 453, 457 (CA).

[97] See Lord Diplock, 'Conventions and Morals', 1 JMLC 525–36 (1970); also A. Diamond, 'The Division of Liability as between Ship and Cargo' [1977] LMCLQ 39–52; and C. W. H. Goldie, 'Effect of the Hamburg Rules on Shipowners' Liability Insurance', 24 JMLC 111–17 (1993); M. F. Sturley, 'Changing Liability Rules and Marine Insurance', 24 JMLC 119–49 (1993).

[98] See below, p. 322 ff.

legislation, not least that which requires liability to be covered by insurance: the liability of motorists under the Road Traffic Acts, and of employers under the Employers Liability (Compulsory Insurance) Act 1969. When the Government published 'Role of Employers' Liability Compulsory Insurance' in late 2003, the response of the ABI was quick and well publicized. Indeed, the very fact of continuing dialogue between government, insurers and employers on the vexed question of employers' liability testifies to the relevance of insurance to liability.

The Insurers' Fears and the Power of Persuasion

A feature of the twentieth century was the industry's power of persuasion. In particular, it mounted an initially successful campaign that the industry should not be regulated, or that rules which were to apply to other sections of society should not apply to insurers. The Law Commission[99] recommended changes in the law on non-disclosure[100] and breach of warranty which an industry campaign managed to block. Equally, the power of the insurance industry as a lobby was seen in the exemption of insurance contracts from the Unfair Contract Terms Act 1977.[101] When, however, the intervention came not from Westminster but from Brussels, the industry's desire for exemption from the EC Directive of 1993 was frustrated. This might be seen as a defeat for an industry that has lost its influence, but it would be nearer the truth to see it as an orderly and tactical retreat in which, within the constraints imposed by the political climate, the industry remained influential. Crucially, the Directive does not apply to 'core provisions' of the insurance contract,[102] and this exemption was developed from a proposal of the ABI that reached the Commission via a European organization of insurers.[103]

The Lessons of Insurance

Lastly, there has been a less direct kind of influence. A number of statutes obtained the necessary support in Parliament in part because of changes in the pattern of insurance, or of changes in attitude brought about by insurance. The Law Reform (Contributory Negligence) Act 1945, whereby it became possible for a plaintiff to recover damages even though the plaintiff had been negligent, owed much to the spread of liability insurance. The abolition of the doctrine of common employment, whereby an employer was not liable to employees for the negligence of other employees, was partly due to the complete change which the practice of employers' liability insurance had produced in the legal treatment of

---

[99] 'Non-disclosure and Breach of Warranty', Cmnd. 8064 (London, 1980). Cf. Lewis, op. cit. above, n. 94.

[100] In March 2005 the Commission agreed to revisit the question. Generally, see Chapter 4, p. 119 ff and Chapter 5, p. 180 ff.   [101] Schedule 1, para. 1(a).

[102] See Chapter 7, p. 269.

[103] Le Comité Européen des Assurances (CEA); see Long (DTI) in (1995) 87 BILA Journal 72, 73.

industrial accidents. The Law Reform (Husband and Wife) Act 1962, which enabled husbands and wives to sue each other in tort, was a response to a situation in which a spouse who had been injured in a road accident through the negligence of the other spouse was the only person in the world who could not claim damages from an insurance company. The influence of insurance has also been traced in the history of product liability.[104] Finally, the very same Unfair Contract Terms Act 1977, which was marked in its gestation by the influence of insurers, also bears the marks of insurance itself: in deciding whether a limitation clause is reasonable, the court is directed by section 11(4)(b) to consider how far it was open to persons seeking to limit their liability to cover themselves by insurance. In practice the courts go further than this and consider the insurance position in relation to most kinds of exemption clause, by asking which of the persons concerned is the better risk bearer.[105] To this we return in the section below entitled 'Contract: Terms'.

Visible Effects: in the Courts

The influence of insurance and insurers on the law developed by the courts is much less clear than the influence on legislation, both as regards patterns of development, the 'invisible' effects,[106] and as regards reasoning in particular cases. The courts may well allow themselves to be influenced by the primary effect of insurance, the magnetic effect of money, that draws the decision to available insurance.[107] The secondary effect, which tailors the law to the 'reality' of the insurance position, is another matter. This effect, the argument runs, is that the very imposition or extent of civil liability is influenced by insurability, or is framed so as to be targeted at a particular kind of insurer rather than some other risk carrier. Notwithstanding the argument, influence in this secondary sense, it is submitted, is to be seen scarcely at all.

Available Insurance

As regards the primary effect, the magnetic effect of available insurance, at one level the influence of insurance may be general and almost subliminal. In the United States it has been contended that 'insurers have repeatedly promoted the fear of liability in order to promote the demand for liability insurance. It is plausible that the fear of liability has been greatly exaggerated and that this exaggeration itself has greatly promoted liability by getting people to insure

---

[104] J. Stapleton, *Disease and the Compensation Debate* (Oxford, 1986) 133. See also in this sense: G. G. Howells (ed.), *Product Liability, Insurance and the Pharmaceutical Industry* (New York, 1991).
[105] See *George Mitchell Chesterhall Ltd v Finney Lock Seeds Ltd* [1983] 2 AC 803; *Smith v Bush* [1990] 1 AC 831.   [106] Above, p. 308 ff.
[107] Below, p. 319 ff.

against it'.[108] In other words, this is the role of insurance as a self-fulfilling prophecy, but, as the author also observes, the magnitude of this effect is unknown and would be hard to measure. In the United Kingdom, the issue is clouded further by the knowledge of the judge, or the lack of it. Whatever judges know or should know about the availability of insurance in general, they were not until recently supposed to know about the insurance cover in place (or not) in the case before the court. In contrast, some courts in Australia have started to follow what occurs in the USA and insist on disclosure of whether insurance cover is in place, and even on what terms. This they have done in pursuance of an official policy to reduce legal costs and increase the speed with which disputes are settled and victims compensated.[109]

In 1994, a Crown Court judge in England found his way into the popular press when he awarded damages against an 82-year-old man, who had shot and injured the claimant at a time when the claimant was attempting to break into the defendant's allotment shed. Whipped into action by certain newspapers, hundreds of their readers responded with anger and with donations to a fund to help the 'poor' old man pay. The judge's reply to the press was what he called the 'cream of the jest', that the 'poor' old man was insured.[110] The judge knew about the insurance because he had been told by counsel at the start of the trial. What he did not know, it seems, is that judges were not supposed to know that sort of thing. That is theory; in practice, they often do.

Judges always know that insurance is in place, of course, when insurance, invariably liability insurance, is compulsory. If a judge goes to lengths to find the motorist negligent, the likelihood is that he does so not because he dislikes motoring but because he believes that, if Parliament has ordained compulsory insurance, public policy favours compensation,[111] and that the motorist has cover and, probably, the claimant does not. If the particular motorist is not insured— and although it is a serious offence, many are not—the liability will be paid by the Motor Insurers' Bureau.[112] Exceptionally, the reverse may also be true. A case in New Zealand concerned whether a motorist whose illegally parked car caught fire and damaged a building, should be liable to the building owner in tort. The likelihood that the owner of the building would have fire insurance being greater than that the motorist would have motor insurance that covered that kind of liability, was a factor against liability.[113] Few objections have been raised, except that it is a factor that may distort the law of tort.

What counts, however, is not whether insurance is available but the court's perception of whether insurance is available. In most instances there is no difference, but controversy continues, for example, over whether and when there

[108] K. D. Syverud, 'On the Demand for Liability Insurance' 72 Tex L Rev 1629–53, 1639 (1994).   [109] See Gill, op. cit. above, n. 33.
[110] The 'poor' old man's appeal to the Court of Appeal was dismissed. See *The Times*, 6 December 1994 and 3 November 1995.   [111] See *Charlton v Fisher* [2002] QB 578 (CA).
[112] See Clarke, ch. 5-9.   [113] *Mayfair Ltd v Pears* [1987] 1 NZLR 459, 462 (CA).

should be liability in tort for economic loss caused by negligence. Whether liability is indeed desirable or not is not our concern, which is with the role of insurance or, rather, perceptions of insurance in the debate.

In a leading case in Canada, a ship with important cargo and a careless captain hit a railway bridge. On a typical day before the accident the bridge was crossed by thirty-two freight trains hauling in total 1,530 freight wagons. The foreseeable consequence of the accident was that traffic could not cross the bridge until it was made safe some weeks later, and that a wide range of manufacturers, carriers, other businesses, and, especially, the plaintiff railway company would lose money. The case was *Norsk*, in which, in an admirable but controversial attempt to get to grips with the economics and insurability of the situation, the Supreme Court decided (by four votes to three) that the loss was recoverable by the railway.[114] Indeed, in *Norsk*, one argument against liability for economic loss (limited by foreseeability alone) was that liability would hit hard non-business people in other cases, such as the holidaymaker who starts a fire. The premise was that such people would be unlikely to have cover against liability to nearby businesses for lost business, which is surely correct. In *Norsk*, however, one argument accepted by the majority in favour of liability for economic loss was that that was the only way the claimant could recover loss of profit, as such loss was not insurable— which is clearly not correct. Loss of profit is an established line of insurance business.[115] Whether or not the decision in favour of a duty was good or not, the Court's knowledge of available insurance, it appears, was not.

In England a claim such as that would have failed; but it is unlikely that the court's perception of available insurance would have been significantly better. The main reason for not imposing a duty in England is the 'floodgates' argument,[116] that otherwise there would be too much liability and that the world of enterprise and of commerce would come to a halt. The assumption, of course, is that the liability is one for which there is no affordable insurance. In England, when the House of Lords decided against the recovery of economic loss in cases such as *Murphy*,[117] it is not apparent that the House was better informed. Did their Lordships know, for example, that, circumscribed by the rules of causation, such loss was recoverable in countries like Holland? The Supreme Court there, as in Italy, had held that when someone negligently cuts a power supply, that person is liable for all foreseeable consequences, physical and pecuniary.[118] Did the House know that, in France, the driver of a vehicle the cause of a crash would be

---

[114] *Canadian National Ry Co. v Norsk Pacific SS Co.* [1992] 1 SCR 1021. See D. Cohen, 'The Economics of *Canadian National Railway v Norsk Pacific Steamship*', 45 U Toronto LJ 143–62 (1995). Cf. B. Feldthusen and J. Palmer, 'Economic Loss and the Supreme Court of Canada' 74 Can B Rev 427–45 (1995).

[115] See, e.g., D. Cloughton (ed.), *Riley on Business Interruption Insurance*, 8th edn (London, 1999).

[116] *Ultramares Corp. v Touche*, 255 NY 170, 179 (1931).

[117] *Murphy v Brentwood DC* [1991] 1 AC 378.

[118] Holland: *HR 14 March 1958*, NJ 1961, 570; *HR 1 July 1977*, NJ 1978. Italy: *Cass civ. 2 April 1965*, D.S. 1965.777.

liable for the foreseeable economic consequences of the congestion? These liabilities were insurable and insured. Last, but surely not least, did the House know that insurance cover for liability for economic loss was available in England, as it is still today?

Again, Lord Denning himself, who was more frank than most other judges about the relevance of insurance, was not always, it seems, better informed. In *Lamb*,[119] for example, he concluded that the householder rather than the local authority should bear the risk of damage by squatters in unoccupied property. He evidently assumed that the householder could and should have had insurance, apparently overlooking the fact that frequently household cover ceased, as it does today, if the property was unoccupied for more than thirty days.

As Lord Bingham conceded many years ago,[120] and Lord Hoffmann more recently,[121] judges cannot be expected to be fully conversant with the insurance background unless fully informed by counsel. Atiyah's assertion that 'it is really high time (in both England and America) that lawyers informed themselves about . . . fundamental matters of insurability in new tort cases and saw to it that the courts were also informed',[122] is apparently no less true now than when he made it in 1992; but can anything really be done about it? The difficulty seems to be that of getting the relevant information[123] and, moreover, information that is up to date. The court can indicate to counsel that it wants the information before the court, but this kind of information, if it concerns claims experience and cost, may well be hard to obtain directly from insurers who regard it as commercially sensitive. However, information sufficient for the enquiry may well be obtainable indirectly by those whose profession it is to find cover for clients: intermediaries and associated panels of experts.

Efficient Insurance

If insurance is available to one side only, that may be all that the court needs to know; then, if it wishes, the court can shift loss in that direction: insurance has its primary effect.[124] If *both* sides are insured, what then? In a leading case, in which both sides were insured, Lord Denning concluded that the insurance factor was cancelled out and turned to other factors in the case.[125] However, if indeed both sides are insured, there remains the further question: which insurance is the more

---

[119] *Lamb v Camden London Borough Council* [1981] 1 QB 625 (CA). R. G. Lee and R. M. Merkin, 'Human Action as Novus Actus Interveniens' (1981) 125 NLJ 965–7.

[120] *Caparo Industries plc v Dickman* [1989] QB 653, 688, *per* Bingham LJ (CA).

[121] *White v Chief Constable of S. Yorkshire Police* [1999] 2 AC 455, 510.

[122] P. S. Atiyah in a lecture quoted by D. Derrington, 'The Effect of Insurance on the Law of Damages', in P. Finn (ed.), *Essays on Damages* (Sydney, 1992) 153–91, 187.

[123] See Chapter 7, p. 277 ff.   [124] See above, p. 304 ff.

[125] *Photo Production Ltd v Securicor Transport Ltd* [1978] 3 All ER 146, 154, (CA); reversed [1980] AC 827.

efficient, and thus perhaps the insurance that should carry the loss? But, again, there remains the preliminary question: is this an issue which the courts are in a position to resolve?

Occasionally, the answer is clear. *Coggin*,[126] for example, concerned vicarious liability for the negligence of a crane driver. The House of Lords held that the driver was the employee of his general employer and not of the client, for whom he was moving goods at the time, because the identity of the client might change from one day to the next; and that the general employer was liable for the driver's negligence. The general employer was the better insurer—not least in the sense of being the one more able and more likely to see to the insurance needs of the driver against illness, unemployment, and accidents.[127]

In many other cases, the answer is less obvious and, in some of them, the judges have reached confident but conflicting conclusions. In a leading case on the liability of auditors for professional negligence, the Court of Appeal took the view that their duty, and thus their liability, could be safely expanded, one judge articulating the underlying assumption that affordable insurance was available.[128] But when the House of Lords reversed the decision, one of the two main judgments took the opposite view of insurance, stating baldly that a foreseeability test of the kind applied by the Court of Appeal 'would open up a limitless vista of uninsurable risk for the professional man'.[129] They cannot both have been right, and one must wonder about their sources. In most cases, however, judges do not mention insurance. The main reason seems to be that they know that the insurance implications of the case are important, but they also know that they know no more than enough 'on which to form anything more than a broad view of the economic consequences of their decisions',[130] and rarely enough to let the decision turn on the point. This is an honest diffidence that is found in the highest courts of the Commonwealth, as well as in England.[131]

This chapter argues that, with the utmost respect, the diffidence is wise. True knowledge knows what it does not know, and it is this that explains why, on the whole, judges do not address the insurance issue. Indeed the issue can be very difficult. In *Norsk*, for example, the issue, as one of the judges saw it, was whether the claimant railway 'was better placed to protect itself from the consequences' of the business losses because, like the other claimants, it had 'access to the full range of protective options', which included not only first party commercial insurance

---

[126] *Mersey Docks and Harbour Board v Coggin and Griffiths Ltd* [1947] AC 1.
[127] See, e.g., ibid., at 17, *per* Lord Porter.
[128] *Caparo Industries plc v Dickman* [1989] QB 653, 703, *per* Taylor LJ.
[129] [1990] 2 AC 605, 643, *per* Lord Oliver.
[130] *Morgan Crucible Co. plc v Hill Samuel & Co. Ltd* [1991] Ch 295, 303, *per* Hoffman J.
[131] High Ct of Australia: *Caltex Oil (Aust.) Pty Ltd v Dredger 'Wilhemstad'* (1976) 11 ALR 227, 265. Sup. Ct of Canada: *Canadian National Ry Co. v Norsk Pacific SS Co.* (1992) 91 DLR (4th) 289, 350. UK: *Morgans v Launchbury* [1973] AC 127, 142–3; *Marc Rich & Co. AG v Bishop Rock Marine Co. Ltd (The Nicholas H)* [1996] 1 AC 211, 228–9, *per* Lord Lloyd; *Wells v Wells* [1999] 1 AC 345, 405, *per* Lord Hutton. *Markesinis and Deakin*, ch. 2.2(c)(vi).

and self-insurance, but also contracts with both the bridge owner and the railway's customers.[132] In *Norsk*, again, the court asked whether the total cost (premiums and transaction costs of all affected businesses) was significantly greater for (their) loss insurance than the cost of liability insurance to potential wrongdoers such as the shipowner. The answers were far from obvious. Again, take the case of claims against a public body such as a health authority in respect of professional negligence. The body may well be self-insured, and the central issue is whether it is 'efficient' to make the public body pay rather than arrange another means of indemnity by society at large; whether it is 'efficient', socially, and politically desirable that the payment should come from funds allocated to public purposes, such as health care, rather than from other sources? It has been well argued that special considerations apply to public bodies as defendants.[133] And, in any of these cases, when the court decides, can it be sure that the loss will be allocated to a sufficient degree and with sufficient certainty to avoid the wasteful cost of overlapping cover?[134] As before,[135] we seem to be encountering the problem of briefing the court. The merits of one kind of insurance over another may be very difficult to assess. Courts are not deterred by difficulty, but the main problem is that the courts have insufficient information to enable them to reach a safe decision.

Even when, arguably, courts are well informed, the ABI has contended strongly that courts are not the appropriate forum in which to settle issues of compensation. In *Heil*,[136] Lord Woolf MR, giving the judgment of a Court of Appeal composed of five judges, addressed that issue as regards whether the Court should bring into consideration a Law Commission report.[137] It was submitted both in writing and orally, on behalf of those representing the defendants, insurance practitioners and the insurance industry, that it would be wrong, as a matter of principle, for the Court to embark on the consideration of the Commission's recommendations. In particular, in the words of Lord Woolf,[138] it was 'contended that it would be unsuitable and inappropriate to seek to alter the level of awards by judicial determination' and that 'Parliament is the appropriate forum in which such a change should be made'. Only then could there be 'a full and proper public debate as to the justification for the increase in general damages which the Commission have recommended'. Parliament 'is in the position to

---

[132] *Canadian National Ry Co. v Norsk Pacific SS Co.*, op. cit. above, n. 131, 349, *per* La Forest J.

[133] B. S. Markesinis and S. Deakin, 'The Random Element of their Lordships' Infallible Judgment' (1992) 55 MLR 619–46, 631.

[134] On this problem, see K. S. Abraham and L. Liebman, 'Private Insurance, Social Insurance and Tort Reform', 93 Col L Rev 75–118, 94 ff. (1993). Similar difficulties have been reported in Australia: M. Mills, 'Insurance and Professional Liability—The Trend of Uncertainty' (2000) 12 Ins LJ 25–47.   [135] See Chapter 7, p. 277 ff.

[136] *Heil v Rankin* [2001] QB 272.

[137] Law Commission Report on Damages for Personal Injury: Non-Pecuniary Loss (1999) (Law Com No. 257) which included the recommendation that the level of damages for non-pecuniary loss for personal injuries should be increased. Among the evidence were submissions from the ABI and the Forum of Insurance Lawyers (FOIL).   [138] *Heil*, op. cit. above, n. 136, at [10].

achieve a change in levels which would be prospective only and can cater for the effects on the insurance industry by means of clearly defined commencement dates and transitional provisions. If the courts interfere, this would create undesirable uncertainty about the prospects of further changes which would not arise if Parliament dealt with the issue.' Moreover, the effect on the insurance industry was likely to be a considerable increase in the amount of liability awards it would have to pay. The significance of this factor was accepted by the Court, which rejected a submission that the effect on the insurance industry should not be taken into account by the Court.[139] Moreover, it did so without taking the findings and values of the Law Commission on trust. Evidently that was an unusual decision. Usually the courts are silent on such matters. Legal writers, of course, are usually no better qualified than judges to decide issues of this kind, but they do have more time to read the views of those who are. One advantage of ivory towers is that the occupant can take a general view and, on a clear day, see what is in the distance. With this caveat, this chapter now looks at some situations in which the perceived efficiency of insurance has been significant.

Tort: Loss or Liability Insurance—in General

An exceptional judge, who 'proves the rule' of judicial silence on the issue of efficient insurance, was Lord Diplock. 'As a judge in the lower courts, Diplock was regarded as analytically outstanding, iconoclastic, and outspoken', and although he shared some of the intellectual ability and the values of Lord Wilberforce, he had 'less of the modesty and caution'.[140] As President of the Restrictive Practices Court, he strode with confidence into the realms of economics. As a leading member of the British Maritime Law Association, he was well able to fathom issues of insurance as they affected the carriage of goods by sea and was deeply involved in the debate when the international liability regime (the Hague Rules) was revised. It was Lord Diplock, with due reverence no doubt as a churchgoer himself, who described the insurer as the 'deus ex machina' of the liability scene. Whether he brought God in or not, he brought to his role as a judge an unusually high degree of experience of the impact of insurance on certain branches of commercial law; and even so, in concluding in favour of loss insurance over liability insurance, he may have got it partly wrong.

Lord Diplock was not the only judge of his time to be aware that a liability system based on fault is an expensive way to administer accident losses;[141] and that the benefits received by victims from the defendant's liability insurance are less in relation to cost than those received under private loss insurance. Back in 1978, the revered report of the Pearson Commission calculated that the system based on tort liability cost 45 pence of every £1 of insurance

---

[139] Ibid., at [32]. On levels of damages, see R. Lewis, 'Increasing the Price of Pain' (2001) 64 MLR 100–111. [140] R. Stevens, *Law and Politics* (London, 1979) 562.
[141] See, e.g., re property damage, Steyn J in *Singer Co. (UK) Ltd v Tees and Hartlepool PA* [1988] 2 Lloyd's Rep 164, 169.

premium.[142] The corollary is the supposition, which is much influenced by motor insurance[143] and which the authority of Lord Diplock established in English judicial thought, that, generally, loss insurance is cheaper and more efficient than liability insurance.[144] But even if one can start from agreement about the appropriate definition and model of economic efficiency, scrutiny shows that both the script and the plot are much less simple than Lord Diplock appeared to suggest.[145] Here are some of the arguments.

First, loss insurance is argued to be more efficient because it is more focused. The estimates of victims of how much loss insurance they need are likely to be more accurate than the estimates of wrongdoers of how much loss they can cause: wrongdoers do not usually know who their victims will be.[146] For example, the railway has a better idea of how much it will lose from closure of a railway bridge than the shipowner who hits it and closes it. The owner of a factory has a better idea of the effect of a fire on the factory and the business than the adjacent road repairer responsible for the fire.[147]

Against this argument, first, it is said that the 'vice' is less vice than virtue; that it is a 'fail-safe' feature that liability cover is usually drafted in more general terms than loss insurance and, consequently, any unexpected dimension of the subject-matter insured is more likely to be covered. Secondly, it is said that liability insurance is preferable because wrongdoers have a better idea of whether they will cause damage at all, being the persons best placed to avoid it. This is true sometimes, but one flaw in this image of the rational wrongdoer is the moral hazard posed, for example, by the macho culture of long hours at desks in the City or at the wheel of a car. Still, as Lord Hoffmann observed:

The rationale, he who creates the risk must bear the risk, is not altered at all by the existence of an insurance market . . . The economic burden of insuring against the risk must be borne by he who creates it and has the control of it . . . The argument that insurance makes the rule unnecessary is no more valid than saying that, because some people can afford to and sensibly do take out comprehensive car insurance, no driver should be civilly liable for his negligent driving. It is unprincipled to abrogate for all citizens a legal rule merely because it may be unnecessary as between major corporations.[148]

---

[142] *Royal Commission on Civil Liability and Compensation for Personal Injury*, 1978, Cmnd. 7054, para. 83.

[143] G. Calabresi, 'First Party, Third Party, and Product Liability Systems', 69 Iowa L Rev 833–51 (1984).

[144] Lord Diplock, 'Conventions and Morals', 1 JMLC 525, 529 (1970). More recently in this sense: Lord Hoffmann in *Transco v Stockport* [2004] 2 AC 1, at [46]. See further Calabresi, op. cit. above, n. 143; S. A. Rea, Jr, 'Economic Analysis of Fault and No-Fault Liability Systems', 12 Can Bus LJ 444, 471 (1987); P. S. Atiyah, 'Personal Injuries in the Twenty-first Century', Paper to the Society of Public Teachers of Law, 16 March 1996. Cf. M. Nell and A. Richter, 'Optimal Liability: The Effects of Risk Aversion, Loaded Insurance Premiums, and the Number of Victims', *Geneva Papers* No. 79 (Apr. 1996), 240–53.   [145] See, e.g., Cohen, op. cit. above, n. 114, 156 ff.

[146] Ibid., at 155 and 157; J. Basedow, *Der Transportvertrag* (Tübingen, 1987) at 486.

[147] *Photo Production Ltd v Securicor Transport Ltd* [1980] AC 827, 846, *per* Lord Wilberforce.

[148] *Transco v Stockport* [2004] 2 AC 1, at [60].

Secondly, it is argued for loss insurance that, in some cases at least, victims, whose interests are paramount, prefer it. This is mainly because it is settled more favourably to victims. On the one hand, victims may be required by their loss policy to bear the first layer (£x) of loss: an excess or a deductible. On the other hand, victims may get less from liability insurance because liability, and thus the amount of indemnity, is reduced by any contributory negligence. Moreover, they may find the money due harder to get: a loss insurer usually hopes to have a continuing relationship with the victim; whereas a liability insurer neither hopes nor expects to see the victim ever again, and has no such incentive to pay promptly or in full, or to give the benefit of any doubt.

Against, however, it might be said that this argument for loss insurance is coloured by motor insurance, and has less relevance, for example, to carriers' liability insurance: carriers may well want to see victims (and their cargo) again, and will be unhappy if the insurer does not pay quickly and in full. Moreover, victims may not be solely concerned with getting the most compensation. There is certainly a feeling in society, but one that is hard to quantify, that it is 'only fair and right' that wrongdoers should be the ones to pay, whether damages or liability insurance premiums. Psychologists tell us that, sometimes, receiving the compensation *from the wrongdoer* is necessary to produce the victim's sense of satisfaction.[149] Journalists tell us that today this is coupled with a sense in victims that someone else should be seen to be to 'blame' and to pay; and this factor has been used to justify insurance covering punitive damages.[150] Moreover, some victims feel that, if the responsibility is left to be carried by own loss insurance, the finger is left pointing too much at the victim rather than at someone else. Indeed, Cane may well be correct in his conclusion that the efficiency argument, that puts the loss on the one who can more efficiently insure against it, is based on notions of paternalism and distributive justice which are alien to the common law tradition[151]—and to the preferences of many victims.

The third argument for loss insurance is the spreading argument, but it is one that cuts both ways depending on the context. Manufacturers, for example, are better able to insure against damage or injury done by their products than most of those who use them, and the cost of liability insurance can be spread with less pain among the buying public as a whole than would be the case if particular users were saddled with all of their own loss.[152] Again, carriers by sea are bigger buyers of insurance (and hence a better known risk) than cargo owners and, as such, can buy cover more cheaply. To this, however, the carrier might reply that, on the contrary, a major loss is more cheaply spread over a number of cargo (loss)

---

[149] G. T. Schwartz, 'The Ethics and Economics of Liability Insurance', 75 Cornell L Rev 313–65, 334 (1990). [150] P. Cane, *Responsibility in Law and Morality* (Oxford, 2002) 246.
[151] P. Cane, *Tort Law and Economic Interests*, 2nd edn (Oxford, 1996), 427.
[152] *Rivtow Marine Ltd v Washington Iron Works* (1973) 40 DLR (3d) 530, 552 (SC), Laskin J; no evidence referred to.

insurers than a single liability insurer.[153] Indeed, in the case of carriage by sea, the argument between loss insurance and liability insurance has been going on for much of the last hundred years, and is far from having been resolved. One reason for that is the inherent difficulty of the issue, but that may not be the only reason. Another, it appears, is that, although apportionment of risk does have some effect on the levels of damage and cost, it is less significant than has been believed in the past; and that consequently carriers have insufficient incentive to research the matter and provide the information needed to fuel the debate to some kind of conclusion: the result is that the data available are unhelpful, and the court which seeks to be helpful may be nothing of the kind. In particular, reasons given in the past for putting a ceiling on the liability of carriers (risk prediction, avoidance of ruinous loss) do not bear serious scrutiny.[154]

Fourthly, an argument for loss insurance is that the liability of wrongdoers to victims and the liability of insurers to wrongdoers are issues more likely to raise difficulties of fact and law than any such questions under loss insurance. This argument reinforces the second, as any difficulties give insurers a stick with which to beat down claims. It is also an argument that the transfer of loss to liability insurers is likely to be less certain and that uncertainty creates cost.[155] However, although bright clear lines do reduce uncertainty, the cost factor cuts both ways. It points to the development of legal rules which spread loss over as few insurers as possible. A no-liability rule may, for example in the case of carriage, lead to multiple first party loss insurance, with greater associated transaction costs.[156]

Further, perhaps this is (again) a point in the debate to suggest that the criterion of efficiency is not low cost alone. For example, said Lord Hoffmann,[157]

in one sense it is true that the fire brigade is there to protect people in situations in which they could not be expected to be able to protect themselves. On the other hand, they can and do protect themselves by insurance against the risk of fire. It is not obvious that there should be a right to compensation from a negligent fire authority which will ordinarily enure by right of subrogation to an insurance company. The only reason would be to provide a general deterrent against inefficiency. But there must be better ways of doing this than by compensating insurance companies out of public funds, and while premiums no doubt take into account the existence of the fire brigade and the likelihood that it will arrive swiftly upon the scene, it is not clear that they would be very different merely because no compensation was paid in the rare cases in which the fire authority negligently failed to perform its public duty.

[153] Diplock, op. cit. above, n. 144, 530–31; M. F. Sturley, 'Changing Liability Rules and Marine Insurance, 24 JMLC 119 (1993), 145.

[154] As regards carriage, see the seminal study: Basedow, op. cit. above, n. 146, 505 ff. More generally, see J. N. Adams, 'The Economics of Good Faith' (1995) 8 JCL 126–37. Symposium: 'Calabresi's *The Cost of Accidents*', 64 Md L Rev 1–736 (2005).

[155] E.g., P. Atiyah, *The Damages Lottery* (Oxford, 1997) ch. 6; and the many publications of Jeffrey O'Connell: http://www.law.virginia.edu/lawweb/faculty.

[156] In this sense Cohen, op. cit. above, n. 114, at 160.

[157] *Stovin v Wise* [1996] AC 923, 955, concerning whether a highway authority should be liable for a collision between two vehicles.

Again, in the central case of motor insurance, the smaller and cheaper is the vehicle, the more vulnerable the occupants, the greater the likely loss, and the more expensive the loss insurance.[158] But if that led to lower premiums for larger vehicles, that would not be acceptable to those who did not run such vehicles, including, for example, those concerned about environmental pollution. In any event, in 2004 some insurers found that certain categories of large vehicle, notably 'four by fours', were a bad risk, and loaded premiums accordingly. Moreover, in some contexts, loss insurance, if associated with strict duties, removes the deterrent effect of tort liability. Not on the roads, it is true, as deterrence derives less from liability than from fear of injury or of disqualification; but in other cases, such as professional liability, the damage to reputation caused by liability may be significant.

After all this time and after much debate, the winner of the argument is not clear. 'It may be that the "insurance argument" cannot be resolved. At the very least, it cannot be resolved without better empirical evidence.'[159] This was the conclusion of the European Commission[160] in 1999, when considering a proposal for an intermodal transport regime[161] and industry response to the proposal. The Commission then commissioned a report, 'The Economic Impact of Carrier Liability on Intermodal Freight Transport'.[162] This was greeted with some 'reserve' by protection and indemnity (P and I) underwriters in London, and by the *Comité Européen des Assurances*. The matter is still under consideration at the Commission.

Whatever the ultimate outcome in the Commission, a somewhat negative conclusion is suggested by the argument that, from the beginning, the debate was false, because it is fruitless to compare things unless, in essential respects, the comparison is of like with like.[163] As Stapleton has pointed out, the risk covered by loss insurance

is the risk of damage being suffered, howsoever caused, be it by someone else's tort or not (let us call this risk T + NT), and this is different from that in relation to which liability insurance is taken out, namely of the insured's tort causing the damage (let us call this risk T).[164]

This may explain why loss insurance has not been universally preferred. Strikingly, liability insurance remains the route to recovery for many victims of personal injury. This is reflected in regimes for the liability of employers and of

---

[158] J. G. Fleming, 'The Pearson Report; Its Strategy' (1979) 42 MLR 249–69, 261. See also Atiyah, op. cit. above, n. 155, 122 ff.
[159] Sturley, op. cit. above, n. 153, 149. Also in this sense B. S. Markesinis et al., *Tortious Liability of Statutory Bodies* (Oxford, 1999) 81 ff.
[160] Directorate-General for Transport (DG VII) at a hearing on 19 January 1999.
[161] 'Intermodal transportation and carrier liability' (Eur OP, Luxembourg, 1999).
[162] europa.eu.int/comm/transport/library/final_report.pdf.
[163] This is also the conclusion drawn by a leading member of the United States' Maritime Law Assn: Sturley, op. cit. above, n. 153.   [164] Stapleton, op. cit. above, n. 44, 831.

producers, as well as motorists. This chapter concludes that the issue is difficult, that the debate has no clear winner, that any general verdict for loss insurance or for liability insurance is suspect, and that perhaps the judge in the High Court of Australia, who said that the merits of loss insurance should not be assumed but should be tested in each situation,[165] was right.

Tort: Loss or Liability Insurance—Commercial Practice

Situations are found—situations that require a degree of cooperation—in which loss insurance is indeed preferable to liability insurance, with the effect that the court may be inclined to negative a duty of care actionable in tort between persons together there. An example is construction work at a major airport, with associated engineering and passenger facilities (shops, parking, conference centre) and, of course, aircraft: larger aircraft hold 400 people, with great potential for loss of revenue if the aircraft are immobilized. The situation poses a formidable liability for any contractor who might carelessly cut wires, or drop a lighted cigarette. For each contractor to have adequate liability cover, the overall cost would be out of all proportion to the value of the global activity, and a disparity that is even more stark in particular cases. The van delivering pre-cooked *cordon bleu* beefburgers would require almost as much cover as the runway repairer. Another situation, posing parallel problems, is the large construction site, such as that associated with the building of an office block or a railway terminal. In such cases, how can the court minded to negative duty justify its decision and draw a line that lawyers can explain to their clients?

Here at least, if the information can be accessed by the lawyers, insurance sometimes provides a broad answer. The practice or pattern of insurance indicates the burden of insurance, and thus the allocation of responsibility, that is preferred by people in the situation and, probably, the one that is most efficient: the practice is not only an explanation for the line but a marker for the line itself. First, the exorbitant cost of a multiplicity of individual liability insurances may, as we have just seen, be the reason for drawing the tort line against liability.[166] But, secondly, if, as is likely, the terminal owner, or the head contractor on the work of construction, has taken out insurance to cover both the loss and the liability of all those legitimately on site, that insurance is both a confirmation of the commercial reality against multiple individual cover, and also a conceptual marker: tort law tells us that the duty of care, which might otherwise have been owed by one person to others, may be limited by the contractual framework created between them.[167] The courts respect this. Commercial practice is a factor important to courts deciding what the law ought to be; this is because certainty and predictability are furthered if the law reflects the practice.

---

[165] Stephen J in *Caltex Oil (Aust.) Pty Ltd v Dredger 'Wilhemstad'* (1976) 11 ALR 227, 265.

[166] See *Petrofina (UK) Ltd v Magnaload Ltd* [1983] 2 Lloyd's Rep 91.

[167] E.g., *Norwich City Council v Harvey* [1989] 1 WLR (CA). See also *Co-operative Retail Services Ltd v Taylor Young Partnership Ltd* [2002] UKHL 17, [2002] 1 WLR 1419, at [39] ff., *per* Lord Hope.

A simpler situation of this kind, and indeed the first to be recognized as such, is that of bailees, who, for goods in their charge, insure not (only) their liability to the goods owner but also the goods themselves, provided, as it often is, that that is clearly the intention of those concerned.[168] The law has responded to clear commercial practice with the 'commercial trust': bailees are allowed to recover from the insurer concerned the full value of goods lost or damaged, even though the loss is not theirs, and they then hold the money for their bailor, the actual loser.[169] Insurance practice overrides the general rule of law that only the loser can enforce a right to indemnity. Again, in the case of the bailee who happens to be a carrier of goods under the Hague Rules, the Rules are both cause and effect of an established pattern of liability based on a certain distribution of risk and of the burden of insurance. This was a significant element in the leading decision of the House of Lords against a duty of care for classification societies to owners of damaged cargo.[170]

Lastly, but less surely, the very practice of *not* taking out insurance may also tell the court something about the appropriate allocation of risk. In *Norsk*, one of the judges agreed that

> if the business community accepts a rule of non-liability for indirect economic losses without securing insurance protection against them by a relatively inexpensive method, then this fact at least suggests that these losses do not present a social problem serious enough to justify the cost to society in providing for their compensation by the most expensive method in its arsenal—liability based on fault. In other words, if the business community is insured, then there is no point in shifting the loss from one insurance company to another at high cost. If the business community is not insured, then that reveals that other ways of defraying such losses are perceived as superior to insurance and the problem is not that serious.[171]

Contract: Terms

The cost of insurance affects the parties' choice of contract terms, for example terms for the carriage of goods. Under the international carriage conventions (such as the Hague-Visby Rules[172] for carriage by sea), shippers can increase the liability of the carrier above the standard conventional limit in amount by making a declaration of the value of the goods shipped; the effect is to transfer risk from the consignor (and the cargo insurer) to the carrier (and its liability insurer). Declarations are rarely made. This is because, in the event of a declaration, although the cargo insurer would lower the premium, the carrier would raise the

---

[168] *Ramco v Int. Ins. Co. of Hannover* [2004] Lloyd's Rep IR 606 (CA).

[169] *Tomlinson (Hauliers) Ltd v Hepburn* [1966] AC 451.

[170] *Marc Rich & Co. AG v Bishop Rock Marine Co. Ltd (The Nicholas H)* [1996] 1 AC 211.

[171] *Canadian National Ry Co. v Norsk Pacific SS Co.* op. cit. above, n. 131, at 350, *per* La Forest J.

[172] International Convention for the Unification of Certain Rules relating to Bills of Lading (Brussels, 25 August 1924), as amended by the Brussels Protocol (23 February 1968) and enacted in England by the Carriage of Goods by Sea Act 1971.

freight charge by an amount greater than the decrease in cargo premium; so, clearly, the consignor would lose more than was saved, and thus has little incentive to make the declaration. All this is because there are so many risks covered by the cargo insurance that the prospect of recovery in respect of one of them has little influence on the amount of the premium, whereas the risk of liability to the cargo owner is one of the main risks insured under the carrier's liability insurance, and is a significant factor in the amount of premiums.[173]

Again, when one party introduces contract terms to exclude or limit that party's liability, the reasonableness (and thus the interpretation) of the terms depends in part on the availability of insurance. The issue arises mainly under section 11(4) of the Unfair Contract Terms Act 1977, but courts had taken this line in disputes arising before the Act came into force. For example, the insurance factor led the court to favour exemption for the supplier of a service for a relatively small fee who was responsible for a large amount of damage to the property serviced;[174] indeed, some clauses purport to 'limit the risk to an amount conveniently insurable'. Another such case is that of bailees of property. If the bailee's charges are low and the property is something like a car, for which owners are likely to have loss insurance, courts favour bailee exemption.[175] If, however, owners are less likely to have cover, for example household furniture insured at home but not while in temporary storage, and given that the law allows bailees to insure the property of others as if it were their own (the 'commercial trust'[176]), courts are less likely to favour exemption. Even the providers of large-scale services may be treated in this way by standard form contracts, such as forms applicable to building contractors whether the work be large or small, and the allocation of risk and of the burden of insurance in this way has been respected and applied by the courts.[177]

Contract: Damages

In *Bredero*, County Council P sold land to defendant D, who developed it and made a large profit. To do so, D broke a covenant with P concerning the density of the development. P's action for damages, the difference between the sale price and the higher price P could have demanded to agree the actual development, failed. P had suffered no loss as a result of D's breach. To award P the sum claimed would, said Lord Steyn, be 'a dramatic extension of restitutionary remedies . . . to confer a windfall in each case on the aggrieved party'. This was not justified, mainly because of its 'wide-ranging impact on our commercial law': uncertainty about the amount of damages and 'a tendency to discourage

---

[173] See Lord Diplock, op. cit. above, n. 144, 539.

[174] *Photo Production Ltd v Securicor Transport Ltd* [1980] AC 827, 851, *per* Lord Diplock. See also, e.g., *George Mitchell (Chesterhall) Ltd v Finney Lock Seeds Ltd* [1983] 1 QB 284, 302, *per* Lord Denning MR, 307 *per* Oliver LJ; [1983] AC 803, 817 *per* Lord Bridge.

[175] See, e.g., *Rutter v Palmer* [1922] KB 87, 90, *per* Bankes LJ.   [176] See Clarke, ch. 5-6.

[177] See *Scottish Special Housing Assn v Wimpey Construction UK Ltd* [1986] 1 WLR 995 (HL).

economic activity'.[178] The latter seems to be reference to the idea of 'efficient breach', which tolerates breach of contract if the effect is to generate more wealth. A further reason, said the judge, was that liability insurance premiums would rise, and that would be against the public interest.

Lord Steyn assumed that relevant insurance is available, but, generally, it is not. Liability insurers usually exclude contractual liability (deliberate or not).[179] Deliberate breach is excluded because it poses a moral hazard: the insurance itself is an inducement to bring about the peril (deliberate breach). If policyholders can get the profit and also get an indemnity for the cost, damages to the aggrieved party, this increases the risk and the unpredictability of the insurer's exposure—which is also heightened in such a case by the 'legal hazard', that is, the relatively high chance that cases of this kind will go to court. So, if breach of contract is covered at all, cover is likely to be costly and limited. Lord Steyn's weighting of the insurance factor is correct only if deliberate breach is covered often enough to have a significant effect on premiums in general—which, it seems, it is not.

The significance of the decision in *Bredero* as regards remedies for breach of contract has largely been removed by later cases, notably the decision of the House of Lords in *Attorney-General v Blake*.[180] The main reasons do not bear on the misconception about available insurance, but *Bredero* does provide another illustration of the reasons for discouraging courts from basing decisions on wider concerns.[181]

Conclusion

The conclusion is that Bishop was right, concerning the efficient distribution of economic loss, when he said that courts do not have enough information to make the requisite technical judgement in each individual case.[182] In many instances this appears to be true also of the insurance factor; and judges are aware of this. Consequently, there is scant reason to believe that judicial perception of insurance has influenced significantly the rules of liability developed by the works. The influence of insurance and insurers is seen most clearly in Parliament, in the form of persuasion, and in the courts in the conduct of litigation. In each case, the influence has been mostly to moderate or restrict liability.

---

[178] *Surrey CC v Bredero Homes Ltd* [1993] 3 All ER 705, 715, *per* Steyn LJ (CA).
[179] See Clarke, ch. 17-4A.   [180] [2001] 1 AC 268. See Treitel, ch. 21.1.1(1)(a).
[181] See above, p. 319 ff.
[182] W. Bishop, 'Economic Loss in Tort' (1982) 1 OJLS 1–29, 13.

9

The Sequel: Perceptions of the Past and of the Future

Certainty and Security

This book has shown that different perceptions of insurance are to be found among those concerned, as well perhaps as too little talking and too much mutual suspicion. One cause of this is ignorance riding on the back of the maxim that 'time is money' and money must be saved at all costs. Another is the state of the law: the nature of its rules, and the degree of uncertainty about what they mean. In particular, people believe that if any dispute arises with insurers, insurers have an unfair advantage under the law; and they do—if insurers choose to use it.

Insurance is a drama in which the actors need to know their lines: what to say and when to say it—which means knowing what the others will say too. Policyholders want peace of mind and security: the certainty of cover against the slings and arrows of outrageous life.[1] A study in Holland[2] suggested that in common law countries there is more emphasis on personal independence and responsibility, and, consequently, less need felt for predictability than in other countries in the study, among them Austria, Belgium, France, Germany, Italy, Spain, and Switzerland. Be that as it may, for order and stability in society, law and what is built upon it must be certain; and there is scant reason to believe that in England people find either insurance or insurance law predictable enough.

Insurers too want certainty—certainty about the particular risk to be insured so that they can rate it and insure it, effectively and profitably. Uncertainty, whether it concerns changes in the law or changes in the weather, is the bane of insurers. To rate risk insurers study both.[3] As regards law, the insurance industry has an effective presence on the benches in Parliament.[4] As regards the physical features of risk, individually, or collectively through the ABI, insurers study ways in which risk can be predicted, managed, and controlled. With this information insurers can circumscribe their exposure by carefully drawn contract terms, including terms designed to encourage and educate policyholders to reduce the risk and the extent of loss. In doing that insurers have moved from the role of actuary to that of adviser and risk manager, with an associated change in the nature of their legal liability to their customers. Enormous energy and skill are behind the very professional drive of the insurance industry to achieve all this. Research about risk and the writing of cover is collective and coordinated to a degree not found in the past, and not found today in many other countries of the world.

In matters of cover large corporate purchasers of insurance have risk managers, who may well be a match for the insurers with whom they deal. Others, small companies or consumers, are not. People have neither the training nor, it seems, the instinct to counter risk, for they are mostly mistaken in both their fears and their certainties.[5] Their fears are not in proportion to the risk; they do not fear what threatens them most, and their responses are misplaced. So are their certainties. They look for anchor points but grab at straws—the comforting anecdote of Uncle Ed who smoked fifty cigarettes a day and lived to the age of 80.

When people respond to risk by buying insurance, frequently they do not understand what they are buying.[6] The persistence of some complainants to the FOS in the teeth of the wording of their policies shows a stubborn devotion to

---

[1] See Chapter 1, p. 3 ff.
[2] I. G. Hofstede, 'Insurance and the Product of National Values', *Geneva Papers* No. 77 (1995), 423–9.   [3] See Chapter 2, p. 48 ff.
[4] See Chapter 8, p. 316 ff.   [5] See Chapter 1, p. 12 ff.
[6] See Chapter 5, p. 145 ff.

perceptions of what cover ought to be, rather than what it is. Evening classes in the interpretation of insurance policies, side by side with scale modelling and Spanish for beginners, are not a serious option. Still, for an educated modern society an understanding of risk is fundamental, and that (in an ideal world) it should be part of the curriculum of continuing education is an attractive suggestion. People would make better decisions about risk and about insurance, and a better deployment of their assets. Moreover, people might learn not to expect too much of insurers, or of the 'plain' English of policies insurers write. People would learn that, in language as in law, certainty is relative, and that absolute certainty is unattainable. The most we can hope for is insurance policies which are as plain as is reasonably possible to the people who buy them, policies which fulfil, as far as sensible rating permits, the reasonable expectations of people with an aversion not only to risk but also to small print; and rules of law which, to their legal advisers at least, are as clear as can be reasonably contrived. It was the celebrated American judge, Cardozo J, who wrote[7] that he was

much troubled in spirit, in my first years on the bench, to find how trackless was the ocean on which I had embarked. I sought for certainty. I was oppressed and disheartened when I found that the quest for it was futile. I was trying to reach land, the solid land of fixed and settled rules, the paradise of a justice that would declare itself by tokens plainer and more commanding than its pale and glimmering reflections in my own vacillating mind and conscience . . . As the years have gone by, and as I have reflected more and more upon the judicial process, I have become reconciled to the uncertainty, because I have grown to see it as inevitable.

Certainty of Law

If absolute certainty cannot be reached, it is nonetheless the end of a road that the law should take as far as it reasonably can. 'It is the province of the law of contract to draw the future into the present.'[8] To ring fence the future requires firm points of reference and clear lines. The 'great object in every branch of law, but especially in mercantile law, is certainty'.[9] These words of Lord Mansfield in 1809 have been echoed down the years. Whether in business or in the affairs of consumers, uncertainty of law means cost—in drafting to provide against what the law might mean and, ultimately, in lost opportunities because of what it might not mean, or in litigation to settle what it does mean.

Lord Goff once observed that for businessmen 'in the end certainty is more important than justice'.[10] Later Lord Hoffmann referred to 'the existence of an

---

[7] B. Cardozo, *The Nature of the Judicial Process* (New Haven, Conn., 1921) 166.
[8] J. Kohler, *Philosophy of Law* (transl. A. Albrecht, New York, 1914) 136.
[9] J. A. Park, A *System of the Law of Marine Insurances*, 6th edn (London, 1809) 202.
[10] 'Opening Address', Second Annual JCL Conference September 1991 (1992) 5 JCL 1–5, 3.

undefined discretion' to refuse to enforce a contract 'on the ground that this would be "unconscionable" ' as being sufficient to create uncertainty, and pointed out that even 'if it is most unlikely that a discretion to grant relief will be exercised, its mere existence enables litigation to be employed as a negotiating tactic'.[11] Moreover, speaking as he often has out of court, Sir Christopher Staughton has pronounced that he did not know 'how otherwise one can demonstrate that business people prefer certainty, unless it be by the choice of English law for their contracts, and standard forms of contract compiled by reference to English law'.[12] Chosen it is. Perfect it is not—neither commercial law in general, nor insurance law in particular.

Certainty of Insurance Law

For insurance law, the certainty sought by Lord Mansfield has been largely achieved on some points. On the one hand, insurers can benefit, for example, from a hard-and-fast interpretation of time limits for notice, as long as they are carefully drafted,[13] and also time limits for payment of premiums: the courts in life insurance cases have not followed land law down the track of relief against forfeiture to soften the effects on life assurance when premiums are tendered late; if policyholders do not pay on time, cover comes to an end. On the other hand, policyholders benefit, for example, when their insurer is hoist by the petard of what is prominent in the insurer's documentation rather than allowed to escape through the interstices of small print. To a very limited degree English law recognizes something like a rule whereby the reasonable expectations of the insured about the cover are fulfilled, as long as those expectations are based on a reasonable view of what the insurer has said.[14]

When the law is hard and fast, however, mostly its effects seem to be hard for policyholders. The courts have responded with exceptions to rules of this kind, but sometimes, for example concerning insurable interest and commercial trust, the exceptions look strained and even puzzling—not only to policyholders, but also to solicitors seeking to explain them.[15] Often insurers do not insist on their strict legal rights; but when insurers have waived a point in people's favour, as Lord Goff was well aware,[16] those people may well wonder whether they can be at all sure that their insurer will do the same next time.

Indeed, the trail of uncertainties starts right at the beginning when a person applies for insurance. The first problem is that the insurance product may not be

---

[11] *Union Eagle Ltd v Golden Achievement Ltd* [1997] AC 514, 519 (PC).
[12] 'Good Faith and Fairness in Commercial Contract Law' (1994) 7 JCL 193–6, 194.
[13] See *McAlpine v BAI*, discussed in Chapter 6, p. 217 ff.
[14] See Chapter 5, p. 153 ff.   [15] See Chapter 1, p. 31 ff.
[16] See his the words quoted above, at p. 336.

easy to understand. The main benefits may be clear; the exclusions and conditions may not. When insurance is sold, the law shows more concern about the accuracy or completeness of what applicants say to the insurer than with what insurers say to applicants.[17] True, there are rules that require insurers and those who sell insurance for them to point up the exclusions. How carefully they do this is disputed. Anyway, insurance buyers are driven by the prospective benefits of what they are buying; most of them, naturally enough, want to believe that the product is as good as it is presented to be, and to get on with the holiday or driving the new car, as the case may be.

If they are wise, insurance buyers are aware of their ignorance and turn to advice; but today they may not find the knowledge they seek. Independent financial advisers (IFAs) are under pressure. They are under pressure of competition from alternative outlets that purport to provide the public with cheaper insurance products. They are under pressure of time not only to save money, but also to meet the expectations of clients; but they lack both the time to learn about new products and the time fully to explain them to clients.[18] Anyway, many insurance buyers are not wise; they simply do not ask for advice. Surveys suggest that many people do not understand what advisers are for, or why they might need them. Indeed, it sometimes seems that some advisers do not either.[19]

Today advisers (intermediaries) are seeking a new role in a changing scene; consequently they are sending out confusing signals to a confused public. The law, too, as it affects insurance intermediaries in general, has sent some confusing signals by allowing dual agency and conflicts of interests,[20] and it remains to be seen to what extent the message will be clearer under the new regulations that came into force in January 2005.[20a] In a scathing judgment back in 1989,[21] Purchas LJ said that:

> To the person unacquainted with the insurance industry it may seem a remarkable state of the law that someone who describes himself as a Lloyd's broker who is remunerated by the insurance industry and who presents proposal forms and suggested policies on their behalf should not be the safe recipient of full disclosure.

Whether a Lloyd's broker or not, if a client ever asks 'Whose side is this intermediary on?', the answer is sometimes surprising.

When people have bought their cover—when they have signed the form and perhaps received a policy—they think that is that and get on with living; but as buyers of insurance they may be in something of a fool's paradise. Although they should have been alerted by the application form or by their adviser that they have to disclose material information, without painstaking advice from an intermediary,

---

[17] See Chapter 4, p. 99 ff.   [18] See Chapter 3, pp. 81–2.   [19] Ibid.
[20] See Chapter 3, p. 66 ff.
[20a] Minor changes in the FSA Rulebook are so frequent that the FSA's front webpage points to a distinct page that lists them. Moreover, major changes are being considered.
[21] *Roberts v Plaisted* [1989] 2 Lloyd's Rep 341, 345 (CA), concerning disclosure of material information. The Law Commission is to publish an Issues Paper on Intermediaries in April 2007. Concerning the new regulations see Chapter 3, p. 60 ff.

buyers will not know what is material and what has to be disclosed.[22] If they have not disclosed the very last detail, the cover can be set aside at the discretion of the insurer. Moreover, if they have paid premium, it is commonly paid to the intermediary, and occasionally a buyer finds that, for one reason or another, the intermediary has not passed it on to the insurer; and that until it is passed on there is no cover at all.

Mostly, of course, people manage to buy perfectly sound and sensible insurance. Then they forget about it until, as is quite usual in practice, they get a reminder to renew (and would be outraged to be told that they are not entitled to reminders and that it is up to them to check dates) or they make a claim. So, for example, having 'sorted out' his accident cover before going on holiday to New Zealand, Peter discovers there the thrills of bungee jumping. When he hits the water and is hurt, however, he discovers that it is a dangerous pastime and, when he claims for his injury, that his insurer agrees; so much so that his insurer has excluded it from all accident cover, including Peter's. Alternatively, Peter jumps safely, but when he comes home and falls on the stairs and claims, he is told by his insurer that his bungee jumping may not have broken his neck but it has broken something called a warranty in the policy; and that when he jumped, weeks before he slipped on the stairs, his cover ended automatically. If he is lucky, Peter may be told about the FOS, where the ombudsmen take a rather different view of these 'warranties', and, eventually, perhaps after many months of 'reconsideration' by the insurer, Peter's claim is paid.

Meanwhile, accountant Jane, who has bought professional liability cover, has a bad day at the office and gives a client some careless advice. When the writ arrives, she finds that her insurer is not obliged to defend her at all, or, if the insurer decides to do so, that the insurer does not want to settle quietly but wants to make a stand, make her a test case on a difficult marginal point about what her lawyer calls economic loss and the rule in *Hedley Byrne*. All this is going to cost Jane a great deal, both in damage to her business reputation and what she will have to pay for liability cover in future.

About the same time, her garage, which bought cover against environmental impairment liability (EIL), finds that the policy definition of pollution is complex and not at all what the garage expected; after all, why should there be cover for damage done by the great flood of petrol from the burst hose on the forecourt, but not for that from the seepage from the defective tank nearby which turned out to have a small crack that nobody noticed?

Jane may, however, feel less foolish, although no less annoyed, than one of her neighbours at home, who thought that 'all-risks' cover meant what it seemed to say, but then found that it does not.[23] Indeed, Jane found that even the very definition of 'insurance' is unclear.[24] That was of little immediate concern to her but of

---

[22] See Chapter 4, p. 101 ff.   [23] See Chapter 6, pp. 189–90.
[24] See below, p. 347 ff.

grave concern to her other neighbour, who is 'something in the City'; for years that neighbour managed a firm that had been selling people life insurance on the basis that that kind of life insurance qualified as a tax-efficient investment, only to be told one day by a court of law that it was not life insurance at all.

Surprises like this are not usually sprung until there is an insurance claim. At that point policyholders may find other surprises too. The exporter whose briefcase was stolen during deep and difficult negotiations in Kabul, when telephone connections were down, is told by his business travel insurer, on getting back to London, that any claim will be rejected because notice of loss is too late, or because the precise contents of the briefcase cannot be proved, or because documentary evidence from the Kabul police was not obtained. Alternatively, the exporter may be told that when he contracted the cover, although not when he went,[25] trips of any kind to Kabul were 'material to the risk', and that what happened there is not covered because the insurer was not told about the planned trip in advance.[26]

In practice, of course, insurance is not such a lottery as these tales might suggest. Whatever the strict black letter of the law may say, insurers, sometimes prompted by the FOS or by the press, often take a softer line. They waive their strict rights under the contract or under the law, they turn blind eyes to late dates, they make 'ex gratia' payments. But if policyholders are to have any real certainty, the sense of security that they seek, they need, as Lord Goff reminded us,[27] to know what their insurer will do *before* the insurer does it; they need to be sure that the insurer who was kind last time will be kind next time. They want to know why so much depends on the discretion, however benign, of insurers. Is there not still something in Williston's belief[28] that most people prefer an inanimate rule to dependence on the 'unbridled will' of their fellow men and women? People who buy locks for their doors wants to be able to sleep peacefully in the knowledge that they are secure from burglars. People who buy insurance also want to know that their cover is secure,[29] and that insurers will pay without undue deliberation or delay. Not so.

No better illustration of insecurity can be found than in the amount of discretion that the law allows insurers, especially when a claim is brought and the insurer's claims department 'smells' fraud. Quite apart from the tried and tested use of 'technical' defences, such as late notice or non-disclosure,[30] the law gives insurers almost infinite discretion to delay payment[31] until claimants crack or simply give up. There is evidence, in the past at least, that a considerable proportion of the stress suffered by claimants in personal injury cases is a product of deliberate strategy by insurers defending the claim and the inability of solicitors, for

[25] Materiality is tested not when the claim arises but when the insurance is contracted: *Associated Oil Carriers v Canton* [1917] 2 KB 184.
[26] See Chapter 6, p. 197 ff, and also p. 215 ff.   [27] Above, pp. 336–7.
[28] S. Williston, *Some Modern Tendencies in the Law* (New Haven, Conn., 1929) 95.
[29] See Chapter 1, pp. 3–4.   [30] Chapter 6, p. 215 ff.   [31] See Chapter 6, p. 244 ff.

reasons of resources, organization, and experience, to move claims forward fast enough.[32]

Insurers are mostly staffed by fair and honourable people, but it was a senior member of the insurance industry who, at a claims conference, warned against claims handlers who pick up a file and look for a spine to shiver down. The evidence of history is that few people can be trusted with power; that discretion is power; and that it does not follow at all that because the power is small on the scale of history, the chances of abuse are small too. 'There never was a man who thought he had not law but his own will, who did not soon find that he had no end but his own profit.' That was the view of an historian many years ago.[33] It is still the view of English law that no man or woman should be judge in his or her own cause. The perception of this book is that too often insurance law is such that insurers are just that. Fair and just perhaps, but judges nonetheless. So, what can be done about the law of insurance? Before trying to answer that question we must first address another. What can be expected of the people who buy insurance, the policyholders?

The Nature of People

Expectations of Speed and Convenience

People tend to assume that if something can be done more quickly than before, it is being done better than before. People who want fast food, convenience food, also want other purchases to be fast and convenient, especially tedious ones like insurance: this once again is ignorance riding on the back of the view that time is money and that money must be saved at all costs, as well as the belief that buying things should be fun. Lingering over the purchase of a new coat may be a plea-sure, lingering over insurance cover is not—that is the perception of insurers afraid of losing market share, and it is probably correct. However, although speedy selling of standard insurance products that have been around for years may well be viable, there is real doubt about that when the products are not standard.

The insurance industry rightly prides itself on product innovation. Scarcely a week passes by without the announcement of some ingenious new policy, with a new range of terms. For common kinds of product, such as house contents insurance, the magazine of the Consumers Association, *Which*, draws up tables to help persistent consumers make meaningful comparisons. However, like the technical specifications of hi-fi, insurance terms are studied only by enthusiasts or obsessives. Too often, insurance buyers do not really know what they are

---

[32] H. Genn, *Hard Bargaining* (London, 1987) 122–3.
[33] Edmund Burke, *Impeachment of Warren Hastings*, 17 February 1788.

buying from sellers, who do not know much more than the buyers about what they are selling.

Moreover, none of this avails the growing number of people who buy by telephone, in particular buyers of motor cover and house contents cover. For these transactions, the most that can be hoped is that terms will be monitored or censored by the FOS,[34] or by the consumers' organizations.[35] Like buyers of canned food, to ensure that they do not get a can of worms, buyers of insurance must depend on the quality control and scrutiny of someone else, whom they trust.

Distrust

Whatever government departments may say about the safety of certain food products, some people will not believe it and will not eat them. Sureness and certainty depend not only on the public perception of the products, but also on their perception of those who provide them or those who offer advice about them. One source of uncertainty and expense in the insurance market today is the mutual distrust between policyholders, on the one hand, and insurers and those who sell insurance, on the other.

Economists, some of them anyway, argue that, generally, business is done better in a spirit of trust and mutual confidence than one of outright competition and hostility. A prominent opponent of competition wrote of trust as a 'rational economic tool' to secure long-term relationships and compensate for market weaknesses such as information imbalance.[36] Even a prominent advocate of competition has contended that the largest costs in a modern economy are transaction costs, and that these are minimized in an atmosphere of trust—in contrast to an atmosphere in which everyone tries to take advantage of everyone else, and no one moves without a lawyer.[37] He went on to warn against economic ideas imported from the United States which come laden with cultural presuppositions, among them the view that, because people cannot be trusted, formal methods of enforcing competition between them are essential. He concluded that the American emphasis on the law as an enforcement mechanism is a part of American culture which does not travel well. Nor has it, as we have seen from the evidence of a compensation culture considered in Chapter 1.

An assessment of the economic argument for trust is beyond the scope of this book and the competence of its author, but there is little in the insurance marketplace to suggest that the argument is misconceived. Indeed, in Europe a leading member of the insurance industry has written that, whatever strategy is adopted by insurance companies to retain market share in future, there is one immutable

---

[34] See Chapter 6, p. 239 ff.   [35] See Chapter 7, p. 268 ff.

[36] F. Fukuyama, *Trust: The Social Virtues and the Creation of Prosperity* (London, 1995).

[37] Samuel Brittan, *Financial Times*, 18 November 1993, with reference to Mark Casson, *The Economics of Business Culture* (Oxford, 1993).

constraint: the insurance industry must have the trust of its customers. It must be seen to honour its commitments, and industry strategy must ultimately be geared to increasing the security underlying each and every policy.[38] This being so, what can be done about it in England?

Trust: Image

For the public to trust insurers requires, it seems, a change in the image of insurers. When a well-known chain retailer of socks and sandwiches started to sell financial products in 1995, it sold only on an 'execution basis': it offered simple and clear information 'on the label' and made it clear that it was not offering advice about the terms. With emphasis on the company's general reputation built up over many years in the retail trade, the centre of the company's marketing strategy was the quality and reliability of what it had sold in the past: 'Trust us again!' Doubtless it was also wary of damaging its image by misselling.

Reliability implies not only consistency of performance but also transparency. People need to 'know where they are' not only with the product, but also with the producer. A relationship in which the stronger party first holds out the hand of friendship but then, come the claim, pulls back in suspicion, or even hostility, is a recipe for nothing but disappointment, disillusionment, and even a sense of betrayal.[39] This does not help the balance sheet either because, usually, it costs insurers less to keep existing customers than to find new customers to replace them. Insurers who were tough on claims in the past now find it hard to shed the distorted image of 'cheats in bowler hats' projected by the press. A better image means a softer response to claims, the point of contact which, all agree, makes the greatest mark on the memory of customers. In the medium term, self-interest alone suggests that insurers should strive for a better relationship with their policyholders, one less of confrontation than of cooperation. Clearly some insurers, especially in the life sector, are moving in this direction. However, they should be aware that both to retain the predictability associated with the paradigmatic contract of the past, and to obtain the trust and cooperation which maximize the mutual benefits of the long-term contract in future, is not possible. The one can be achieved only by some sacrifice of the other.

Trust: Information

For insurers to trust the public will, it seems, also require a change in the insurers' image of the public. Here, however, the initiative lies not with the public but with

---

[38] H. Schulte-Noelle, 'Challenges for Insurers in the Nineties', *Geneva Papers on Risk and Insurance*, No. 72 (1994), 287–303, 301.
[39] T. Baker, 'Constructing the Insurance Relationship' 72 Tex L Rev 1395–1433, 1414 (1994). See Chapter 6, pp. 209–10.

insurers to educate the public: to educate those who buy insurance against false expectations of cover and those who have bought insurance against fraud. There are signs now that people are beginning to understand that insurance fraud is not a sport but a form of cheating, and that it is they who, ultimately, bear the cost of fraud. Moreover, as with other kinds of crime, the best way of reducing the level of fraud is to raise the level (and thus the fear) of detection. Significant, therefore, is that the chance of detection has been increased by the computer record and data sharing between insurers, such as the Claims and Underwriting Exchange (CUE).[40]

Although the CUE may increase the confidence of insurers that they can spot fraud, it does not, of course, necessarily lead to trust—on either side. On the contrary, one consequence of the CUE may be that there is not more but less trust on each side—on the insurers' side because they may feel that with the CUE behind them they do not need to trust policyholders, and on the side of policyholders because of what they feel about computers, confidential data, and the archetypal Orwellian image of Big Brother. The perception persists that, like speed cameras on roads, computer checks are 'not cricket'; that like some other miracles of science, computers put too much power in the hands of the wrong people or, at least, people who cannot always be trusted. Many are deeply suspicious about the use of information by networks of computers available to public authorities, to branches of government, and to the police. Some will see the CUE as one more strand in the web of the Orwellian State. In 1993 the ABI published a Data Protection Code of Practice, but then withdrew it.

The Law of Cooperation

For the last thirty years writers on the law of contract have stressed the importance of long-term contractual relationships, and some have argued for changes in the law of contract to accommodate and encourage these 'relational' contracts. They argued that 'classical' rules of contract law were developed in the context of discrete market transactions concluded at arm's length, which are no longer typical. Others counter with the contention that all of the concerns behind that argument can be accommodated by the traditional 'classical' rules,[41] that long-term commercial relationships are best nurtured like other human relationships, and that therefore the less the law is brought in the better.

Be that as it may, this book suggests,[42] however, that the insurance relationship, long term as it may well be, differs in significant respects from other long-term contractual relationships; that insurance is still served adequately by traditional rules of law that are black in letter and clear in outline; and indeed that some

---

[40] See Chapter 6, p. 210 ff.
[41] E.g., R. Austen-Baker, 'A Relational Law of Contract?' (2004) 20 JCL 125–44.
[42] See Chapter 5, p. 172 ff.

existing rules are not clear enough. While advocating more trust between insurers and their policyholders, it is argued here nonetheless that policyholders should not have to trust insurers in the way they exercise discretion about resort to rules of law, such as technical defences, which favour insurers; but that, as far as can reasonably and possibly be, policyholders should have the firm support of predictable insurance contract law.

Still, some aspects of the relationship cannot be based entirely on law like that. Indeed, one suggestion is that long-term contractual relationships are a sociological rather than a legal category in which, as some writers have put it, 'short-term maximizing behaviour is rejected as opportunistic'. On the contrary, it is said, as in any kind of partnership, the parties should aim at 'utility-maximization indirectly through long-term co-operative behaviour manifested in trust and not in reliance on obligations specified in advance'.[43] One way of facilitating cooperation is by resort to external norms deriving from trade or industry practice. Relational contracts, they argue, require the rejection of immediate *individual* self-interest as the measure of economic rationality, and its replacement by common interest as this measure. Self-interest in these contracts is sufficiently served by cooperation.

The interest of that argument for relational contracts lies not only in its intrinsic merits but in its resonance with current legal developments on a wider front, in particular with the doctrine of contractual good faith, which has now crossed the sea from Brussels to underpin contracts at large. To date English courts have taken a narrow view of good faith under the EC Directive;[44] however, one day soon, good faith based on a spirit of cooperation,[45] together with assessment of the reasonable expectations of contracting parties,[46] may well offer a new legal foundation for the insurance relationship as well as other kinds of contractual relationship.

The Nature of Law and of Language

Language

Like many goals in life, certainty of law is one that should be sought, but sought in the awareness that it is a goal that will never be perfectly attained; and that it is 'not a valid objection to legal doctrine that it will not always be easy to know whether the doctrine is to be applied in a particular case. The law has to face such embarrassments.'[47] Answers to questions of law often shade one into another.

---

[43] D. Campbell and D. Harris, 'Flexibility in Long-term Contractual Relationships: The Role of Co-operation' (1993) 20 J Law & Society 166–91, 167, 180.   [44] See Chapter 7, p. 269 ff.
[45] R. Brownsword, 'Two Concepts of Good Faith' (1994) 7 JCL 197–244, 209.
[46] H. K. Lucke in P. Finn (ed.), *Essays on Contract* (Sydney, 1987) 162 and 164. See Chapter 5, p. 153 ff.   [47] *Dashwood v Magniac* [1891] 3 Ch 306, 364, *per* Bowen LJ (CA).

An associated problem lies in conflicting traditions of the common law. On the one hand, as we have seen, the law seeks to respect people's need to know where they stand. On the other hand, the common law distrusts rules that are general, and prefers the 'incremental' development of rules case by case, inch by inch. It was once said in the Canadian Supreme Court that uncertainty 'is inherent in the common law generally. It is the price the common law pays for flexibility, for the ability to adapt to a changing world. If past experience serves, it is a price we should willingly pay, provided the limits of uncertainty are kept within reasonable bounds.'[48] If the law is too rigid, it may inhibit developments in law and practice which become desirable as conditions change. Nonetheless, the limits of uncertainty should be tight.

To this end, the terms of insurance contracts are drawn with care and consideration; but neither the quest for precision nor the scarcely consistent campaign for 'plain' English will ever avoid all ambiguity.[49] Because the law has to be expressed in words, and words have a penumbra of uncertainty, marginal ambiguity is bound to occur. This being so, the function of the judge is not simply to administer the law and apply the contract. The judge must sometimes look not only to the letter of the law and the wording of the contract, but also to the spirit and purpose of both. The application of the EC Directive, for example, to unfair insurance terms,[50] while good for policyholders in the longer run, created a cloud of uncertainty in the shorter term, but one which is being steadily lifted by the work and publications of the Office of Fair Trading (OFT).[51]

The work of the OFT is part of the important process of demystification, whereby insurance law is being brought more clearly into the frame of the general law of contract. This, it is submitted, is something that can and should be done in the cause of certainty. If, as is also submitted here, it is too much to expect policyholders to understand every clause of their contract and the law that sustains it, at least something can be done to ensure that their advisers, solicitors, or barristers can do it for them.

Lawyers

The law, said Williston, 'must be applied by men engaged in practical affairs and by so many of them that to be useful legal doctrine must be capable of being understood and stated by men who are neither profound scholars nor interested in abstract thought'.[52] Insurers are specialists in insurance and, as needs must, some of them know a lot about insurance litigation. Mostly, solicitors are not; and in the field of litigation in particular solicitors are often no match for insurers.

---

[48] *Canadian National Ry Co. v Norsk Pacific SS Co.* (1992) 91 DLR (4th) 289, 368, *per* McLachlin J, concerning liability for economic loss.   [49] See Chapter 5, p. 147 ff.
[50] See Chapter 7, p. 268 ff.   [51] See www.oft.gov.uk and follow 'bulletin'.
[52] Williston, op. cit. above, n. 28, 127.

Of course, barristers and some solicitors too do specialize in litigation at large, but for the majority insurance law is likely, at best, to be a dim recollection of a chapter tucked away at the end of a course on commercial law. In the third and latest edition of a leading book entitled *Commercial Law*,[53] there are at most four pages of print devoted to the law of insurance, scattered in four different places in a total text of 1,210 pages.

In the UK, general (non-marine) insurance law is taught by the Chartered Institute of Insurers as a small part of a professional course for those entering the industry. For those heading for legal practice, it is taught in less than a handful of university courses. Sheffield University has 150 undergraduates on such a course, but elsewhere there is no class exceeding fifty students. London University offers it as an LLM option and has more external students in Hong Kong than students in residence in London. In France, however, there are three institutes of insurance law, the largest in Paris, teaching French insurance law to hundreds of students. In Germany there are hundreds more. In the UK the position is unlikely to change. With diminishing resources to meet the increasing demands of other, often more novel and more fashionable options, more space in the university syllabus for insurance law is unlikely.

In practice, lawyers with less and less time to meet the demands of courts and clients for more and more speed, do not have the resources either of time or of training to learn enough. Lawyers in practice have to make do with what training they have got; and as regards insurance disputes, that means, mainly, the law of contract. Sooner or later questions of insurance contract law will land on their desk, whether the drafting of documents or of handling disputes. How well equipped they are for the task depends significantly on what we mean by insurance contracts and to what extent insurance contracts require special rules, issues to which we now turn.

The Nature of Insurance Contracts

Definition or Description?

All-embracing 'definitions' of insurance, such as are sometimes sought in Canada and in the USA, even in the Supreme Court,[54] tend to be too broad and too bland, as it seems in England, to be useful.[55] There is an element of insurance in any measure against an adverse event of any kind, if someone agrees that they will thereupon compensate the loser or help out with repair, maintenance, cure, and so on. The helper's promise, if it is a binding promise, is what the law recognizes as an assumption of risk. Clearly, not all such arrangements are to be regarded

---

[53] R. M. Goode, *Commercial Law*, 3rd edn (London, 2004).
[54] E.g., *Group Life & Health Ins. Co. v Royal Drug Co.*, 440 US 205, 211 (1979).
[55] See Clarke, ch. 1.

as insurance contracts. Clearly, Parliament does not wish to regulate all these contracts as insurance, or indeed as anything else; it does not, for example, wish to monitor the solvency of every computer support firm. At what point, then, does such a contract become one of insurance, and one that perhaps should be regulated as such?

Judges have sometimes referred grandly to 'those who are generally accepted as being insurers', evidently not feeling that they had to stoop to particularity. The general attitude of courts in England remains that of Lord Templeman, that 'no difficulty has ever arisen in practice, and therefore there has been no all-embracing definition'. He went on to explain that this is not intellectual idleness but that it is undesirable that there should be a definition 'because definitions tend sometimes to obscure and occasionally to exclude that which ought to be included'.[56] Whereas it is true that in most cases it is clear whether there is insurance or not, it is also true that there is a marginal penumbra of obscurity where traditional insurance products meet the ingenuity of innovative financial markets. There, at the cutting edge of the City of London, there is no definition which is sufficiently definite to be either useful or inhibiting. The best we can say is that the 'generally accepted' archetype of insurance appears to have certain features, what Lord Templeman called the essential requirements of an insurance contract.[57] The features of insurance were established a century ago in a judicial statement which was adopted as recently as 2004 by the FSA as the best statement of the common law.[58] The prominence of any one feature varies from case to case, but all of them are necessary for there to be insurance. We return to them below.

Statutory Definitions

The Financial Services and Markets Act 2000

Parliament might have appeared to have 'defined' insurance in the Financial Services and Markets Act 2000, but scrutiny indicates that Parliament did not do so in terms that many would regard as a working definition. For the purpose of the Act what counts is a 'regulated activity' either relating to 'an investment of a specified kind', or relating to a specified activity 'in relation to property of any kind'.[59] The Regulated Activities Order, Article 3, states that a 'contract of insurance means any contract of insurance which is a contract of long-term insurance or a contract of general insurance'. Long-term and general insurance contracts are in turn defined, by reference to Parts I and II of Schedule 1 to the Order, in the

---

[56] *Dept of Trade and Industry v St Christopher Motorists' Assn* [1974] 1 Lloyd's Rep 17, 18 ff., *per* Templeman J.   [57] Op cit.
[58] http://www.fsa.gov.uk/pubs/policy/ps04_19.pdf , para. 6.3.4, with reference to *Prudential Ins. Co. v Commissioners of Inland Revenue* [1904] 2 KB 658, 664.
[59] Section 22. The specification is found in the Financial Services and Markets Act 2000 (Regulated Activities) Order 2001 (SI 2000/544).

same terms as the description of the classes of insurance activity to be found in the First Life and Non-Life Directives.[60] However, these EC Directives on insurance do not define insurance, and the European Court of Justice has resisted the temptation too.[61] So, even for the purpose of the Act of 2000, little has changed; and the most we can say is that, as before, definition must be done *ad hoc* by reference to the features of the activity that concern the legislation in question.

The View of the FSA

In August 2002 the FSA published a Consultation Paper (CP 150). In 2004 the FSA published a response paper, which it called a policy statement,[62] that explains its response to the consultation exercise and sets out the final text that is now part of the FSA's *Authorization Manual* (AUTH). Compliance with AUTH will be required of, notably, insurance intermediaries. One of the FSA responses is a 'further explanation of how the FSA assesses whether or not there has been a sufficient assumption of risk for a particular contract to be classified as a contract of insurance at common law'.[63] However, Appendix 1 of the policy statement, which contains the Final Text of the Handbook which is to be part of AUTH, makes it clear[64] that the Regulated Activities Order, which sets out the activities for which authorization is required, does not attempt an exhaustive definition of contracts of insurance. Instead it makes specific extensions to and limitations on the common law concept. For example, it extends the concept of insurance to contracts of guarantee. It is not the intention of the FSA to supersede or replace the common law on the issue. The FSA will still consider each case on its merits,[65] in the light of the FSA's interpretation of the common law.

As for the common law, the FSA takes as a starting point the statement of essential elements of insurance by Channell J in *Prudential*,[66] on the premise that any contracts lacking those elements are unlikely to be classified as insurance.[67] This statement will be interpreted by the FSA in the light of subsequent legislation and case law, and in particular in the light of the purpose of the legislation to be applied by the FSA, giving more weight to substance than to form.[68] The document continues with a scholarly exposition of the common law running to several pages, as it will be interpreted and applied by the FSA, with examples of how, in the view of the FSA, it would apply to certain marginal cases.

[60] 73/239/EEC and 79/267/EEC, as amended.
[61] See *Card Protection Plan v Customs and Excise Commissioners*, ECJ Case C-349/96, [1999] 2 AC 601.   [62] http://www.fsa.gov.uk/pubs/policy/ps04_19.pdf.
[63] Ibid., para. 3.2.2.(a).   [64] Ibid., para. 6.3.2.   [65] Ibid., para. 6.4.3.
[66] *Prudential Ins. Co. v Commissioners of Inland Revenue*, op. cit. above, n. 58. Also set out in AUTH, App. 6.3.4G.   [67] Op. cit. above, n. 62, at para. 6.5.1.
[68] Ibid., para. 6.5.4, with reference to *Fuji Finance Inc. v Aetna Life Ins. Co. Ltd* [1997] Ch 173 (CA) and *Re Sentinel Securities* [1996] 1 WLR 316.

Thus, in the work of the FSA, helpful as it is, a clear two-dimensional and universal definition of insurance is neither sought nor to be found. Lawyers must content themselves still with views such as that of a widely respected economist, the late Reimer Schmidt, who said that the changing concept of insurance is 'a many-sided prism'.[69]

Features Required by the Courts and Common Law

One obvious feature of insurance is that the company in question must be in the business of insurance business,[70] albeit business in the broadest sense. The insurer may be a charity and insurance may be just one part of its business, but that is insurance business nonetheless. This is a requisite feature, because only insurance 'business' of a certain degree of regularity is an activity which warrants regulation by statute.

The second feature of insurance is the insurer's promise to pay—in money or in kind.[71] We think first of money, but in many cases insurers provide something other than money, or something in addition to money: services that range from the reinstatement of damaged buildings to the provision of a driver or a car while the policyholder needs one, or even of bereavement counselling for a survivor on the death of the life insured. If a policyholder 'goes down' and breaks a leg, an accident insurer pays money and perhaps transport home, as well as medical treatment. If a policyholder's computer 'goes down', a business interruption insurer may provide computer back-up so that the business can continue.

The third feature of insurance, closely associated with the second feature, is that the alleged insurer must be legally (i.e., contractually) bound to pay the money or provide the benefit in kind[72] which constitutes the second feature; and the beneficiary must have a legally enforceable right to receive it.[73]

The fourth feature of insurance is that the benefit is due only if a specified insured event occurs. Moreover, at the time of contracting, it must be uncertain whether the specified event will occur.[74] The uncertainty may be as to whether it will occur at all (e.g., burglary), as to its timing (e.g., death), or as to how often it will occur (e.g., damage to taxis).

The fifth feature of insurance is that the insured event must be one that is adverse to the policyholder. Fire or burglary at home, damage to the roof, and so on, are clearly adverse to policyholders. In the case of a life policy maturing when the person insured reached a stated age, such as 65, however, it has been suggested in England that, far from being adverse to the person concerned, reaching that

---

[69] R. Schmidt, 'Considerations on the Significance for Insurance Law of the Consequences of Economic Studies', *Geneva Papers* No. 74 (Jan. 1995), 74–83, 77.

[70] *Hall d'Ath v British Provident Assn* (1932) 48 TLR 240.

[71] *Dept of Trade and Industry v St Christopher Motorists' Assn*, op. cit. above, n. 56.

[72] *Hampton v Toxteth Co-operative Provident Sy Ltd* [1915] 1 Ch 721 (CA).

[73] *Medical Defence Union Ltd v Dept of Trade* [1980] Ch 82.   [74] Ibid., 89.

age is an event to be celebrated. According to Sir Robert Megarry, who went on to pass the age of 90, a 'feat of survival can hardly be called an event that is adverse to his interests'.[75] It is to be hoped that he still takes that view. However, be that as it may, the answer given in England was also that given in Australia: 'a whole life policy is an insurance against dying too soon, an endowment policy an insurance against living too long'.[76] For some the passage of the years is unkind and uncomfortable. Cash can often ease the discomfort.

Rough Edges

Distinguishing the Payment of Contract Damages

The five features described in the last section do not sufficiently distinguish insurance in all cases. Notably, insurance shares the third and fifth features, an adverse event that triggers an obligation to pay money, with the (secondary) promise of any contractor to pay money (damages) on the occurrence of an adverse event for which the contractor is responsible, that is, a breach of the primary promise,[77] for the consequences of which that contractor has assumed responsibility.[78] If a policyholder's computer 'goes down', a business interruption insurer may provide computer back-up so that the business can continue, as well as cash indemnity for business lost nonetheless. Alternatively, the business may call on the computer supplier to pay compensation for breach of contract. Why is that not insurance?

To distinguish the secondary promise of a contractor to pay damages, one answer[79] is that the archetypal insurance promise must concern an adverse event outside the control of either party, something which neither, notably the policyholder, has in any sense brought about. That is correct but still not enough, because that is also true of some ordinary contracts. The failure of the computer, for which the supplier is liable, may well be due to components defectively assembled many thousands of miles to the east. Again, it is not uncommon in international commerce, where one party undertakes a strict obligation and is liable for failure to perform resulting from circumstances completely outside his control, such as intended (even sole) sources of supply[80] or chosen sub-contractors.[81]

An alternative and more helpful answer is found in the USA to draw a line between insurance and product guarantees (also called product warranties). This is the 'principal object' test, which is also referred to as the primary or dominant

---

[75] Ibid., 93.

[76] *National Mutual Life Assn v FCT* (1959) 102 CLR 29, 45, *per* Windeyer J (HCA).

[77] The analysis of contracts in terms of primary and secondary promises is that of Lord Diplock, e.g., in *Photo Production Ltd v Securicor Transport Ltd* [1980] AC 827, 848.

[78] The 'assumption of responsibility' analysis of Lord Goff, e.g., in *The Pegase* [1981] 1 Lloyd's Rep 175, at 182–3.

[79] E.g., J. Birds and N. J. Hird, *Birds Modern Insurance Law*, 5th edn (London, 2004) 14.

[80] E.g., *Intertradex SA v Lesieur Tourteaeaux SARL* [1978] 2 Lloyd's Rep 509 (CA).

[81] E.g., *Lebeaupin v Crispin* [1920] 2 KB 714.

purpose test. Clearly, a product guarantee is ancillary to the sale of the product, which is what characterizes the transaction and distinguishes it from insurance.[82] Moreover, the test has been applied to distinguish health insurance from the provision of medical services,[83] and to classify contracts which mix pure risk (death) and investment risk.[84] In England such a test might also be of use when, as is increasingly common today,[85] insurers offer not only insurance in the traditional sense, but also advice about risk management and loss prevention.

Conflicting Purposes

The correct classification of contracts which mix pure risk (death) and investment risk, referred to above with the view of Sir Robert Megarry, also illustrates another difficulty, that of conflicting purposes. This was one of the problems in the leading case of *Fuji*.[86] The case concerned the nature of a single premium capital investment bond taking the form of life insurance. Under the terms of the bond, there was uncertainty about when the money would become payable, however, the uncertainty did not chiefly depend on the length of the life insured. Therefore, the first court held, contrary to the view of both the market and the Government, that the bond was not insurance but an instrument of investment. The decision was in line with the purpose of the relevant legislation, the Life Assurance Act 1774, that insurance should be used for insurance cover and not for anything else, albeit in this case not something the Act aimed to control, which was wagering. However, in reality the purpose of life insurance has always been to make financial provision for the uncertainties of life (and death) and of the future. This was also the purpose of investment of the kind found in *Fuji*. In these circumstances, the Court of Appeal reversed, concluding that, to be life insurance, it is enough that the right to benefits is not determined by life or death but 'related' to life or death; and that therefore the bond was indeed insurance.

The Nature of Insurance Contract Law

Neither insurance nor insurance law functions or develops in isolation. Fleming spoke of 'a symbiotic relationship' between the law of tort and liability insurance.[87] Indeed, an interrelationship can be seen between the conditions of

---

[82] See S. J. Williams, 'Distinguishing Insurance from Investment Products', 98 Col L Rev 1996–2027, 2019 ff. (1998).

[83] Williams (ibid.) cites, e.g., *Jordan v GHA*, 107 F 2d 239 (DC Cir, 1939).

[84] Williams (ibid.) cites *Securities and Exchange Commission v VALIC*, 359 US 65 (1959).

[85] See Chapter 2, p. 53 ff.

[86] *Fuji Finance Inc. v Aetna Life Ins. Co. Ltd* [1997] Ch 173 (CA).

[87] J. G. Fleming, *The American Tort Process* (Oxford, 1988) 21. See also C. von Bar, *Das Trennungprinzip*, AcP 181 (1981) 289–327; and above, Chapter 8, p. 308 ff.

insurance contracts, not only for liability but for other risks, and a whole range of behaviour on the part of policyholders. Behaviour has been the traditional concern of criminal law, tort, and, in specific ways, contract law. Now behaviour has become one of the concerns of insurers and their insurance contracts; to a degree insurers too have become regulators. Insurers, concerned with risk management and loss prevention, and thus with the moral hazard, promise cover only if policyholders observe a 'code' of conduct: they cover house contents only if certain locks are fitted; they cover road hauliers' liability only if certain anti-theft devices are installed. One set of rules (contract) supports another set of rules (conduct).

The main questions of symbiosis here, however, concern the role of insurance *law*. Is there such a degree of conceptual affinity between insurance law and the general law that the one influences the other? And, if so, can insurance law be understood in terms of the general law? In their role as advisers, both insurers and intermediaries operate squarely within the general law of contract and, to a marginal degree, the law of tort. So the question of affinity becomes whether and to what extent insurance contract law is different in content from the general law of contract.

Common Law: Similarities

The work of insurance intermediaries, whether they act for insurers or for buyers of insurance, is governed by the general law of agency. Although the law is some-times ignored in practice, it has been supplemented recently by regulation, much of which brings practice back in line with the general law, on the part of the FSA.[88] Insurance contracts, whether contracted through intermediaries or not, are concluded like other contracts. Acceptance meets offer or counter-offer in the usual way.[89] Even at Lloyd's the customary market rituals have been squeezed into the template of offer and acceptance. Insurance contracts do not require any spe-cial form and, apart from marine contracts, do not even have to be in writing—although in practice a document such as a policy is commonly used. In short, insurance contracts are concluded like other contracts.

Performance of the contract of insurance by policyholders is mainly the payment of premium. With the exception of some special rules about the recov-ery of premium, the rules of law that apply to the payment of premium are the general rules of law for the payment of money.[90] When the courts have sought to soften the consequences of non-payment (forfeiture), they have done so with general rules of law such as waiver.[91] Performance of the contract by insurers is mainly the provision of cover—the promise of payment in the event of a stated

---

[88] See Chapter 3, p. 60 ff. The Law Commission is to publish an Issues Paper on Intermediaries in April 2007.   [89] See Chapter 4, p. 90 ff.
[90] See Chapter 4, p. 132 ff.
[91] *The Scaptrade* [1983] 1 Lloyd's Rep 146 (CA), aff'd [1983] 2 AC 694.

contingency.[92] If insurers pay too much insurance money they can recover it. Mostly the rules of recovery are rules of the general law of obligations, the law of contract and the law of restitution.[93] If insurers provide services or things in lieu of, or as well as, money, they are liable under the general law applicable, for example, to shops that sell goods.

Cover as an insurance 'product' is, of course, quite different from what is sold in a supermarket, but one important similarity in law lies in (the rules of) interpretation, that is, the specification of the kind of product being sold, its quality, and contents. Again, in general no difference: insurance contracts are interpreted like other contracts.[94] In particular, there is a presumption that any word that has an established meaning in some other part of the law is used in the same sense in insurance contracts; but, of course, a presumption can be rebutted to give way to exceptions (see the next section).

Lastly, interpreters of insurance contracts have begun to talk about the 'reasonable expectations' of the insured; this kind of heresy, if that is what it is, is not limited to insurance contracts.[95] Whether this approach (to all contracts) is truly contractual, or whether it is so 'objective' and removed from the likely intentions of the parties as to be really 'tortious', as it has been described in the United States, is another matter; the point here is that on this issue insurance contracts are treated in the same way as other contracts.

Common Law: Differences

One exception to the similarities in the application of rules of interpretation (above) is to be found in the insurance rule of causation, which is often regarded as a rule of interpretation. The insurance rule of proximate cause is narrow in order to accommodate the desire of insurers for predictable levels of exposure.[96] A strict rule of this kind is sometimes applied to general contractual exclusions, but it is prominent in insurance law. A second exception is that some words and phrases (e.g., loss, fire, all-risks: see Chapter 6) have acquired a crust of case law which gives them their own colour, and this, of course, is the colour of the insurance context. Moreover, certain categories of insurance term are not only different from general contract categories but utterly confusing in their apparent similarity.

In particular, although insurance 'exclusions' are like other 'exclusions', 'conditions' and 'warranties' are understood quite differently in insurance contracts.[97] Even so, to some extent the same can be said of other standard contracts, such as charterparties or building contracts; and on the important issue of the effect of a

[92] The subject of Chapter 5.   [93] See Chapter 6, p. 226 ff.
[94] See Chapter 5, p. 139 ff.   [95] See Chapter 5, p. 153 ff.
[96] See Chapter 6, p. 184 ff.   [97] See Chapter 5, p. 155 ff.

breach of warranty, the House of Lords has now brought insurance law back into the broad line of general contract law.[98]

Elements, notably mistake and misrepresentation, that vitiate other contracts also vitiate insurance contracts, and in the same way. Strikingly, however, insurance contracts are also vitiated by non-disclosure; this is indeed a very special rule of insurance law.[99] In 1915, a treatise on non-disclosure set out a general principle of disclosure which, it was maintained, applied to most kinds of contract. In the second edition of that work, not published until 1990, the authors had retreated from such a general view of the impact of non-disclosure.[100] Explanations of the non-disclosure rule based on general ideas of implied term or fiduciary duty have also been rejected. The rule is an aspect of the insurance duty of good faith. This is not the rule of good faith which is beginning to emerge in the general law of contract, as that goes beyond disclosure; but the convergence of the two, or, more likely, the absorption of the narrow insurance rule in a wider contract rule for all contracts, is a real prospect in future. Even now, as regards the degree of inducement that triggers a remedy, the House of Lords has aligned non-disclosure with misrepresentation, and thus with general contract law.[101] Moreover, except that the Misrepresentation Act 1967 does not apply to non-disclosure, the insurer's remedy for non-disclosure, rescission, is *mutatis mutandis* the same as that for misrepresentation, and thus a remedy of the general law.[102]

In the case of contingency insurance, such as life insurance, the action to enforce the insurer's promise is an action for debt like any other. In the case of indemnity insurance, however, the action has been described by Lord Pearson as an action for damages, but damages 'in a somewhat unusual sense'.[103] These words demonstrate the politeness demanded of a judge inhibited by precedent: if the payment of indemnity is indeed a payment of damages, as precedent still insists today, insurance law is eccentrically out of line. This apart, in other respects, such as the assessment of loss under the basic rule of indemnity, according to which policyholders recover no more than their actual loss, it is very similar to the principle of indemnity in tort; and cases from tort are often relied on.[104]

Lastly, when insurers raise defences to claims, such as non-disclosure on the part of the policyholder, that is often countered by legal argument often based on waiver or estoppel[105]—very much the same refrain heard again and again in

---

[98] *The Good Luck* [1992] 1 AC 233, discussed in Chapter 5, p. 157 ff. Moreover, the latter is now also true of the legal consequences of a claimant being late in giving the insurer notice of loss: see Chapter 6, p. 216 ff.   [99] See Chapter 4, p. 98 ff.

[100] G. S. Bower, *The Law Relating to Actionable Non-Disclosure,* 2nd edn (London, 1990) 85 ff.

[101] *Pan Atlantic Ins. Co. Ltd v Pine Top Ins. Co. Ltd* [1995] 1 AC 501.

[102] See Chapter 4, p. 116 ff. The Law Commission is to publish a Consultation Paper on the Law of warranties and non-disclosure in July 2007.

[103] *Jabbour v Custodian of Israeli Absentee Property* [1954] 1 WLR 139, 144, *per* Pearson J; see Chapter 6, p. 244 ff.   [104] See Chapter 6, pp. 220–21.

[105] See, e.g., Chapter 4, p. 110 ff.

relation to other kinds of contract. Indeed, waiver has a prominent part in insurance law and practice. Insurers sometimes choose to respond to insurance claims in a way that is more generous to the insured than is strictly required, either by the letter of the contract or by the letter of the law. Nothing special about that alone, of course, except perhaps in the degree. Not only do insurers pay against the 'better' judgement of their lawyers or the 'uncharitable' views of their own claims departments, but the industry has had codes of conduct which urged insurers not to insist on certain of their legal rights, for example, not to rescind unless the insured's misrepresentation was careless or fraudulent. Moreover, these and other extra-legal considerations of 'good insurance practice', and of what is 'fair and reasonable in all the circumstances', are the 'rules' that have guided the Insurance Ombudsman and now guide the FOS.[106]

Statute

Apart from the long-standing requirement of disclosure, the distinctive legal features of insurance contracts have come not from the courts, not from those with any conceptual feel for the jurisprudence and the wider contractual context, but from elsewhere, mainly from Parliament. When new rules of law were brought in by statute for exclusion clauses in contracts, they did not apply to insurance contracts: the Unfair Contract Terms Act 1977. However, on the one hand, exclusion of insurance in that Act is evidence of the persuasive power of the industry rather than of any inherent difference between insurance contracts and other contracts; and, of course, some other kinds of contract were also excluded. On the other hand, similar legislation of European origin did not exclude insurance contracts.[107] Moreover, not surprisingly, there are some other, special statutory rules for insurance contracts. But, with two reservations, they are of marginal importance.

The first reservation concerns the Contracts (Applicable Law) Act 1990. The Act brings in a regime for Europe at large, which establishes rules for all contracts, with certain exceptions. The exceptions include insurance contracts (but not reinsurance contracts) on risks situated in the EC, which are not left to be governed by national rules (previously governing all kinds of contract) but for which a special regime is established. This is a marked differentiation of insurance contracts, but its significance to the present discussion is tempered in two respects. First, the special regime allows a result that does not differ as markedly as first impressions might suggest from the general contract rules in the Act. Secondly, the view is widely held, as an objection to the regime, that a special regime for insurance contracts is not justified.[108]

---

[106] See Chapter 6, p. 243 ff.   [107] See Chapter 7, p. 268 ff.

[108] See F. Reichert-Facilides (ed.), *International Insurance Contract Law in the EC* (Deventer, 1993).

The second reservation concerns insurance intermediaries. Largely ruled in the past by the law of agency and the law of tort, this underlying law has now been overlaid by regulations which are the work of the FSA and have a statutory basis. However, it should be recalled that most of these regulations are not exclusive to insurance intermediaries but apply to a wider group of persons offering financial services of which insurance intermediaries are part.[109]

Contract or Contracts?

In the past decisions in certain contexts, such as shipping, construction, and insurance, have had considerable influence on the development of English contract law. The influence has been mutual. Again and again, courts faced with particular issues in insurance cases have recognized a familiar issue of general contract law and treated it as such. The general law, mostly the law of contract, provides a frame of reference from which, by education, inclination, and tradition, the English lawyer proceeds. The general law provides a substratum from which the judge can draw if a rule of 'insurance law' is not apparent. This is not a weakness of insurance law but a source of strength. It is not a palliative; it is a standard procedure because, in the words of Lord Roskill, it is desirable 'that the same legal principles should apply to the law of contract as a whole and that different legal principles should not apply to different branches of that law'.[110]

In the last 100 years, many established branches of law have developed new branches. This is partly the complexity that comes with growth; but it is also partly the result of the associated concentration of human time and energy—and the associated ignorance of wider perspectives of law—the 'high priest syndrome', that revels in modern legal mystique, that elevates a narrow view and the associated vice of ignorance into the virtue of specialization. The law is better applied if it is better understood. Insurance contract law should be something which the legal profession recognizes and to which it can relate. The presumption should always be against those who assert that it is, or should be, different. This book shares the view of a leading American writer in the field, that insurance law is 'not an exotic species that belongs in a legal zoo, but a system that is subject to and part of the same regime of principles and policies that constitutes the rest of the law'.[111] Insurance contracts are still largely seen by lawyers as commercial contracts, and it is in the area of commercial contracts that classical contract law survives in its purest form.[112]

---

[109] See Chapter 3; p. 60 ff.   [110] *The Hansa Nord* [1976] 1 QB 44, 71, *per* Roskill LJ (CA).
[111] K. S. Abraham, *Distributing Risk* (New Haven, Conn., 1986) 9.
[112] L. J. Priestley, 'Contract—The Burgeoning Maelstrom' (1988) 1 JCL 15–32, 17. Cf. S. W. Hedley, 'Contracts as Promises' (1993) 44 NILQ 12–33.

Effective insurance depends on effective insurance contract law, and that depends on effective contract law—depends, however, only to a degree. The court, the draftsman, the commentator, each might do worse than to recall the words of Samuel Johnson: 'How small the part of all the hearts of men endure, that laws or kings can cause or cure.' Insurers are neither gods nor kings, but they can and do much to ease the financial and psychological burdens of what men and women must endure. So too the law with which insurers must work. It could do more.

Index

Lightning Source UK Ltd.
Milton Keynes UK
UKOW06f1051110216

268162UK00008B/113/P